HUME'S ENLIGHTENMENT TRACT

Hume's Enlightenment Tract is the first full study for forty years of David Hume's *Enquiry concerning Human Understanding*. The *Enquiry* has, contrary to its author's expressed wishes, long lived in the shadow of its predecessor, *A Treatise of Human Nature*. Stephen Buckle presents the *Enquiry* in a fresh light, and aims to raise it to its rightful position in Hume's work and in the history of philosophy. He argues that the *Enquiry* is not, as so often assumed, a mere collection of watered-down extracts from the earlier work. It is, rather, a coherent work with a unified argument; and, when this argument is grasped as a whole, the *Enquiry* shows itself to be the best introduction to the lineaments of its author's general philosophy. Buckle offers a careful guide through the argument and structure of the work. He shows how the central sections of the *Enquiry* offer a critique of the dogmatic empiricisms of the ancient world (Stoicism, Epicureanism, and Aristotelianism), and set in place an alternative conception of human powers based on the sceptical principles of habit and probability. These principles are then put to work, to rule out philosophy's metaphysical ambitions and their consequences: religious systems and their attendant conception of human beings as semi-divine rational animals. Hume's scepticism, experimentalism, and naturalism are thus shown to be different aspects of the one unified philosophy—a sceptical version of the Enlightenment vision.

D1614778

Hume's Enlightenment Tract

The Unity and Purpose of *An Enquiry concerning Human Understanding*

Stephen Buckle

CLARENDON PRESS · OXFORD

OXFORD
UNIVERSITY PRESS

Great Clarendon Street, Oxford OX2 6DP

Oxford University Press is a department of the University of Oxford.
It furthers the University's objective of excellence in research, scholarship,
and education by publishing worldwide in

Oxford New York

Athens Bangkok Buenos Aires Cape Town Chennai
Dar es Salaam Delhi Hong Kong Istanbul Karachi Kolkata
Kuala Lumpur Madrid Melbourne Mexico City Mumbai Nairobi
São Paulo Shanghai Taipei Tokyo Toronto

Oxford is a registered trade mark of Oxford University Press
in the UK and certain other countries

Published in the United States
by Oxford University Press Inc., New York

British Library Cataloguing in Publication Data

Data available

Library of Congress Cataloging in Publication Data

Buckle, Stephen.
Hume's enlightenment tract : the unity and purpose of An enquiry concerning human
understanding / Stephen Buckle.
p. cm.
Includes bibliographical references and index.
1. Hume, David, 1711–1776. Philosophical essays concerning human understanding.
2. Knowledge, Theory of. I. Title.
B1484 .B83 2001   121   dc21   00 060633

ISBN 0-19-825088-6 (hbk.)
ISBN 0-19-927114-3 (pbk.)

1 3 5 7 9 10 8 6 4 2

Typeset by SNP Best-set Typesetter Ltd., Hong Kong
Printed in Great Britain
on acid-free paper by
Biddles Ltd., King's Lynn, Norfolk

*to my students
at the University of Sydney
1993–1998*

PREFACE

This is a study of Hume's *An Enquiry concerning Human Understanding*, a work that is much read, but little studied. This unusual state of affairs reflects its widespread reception as a toned-down version of its author's serious philosophy in *A Treatise of Human Nature*: thus the *Enquiry*'s parts are widely used in undergraduate introductions to various philosophical topics, but serious studies of 'Hume's philosophy' concentrate, sometimes exclusively, on the *Treatise*. Moreover, since the different parts of the work are employed separately, as introductions to different philosophical topics—most obviously, Sections IV and VII to epistemology, Section X to philosophy of religion—the modern university curriculum fragments the work according to its own distinctive needs. The result is the neglect of the whole as a whole, and, further, the misunderstanding of the parts themselves.

The aim of this study is to correct these errors. It will show Hume to be a philosopher of the Enlightenment, and that taking the fact seriously is the key to understanding his central themes and arguments: that, in particular, his scepticism is not the project of radical doubt, but a form of ancient scepticism, directed against philosophical dogmatism, not against ordinary belief; and that his employment of it reflects the characteristic Enlightenment strategy of appealing to ancient schools of thought opposed to Aristotle in order to attack scholastic philosophy and its religious fruits. The *Enquiry*'s argument falls into place against this background, and so reveals itself to be a unified work, and the best introduction to the coherence of Hume's mature thought.

A brief outline will indicate the shape of the book. Part One sketches the interpretation pursued in detail in Part Two, the main body of the work. Chapter 1 clears away some obstacles to an unprejudiced understanding of the work. These obstacles derive in large part from an indefensible, but tenacious, conception of Hume's intellectual career, fostered by some scattered remarks in his short autobiography. Chapter 2 provides a sketch of the circumstances in which the work was produced, and of the organization of the argument, in order to throw light on Hume's aims. It is argued that the critique of religion is not incidental, but central, to the work's purpose, and is so because Hume is not a

modern professional epistemologist, concerned with the theory of
knowledge for its sake alone. He is, rather, a philosopher greatly
influenced by ancient thought and ideals, and thus someone who,
like the ancients, aims to put epistemological principles to work
in a practical philosophy of life. His view is, in a nutshell, that
the revolution brought to completion in natural philosophy by
Newton shows the necessity, for the human sciences, of reviving
the standpoint of ancient Academic scepticism. Chapter 3 resolves
the apparent tensions in this position by showing how Hume's
philosophical self-understanding integrates experimental philosophy, naturalism, and scepticism into a coherent whole.

Part Two then offers a detailed section-by-section commentary
on the work. The aim there is to interpret the meaning of Hume's
claims, and to indicate his more prominent intellectual debts.
With few exceptions, the truth or falsity of Hume's views is not
considered; and for this reason there is less attention to debates in
modern secondary literature than might be expected. My aim has
been to offer a coherent interpretation of Hume's text, and to leave
as uncluttered as possible the outlines and development of his
thought. Part Three provides a very brief summary of the conclusions reached, and of the overall picture that emerges.

This study therefore provides an interpretation of Hume's
mature philosophical outlook. The account offered is not without
its tendency: the Hume who emerges is not the self-undermining
sceptic who denied the reality of causal powers before turning,
inexplicably, to essays and histories that appealed to the very
notions denied, but the (so-called) new Hume, who denied that
we could *know* what such powers were, while at the same time
affirming that we are determined—by the irresistible instinctive
processes of the human mind—to believe in the existence of such
powers, and to frame our actions accordingly. Although I do not
mean to give the impression that my Hume is identical to John
Wright's, Wright's description of Hume as a 'sceptical realist' seems
to me apposite. Hume is indeed a sceptical realist in the sense that
he denies that we can attain to philosophical knowledge of the
causes of things, while accepting (as he believes we must) that we
inhabit a real world in which real but hidden powers bring about
what we observe to come about. He is, in short, a sceptic about
essences, but a realist about *existences*; and early modern philosophy's tendency, borrowed from ancient thought, to organize philosophical questions around this distinction—and plainly illustrated
in Descartes's division of his subject in the *Meditations*, as well as
Hume's distinctions between the divine nature and being in his

religious works—makes the term 'sceptical realism' particularly apt. It is not, however, a *necessary* label for Hume's thought, since sceptical realism, thus defined, is nothing but a version of Academic scepticism.

Of course, to claim that this is the standpoint of the *Enquiry* is considerably less controversial than to claim it of the *Treatise*; and I make no claim that the earlier work will fit this picture unproblematically. However, once it is seen just how thoroughly, and coherently, the *Enquiry* does fit this picture, any thought that it is no more than an unphilosophically motivated grab for fame becomes untenable. Moreover, to discover the work's coherence is also to encourage a fresh look at its precocious predecessor, because it serves to highlight how the *Treatise*'s more extreme moments threaten even Hume's project itself. The search for a more stable philosophical outlook, in the form of a 'durable and useful' mitigated scepticism, is thus evidence not of Hume's abandonment of serious philosophy, but of an ongoing attempt to fashion his thought into a unified whole. The coherence of the *Enquiry*'s argument is itself the evidence that the attempt succeeds. Hume knew what he was doing when he recast parts of the *Treatise* for republication, and sympathetic attention to the *Enquiry*'s text reveals the fact, by revealing there a unity that is not commonly suspected.

In fact, it is because this is so commonly assumed not to be so that the *Enquiry* is rarely studied on its own terms. It is usually, if implicitly, treated as a work best suited only for beginning students, being no more than a savagely pruned, and excessively *tamed*, version of Hume's thought. This view has its reasons, of course: it is certainly true that the *Enquiry* lacks the plenitude of the *jardin anglais* from which it was constructed, and that fossicking in such dense thickets has its virtues and its pleasures. However, the controlled execution of a well-wrought design is, in the end, the measure of a philosophical work, and it is against this standard that the *Enquiry* deserves to be judged. This study aims to show that the *Enquiry* is just such a construction: that its apparently disconnected sections comprise a coherent argument, and reflect a coherent point of view: that Hume's scepticism and experimentalism, his religious criticisms and his positive naturalism, are all aspects of a unified philosophical outlook. This coherence and order have largely been ignored or misunderstood because they are presented in a firmly pruned *jardin français* whose design has resisted the eye of lovers of English wildness.

Every author hopes that his or her book will be read in whole. The fate of the *Enquiry* is plain evidence of how rarely this hope is realized. In the case of a work of this kind, it is almost inevitable that, despite its central message, it will be mined according to the demands of the undergraduate curriculum. For this reason, I have thought it necessary occasionally to repeat myself, by offering some brief summaries of what has gone before, especially in the treatment of Sections VII and X, where such mining is surely inevitable. I hope that this is not irritating to the orderly reader, and console myself with the thought that comparable, if not identical, factors led Hume to adopt the same strategy in the *Enquiry* itself.

The primary intellectual debts incurred in the writing of this book must begin with Edward Craig, Galen Strawson, and John Wright, whose influence on the outcome will be plain to all. For their very helpful comments on (what became) the final product, I must thank Tom Beauchamp, Sandy Stewart, David Fate Norton, Terence Penelhum, and the readers for the Press. Thanks are also due to David Smith for late-night whisky and discussion when the enterprise was in its formative stages; to the late George Molnar for his vigorously expressed disagreement, on our casual intersections on Glebe Point Road, with (what seemed to be) all of my views on Hume; and to Max Deutscher, who, in 1976, decided to teach his Honours class *Treatise* Book II rather than the usual Hume diet, and so first posed for me the question of the unity of Hume's thought.

Various parts of the work were delivered to audiences at the Universities of Auckland, Sydney, Melbourne, and Wollongong, the Australian Catholic University, and the Seventeenth-Century Studies Group at Birkbeck College. A related paper was also presented at the 'Hume and Contemporary Pragmatism' conference in Sydney in 1997. That conference, organized by Cathy Legg, was supported from an Australian Research Council Large Grant shared with Huw Price. The ARC grant also created the time to complete the penultimate draft, for which I am grateful. The book draws heavily, in places, on material that has previously appeared elsewhere, so my thanks to Blackwell Publishers for permission to include material from 'British Sceptical Realism: A Fresh Look at the British Tradition', *European Journal of Philosophy*, 7 (1999); and to Oxford University Press for permission to re-use material from 'Hume's Biography and Hume's Philosophy: "My Own Life" and *An Enquiry concerning Human Understanding*', and 'Marvels, Miracles, and Mundane Order: Hume's Critique of Religion in *An Enquiry concerning Human Understanding*', *Australasian Journal of Philosophy*, 77 (1999) and 79 (2001), respectively.

This book was completed in difficult circumstances. For this reason, it is with a very keen sense of appreciation that I thank Jean Curthoys, Knud Haakonssen, John Kleinig, Alan Olding, Onora O'Neill, Aleksandar Pavkovic, Robert Young, and, not least, my parents for unflinching support in very trying times. Many others also deserve thanks for practical or moral support. Unfortunately, I cannot mention them all here. The following is a list of those whose responses and support have gone beyond the call of duty: Keith Anderson, David Armstrong, Rick Benitez, Nick Bunnin, Keith Campbell, Dario Castiglione, Alan Chalmers, Aviva Cohen, Deirdre Coleman, John Colman, Chris Cordner, Roger Crisp, Fred D'Agostino, Peter Dews, Gordon Finlayson, Peter Forrest, Jim Franklin, André Fuhrmann, Bob Fullinwider, Raimond Gaita, Jerry Gaus, William Grey, Paul Griffiths, Richard Hare, Drew Khlentzos, Veronica Leahy, George Leung, Karen Lines, Pawel Łukow, Jeff Malpas, Peter Marks, Graeme Marshall, Thomas Mautner, John McCloskey, Peter Menzies, Robert Nola, Barry Oakley, Graham Priest, Julius Rocca, Leila Shotton, Peter Singer, Jack Smart, Vince Stefano, Kim Sterelny, Sandy Stewart, Galen Strawson, Alessandra Tanesini, Marion Tapper, Udo Thiel, Neil Thomason, Janna Thompson, Bernadette Tobin, Suzanne Uniacke, and John Wright. I hope I have not overlooked anyone; prudence has required omitting the names of the vulnerable.

The circumstances have had one regrettable practical consequence, in that some recent works on Hume have not received the attention they deserve: most conspicuously, Don Garrett's *Cognition and Commitment in Hume's Philosophy*. Other potential difficulties, however, have been smoothed away by Peter Momtchiloff's sane advice. My colleagues at the Australian Catholic University have had a similar effect by providing a refreshingly pleasant environment in which to complete the final revisions. Finally, my former colleagues at the University of Sydney can be thanked for placing me in the excellent company of (in temporal order) Udo Thiel, Ted Sadler, Christiane Schildknecht, Norbert Zmijewski, and Damian Byers. But my students at Sydney deserve thanks: for cheerfully accepting their fate as my guinea pigs, and for constituting a material refutation of the barbaric assumptions of Australian higher education policy.

Stephen Buckle

Sydney
March 2000

CONTENTS

The experimental reasoning itself, which we possess in common with beasts, and on which the whole conduct of life depends, is nothing but a species of instinct or mechanical power, that acts in us unknown to ourselves; and in its chief operations, is not directed by any such relations or comparisons of ideas, as are the proper objects of our intellectual faculties. (Section IX)

As nature has taught us the use of our limbs, without giving us the knowledge of the muscles and nerves, by which they are actuated; so has she planted in us an instinct, which carries forward the thought in a correspondent course to that which she has established among external objects; though we are ignorant of those powers and forces, on which this regular course and succession of objects totally depends . . . Here, then, is a kind of pre-established harmony between the course of nature and the succession of our ideas; and though the powers and forces, by which the former is governed, be wholly unknown to us, yet our thoughts and conceptions have still, we find, gone on in the same train with the other works of nature. Custom is that principle, by which this correspondence has been effected; so necessary to the subsistence of our species, and the regulation of our conduct, in every circumstance and occurrence of human life . . . Those, who delight in the discovery and contemplation of *final causes*, have here ample subject to employ their wonder and admiration. (Section V Part II)

The justest and most plausible objection against a considerable part of metaphysics, [is] that they are not properly a science; but arise either from the fruitless efforts of human vanity, which would penetrate into subjects utterly inaccessible to the understanding, or from the craft of popular superstitions, which, being unable to defend themselves on fair ground, raise these entangling brambles to cover and protect their weakness. Chaced from the open country, these robbers fly into the forest, and lie in wait to break in upon every unguarded avenue of the mind, and overwhelm it with religious fears and prejudices. (Section I)

We have, in the following enquiry, attempted to throw some light upon subjects, from which uncertainty has hitherto deterred the wise, and obscurity the ignorant. Happy, if we can unite the boundaries of the different species of philosophy, by reconciling profound enquiry with clearness, and truth with novelty! And still more happy, if, reasoning in this easy manner, we can undermine the foundations of an abstruse philosophy, which seems to have hitherto served only as a shelter to superstition, and a cover to absurdity and error! (Section I)

PART ONE

Approaching the Text

Chapter 1

Clearing the Ground

A study of *An Enquiry concerning Human Understanding* immediately confronts an obstacle. Hume's first *Enquiry* is widely regarded as a milk-and-water version of the author's serious philosophy, appropriate perhaps for the beginning student: but for the serious engagement with Hume's philosophy, it is thought, the *Enquiry* must be left behind, and the more challenging and more demanding product of its author's earlier years, *A Treatise of Human Nature*, should take its place. It is not that the *Enquiry* is unread, or even unstudied; but it remains true—especially, but not only, amongst non-specialist readers—that to give priority to the *Enquiry*, whether in whole or in part, requires justification.[1] This contrasts sharply with the tendency of no small number of Hume's commentators to equate studies of the *Treatise* (and even of parts of Book I of the *Treatise*) with studies of Hume's philosophy.[2] In this light, it comes as no surprise that studies of the first *Enquiry*, as a work worthy of attention in its own right, are rare.[3] This book is, then, out of step with some well-established verities in the interpretation of Hume's philosophy. And not accidentally so:

[1] See e.g. P. J. R. Millican, 'Hume's Argument Concerning Induction: Structure and Interpretation', in S. Tweyman (ed.), *David Hume: Critical Assessments* (London: Routledge, 1995), ii. 93–4. T. Penelhum, *David Hume: An Introduction to his Philosophical System* (West Lafayette, Ind.: Purdue University Press, 1992), is largely based on extracts 'from the two *Enquiries*, and primarily from the first', because 'these are the works most easily extracted and were intended by Hume himself to be more accessible presentations of his ideas than the *Treatise* had been. The *Treatise* and *Dialogues* remain indispensable, however . . .' (p. x). For the serious student, that is of course true. But it is notable that the reliance on the *Enquiry* is explained by reference to the book's introductory character.

[2] Some recent examples are the following: D. Pears, *Hume's System: An Examination of the First Book of his* Treatise (Oxford: Oxford University Press, 1990); W. Waxman, *Hume's Theory of Consciousness* (Cambridge: Cambridge University Press, 1994) (according to its abstract 'a comprehensive analysis and re-evaluation of the first book of Hume's *Treatise of Human Nature*'); O. A. Johnson, *The Mind of David Hume: A Companion to Book I of* A Treatise of Human Nature (Urbana, Ill.: University of Illinois Press, 1995); H. W. Noonan, *Hume on Knowledge* (London: Routledge, 1999) (described in the Preface as 'a study of the most important themes in Book I of Hume's first, and greatest work: *A Treatise of Human Nature*').

[3] The only notable book-length studies of the first *Enquiry* are A. Flew, *Hume's Philosophy of Belief* (London: Routledge & Kegan Paul, 1961; repr. Bristol: Thoemmes Press, 1997), and G. Stern, *A Faculty Theory of Knowledge: The Aim and Scope of Hume's First* Enquiry (Lewisburg, Pa.: Bucknell University Press, 1971).

although criticism of the *Treatise* is no part of the burden of this work, it will be argued that the widespread preference for (primarily) Book I of the *Treatise* over the first *Enquiry* is, in important respects, misguided.

The preference is misguided in at least two respects. In the first place, it reflects certain convictions about the nature of Hume's philosophy—convictions derived from selected passages in the *Treatise*—that necessarily subordinate the first *Enquiry* to the earlier work; and so, where they differ, rules it out of serious consideration. These convictions will not be addressed directly, but will be countered by the study as a whole: the aim is to show that the *Enquiry* is a unified work with a coherent argument, and that the very coherence, and significance, of the argument shows it to be the best short guide to Hume's philosophy. Secondly, the preference for the *Treatise* is misguided because it depends on a misleading picture of the course of Hume's intellectual career. In fact, it is because of a pervasive view about the shape of Hume's intellectual career that the conviction of the superiority of *Treatise* Book I over the *Enquiry* has petrified into orthodoxy. Ironically, this view of his intellectual career is due in part to comments of Hume's own, so part of the blame for this outcome (which, as we shall see, he did not welcome) must be laid at his own door. It is necessary to begin this study, then, by clearing away some of the obstacles that stand in the way of a fresh look at the *Enquiry*, not least those left by Hume himself.

Much of the trouble has been caused by the short autobiography, 'My Own Life'. It has made it difficult for the first *Enquiry* to find friends partly because of two sentences there concerning the *Enquiry*'s content, but especially because of a brief act of authorial self-disclosure: Hume's remark, towards the end, that 'the love of literary fame' was his 'ruling passion'.[4] The influence of this brief, almost parenthetical, remark—amongst Hume's friends as much as his enemies—is difficult to exaggerate. It has encouraged the view that, after writing the *Treatise*, Hume abandoned philosophy for popular success; and this view has in its turn underpinned a method of interpretation of Hume's works in which his later reworkings of his views, most particularly in the two *Enquiries*, have been relegated to secondary status, mere 'literary' reworkings of the serious philosophy of the *Treatise*.

If Hume had imagined what would be made of some of his brief remarks there, in particular those concerning his later philo-

---

[4] David Hume, 'My Own Life', in *Essays, Moral, Political, and Literary*, rev. edn., ed. E. F. Miller (Indianapolis: Liberty Fund, 1987), p. xl.

sophical endeavours, he would have spent more time and care in the drafting of that short document. The fault is not, however, simply to be laid at the door of 'My Own Life'. The interpretation of Hume's intellectual career fostered by the scattered remarks in that work also depends heavily on a very selective, and equally prejudicial, reading of those remarks. A less hasty assessment of 'My Own Life', and, in addition, a less selective reading of his remarks intended for posterity, offer a different picture of his intellectual career; and, not least, are able to reveal the first *Enquiry* in a considerably more positive light.

Before turning to that task, it will be useful to pause to illustrate just how profound the influence of the picture of Hume as a mere lover of literary fame can be. As noted, its pervasive effect is to limit Hume's serious philosophy to the *Treatise*. Not uncommonly, a more extreme version is encountered, in which the serious philosophy ends with the sceptical crisis at the end of *Treatise* Book I. None of this compares, however, with the truly feral form of the thesis, in which the whole of the *Treatise* itself is dismissed as pure opportunism, as a (diabolically) clever young man's unprincipled grab for fame:

Hume wrote for two purposes: to make money, and to gain a literary reputation. He acknowledged, 'My ruling passion is the love of literary fame.' As a youth he studied Locke and Berkeley, and Cicero and the ancient Academic skeptics; in their thought he saw the chance to reach startling conclusions and become a shocking success. Berkeley had attacked Newtonian science for serious reasons; he was a crusader, interested in a sound and consistent science. Hume subtly criticized it primarily to attract attention to the Scotsman David Hume. He hated Locke and Newton as Englishmen, besides; for next to priests Englishmen were his most cordial hatred.[5]

Mercifully, extremism of this kind is rare, but more moderate assessments of Hume's work, encouraged by the autobiographical remark, have also stumbled over the relationship of the *Treatise* to

[5] J. H. Randall, 'David Hume: Radical Empiricist and Pragmatist', in S. Hook and M. R. Konvitz (eds.), *Freedom and Experience* (Ithaca, NY: Cornell University Press, 1947), 293. The passage is quoted in J. Noxon, *Hume's Philosophical Development* (Oxford: Clarendon Press, 1973), 79 n. Noxon refers to it as an 'unscrupulous and irresponsible fabrication'. He provides some other examples of the charge that Hume was wanting in philosophical seriousness in his 'Hume's Agnosticism', in V. C. Chappell (ed.), *Hume: A Collection of Critical Essays* (London: Macmillan, 1966), 362. A more sympathetic handling of Randall's charge is provided by Richard Popkin. Despite firm disagreements with Randall's opinions, Popkin shares sympathy with his targets, and so observes: 'As an antidote to hero-worship and the self-congratulation of the [twentieth-century] empiricists, Randall's approach is appealing, intriguing, and often shocking' ('Randall and British Empiricism', in R. H. Popkin, *The High Road to Pyrrhonism*, ed. R. A. Watson and J. E. Force (Indianapolis: Hackett, 1993), 47). An antidote to the complacent vices of the modern empiricists is, perhaps, no bad thing; but the antidote would have been more effective if it had partaken more of the truth.

the later works, and over the relationship of Book I to the remainder of the *Treatise* itself.[6] Of course, the autobiographical remarks
do not produce this effect on their own. The heart of the problem
here is the not uncommon interpretation of Book I of the *Treatise*
as wholly destructive. Once this is accepted, then its relationship
to the subsequent works, including the subsequent parts of the
Treatise itself, must be problematic. The autobiographical remarks
are then seized on in order to show the problem to stem from
Hume's personality. A wholly destructive work can be followed
by apparently constructive works written in an urbane manner
because the author neither is nor was seriously concerned with the
issues. Here we see how Randall's Hume is generated.

Putting the issue in these terms gives priority to the interpretation of the *Treatise*, and then appeals to 'My Own Life' only after
the fact. In so doing it shifts the blame away from the autobiography itself, implying that it is not an independent cause of
this interpretative landscape. Whatever the strengths and weaknesses of this position, however, it remains true that the autobiographical remarks have been the primary cause by which this
landscape has been *petrified*. Once it has been accepted that Hume's
love of literary fame meant that he abandoned philosophy, the
point can then be *illustrated* by a hasty acquaintance with the more
dramatically sceptical moments in the later parts of *Treatise* Book
I. Hume the purely destructive sceptic, the disingenuous exploiter
of the public's taste for literary entertainments, is then proved *from*
the autobiography, and applied *to* the *Treatise*. In this way a thinly
based construction is transformed into an interpretative edifice
hewn in stone.

This study will attempt to shake this edifice, but not by any
detailed re-examination of the *Treatise*. In recent years, there has
been a good deal of scholarly endeavour directed at just that
end. The upshot has been a significant re-evaluation: both of the
Treatise itself, including the relations between its parts, and of
Hume's corpus as a whole.[7] My aim is to concentrate attention on

---

[6] T. H. Grose, for example, was struck by 'the suddennness with which his labours in philosophy came to an end'—that is, with the publication of the *Treatise*—and then goes on to
claim that Hume 'certainly lacked the disposition, and probably the ability' to engage in any
positive reconstruction after the destructive achievements of the *Treatise*. See 'History of the
Editions', in *The Philosophical Works of David Hume*, ed. T. H. Green and T. H. Grose (London:
Longmans, Green, 1889), iii. 75–6. Remarks like these leave Books II and III of the *Treatise*
in limbo; but for the purposes of this study, the key feature is the interpretation of Book I as
entirely destructive.

[7] N. Kemp Smith, *The Philosophy of David Hume* (London: Macmillan, 1941), is the ground-
breaking work that revitalized the study of Hume's thought. Perhaps the most important of
the recent works are D. F. Norton, *David Hume: Common-Sense Moralist, Sceptical Metaphysi-*

the *Enquiry*, to draw out its overall argumentative strategy, and to show by example the merits of the work—and in this indirect way to encourage a fresh perspective. In this sense, then, this study finds common cause with the shift in the interpretative landscape, and reflects its implication that the later works deserve serious consideration in their own right. The proof of the pudding will, of course, depend upon the coherence of the interpretation offered in these pages. The immediate task, however, is to return to 'My Own Life' and the obstacles it sets in the way of taking Hume's later works seriously.

The Popular View

The popular view,[8] that the first *Enquiry* is merely an edited-down and 'literary' reworking of the *Treatise*, is not without its textual support. In 'My Own Life' Hume explains the advent of the first *Enquiry* as an attempt to gain the readership that the *Treatise* had failed to attract. The reception of the *Treatise*, he says, was disastrous: 'Never literary attempt was more unfortunate than my Treatise of Human Nature. It fell *dead-born from the press*, without reaching such distinction, as even to excite a murmur among the zealots.'[9] This publishing failure is then invoked to explain the writing of the first *Enquiry*. A few paragraphs later, he remarks:

I had always entertained a notion, that my want of success in publishing the Treatise of Human Nature, had proceeded more from the manner than the matter, and that I had been guilty of a very usual indiscretion, in going to the press too early. I, therefore, cast the first part of that work anew in the Enquiry concerning Human Understanding, which was published while I was at Turin. But this piece was at first little more successful than the Treatise of Human Nature.[10]

cian (Princeton: Princeton University Press, 1982); J. P. Wright, *The Sceptical Realism of David Hume* (Manchester: Manchester University Press, 1983); and D. W. Livingston, *Hume's Philosophy of Common Life* (Chicago: University of Chicago Press, 1984). Two other books have done much to revivify philosophical thinking about Hume's project in the wider (non-specialist) philosophical community: E. Craig, *The Mind of God and the Works of Man* (Oxford: Clarendon Press, 1987), and G. Strawson, *The Secret Connexion: Causation, Realism, and David Hume* (Oxford: Clarendon Press, 1989). The invigorating effect of studies such as these (including, of course, the invigoration of their critics) is well illustrated in D. F. Norton (ed.), *The Cambridge Companion to Hume* (Cambridge: Cambridge University Press, 1993).

[8] I mean 'popular' in much the sense that Hume uses 'vulgar', that is, 'common', in both senses of the word: widespread, and unsophisticated. The view is less common amongst Hume scholars; but it is not extinct, and neither is its influence. Amongst non-specialists, it remains a vigorous presence, and, for this reason, continues to exercise considerable influence on the undergraduate curriculum (on which more below).

[9] Hume, 'My Own Life', in *Essays*, p. xxxiv.

[10] Ibid., p. xxxv.

This account of the genesis of the first *Enquiry* provides as good a defence of the popular view as one is likely to find. It implies that the differences between the early and later work are more stylistic than substantial; and it licenses an approach to Hume's corpus that mines the earlier, larger work for the essential elements of the author's position, scanning the later work only for any additional details or *bons mots*.

However, there is considerably more art in Hume's comments here than may meet the (modern) eye, and bringing it to the fore immediately gives a somewhat more complex impression. The famous remark that the *Treatise* 'fell *dead-born from the press*' is the key: to the eighteenth-century reader, it would have had a somewhat contrived air, because, as Marina Frasca-Spada has pointed out, it is in fact a quotation from Pope's 'Epilogue to the Satires' (and Hume's italicizing is presumably meant to signal the fact). Moreover, once this is recognized, Hume's remark takes on a new meaning. This is because the original line—'All, all but truth, drops dead-born from the press'[11]—connects publishing failure with falsehood, and therefore with *deserved* failure. So Hume seems to be saying, not merely that the *Treatise* did not attract a wide readership, but also that this is what one should expect, given its flaws.[12] If this is right, then the popular reading of these remarks is well astray, and the resultant priority accorded the *Treatise* quite the opposite of Hume's intention.

Whatever the exact meaning of Hume's remark, its consequences for the *Enquiry* are clear-cut. This is because the popular view typically leads to the conclusion that the *Enquiry* is of little independent value, and so may be set aside (more or less) altogether, the decision justified by a brief explanatory note. Examples are not hard to find. One recent study of Hume's philosophy ignores the *Enquiry* in the main text. It is not until the 'Postscript', on the final page of the work, we read:

This study of Hume's basic system has concentrated exclusively on *A Treatise of Human Nature* and neglected *An Enquiry concerning Human Understanding*.

[11] Alexander Pope, 'Epilogue to the Satires', ii. 226, in *Alexander Pope*, ed. P. Rogers (Oxford Authors; Oxford: Oxford University Press, 1993), 407; M. Frasca-Spada, *Space and the Self in Hume's* Treatise (Cambridge: Cambridge University Press, 1998), 86.

[12] If we take this to be his meaning, the discrepancy between the book's implied and actual sales is resolved: for, although the *Treatise* did not hit the best-seller lists, it did receive a steadily increasing degree of recognition. Nonetheless, the very fact of Hume's decision to write the first *Enquiry* is sufficient to show that the book's steady progress in the world was insufficiently satisfying to a young man who hoped to take the educated world by storm. For the details of the *Treatise*'s reception, see E. C. Mossner, *The Life of David Hume*, 2nd edn. (Oxford: Clarendon Press, 1980), ch. 10; and for Hume's varying assessments of its fate over time, see Frasca-Spada's neat collation, *Space and the Self in Hume's* Treatise, 96–101.

The reason for this procedure was not that the *Enquiry* throws no light on the matter. It was that the light that it does throw is softer and more diffuse, whereas the *Treatise* is a young man's book in which the structure of his thought emerges more starkly and with sharper outlines. In his first presentation of his system paradoxical implications are never blunted to reduce the shock of their impact.[13]

Orthodoxies often flourish unconstrained by their inconsistencies, and in this light the last sentence here should give us pause. If the failing of the *Treatise* had been the manner rather than the matter, why should the paradoxical implications be a casualty of rewriting? Why might not their disappearance be due to authorial second thoughts? Perhaps the most tempting reply, for adherents of the popular view, is that Hume's search for acceptance by a polite audience is once again the cause. But this will not stand up.

In the first place, this response ignores the fact that many of the 'paradoxical' theses not only survive in the *Enquiry*, but play central roles. The accounts of causation and belief are cases in point, as is (perhaps) the account of liberty and necessity. Secondly, the inclusion in the *Enquiry* of the section on miracles, which had been left out of the *Treatise* precisely because it may have caused offence, can hardly be understood as part of an attempt to massage the sensibilities of the literary public. These aspects are, I think, sufficient to challenge the assumption underlying the above response—that is, that Hume believed that the way to find a reading audience is to tell them what they want to hear. Whether or not the assumption is true in fact, it does not seem to have been Hume's own. He certainly sought an audience, and was disappointed when it was hard to find. But he did not seek his audience by trying to tell polite society what it wanted to hear. In fact, much of his work, early and late, seems to have sought to excite the interest of the reading public precisely by provoking the zealots. 'My Own Life' can itself be reasonably regarded as just such a work.[14]

If this seems plausible, then there is little good reason for not taking Hume at his word when he effectively disowns the *Treatise* in the 'Advertisement' to the 1777 edition of his works. It is worth remembering that, although the precise date of composition of

[13] Pears, *Hume's System*, 199.
[14] There are quite a number of remarks of this kind to be found there. For example, he says, speaking of the period 1749–51: 'Meanwhile, my bookseller, A. Miller, informed me, that my former publications (all but the unfortunate Treatise) were beginning to be the subject of conversation; that the sale of them was gradually increasing, and that new editions were demanded. Answers by Reverends, and Right Reverends, came out two or three in a year; and I found, by Dr. Warburton's railing, that the books were beginning to be esteemed in good company'. ('My Own Life', in *Essays*, p. xxxvi).

this 'Advertisement' is not known, it does belong to the later years of Hume's life.[15] Its inclusion in the 1777 edition shows it to be, like 'My Own Life', intended for posterity, not for present acclaim. There is no solid basis, then, for treating the two pieces as differently motivated, with one telling the truth and the other hiding it. The account given there of the *Treatise*, and of its relation to the first *Enquiry* (and other later writings), is similar to the account provided in the autobiography.[16] There are some significant differences, however, and attending to them will be enlightening.

The reason for writing the *Enquiry* and the other works is there given in terms of the lessons the young author learnt from the *Treatise*'s poor reception: the *Treatise* was, he says,

a work which the Author had projected before he left College, and which he wrote and published not long after. But not finding it successful, he was sensible of his error in going to the press too early, and he cast the whole anew in the following pieces, where some negligences in his former reasoning and more in his expression, are, he hopes, corrected.[17]

This remark seems to be in much the same spirit as the 'more from the manner than the matter' judgement of 'My Own Life', although the lack of success here referred to may well mean not merely lack of readers but lack of critical approval. Moreover, both passages, in their different ways, do acknowledge changes in the 'matter', even if less than those of 'manner'; and, given the extent to which the *Treatise* was criticized for its style, this does allow that the changes of substance need not be negligible. Of course, if there were nothing further to go on, the point would not be established. However, the 'Advertisement' continues with Hume castigating those who have based their criticisms on the *Treatise* rather than on the later works:

several writers, who have honoured the Author's Philosophy with answers, have taken care to direct all their batteries against that juvenile work, which

---

[15] Hume mentions it in a letter of October 1775, to his printer William Strahan: 'There is a short Advertisement, which I wish I had prefix'd to the second Volume of the Essays and Treatises in the last Edition. I send you a copy of it. Please to enquire at the Warehouse, if any considerable Number of that Edition remain on hands; and if there do, I beg the favour of you, that you woud throw off an equal Number of this Advertisement, and give out no more Copies without prefixing it to the second volume.' He adds: 'It is a compleat Answer to Dr Reid and to that bigotted silly Fellow, Beattie.' See *The Letters of David Hume*, ed. J. Y. T. Greig (Oxford: Clarendon Press, 1932), ii. 301.

[16] It is also consistent with the steady shift of his attitude over time, as revealed in his letters. See Frasca-Spada's collation of these, *Space and the Self in Hume's* Treatise, 96–101.

[17] 'Advertisement', in David Hume, *Enquiries concerning Human Understanding and concerning the Principles of Morals*, 3rd edn., ed. L. A. Selby-Bigge, rev. P. H. Nidditch (Oxford: Clarendon Press, 1975), 2.

the Author never acknowledged, and have affected to triumph in any advantages, which, they imagined, they had obtained over it: A practice very contrary to all rules of candour and fair-dealing, and a strong instance of those polemical artifices, which a bigotted zeal thinks itself authorized to employ. Henceforth, the Author desires, that the following Pieces may alone be regarded as containing his philosophical sentiments and principles.[18]

This may seem something of an overreaction—unfair to the *Treatise*—but there would have been no need for it, were it not the case that attending to the *Treatise* alone easily gave a reader a false impression of the author's philosophy. Whether the errors arose because of the *Treatise*'s defects of manner (such as its occasional obscurities and stylistic infelicities), or because of its defects of matter (as discovered by comparing its theses with the later works), the cure is in both cases the same: recognizing that the *Treatise* cannot be taken to represent the author's settled opinions.

Of course, the value of the *Treatise* is not reducible to its value as a guide to Hume's settled opinions. It may well be thought, for example, that Hume's first thoughts were his best; even that he modified them too readily, perhaps because wounded by the book's unfavourable reception.[19] However, if our concern is with Hume's own mature position, then the status of the *Treatise* is to be settled only by carefully surveying its doctrines in the light of the later works. If the task seems too onerous, the alternative would be to attend to the later works first and foremost, to the *Treatise* little if at all. To the student seeking an introduction to Hume's thought, then, it would seem most appropriate to begin, and perhaps even end, with the reading of the *Enquiries*, *Essays*, and works on religion. The *Treatise*, on this view, should be left to the professional: not, however, because it contains an esoteric truth too demanding for the mere amateur, but because to read it is not to discover Hume's considered philosophy: it is only to discover the detail on which professionals thrive—in this case, the early history of Hume's opinions.

This is certainly a conclusion a long way from the popular view. Why does it seem so unsatisfactory? One reason has already been given: that the views he later gave up—or, at least, failed later to endorse—were in fact of greater philosophic worth than those upon which he eventually settled. This is certainly possible, but it applies equally to every philosopher, not to Hume alone. So why does it seem *especially* unsatisfactory as a view about Hume? The sheer intellectual force of the many admired sections of the

---

[18] Ibid.
[19] This is not an uncommon view. See e.g., Noonan, *Hume on Knowledge*, 5.

Treatise is surely much of the answer; but this positive case is, I think, supported by a nagging doubt that stems from the popular view. Unless a direct sally on the question of Hume's 'love of literary fame' can show that this remark is not evidence of philosophically disreputable motives, the suspicion will linger that Hume's rewritings were part of a retreat from philosophy to polite entertainments. So to that task we must now turn. In the next section it will be argued not only that Hume did not retreat from philosophy, but that a proper understanding of the famous remark shows it to imply the opposite: that it is a part of Hume's *defence* of his philosophical work (if not of it alone).

The Love of Literary Fame

Hume's declared 'love of literary fame' has two aspects, and it will be best if these are considered independently. So the meaning of 'literary' and its cognates in Hume's work will be examined, before turning to the question of the love of fame. Finally, a word will be offered on the significance of referring to this love as a 'ruling passion'.

The popular view, that Hume turned from philosophy because of his overriding love of literary fame, depends on assuming that he regarded the philosophical and the literary as quite distinct spheres. There are some examples that support this: the remark, in 'My Own Life', that the second *Enquiry* was, of all his writings, 'historical, philosophical, or literary, incomparably the best';[20] and the very title of the *Essays, Moral, Political, and Literary*. Nevertheless, stated as a general principle, the assumption is false. This is readily shown by a brief survey of Hume's use of the relevant terms. He regularly uses 'literary', 'literature', and so on to refer to the activity of writing in general, and the norms appropriate to it. He does not, in other words, consistently distinguish philosophy from literature, but regularly includes philosophy *within* the realm of literature. Strikingly, 'My Own Life' is itself a principal source of examples of such usage. Three passages serve to illustrate this.

The first occurs when Hume is outlining the early development of his intellectual interests. He says:

I passed through the ordinary course of education with success, and was seized very early with a passion for literature, which has been the ruling passion of my life, and the great source of my enjoyments. My studious disposition, my

---

[20] Hume, 'My Own Life', in *Essays*, p. xxxvi.

sobriety, and my industry, gave my family a notion that the law was a proper profession for me; but I found an unsurmountable aversion to every thing but the pursuits of philosophy and general learning; and while they fancied I was poring upon Voet and Vinnius, Cicero and Virgil were the authors which I was secretly devouring.[21]

In this passage, the 'passion for literature' explains a preoccupation with 'philosophy and general learning'; and, while Virgil may be thought to represent literature *rather than* philosophy, the same cannot be said of Cicero. Hume explicitly acknowledges his debt to Cicero as a moral philosopher: in a famous letter to Francis Hutcheson, he remarks that 'upon the whole, I desire to take my catalogue of virtues from Cicero's *Offices* . . . I had, indeed, the former book in my eye in all my reasonings'.[22] At the risk of labouring the obvious: this shows Cicero being treated as a thinker, and not merely as an exemplar of Latin literary style.

The second example, ironically, refers to the *Treatise* itself—the work alleged to pre-date Hume's 'literary turn'. In the sentence immediately preceding the famous remark that the *Treatise* 'fell *dead-born from the press*', Hume says: 'Never literary attempt was more unfortunate than my Treatise of Human Nature.' This can only mean that, in his eyes, the *Treatise* was itself a literary work; and its failure 'even to excite a murmur amongst the zealots' indicates that literary works can fail not simply through lack of readers or stylistic failings, but also because of their philosophical reception.

The significance of the third example may not be immediately obvious. Hume says: 'In 1751, I removed from the country to the town, the true scene for a man of letters. In 1752, were published at Edinburgh, where I then lived, my Political Discourses, the only work of mine that was successful on the first publication.'[23] The publication of the *Political Discourses* (later to become the second volume of the *Essays*) is here part of the activity of a 'man of letters', and, although the essays in question might not *now* be termed 'philosophical', being largely concerned with political and economic questions, they are nonetheless serious intellectual pieces. They are not productions designed merely for the exercise of refined aesthetic sensibilities. Nor is this usage itself a mere 'literary' indulgence on Hume's part. In a passage from one of the early essays withdrawn from the later editions of the *Essays*, 'Of

---

[21] Ibid., pp. xxxii–xxxiii.
[22] Hume to Hutcheson, 17 Sept. 1739; in *Letters*, ed. Greig, i. 34 (repr. in D. D. Raphael (ed.), *British Moralists 1650–1800* (Oxford: Oxford University Press, 1969), ii. 109).
[23] 'My Own Life', in *Essays*, p. xxxvi.

Essay Writing',[24] Hume uses the term again, and in a way that makes its proper reference clear: ' 'Tis with great Pleasure I observe, That Men of Letters, in this Age, have lost, in a great Measure, that Shyness and Bashfulness of Temper, which kept them at a Distance from Mankind; and at the same Time, That Men of the World are proud of borrowing from Books their most agreeable Topics of Conversation.'[25] A man of letters is presented here as a writer, a producer of books, and is contrasted with a man of the world, who lives the life of active involvement in practical affairs. Since it is still the educated classes Hume has firmly in mind, the politician and the diplomat would be the best examples. Given this distinction, then, we should not find it surprising that Hume includes philosophical writing within the world of the literary. The philosopher is a man of letters, and his works are literary works. The assumed clear distinction between the philosophical and the literary, on which the common view depends, is therefore mistaken.

Further support for this conclusion is not difficult to come by. One in particular is worth mentioning, because it occurs in the same context as the above quotation. In the immediately preceding paragraph, Hume uses the term *'Belles Lettres'* to refer to the products of 'Learning'—although the context leaves it unclear whether it is the whole, or merely a part, of those products.[26] Secondly, in a letter to Hugh Blair from Paris in late 1763, he remarks that 'The Men of Letters here are very agreeable', adding 'Those whose Persons & Conversation I like best are d'Alembert, Buffon, Marmontel, Diderot, Duclos, Helvetius'.[27] Obviously, this is not a list of the *merely* literary. Hume's use of the term can also be instructively compared with Voltaire's: in Letter 23 of his *Letters on England*, 'On the Consideration Due to Men of Letters', the young Voltaire implicitly identifies the concerns of the man of letters with the world of the arts—a world that includes 'astronomy, all branches of mathematics, medicine, antiquarian researches, painting, sculpture and architecture'.[28] Thirdly, a survey of the contents of the journals on which the 'republic of letters' was built, membership of which defined the 'man of

---

[24] Given the work's dependence on extended (and rather heavy-handed) metaphors, a feature not characteristic of Hume's work, it is hard to resist the conclusion that one reason for the exclusion of this piece from later editions was precisely for aesthetic reasons. Alternatively, it may be that Hume later judged the tone of the work to be inappropriate for a successful publication, since the essay's use of metaphor is in part a plea that the following, more intellectually demanding, essays be taken seriously by the refined reading public. The essay thus played, in the first edition (the only edition in which it appeared), the same role as the opening section of the first *Enquiry*.

[25] 'Of Essay Writing', in *Essays*, 535.   [26] Ibid. 534.   [27] *Letters*, ed. Greig, i. 419.

[28] François-Marie Arouet Voltaire, *Letters on England* [*Lettres philosophiques*], trans. L. Tancock (Harmondsworth: Penguin Books, 1980), 111–14.

letters', shows a similar breadth and depth. In the *Gentleman's Magazine*, for example, 'amongst all the travel reports, political opinions, literary satires, and general news of the happenings in the republic of letters . . . the most random sampling reveals a dazzling range of scientific news and opinion in juxtaposition with theological and doctrinal controversies'.[29] John Valdimir Price's conclusion is apposite: 'The "man of letters" in the eighteenth century had to be philosopher, historian, and literary craftsman if he wanted to have any impact on his readers.'[30] The explanation for this very broad use is that to be a man of letters was to be *educated*. The domain of the man of letters was literature, and literature was the written word. It embraced all written— that is, all educated—pursuits, the seriously intellectual no less than the purely aesthetic. Therefore, terms such as 'literature', 'literary', or 'man of letters', in their eighteenth-century employment, do not indicate polite amusements rather than serious intellectual endeavours. If anything, they imply the opposite.[31]

Finally, it is also in 'Of Essay Writing' that Hume makes the famous remark that he considers himself 'a Kind of Resident or Ambassador from the Dominions of Learning to those of Conversation'. Taken at face value, this remark might seem to support the popular view, but once again a closer inspection shows that it does not. This is because the point of being such an ambassador is, for Hume, to improve *both* domains, not simply to improve the latter by reporting to it the discoveries of the former. This is often not recognized, because it is not obvious how the 'conversible' world can improve the world of learning. But Hume is clear on the matter. Without constant contact with the world of affairs, learning becomes self-indulgent, irrelevant, in a word, 'barbarous': 'Even Philosophy went to Wrack by this moaping recluse Method of Study, and became as chimerical in her Conclusions as she was unintelligible in her Stile and Manner of Delivery.'[32] Philosophy

---

[29] J. E. Force, 'Hume's Interest in Newton and Science', *Hume Studies*, 13 (1987), 188.

[30] J. V. Price, review of J. W. Yolton (ed.), *Philosophy, Religion and Science in the Seventeenth and Eighteenth Centuries*, in *British Journal for the History of Philosophy*, 1 (1993), 153.

[31] For broadly similar conclusions, see also J. J. Richetti, *Philosophical Writing: Locke, Berkeley, Hume* (Cambridge, Mass.: Harvard University Press, 1983), ch. 4; and J. Christensen, *Practicing Enlightenment: Hume and the Formation of a Literary Career* (Madison: University of Wisconsin Press, 1987), introduction.

[32] *Essays*, 534–5. Eugene F. Miller, in his Foreword to the *Essays*, concurs: 'Hume's essays do not mark an abandonment of philosophy, as some have maintained, but rather an attempt to improve it by having it address the concerns of common life' (*Essays*, p. xviii). It is worth emphasizing that this is no eccentric opinion, nor one limited to Humean apologists. Many philosophers have felt the force of the point. Thus, for example, C. A. J. Coady: 'If philosophical concerns are not, at certain points, turned outwards towards the broader community and its intellectual condition, they lose focus and nourishment, and if the community has no access to the reflections of philosophers, it is deprived of valuable insights and

becomes no good, even to itself, when it turns its back on the world of public affairs. For the public world itself, it is actually pernicious, since its unintelligible jargon becomes an obstacle to social improvement. Hume's concern for the 'conversible' world is evidence not of shallow populism, but of his reforming concern that intellectual advances be translatable into social improvements. It shows him to belong with other reforming public thinkers—for example, Bacon and Voltaire.

To turn now to the second aspect, the love of fame. The popular view depends on treating this as the desire for applause, or popularity, however fleeting: fame in the Andy Warhol sense. The quintessential creation of this form of fame is the modern *celebrity*, aptly described as 'someone well-known for their well-knownness'. In its negative aspect, it is simple notoriety. This is emphatically not what Hume has in mind.

What he does have in mind is shown by two passages from *An Enquiry concerning the Principles of Morals*. In Section VIII, entitled, appropriately, 'Of Qualities immediately agreeable to Others', Hume argues that we become liked and admired by others through the possession and exercise of social virtues. These include, first of all, good manners and social ease, but also intelligence, especially creative intelligence:

Among well-bred people, a mutual deference is affected; contempt of others disguised; authority concealed; attention given to each in his turn; and an easy stream of conversation maintained, without vehemence, without interruption, without eagerness for victory, and without any airs of superiority ... But, in order to render a man perfect *good company*, he must have Wit and Ingenuity as well as good manners.[33]

The man who possesses these virtues will be well thought of by others, and will thus possess a public *reputation*, or *fame*. Fame in this sense is entirely laudable, as is the desire for such a reputation: the 'love of fame'. This is what Hume means by the term, so it is not surprising to find that he also considers it entirely virtuous: 'A desire of fame, reputation, or a character with others, is so far from being blameable, that it seems inseparable from virtue, genius, capacity, and a generous or noble disposition.'[34]

In the following section, the point is pressed:

self-understanding ... I have tried here to keep philosophical technicalities to a minimum, and to write in a way that I hope will engage the attention and interests of philosophers and non-philosophers alike' (C. A. J. Coady, *Testimony* (Oxford: Clarendon Press, 1992), p. x). In affirming this position, Coady is not abandoning philosophy, but seeking to do it well. The same is true of Hume.

[33] *Enquiries*, 261–2.   [34] Ibid. 265.

A spring of our constitution, that brings a great addition of force to moral sentiment, is the love of fame; which rules, with such uncontrolled authority, in all generous minds, and is often the grand object of all their designs and undertakings. By our continual and earnest pursuit of a character, a name, a reputation in the world, we bring our own deportment and conduct frequently in review, and consider how they appear in the eyes of those who approach and regard us. This constant habit of surveying ourselves, as it were, in reflection, keeps alive all the sentiments of right and wrong, and begets, in noble natures, a certain reverence for themselves as well as others, which is the surest guardian of every virtue. The animal conveniencies and pleasures sink gradually in their value; while every inward beauty and moral grace is studiously acquired, and the mind is accomplished in every perfection, which can adorn or embellish a rational creature.[35]

This long passage shows conclusively that, when Hume identifies his ruling passion as the love of literary fame, nothing could be further from his meaning than the opportunistic desire for ignorant applause. The love of fame is the desire to be respected and admired by others, and respected and admired by being seen to *deserve* such respect and admiration, because genuinely in possession of the relevant virtues. It is, in other words, the concern to have a good reputation—a good name—and in this sense fame is a measure of virtue.

This connection, between fame and virtue, is implied by the fact that 'fame', when unqualified, usually meant 'known to possess *good* reputation or character'. This is acknowledged in *The Oxford English Dictionary*, which treats 'fame', when unqualified, as a term of praise, because the pejorative sense is typically qualified by an adjective: thus 'cruel fame' and 'ill fame'. The archaic air of these expressions indicates that such uses are less common today, but it is worth noting that they have not disappeared. Thus we show ourselves to be lovers of fame when we seek to avoid *infamy*, in particular by ensuring that we are never *defamed*. Of course, attributions of fame can be misplaced, and the point was not lost even on a world innocent of modern mass media. Thus Francis Bacon observes, in his essay 'Of Praise', that its objects are not always deserving:

Praise is the reflection of virtue: but it is as the glass or body which giveth the reflection. If it be from the common people, it is commonly false and naught, and rather followeth vain persons than virtuous. For the common people understand not many excellent virtues . . . Certainly fame is like a river that beareth up things light and swollen and drowns things weighty and solid.

---

[35] Ibid. 276.

But if persons of judgment and quality concur, then it is (as the Scripture saith), *Nomen bonum instar unguenti fragrantis.*[36]

Bacon's view is useful here, for it provides an independent test for Hume's own love of fame. If Hume's concern is for the estimation of the learned, rather than of the ignorant multitude, then his concern for fame is, once again, to be distinguished from the desire for mere applause. This is what we find, not least in the young man anxious for making a splash: in letters written to his cousin Henry Home during the period when the *Treatise* was about to see the light of day, Hume shows himself to be very concerned, not with ignorant applause, but with the judgement of those readers capable of understanding the work; and his concern with style there is with the means by which such understanding is brought about.[37] Much the same point is made in the *Abstract*, where Hume acknowledges that in this work (that is, in the *Treatise*) he must be judged by 'the *Few*' who are capable of the necessary judgement, rather than by 'an *appeal to the people*'.[38] The young Hume thus passes Bacon's test for merited praise.

The love of literary fame is the desire to be esteemed, and *correctly* esteemed, as someone who possesses the virtues relevant to the writer's craft. In Hume's case, this means the general virtues necessary for a pleasing style; but it also means the specific virtues appropriate to the different species of Hume's writings: historical, philosophical, and 'literary'. The popular view, then, that Hume abandoned philosophy because of his 'love of literary fame', will not stand up. The love was real: but the supposed contrasts on which the common view depends are entirely fictitious.

As a tailpiece to these considerations on the love of fame, an earlier treatment of the subject is enlightening. The French Arminian theologian Jacques Abbadie had argued, in his *The Art of Self-Knowledge* (1692), that the desire for praise is a providentially implanted tool for the perfection of society:

It pleased the wisdom of the Creator to give us, for judge of our actions, not only our reason, which allows itself to be corrupted by pleasure, but also the reason of other men, which is not so easily seduced . . . [since] they are not so partial to us as we are to ourselves. It is this desire of being esteemed that

---

[36] 'A good name is like a fragrant ointment' (Eccles. 7: 1); Francis Bacon, *The Essays*, ed. J. Pitcher (Harmondsworth: Penguin Books, 1985), 215.

[37] See *Letters*, ed. Greig, i. 23–7.

[38] *Abstract*, in *A Treatise of Human Nature*, 2nd edn., ed. L. A. Selby-Bigge, rev. P. H. Nidditch (Oxford: Clarendon Press, 1978), 644. (My thanks to D. F. Norton for drawing my attention to this and the preceding reference.)

makes us courteous and considerate, obliging and decent, makes us wish for decorum and gentle manners in social relations.[39]

Abbadie's point is part of a larger critique of the predestinarian views of the Jansenists and Calvinists, and as such is part of an attempt to show the positive features of social life. This general concern would have been very congenial to Hume, and Abbadie's specific points in this passage could have been written by Hume himself: that social life serves to correct our tendency to over-value ourselves, makes us considerate of others, encourages gentle manners, and so on. All this suggests that Hume's affirmation of fame, including, we may surmise, its literary variety, would have been understood by his (unprejudiced) contemporaries as an affirmation of the value of society for human beings—not simply for the friendships it can offer, but because it is in society that both social and intellectual virtues are cultivated. This picks out a thread running all the way through Hume's works. For the affirmation of the social in the love of literary fame in 'My Own Life', Hume's last work, reflects precisely the value placed on the judgement of the educated public in his first, as the 'Advertisement' to the *Treatise* shows: 'The approbation of the public I consider as the greatest reward of my labours; but I am determin'd to regard its judgment, whatever it be, as my best instruction.'[40]

Finally, it is worth making some observations about the likely impact of Hume's use of the expression 'ruling passion'. Amongst modern philosophers, the words are commonly taken at face value, as if simple self-disclosure. The term has a history, however, and it is unlikely that Hume's readers were unaware of the fact. The consequence is that the whole remark with which we are concerned—'my love of literary fame, my ruling passion'—has, to its intended audience, a 'literary' air of its own. It bears the stamp of artifice.[41]

To bring this out, we can begin with Locke. Towards the end of *An Essay concerning Human Understanding*, Locke turns to questions concerning the causes of irrationality and error in human behaviour. One of these causes is 'Men's Appetites, and *prevailing Passions*', which resist the counsels of reason as 'Mud-Walls, resist the strongest Batteries', and thereby 'keep out the Enemy Truth,

---

[39] Quoted in J. Z. Muller, *Adam Smith in his Time and Ours: Designing the Decent Society* (New York: Free Press, 1993), 52.

[40] *Treatise*, p. xii.

[41] The connections are pointed out by Frasca-Spada: 'Ruling passion', she suggests, 'was, presumably, a cliché' (*Space and the Self in Hume's* Treatise, 107).

that would captivate, or disturb them'.[42] In this sense, a ruling
passion is what governs us, even in the face of our best efforts to
the contrary. It is not so much our explicit occurrent motive, but
the underlying cause visible to others who understand our character flaws, or to ourselves when we reflect upon our pasts and
discern patterns of which we were not conscious at the time. As
such, it is a two-edged sword—including in Hume's case. It is so
because for Hume to invoke a ruling passion is, in this sense of the
term, implicitly to deny that his decision to rewrite his philosophy in various works was motivated by a conscious pursuit of
fame—even of deserved fame in the sense spelt out above. On the
other hand, it is to concede that the mature man, looking back on
his past, sees the reality of his search for recognition, albeit hidden
at the time in the consuming pursuit of the argument, or later
in the forging of a diplomatic career. It does allow us to think of
Hume's remark as a possibly wry observation on the unexpected—
unexpectedly coherent—shape of a life when viewed from its final
vantage point.

  Hume may or may not have intended his remark to have the
obdurate, self-ironical, air the notion possesses in Locke's employment. He may have had in mind a more recent, and more widely
recognized, literary employment, in the first of Pope's *Moral Essays*,
the 'Epistle to Cobham'. If it was this use that Hume had in mind,
his remark lacks the wry air of the Lockean use—of insight into
one's foibles. It would be the more neutral recognition of one's
general motivations, without any sense of being at odds with
reason. It would be, in fact, simply the most salient of the 'calm
passions' described in Book II of the *Treatise*. However, Pope's use
of the term does offer support for the view advanced above, that
Hume saw his love of literary fame as a virtue, and expected others
to see it so as well. An examination of the passage makes this clear.
Pope contrasts the changeability of human behaviours, before
unifying them under the head of the 'ruling passion':

> Judge we by nature? Habit can efface,
> Interest o'ercome, or policy take place:
> By actions? those uncertainty divides:
> By passions? these dissimulation hides:
> Opinions? they still take a wider range:
> Find, if you can, in what you cannot change.
>   Manners with fortunes, humours turn with climes,
> Tenets with books, and principles with times.

---

[42] John Locke, *An Essay concerning Human Understanding*, ed. P. H. Nidditch (Oxford:
Clarendon Press, 1975), IV. xx. 12.

> Search then the RULING PASSION: there, alone,
> The wild are constant, the cunning known;
> The fool consistent, and the false sincere;
> Priests, princes, women, no dissemblers here.

Further, once the general principle is established, the particular ruling passions of given individuals can then be identified. Thus Pope continues:

> This clue once found, unravels all the rest,
> The prospect clears, and Wharton stands confessed.
> Wharton, the scorn and wonder of our days,
> Whose ruling passion was the lust of praise . . .[43]

It is not certain that Hume is alluding to these lines, of course; but if he is, the message is clear. Philip, Duke of Wharton (1698–1731), ruled by the lust of praise, 'blazed across the early Hanoverian sky and burnt himself out by the age of 33', becoming, thereby, an 'object of cautionary tales'.[44] Hume, in contrast, ruled by the love of literary fame, was, as he is happy to tell us himself, 'a man of mild dispositions, of command of temper, of an open, social, and cheerful humour, capable of attachment, but little susceptible of enmity, and of great moderation in all [his] passions'.[45] Hume's 'confession' of his ruling passion, may, then, be just another way to remind the reader of his moral virtues. It is certainly not a penitent's confession of an intellectual vice.

Two Final Obstacles

Doubts may yet linger. After all, is it not the case that, however one construes Hume's explicit remarks about literary fame, he shows by his practice that he gives up serious philosophy after the *Treatise*? He offers, in the first *Enquiry*, only short and superficial accounts of the problems he had considered at some length in the *Treatise*, avoiding some of the toughest problems entirely; he resorts, on political and social topics, to the polite essay form of Addison and Steele, a form, however accessible, not suited to the resolution of difficult problems; he devotes his intellectual time and energy, in his maturity, to writing the massive *History of England*, easily the longest of all his works; and in his later years

---

[43] Alexander Pope, 'An Epistle to Sir Richard Temple, Lord Cobham', 166–81, in *Alexander Pope*, ed. Rogers, 324.
[44] As Pat Rogers puts it in the Biographical Index (ibid. 732).
[45] 'My Own Life', in *Essays*, p. xl.

he retires to the pleasures and rewards of the diplomatic life. Does he not therefore show, in his own life, his adherence to his remarks, in the first *Enquiry*, to the effect that Man is not only a 'reasonable being', but also a 'sociable being' and an 'active being', and that living well requires keeping these three elements in harmony, in particular by preventing the first, intellectual, aspect, from dominating the others? Does he not, in other words, *show* his abandonment of philosophy, and in doing so show how faithfully he adheres to his own maxim, 'Be a philosopher; but, amidst all your philosophy, be still a man'?[46]

This question has many strands, and it would be tedious to attempt to answer them all. The relation of the first *Enquiry* to the *Treatise* is of central importance here, but cannot, of course, be settled independently of an understanding of the *Enquiry*'s own purpose—the identification of which is, of course, the main ambition of this study. Other relevant strands, such as the proper interpretation of the *Essays* and *History*, would lead too far afield, and so must be left to another occasion.[47] Two questions can, however, be profitably examined at this point: one is the conception of philosophy implicit in several of the objections, and embodied in no small percentage of philosophy curricula; the other is the meaning of the famous remark that concludes the paragraph above. The second of these can be considered first.

'Be a philosopher; but, amidst all your philosophy, be still a man.' This famous remark, from the opening section of the first *Enquiry*, has seemed to many, friend and foe alike, to sum up Hume's outlook. To the friend, it has seemed to capture the humane, balanced nature of Hume's mitigated scepticism, and for this reason it finds itself on the title page of Ernest Mossner's admiring biography.[48] To the foe, it has seemed to sum up Hume's regrettable willingness, when confronted by real philosophical difficulties, to abandon the challenge and opt for the comfortable life.

Both views are mistaken, but not because they misunderstand the point of the remark. The point is indeed to affirm that 'the mere philosopher is a character, which is commonly but little acceptable in the world', and that the appropriate response is to

---

[46] *Enquiries*, 9.
[47] Some of the more important discussions of these are the following: D. F. Norton and R. H. Popkin (eds.), *David Hume: Philosophical Historian* (Indianapolis: Bobbs-Merrill, 1965); Livingston, *Hume's Philosophy of Common Life*; N. Capaldi and D. W. Livingston (eds.), *Liberty in Hume's History of England* (Dordrecht: Kluwer, 1990); and M. A. Box, *The Suasive Art of David Hume* (Princeton: Princeton University Press, 1990).
[48] Mossner, *The Life of David Hume*, p. iii.

limit one's pursuit of hard intellectual endeavours, to preserve in one's life space for company and action, space unfettered by wearisome and alienating intellectual labour. The misunderstanding, however, is the presumption that the point being affirmed is Hume's own. It is not. The opening section of the *Enquiry* is an *apologia* for the work itself, and attending to its structure reveals the role that this famous remark actually plays. The basic structure is as follows: in paragraphs 1–2, Hume describes two kinds of philosophy, the 'easy' and the 'abstruse'; in paragraphs 3–4, he presents the case for the 'easy' philosophy'; in paragraphs 5–10, he provides the reply of the 'abstruse' philosophy. In the closing sentences of paragraph 10, he then offers a harmonizing conclusion: the best course is to attempt to combine the merits of each of the two kinds, 'by reconciling profound enquiry with clearness, and truth with novelty'.[49] Where does the famous remark fit in this structure? It is the summation of the view of the 'easy' philosophy. As such, it is not Hume's own considered view. In fact, he explicitly rejects it.

The modern reader easily fails to notice this because of the very leisurely pace with which Section I unfolds. It is itself, of necessity, more in the style of the 'easy' philosophy, since its task is to persuade the reader to persevere through the difficult passages that lie ahead. In this respect, its very existence is testimony to the fact that difficulty *does* lie ahead—and also to Hume's awareness that his success in combining the two kinds of philosophy was likely to be judged (or prejudged) as less than total, at least by his expected audience. Even so, the text does provide sufficient immediate clues to alert the attentive reader to the fact that the remark is not Hume's own position, however sympathetically he may have viewed it. Immediately following the three carefully balanced sentences proclaiming that Man is 'reasonable', 'sociable', and 'active', a conclusion is drawn and then elaborated, and summed up with the remark in question. The first statement of this conclusion indicates, however, that it concerns only appearances: 'It *seems* . . . that nature has pointed out a mixed kind of life as most suitable to human race . . .'.[50] Hume is usually very careful in his use of appearance terms, so when he says 'seems' here he is best understood to mean just that. Nevertheless, it may itself seem contentious to pin a heavy interpretative load on just one word—so this interpretation will be strengthened considerably by further contextual support.

[49] *Enquiries*, 16.   [50] Ibid. 9 (emphasis added).

The support is available, because the opening sentences of paragraph 5, immediately following the famous remark, can be read only as a (sympathetic) rejection of the preceding paragraphs, including the remark itself. To show the point of the passage most clearly, it is best to include its immediate context:

Be a philosopher; but, amidst all your philosophy, be still a man.

Were the generality of mankind contented to prefer the easy philosophy to the abstract and profound, without throwing any blame or contempt on the latter, it might not be improper, perhaps, to comply with this general opinion, and allow every man to enjoy, without opposition, his own taste and sentiment. But as the matter is often carried farther, even to the absolute rejecting of all profound reasonings, or what is commonly called *metaphysics*, we shall now proceed to consider what can reasonably be pleaded in their behalf.[51]

This passage is clearly meant to bridge two sections: to respond to an argument for the 'easy' philosophy by introducing a defence of the 'abstruse' philosophy. The author has not yet revealed his hand, but it is sufficiently evident that his position is not to be identified with that summed up in the famous remark. Not for the first time, Hume's facility with the 'quotable quote' has served to mislead his readers.

We can now turn to the second of the two obstacles mentioned above—the assumption hidden in the standard assessment of the *Enquiry* as less sophisticated in its treatment of important philosophical problems. The assumption is the equation of philosophy with the discussion of 'philosophical problems': that to engage in the philosophical enterprise is precisely to be concerned with a distinctive set of problems, identifiable independently of any substantive philosophical position. In its extreme form, it is to assume that to be a philosopher is to be someone who *does* address these problems, no more and no less; that philosophical activity is defined by contributions to debates in professional journals of philosophy. This assumption, especially in its stronger forms, is an important obstacle to an independent evaluation of the *Enquiry*. It is also very difficult to shake off, in part because of the pressure to rank—and therefore to place on a uniform scale—the members of a profession that rewards according to achievement, but especially because of the ubiquitous influence of that powerful interpretative filter and inertial force: the undergraduate curriculum. The curriculum tends to marginalize the *Enquiry* precisely because of its characteristic divisions.

[51] *Enquiries*, 16.

The teaching of early modern philosophy in university philosophy departments is typically arranged around a narrow range of themes, topics, or debates, most of which are at some remove from the actual concerns of the authors studied. The following four titles would come pretty close to exhausting the actual content of most courses in which the study of Hume's writings comprises a non-negligible part: Rationalism versus Empiricism; Topics in Empiricism; Forerunners of Modern Positivism; and (of course) Problems of Philosophy. In fact, Hume is taught in undergraduate philosophy courses precisely because it is thought possible to fit him into courses of this kind. If he did not fit, he would not be taught—and would therefore enjoy the profound neglect of, say, Gassendi or Montaigne. However, once questions like these are in the air, the *Enquiry*'s chances of being taken on its own terms are immediately in trouble, since, as already observed, the *Treatise* offers a fuller discussion of the various topics. Even if one starts from the *Enquiry*—as indeed is not uncommon in introductory philosophy courses—the problems will almost inevitably be 'clarified' by referring the student to the *Treatise*; and the hyperabundance of literature available on the *Treatise*'s handling of the issues ensures that, however much the course focuses on the *Enquiry*, the students' essays (and thus, in time, the unreflective assumptions of a new generation of philosophers) will be shaped by the earlier work.[52]

No less important, in terms of Hume's role in the curriculum, is that it is the *Treatise* that affirms, or appears to affirm, the views that the curricular distinctions require. Hume is taught in order to present the figure known as the 'Humean', a figure with a clear and (no less usefully!) a questionable view on the relevant topics. This figure—especially its more 'destructively sceptical' aspects[53]— is far more clearly represented in the earlier work, especially in

---

[52] This is the voice of experience!

[53] Hume is canonized as an essentially destructive thinker, first, because Reid so understood him, and saw this outcome to be the inevitable tendency of the theory of ideas. Hume himself sought to oppose Reid's interpretation of his philosophy: as indicated above, the 'Advertisement' affixed to the later editions of his works was intended as 'a compleat Answer to Dr Reid and to that bigotted silly Fellow, Beattie'. Secondly, and, in the end, more influentially, Hume's reputation as a wholly destructive thinker reflects the impact of Kantian philosophy and subsequent Kantian historiography. The Critical Philosophy understood itself as overcoming a species of scepticism—of which Hume was the exemplar—which, although rightly opposed to the dogmatic philosophies of the past, left no firm foundation for constructive philosophy. Hume's philosophy was effectively defined as a problem to be overcome. Such was the Kantian influence in the nineteenth century that this account of Hume triumphed even amongst those who rejected Kant's solution. Thus Hume's philosophy became canonical principally because of what it was understood to be against, and in this way it came to be understood as a philosophy almost wholly concerned to be oppositional— that is, to all constructive traditions in philosophy. See e.g. F. C. Beiser, *The Fate of Reason* (Cambridge, Mass.: Harvard University Press, 1987), introduction.

some of its catchier phrases, so its value for the curriculum comes as no surprise. The *Enquiry*, in contrast, often seems to fail to say what readers familiar with the *Treatise* (the teachers) are confident he *must* (or at least *should*) be saying, and so, in the end, it tends to be set aside as a somewhat disappointing work.

In all of this, the conviction that philosophy is essentially the analysis of a cluster of problems (and an *invariant* cluster at that) is doing a large share of the work. However, there is readily available a quite different conception of philosophy, a conception held by perhaps the majority of students when they first enrol in a philosophy course—and which their teachers often devote some energy to knocking out of them. The energy is probably unnecessary, however, since osmosis alone will do the job: after several years of study, students have either forgotten, or learnt to dismiss, views that imply that a philosophy is a coherent world view, that what its study might provide, above all, is a 'philosophy of life'. This is, in my view, a deeply regrettable development; but here it is appropriate only to point out the way in which it conspires to obstruct the reading of the first *Enquiry*. This is because, as this study will attempt to show, the *Enquiry* is precisely an attempt to work out a coherent philosophical outlook, with significant implications for the conduct of one's life. In the working-out of this position, what we now refer to as Hume's 'empiricism' plays a crucial role—but in describing it thus we are led into the wrong set of disjunctions.

Hume understood his intellectual activity not as the construction of 'empiricist' (dogmatic sensationalist) philosophy, but as the working-out of a consistent 'experimental philosophy'. The key to understanding his aims in the *Enquiry* can be described in terms of finding the proper interpretation of experimental philosophy, and of its application to the sphere of human affairs. Hume made it plain that he understood this proper interpretation to amount to a form of scepticism, but not of a wholly destructive or self-defeating scepticism. He made it equally plain that this scepticism had a cutting edge, and a very discriminating one at that. The task of reading the *Enquiry* aright, then, depends on understanding the connections between experimentalism, scepticism, construction, and criticism. The next chapter will identify the *Enquiry*'s main critical target, and thereby sketch in the outlines of Hume's intellectual project.

Chapter 2

Circumstances and Aim

From its opening section, the first *Enquiry* signals that it has a polemical purpose. It is not merely a polemic, of course, but identifying the work's apparent (and real) targets assists in bringing out the underlying unity of its argument; and that argument, once its outlines have been sketched in, also illustrates the connections Hume discerns between experimentalism and scepticism. The immediate task, then, is to emphasize the significance of the *Enquiry*'s distinctively sharp edge, and to identify its primary targets. Attending to the particular circumstances in which the work was produced will be a useful preparation.

The Circumstances of Production

Hume published the *Philosophical Essays concerning Human Understanding* (as the *Enquiry* was first titled) in 1748. This places it at the end of one of the most eventful periods of his life, events that are played down in the autobiography. Mossner suggests, mainly on the basis of a letter from Hume to his older cousin Henry Home—which refers to work in progress on some 'philosophical & moral Essays'—that Hume began work on what became the *Enquiry* in 1745, when living near London, employed as a tutor to the Marquess of Annandale.[1] The Marquess's mental instability led to Hume's departure from the position, and subsequent move to London, on 16 April 1746, the day of the final defeat of Bonnie Prince Charlie at Culloden. Further troubles with France—the War of the Austrian Succession—provided Hume with employment, as secretary to General James St Clair, a distant relative. This led to a brief, and comically mismanaged, military adventure in Brittany. St Clair was instructed to mount an expedition against French Canada, but a mixture of unfavourable weather and Admiralty

---

[1] Mossner, *The Life of David Hume*, 174.

indecision saw the expedition redirected at short notice to a frontal assault on the coast of France. The assault was a complete botch-up, as might be expected given the lack of preparation—St Clair even had to buy a map of France from a shop in Plymouth before the fleet could set sail—but Hume did manage to survive a few days in Brittany as an enemy alien before the expedition retreated to the safety of England. The whole misadventure is covered by a sentence in 'My Own Life'; Voltaire exposed its absurdities at greater length in an appendix to his *History of the War of 1741*.[2] Serious military expeditions now behind him—but wearing 'the uniform of an officer' while accompanying St Clair's military embassy to Vienna and Turin—Hume was able to return to the work in mid-1747, finishing it by the beginning of the following year. It appeared while he was still in Turin.[3]

The *Enquiry* was thus composed in the years 1745–8, a period in which Hume was not living the quiet life of the man of letters, but was caught up in wider political tensions. If the main source of those tensions is brought to the fore, it becomes possible to see the *Enquiry* as owing some of its features to political developments. The background event that raised tensions with France was the Revolt of 1745: Bonnie Prince Charlie's attempt, supported mainly by Highland Catholics, to reclaim the British throne for the Stuarts; an attempt that, after impressive early successes, finally came to grief at Culloden in 1746. This was the third Jacobite uprising in Hume's lifetime, after the Great Rising of 1715 and the Little Rising of 1719. It was also to be the last; but this was not, of course, evident at the time. Rather, it seemed to show that Scottish Catholicism was a political force to be feared, and did indeed show that the religiously embedded political conflicts of Great Britain in the 1640s, the revival of which had been only narrowly averted in 1688, were far from ancient history.[4] To the reflective citizen of the mid-eighteenth century, the politics of Catholicism was a force to be reckoned with; for Hume, a Lowland Scot sympathetic to the Hanoverian succession, it was a danger to be opposed.[5]

A second important factor in Hume's life in this period—although passed over in 'My Own Life'—is that in 1745 he applied, unsuccessfully, for the vacant Chair in Moral Philosophy at the University of Edinburgh. This was his first attempt to gain an aca-

---

[2] For the details, see ibid. 187–204.   [3] 'My Own Life', in *Essays*, p. xxxv.
[4] See e.g. B. Lenman, *The Jacobite Cause* (Glasgow: Richard Drew Publishing, 1986).
[5] See Hume's discussion of the issue in 'Of the Protestant Succession', in *Essays*, 502–11. This essay was itself written for publication in 1748, but, because of the temper of the times, it was withheld. See the editorial comments by E. F. Miller, 502 n.

demic appointment, and the failure must have hit him hard. The fact that his lack of success was largely due to factional machinations within the Edinburgh establishment (that is, within the upper echelons of the Church of Scotland) would not have escaped him; and it is clear that he took strong exception to one volley in that factional war, the publication of a pamphlet attacking his suitability for the position. The pamphlet alleged that the *Treatise* was both atheistic and a threat to morality. Upon learning of its existence, Hume immediately dashed off a reply—as he tells us, the very same day. This reply, entitled *A Letter from a Gentleman to his Friend in Edinburgh*, rebuts the pamphlet's charges one by one— a fact sufficient in itself to show that he cared greatly about the outcome of the disputes concerning the Chair. His failure can only have left him very uncertain about the possibility of an intellectual career, and so extremely disappointed.[6]

The two events together—the personal and the political—can reasonably be supposed to have left him markedly more hostile to religion, especially to the extremism fostered in religious politics and morals. On this supposition, it would not be surprising to find more sharply expressed criticisms of religion in the subsequent works. This is indeed what we find. To name just two: the second *Enquiry*, with its blunt estimation of the 'monkish virtues';[7] and the Stuart volumes of *The History of England* (published in 1754), with their sharp criticisms of the Puritans in particular. The same is true of the first *Enquiry*: it has a sharp edge quite lacking in the *Treatise*, and it is religion in particular that is made to feel the blade.[8] Hume makes his official target very plain: as will be shown

[6] David Hume, *A Letter from a Gentleman to his Friend in Edinburgh*, ed. E. C. Mossner and J. V. Price (Edinburgh: Edinburgh University Press, 1967). Mossner and Price provide, in the Introduction, a helpful account of the politics surrounding the appointment. See also R. B. Sher, 'Professors of Virtue: The Social History of the Edinburgh Moral Philosophy Chair in the Eighteenth Century', in M. A. Stewart (ed.), *Studies in the Philosophy of the Scottish Enlightenment* (Oxford Studies in the History of Philosophy, 1; Oxford: Clarendon Press, 1990), 102–9.

[7] *Enquiries*, 270.

[8] See Noxon, *Hume's Philosophical Development*: 'It is no conjecture, but a fact that confronts anyone who reviews his philosophical books in order, that Hume became increasingly hostile toward religion . . .' (77–8). Noxon attributes this to Hume's becoming 'increasingly concerned to check the speculative excesses of the Newtonians' (77), and goes on to claim that 'an appreciation of Hume's response to the religious aspect of the Newtonian movement is as important for understanding his mature philosophy as recognizing the impact of the Newtonian method for understanding his first work' (78–9). This is, I think, to head in the right direction, but its focus is too narrow. On the account to be offered here (which, unlike Noxon's thesis, admittedly, concerns only the first *Enquiry*), although the Newtonians are indeed in Hume's field of fire, they are not his particular target. His focus is very broad, and the religious views of the Newtonians come in for attention principally because Hume's concerns so centrally revolve around religion, but also because he believes they have misunderstood the lessons of Newtonian philosophy. Strikingly, he also believes the misunderstandings to infect Newton himself. Newton and his followers developed religious

below, the book presents itself as a Protestant attack on Catholicism, and the innocent eighteenth-century reader would not have missed the message. Of course, the actual argument has ramifications that are considerably wider, and of little comfort for Protestants—and it is plain that the author is well aware of the fact. So the gap between official and actual targets shows that Hume deliberately presented the work as if aligned to a cause to which it was opposed: the official target must be described as, in part, a rhetorical smokescreen intended to disarm, or at least perplex, the intending critic. Nevertheless, bringing that target to centre stage is an important step in discerning the direction of the argument.

The Target

The opening section of the first *Enquiry* is principally an apology for some of the difficult and abstract issues that are to confront the reader in the subsequent sections. Hume argues that the difficulties of the road ahead are worth it, because the end result will be accuracy and clarity. He does not rest content with this assurance, but further argues that the greatest value of coming to possess accurate knowledge is that it enables us to identify superstition for what it is, and so to inoculate ourselves against all such imprisoning philosophies by recognizing the false promises on which they do, and must, rely.

The first step towards this goal is to identify why difficult philosophy—'metaphysics'—is not always held in high regard:

the justest and most plausible objection against a considerable part of metaphysics [is] that they are not properly a science; but arise either from the fruitless efforts of human vanity, which would penetrate into subjects utterly inaccessible to the understanding, or from the craft of popular superstitions, which, being unable to defend themselves on fair ground, raise these intangling brambles to cover and protect their weakness. Chaced from the open country, these robbers fly into the forest, and lie in wait to break in upon every unguarded avenue of the mind, and overwhelm it with religious fears and prejudices.[9]

apologetics that they took to be faithful to their scientific revolution, and that they stressed in public discussion in order to rebut charges of implicit atheism. The second prong of Hume's critique of religion in the *Enquiry* is designed to show that the Newtonians' apologetics depend on misconstruing their own revolution.

[9] *Enquiries*, 11.

Against such dangers, there is only one reliable defence:

> Accurate and just reasoning is the only catholic remedy, fitted for all persons and dispositions; and is alone able to subvert that abstruse philosophy and metaphysical jargon, which, being mixed up with popular superstition, renders it in a manner impenetrable to careless reasoners, and gives it the air of science and wisdom.[10]

In these passages we see the *Enquiry* announcing a polemical purpose that distinguishes it quite sharply from the *Treatise*.[11] The *Treatise* had announced itself as part of a revolution in philosophy, which in England was already under way: the revolution is described on the title page as 'An Attempt to introduce the experimental Method of Reasoning into Moral Subjects', and the Introduction names the co-revolutionaries as 'Mr. *Locke*, my Lord *Shaftesbury*, Dr. *Mandeville*, Mr. *Hutchinson*, Dr. *Butler*, & c.'.[12] The tone of these remarks is one of youthful optimism: the old has been discarded, and the new, not yet complete, is making sure and steady progress that will redound to the great benefit of all. In the *Enquiry*, things are quite different: the sanguine expectation of progress has disappeared, and been replaced by a determination to sweep away a stubborn rival. The *Enquiry* will achieve its aim if it can set out the limits of human understanding, do so in an accessible style, and thereby display, for all to see, the failings and debilitating effects of an established rival view:

> we have, in the following enquiry, attempted to throw some light upon subjects, from which uncertainty has hitherto deterred the wise, and obscurity the ignorant. Happy, if we can unite the boundaries of the different species of philosophy [i.e. the accurate and the accessible], by reconciling profound enquiry with clearness, and truth with novelty! And still more happy, if, reasoning in this easy manner, we can undermine the foundations of an abstruse philosophy, which seems to have hitherto served only as a shelter to superstition, and a cover to absurdity and error![13]

From its opening section, then, the *Enquiry* announces that it is taking aim at a rival view, a view that is a haven for 'superstition'. There is a plain meaning to this claim. In the idiom of the day, at least in the Protestant world, 'superstition' is code for Catholicism.

---

[10] Ibid. 12.

[11] See Noxon's remark that, in contrast to the *Treatise*, Hume's aims in the *Enquiry* 'are essentially critical, not constructive' (*Hume's Philosophical Development*, 157). This overdoes it, however, since construction is a necessary part of the overall argument. A critical work unable to avoid sliding into Pyrrhonism would lose its appeal, even to the critically minded, and Section XII, in particular, is intended to address this problem.

[12] *Treatise*, pp. xi, xvii.

[13] *Enquiries*, 16.

Thus, in the essay 'Of Superstition and Enthusiasm', Hume clearly
has Catholicism in mind when he explains what superstition is,
its origin and tendency: its source, he says, lies in 'weakness, fear,
melancholy . . . [and] ignorance'; it is favourable to priestly power
and hostile to civil liberty.[14] The *Enquiry* thus gives a firm impression, right from the start, that the principles it will expound and
defend will provide a critique of Catholicism, and of the abstruse
philosophy that underpins it. Although the actual targets are, as
noted, much wider, the relevant point is that the *Enquiry* quite
explicitly presents itself as, among other things, a critique of
religion.

For this reason, it is very surprising to see L. A. Selby-Bigge, in
his Introduction to the standard Oxford edition of the *Enquiries*,
treating the sections that directly criticize religious belief as if they
are somehow incidental to the work. The surprise is lessened by
the strong hints within that essay that suggest Selby-Bigge to share
the assumption criticized above, that the *Enquiry* is no more than
a more accessible version of parts of the *Treatise*. This much can
be gleaned from his comments on the sections in question:

Miracles, providence, and a future state. §§ x and xi of the Enquiry, in which these
subjects are treated, belong to Hume's applied philosophy, and, important and
interesting as they are in themselves, they do not add anything to his general
speculative position. Their insertion in the Enquiry is due doubtless rather to
other considerations than to a simple desire to illustrate or draw corollaries
from the philosophical principles laid down in the original work.[15]

Indeed it is true that Hume's concern is more than 'a simple
desire to illustrate'; but the contrasts supposed here impose a spurious other-worldliness on Hume's philosophical ambitions, as if
his concerns were simply those of a modern-day professional epistemologist. The 'other considerations' are announced in Section I
as a central part of the author's aims, and nowhere in that section
is there any suggestion that the *Enquiry* (in contrast to the *Abstract*)
exists in order to make the *Treatise* accessible, by 'illustrating', or
drawing 'corollaries' from, the principles laid down in the earlier
work.[16]

---

[14] 'Of Superstition and Enthusiasm', in *Essays*, 74, 75, 78. 'Enthusiasm', the contrasting
form of 'false religion', corresponds to dissenting Protestantism. This means that a moderate
Anglican could find much to accept in Hume's critique; it would be hasty to suppose that
his critique of the different religious tempers could not find religiously minded allies.
[15] *Enquiries*, p. xix.
[16] Selby-Bigge is ably castigated by Flew, *Hume's Philosophy of Belief*, 7–8. Noxon also
observes that these new sections show Hume's 'increasing preoccupation with religious
questions', pointing out that 'a full quarter of his first *Enquiry* is exclusively concerned with
them' (*Hume's Philosophical Development*, 78).

Given, then, that the *Enquiry* acknowledges that it is an attack on 'superstition', and that most of Hume's readers would immediately have assumed this to mean Catholicism (and other kinds of false religion), what then of the abstruse philosophy on which it relies, and which is also identified as a target? The natural answer here would be that Aristotelianism, in particular its scholastic varieties, must be meant. This answer gains strong support from the *Enquiry*'s famous closing paragraph, where Hume picks out the work's explicit and obvious targets:

When we run over libraries, persuaded of these principles, what havoc must we make? If we take in our hand any volume; of divinity or school metaphysics, for instance; let us ask, *Does it contain any abstract reasoning concerning quantity or number?* No. *Does it contain any experimental reasoning concerning matter of fact or existence?* No. Commit it then to the flames: for it can contain nothing but sophistry and illusion.[17]

This famous passage, by returning to the critical purpose announced right at the beginning of the work, underlines the unity of the whole. The content similarly reflects this unity, since the 'superstition' and 'abstruse philosophy' of Section I can be mapped onto the 'divinity and school metaphysics' picked out here for special mention. This conclusion is not, then, a hostile burst that comes from the blue—not Hume taking random pot-shots at doctrines he happens to have undermined—but the culmination of the critical enterprise flagged from the beginning. The particular form of 'abstruse philosophy' which has been 'a shelter to superstition' is here identified as the metaphysics of the schools, and the 'superstition' is the divinity that has flourished under its wing. So the express target of the *Enquiry* is medieval Aristotelianism and Aristotelian religion—that is, (Catholic) 'superstition'.

Presumably, this was a message that Hume's largely Protestant readership would have been happy to hear. For the modern reader, however, it may seem surprising and implausible to interpret the *Enquiry* in this light. This is first because, as noted, the religious arguments of the work cut deeper, giving no comfort to orthodox Protestants; and, secondly, because the philosophical curriculum, with its division of the period into rationalists and empiricists, encourages the belief that his target must be modern rationalism. These reservations will be considered in turn.

In the first place, it is not controversial that Hume's arguments cut more deeply; and it is not being denied. Rather, Sections X and

---

[17] *Enquiries*, 165.

XI of the *Enquiry* show what Hume believes experimental reasoning to imply for religion, and these implications are clearly profound. Section X, 'Of Miracles', argues that belief in testimony to a miracle, no matter how well supported, is at odds with the principles of experimental reason, concluding that 'the *Christian Religion* not only was at first attended with miracles, but even at this day cannot be believed by any reasonable person without one'.[18] And Section XI, 'Of a particular Providence and of a future State', denies the possibility of arguing from the natural world to any form of deity worth caring about, and, for good measure, raises doubts about the very legitimacy of arguing from the world to a deity at all.

However, what this shows is not that the express target is not Catholicism, but that, as mentioned above, Hume is not entirely guileless in his handling of his audience. The work presents itself in such a way that it leads the Protestant reader in confidently, only for the ground eventually to be undermined. In fact, even this undermining is not carried out without further instances of authorial guile. Thus Hume's conclusion in Section X is presented as if it were a form of fideism, pinning the justification for religious belief not at all on reason, but on faith alone. This claim is not to be taken at face value, as will be shown; but it is important to notice that not all of Hume's readers would have been entirely confident in dismissing it as disingenuousness. For example, such a claim would strike a 'fundamentalist' Protestant nerve, making religious belief a gift from God rather than an achievement of hubristic human reason. For such a Protestant, even the quoted remark that belief requires a miracle would have pulled in two directions. Furthermore, not dissimilar claims stemmed from intellectually more sophisticated sources: thus Robert Boyle, and, following him, John Locke, both defended the idea that some truths are 'above reason'.[19] No less significantly, forms of fideism had been held by Christian sceptics on both sides of the confessional divide, by both the Protestant Pierre Bayle and the Catholic Michel de Montaigne.[20] So Hume's fideistic appeal at the end of Section X

---

[18] *Enquiries*, 131.
[19] See Locke, *Essay*, IV. xviii; and, for a recent discussion of Boyle's view and its sources, see J. W. Wojcik, *Robert Boyle and the Limits of Reason* (Cambridge: Cambridge University Press, 1997).
[20] Montaigne's defence of faith is not unalloyed, but by denying reason he does make room for faith, particularly in 'An Apology for Raymond Sebond', in *The Complete Essays*, trans. M. A. Screech (Harmondsworth: Penguin Books, 1991), 489–683. The essay concludes: 'Nor may a man mount above himself or above humanity: for he can see only with his own eyes, grip only with his own grasp. He will rise if God proffers him—extraordinarily—His hand; he will rise by abandoning and disavowing his own means, letting himself be raised and pulled up by purely heavenly ones. It is for our Christian faith . . . to aspire to that holy and miraculous metamorphosis' (683).

is sufficiently similar to some notable precedents, not least of self-confessed sceptics who sought to reconcile scepticism with faith, to prevent many of his contemporary readers from dismissing his claimed position.

Furthermore, Hume's claimed position would, at first sight, have gained credibility by attacking miracles. This is because a differentiating belief between Catholics and most Protestants was and is whether miracles still occur, or were restricted to biblical times. Unlike Protestants, Catholics accept the continuing occurrence of miracles, attested to by non-apostolic witnesses: so a critique of reports of miracles, as long as biblical miracles are somehow protected, is at home in a Protestant critique of Catholicism. This is, I believe, the impression Hume hopes to give; and his commencing Section X with an appeal to Archbishop Tillotson's anti-Catholic argument against the 'real presence', together with the claim that his own argument will be a 'of a like nature', and will therefore likewise be a check on 'superstitious delusion',[21] are best read in that light. Nevertheless, he *is* being disingenuous: in trading on these impressions, he is, as with his explicitly identified target at the beginning and end of the work, covering his tracks, pretending that a damaging critique of religion leaves some species of Protestant Christianity unscathed. The official targets are Catholicism and its metaphysical foundation, scholastic Aristotelianism. But that the explicit identification of these targets is a rhetorical smokescreen does not imply them to be irrelevant; indeed, they can only serve their purpose—only *be* a smokescreen—if a significant part of the book's argument is genuinely aimed at Aristotelian views; if not, necessarily, at them alone.

This returns us to the second reservation. To identify Hume's targets in this way seems to be at odds with the easy assumption that Hume's philosophical target must be the modern rationalism of Descartes, his followers, and his successors. The assumption finds its source in the textbook histories of philosophy that understand early modern philosophy as a contest between two warring schools of thought: rationalism and empiricism. Hume is plainly no rationalist, and so, if early modern philosophy is a contest between rationalism and empiricism, it seems that Hume's arguments *must* be aimed at the opposing doctrines or arguments of the rationalists.

There are several ways in which this conclusion can be resisted. In the first place, the textbook history, by its preoccupations with 'warring schools', forces different views into artificially opposed

---

[21] *Enquiries*, 110.

camps, thereby distorting their more complex interrelations.[22] Secondly, it supposes that, in the early modern world, the story of philosophy is the story of epistemology—an assumption that is misleading because anachronistic. Before the advent of modern professional philosophy, with its entrenched subdivisions between different branches of philosophy, epistemological positions were advanced in order to establish or undermine substantive physical or metaphysical conclusions, and they were usually supported or rebutted for much the same reasons. This means that an attack on a certain doctrine or method may be no more than a part of an attack on a metaphysical position: identifying the target of a specific argument need not be instructive, unless it can be related to larger issues. And, since it is not uncommon for quite different conclusions to depend on one form or other of a similar argument, an attack on that argument can serve as an attack on a whole cluster of views. So, even if some of Hume's arguments are thought to be directed at rationalist views, it does not follow that they are directed solely—or even primarily—at rationalism. A critique of a rationalist argument could be pressed into serving a larger critique of philosophies that are, in the relevant respect, similar. Thus the official aim, of attacking Aristotelianism, is not ruled out by the discovery of anti-rationalist arguments.[23]

In fact, the evidence that the *Enquiry* affords seems to fit just such a conclusion, for it is very difficult to find any evidence that Hume has rationalist views at the forefront of his mind. It is, of course, true that, in developing his position, he opposes or rejects many rationalist theses; but it is also true that rarely, if at all, can rationalism be picked out as the central philosophical target of the work. This is revealed by surveying Hume's rhetoric and arguments.

In the first place, Hume's rhetoric makes most sense if he is referring to a philosophy that has been around for some length of time: he seeks to 'combine truth with novelty' in opposing 'an abstruse philosophy which seems to have *hitherto* served only as a shelter to superstition'.[24] True, Cartesian rationalism has, at the time he is writing, managed to chalk up its century, but since in the *Trea-*

---

[22] For a critical assessment of the view that the history of philosophy can be resolved into a series of battles between 'warring schools', see J. Rée, *Descartes* (London: Allen Lane, 1974), 151–7; and 'Philosophy and the History of Philosophy', in J. Rée, M. Ayers, and A. Westoby, *Philosophy and its Past* (Hassocks, Sussex: Harvester Press, 1978), 3–18.

[23] However, since Aristotelianism is a form of empiricism, not of rationalism, the presence of anti-rationalist arguments might also encourage the view that the *actual* target of the work is surprisingly inclusive, lumping all these different views together because it is opposed to what they all have in common. This will be argued below.

[24] *Enquiries*, 16 (emphasis added).

tise this length of time is suggested to be necessary for digesting the moral significance of the revolution in natural philosophy,[25] it cannot convincingly be held of Cartesian rationalism that it has 'served only as a shelter for superstition'. Perhaps by some it had been *thought* to be, but Hume would have to allow that such a state of affairs would be attributable, at least in part, to a hasty attempt to digest its implications—and that would be to level quite a different charge. Whichever way the charge is taken, however, it would be unfair to the facts. The uncomfortable relations between the Cartesians and the Catholic Church, including the placing of Descartes's works on the Index shortly after his death, show how unconvincing it is to charge Cartesianism with being 'a shelter for superstition'. However superstitious Hume may have judged the Cartesians or their philosophy to be, it was certainly no shelter.

The point is reinforced when extended to cover the other principal rationalists. Spinoza's heterodoxy rules out his philosophy as a possible target—even though Hume accuses him of harbouring absurdities, many of which can also be found in the theologians. Moreover, since Hume observes that these 'absurdities' are denounced when encountered in Spinoza, but a subject of approval when found in the theologians, it is clear that Spinozism is not, for him, the shelter under which religious superstition hides itself.[26] Nor can Leibniz be fitted into this mould, since, despite the central concern in all his philosophical work to defend Christianity, the means he chose was to accommodate the new philosophy of Cartesian mechanism with the old Aristotelian philosophy of 'natures' or substantial forms.[27] So the new philosophy, however described, cannot be isolated as the servant of his religious apologetics. In fact, it would seem truer to say that the new philosophy was the cause of his religious discomforts, and that he sought accommodation with the old in order to ease them.

Secondly, when Hume criticizes the occasionalists' account of

---

[25] ''Tis no astonishing reflection to consider, that the application of experimental philosophy to moral subjects should come after that to natural at the distance of above a whole century; since we find in fact, that there was about the same interval betwixt the origins of these sciences; and that reckoning from THALES to SOCRATES, the space of time is nearly equal to that betwixt my Lord BACON and some late philosophers in *England*, who have begun to put the science of man on a new footing, and have engaged the attention, and excited the curiosity of the public' (*Treatise*, pp. xvi–xvii).

[26] Ibid. 243. The 'superstitious' were not attracted to his views because, like Hume, they believed his doctrine of substance to be a 'hideous hypothesis' which amounted to 'a true atheism' (240–1).

[27] Leibniz's spokesman Theophilus emphasizes the accommodation between ancient and modern philosophies achieved in his system, and defends Scholastic substantial forms, in G. W. Leibniz, *New Essays on Human Understanding*, ed. P. Remnant and J. Bennett (Cambridge: Cambridge University Press, 1996), 71–3, 317–18.

causation at the end of the first part of Section VII, 'Of the Idea of
necessary Connexion', he makes it very clear that they *are* the
target.[28] That is, he treats them in much the same way as he treats
Locke and other fellow-travellers or allies on the experimental
road: that is, when he has an objection to raise against them, he
specifies that they are the object of the criticism. Since occasionalism was a major strand of rationalism, one would expect
that a work aiming at criticizing rationalist views would object to
versions of those views as somehow *typical* of the views produced
by that school of thought.[29] But Hume does not proceed in that
way: he picks the occasionalists out as a distinct position on causation, and criticizes them accordingly.[30]

Thirdly, if the modern rationalists were the target, one would
expect the doctrine of innate ideas to come in for some harsh treatment. But nothing could be further from the truth: the issue is
almost entirely ignored in the *Enquiry*, and, when it is discussed,
Hume's attitude towards it is surprisingly relaxed. Although he
makes it perfectly clear that all ideas arise from impressions, and
initially from impressions of sensation, he treats the point as
almost too obvious to deserve any detailed defence: it is a point
that 'every one will readily allow'.[31] The direct discussion of 'innate
ideas' is relegated entirely to a footnote at the end of Section II,
'Of the Origin of Ideas', where he affirms that, in the most appropriate sense of such an obscure term, ideas are *not* innate. This
seems straightforward enough; but it then comes as a shock to

[28] *Enquiries*, 70–3.
[29] Daniel Garber has argued that Descartes was more of an occasionalist than is usually
conceded: 'even though Descartes posits causes of change in the world in addition to God,
finite minds, and angels at the very least, he does seem to agree with his occasionalist followers in denying that bodies are genuine causes of motion, and may well agree with them
in denying that bodies can cause sensations as well. Can we say, on the basis of this that
Descartes is a quasi-occasionalist, an occasionalist when it comes to the inanimate world,
though not in the world of bodies connected to minds? The doctrine of occasionalism is certainly flexible enough to allow this' (*Descartes' Metaphysical Physics* (Chicago: University of
Chicago Press, 1992), 304; see also his 'Descartes and Occasionalism', in S. Nadler (ed.), *Causation in Early Modern Philosophy: Cartesianism, Occasionalism, and Preestablished Harmony* (University Park, Pa.: Pennsylvania State University Press, 1993), 9–26). Garber does go on to
distinguish Descartes's quasi-occasionalist view from that of his successors. The relevant
issue here is that, if Hume's view of Descartes was in any way comparable, a critique of occasionalism just would be part and parcel of a critique of rationalism. The evidence there is on
this issue, however, does not offer support. It is clear that, in the *Enquiry* passage in question, Hume has the thoroughgoing Malebranchean thesis in mind: the doctrine he attacks
holds that minds and bodies alike are mere occasions for divine causal activity, and he sums
up by observing that, 'for these philosophers, everything is full of God' (*Enquiries*, 71).
[30] He also criticizes them in ways that do not sit at all comfortably with the common view
that he reduces causation to regularity. The failings of the occasionalists include the fact that
'they rob nature, and all created beings, of every power' (*Enquiries*, 71). Strange words indeed
from a man who is widely believed to have done the same! The issue will be examined in
more detail in Part Two; see also Strawson, *The Secret Connexion*, 199–204.
[31] *Enquiries*, 17.

see Hume add that, although ideas are not innate, nevertheless impressions, the source of ideas, *are*: 'admitting these terms, *impressions* and *ideas*, in the sense above explained, and understanding by *innate*, what is original or copied from no precedent impression, then may we assert that all our impressions are innate, and our ideas not innate.'[32]

The surprising conclusion cannot mask the fact that Hume is not affirming any view with which a rationalist would agree. He elsewhere insists that the source of ideas is indeed in experience alone. Thus in a long footnote in Section V, in an examination of the common distinction between reason and experience, he effectively rules out innate ideas in the rationalists' sense. He says: 'notwithstanding that this distinction be thus universally received, both in the active and speculative scenes of life, I shall not scruple to pronounce, that it is, at bottom, erroneous, at least, superficial.' This is because, when we examine those arguments or explanations attributed to reason, we discover that 'it is experience which is ultimately the foundation of our inference and conclusion'.[33] There is no source of ideas outside experience, so, when we reason, we call on only the materials experience has provided.

Hume's position is thus quite at odds with the rationalist view on innate ideas. It is very surprising, however, to see such a casual handling of the terminology, allowing as it does the conclusion that the original sources of our knowledge are indeed innate, as the rationalists had argued. This is surely the strangest method of defending one's views against one's opponents! It is difficult to resist the conclusion that these remarks are intended as little more than an aside—passing observations on an issue concerning which he expects his readers to be aware, but not deeply engaged. An epistemological litmus test for dividing rationalists from empiricists seems, in other words, to be treated as little more than a historical curiosity. One lesson to draw from this is that, here as elsewhere, Hume seems to be preaching to the converted: addressing a British audience who do not have much truck with curious Continental thinkers, and so do not need to be persuaded on all points equally. Another is that Hume does not need to argue for or against innate ideas, for his account of human nature denies them any significance. Innate ideas matter to rationalism because they are taken to bear the stamp of truth. Thus it is by isolating innate ideas that Descartes searches out a stable foundation for his system. Thus also Locke denied the existence of any such

---

[32] Ibid. 22.   [33] Ibid. 43 n.

ideas because he denied us possession of any infallible knowledge. Thus his pupil Shaftesbury attacked him for undermining morality. And so on. Hume, however, is casual on innateness because his account of the origin and development of ideas is part of an account of human functioning in which certainty is ruled out, and error shown to be built into the very fabric of our minds. The analysis of the *Enquiry*'s argument in Part Two will show this to be so.

Fourthly, although Hume cannot develop his position without having frequently to elaborate anti-rationalist theses, it is not the case that these are *exclusively* anti-rationalist. So, for example, when he stresses, in Section XII, 'Of the academical or sceptical Philosophy', that 'the non-existence of any being, without exception, is as clear and distinct an idea as its existence',[34] the appearance of Cartesian terminology suggests who is in the front of his mind. But the doctrine being attacked, that some beings (or, more particularly, some Being) could exist necessarily, is not exclusively Cartesian, nor even exclusively rationalist.[35] Hume's readers, for their part, would have had no trouble recognizing that scholastic theology is conspicuously in the firing line at this point. Similarly, Hume's positive account of belief as instinctive and passive, in Section V Part II, is plainly at odds with Descartes's neo-Augustinian account of belief as an activity of the will;[36] but it is equally at odds with the role of active *noûs* in the Aristotelian account.[37] What is more, Hume signals that this part of the argument is not central to his purposes, since he declares it to be entirely *optional* for readers who do not 'love the abstract sciences': 'the remaining part of this section is not calculated for them, and the following enquiries may well be understood, though it be neglected.'[38]

However, not all discussions of apparently rationalist theses in the *Enquiry* are peripheral to the main argument. In fact, some of the central arguments appear to indicate rationalist concerns. Thus

---

[34] *Enquiries*, 164.

[35] The same can even be said about the terminology: clarity and distinctness are Stoic notions that Descartes adopted, and it seems to be true that in other parts of the *Enquiry* Hume has Stoic ideas in mind. (See below.)

[36] René Descartes, *Meditations on First Philosophy*, Fourth Meditation, 'Truth and Falsity', in *The Philosophical Writings of Descartes*, trans. J. Cottingham, R. Stoothoff, and D. Murdoch (Cambridge: Cambridge University Press, 1984), ii. 37–43. See S. Menn, *Descartes and Augustine* (Cambridge: Cambridge University Press, 1998), ch. 7; and his 'Descartes, Augustine, and the Status of Faith', in M. A. Stewart (ed.), *Studies in Seventeenth Century European Philosophy* (Oxford Studies in the History of Philosophy, 2; Oxford: Clarendon Press, 1997), 1–31.

[37] Aristotle, *On the Soul*, III. ii–v, in *A New Aristotle Reader*, ed. J. L. Ackrill (Oxford: Clarendon Press, 1987), 188–97. See J. Lear, *Aristotle: The Desire to Understand* (Cambridge: Cambridge University Press, 1988), 116–41.

[38] *Enquiries*, 47.

in Section IV Part I, 'Sceptical Doubts concerning the Operations of the Understanding'—and again in Section VII Part I, 'Of the Idea of necessary Connexion'—it is argued that 'reasonings *a priori*' do not give us insight into the causal powers or natures of objects.[39] The rationalists affirmed precisely such insight to pure reason, as exemplified in Descartes's entirely a priori arguments in the *Meditations* to establish the nature and existence of *res extensa* and *res cogitans*. The Aristotelians, in contrast, held no such brief for pure reason. So in those two parts of the *Enquiry* it may seem that the rationalists are the particular target, and therefore that they loom more largely in Hume's mind than has so far been conceded.

However, it is far from clear that distinctively rationalist views are at stake. A closer inspection of the argument in Section IV will show Hume's concerns to be somewhat different. The first thing to notice is that the sense in which Hume uses the expression 'reasonings *a priori*' is not what the modern reader might expect. This is shown by the example he employs to deny a priori insight into causal powers: 'Let an object be presented to a man of ever so strong natural reason and abilities; if that object be entirely new to him, he will not be able, *by the most accurate examination of its sensible qualities*, to discover any of its causes and effects.'[40] This is hardly a point that Descartes, for example, would have contested. The famous example of the wax in the Second Meditation is designed (in part) to make a similar point about the limited powers of sensory inspection.[41] But for Descartes the lesson of such examples is to rely on reason by *turning away from* the senses.[42] Hume clearly does not have in mind any such radical procedure. The 'reasonings *a priori*' of which he is critical is reasoning that is *attentive to* sensory information. He is not thinking of Descartes, nor, it seems, of any modern rationalist. So who or what does he have in mind? The position he is attacking appears to be the Stoic view that knowledge arises through 'cognitive impressions': that is, that there are some sense perceptions that are the basis of true judgements about the natures of things.[43] And, when he goes on, in Part

---

[39] Ibid. 27.   [40] Ibid. (emphasis added).

[41] *The Philosophical Writings of Descartes*, ii. 20–2.   [42] Ibid. ii. 121.

[43] See e.g. Diogenes Laertius: 'They [the Stoics] say that the cognitive impression is the criterion of truth, i.e. the impression arising from what is . . . [it] is the criterion of things . . . that which arises from what is and is stamped and impressed exactly in accordance with what is. The incognitive is either that which does not arise from what is, or from that which is but not exactly in accordance with what is: one which is not clear or distinct' (*Lives of Eminent Philosophers*, VII. 54, 46, in A. A. Long and D. N. Sedley (eds.), *The Hellenistic Philosophers* (Cambridge: Cambridge University Press, 1987), i. 241–2). See also A. A. Long, *Hellenistic Philosophy: Stoics, Epicureans, Sceptics*, 2nd edn. (London: Duckworth, 1986), 126–8.

II, to argue that experience—understood not as individual sense perceptions but as *connected experience* over time—likewise fails to deliver knowledge of causes and effects, he appears to be modifying an argument Locke had brought against the Aristotelian (and Epicurean) account of the acquisition of knowledge of substances, and therefore of their qualities or powers.[44]

Hume's argument is, in other words, directed against the major schools of ancient empiricism, not against rationalism, ancient or modern. He is arguing thus, I suggest, because these ancient schools represent, for his audience, the main types of optimistic (or dogmatic) empiricist philosophy—empiricist defences of the belief that, through individual sensations or connected experience, it is possible to derive certain knowledge of the natures or powers of objects, of what there is. But it is the Aristotelian (and Epicurean) view that seems the prime target. This is, in part, because Part I prepares the ground for the argument of Part II. But a further reason is because Hume's unfamiliar use of 'a priori' makes sense if placed against a background of Aristotelian thought: the inspection of the sensory properties of an object will properly be described as a priori—as prior to experience—if by 'experience' we mean, not individual sensations, but the Aristotelian sense of connected experience of the world—experience in the sense of 'being experienced', the fruit of extended contact with the world over time.[45]

It also deserves mentioning that Hume's concern in this section is not so much with the *sources* of knowledge—the sticking point between rationalism and (constructive) empiricism—but with its *possibility*. The issue is, then, the competing claims of dogmatism and scepticism, as the following section makes explicit. Scepticism of some kind is there presented as the outlook most congenial to the experimental philosopher. The views rejected in Section IV— claimed empirical sources of knowledge of natures or causal powers—are attempts to establish philosophical dogmas through the standards recognized by experimental philosophy—that is, through sensation and experience. They are rejected because they have failed fully to comprehend the new philosophy's implications for accounts of perception and causation. So what appeared to be

[44] See Locke, *Essay*, II. xxiii. 1; and Michael Ayers's account of this passage in his 'The Foundations of Knowledge and the Logic of Substance: The Structure of Locke's General Philosophy', in G. A. J. Rogers (ed.), *Locke's Philosophy: Content and Context* (Oxford: Clarendon Press, 1994), 60–71. See Aristotle, *Metaphysics*, I. 1; in *A New Aristotle Reader*, ed. Ackrill, 255–7.

[45] Hume's use of 'a priori' is discussed in R. F. Atkinson, 'Hume on Mathematics', *Philosophical Quarterly*, 10 (1960), 127–37, and W. A. Suchting, 'Hume and Necessary Truth', *Dialogue*, 5 (1966–7), 47–60. See also L. W. Beck, 'Analytic and Synthetic Judgments before Kant', in his *Essays on Kant and Hume* (New Haven: Yale University Press, 1978), 80–100.

a critique of the rationalists is in fact a sceptic's rejection of dogmatic empiricism—especially, but not only, of Aristotelianism—from the standpoint of a consistently applied (mechanical) experimentalism.

An Enlightenment Tract

It has been argued that the *Enquiry* is explicitly an attack on Catholic 'superstition' and the 'abstruse philosophy' under which it has sheltered, scholastic Aristotelianism. Its actual targets, however, include all forms of religion worthy of the name, and all forms of metaphysics that violate the principles of a properly formulated experimental philosophy. The modern rationalist philosophies stemming from Descartes are included in this last category, but they are not singled out for any special attention. Hume seems to be working on a broader front, and the outline of the argument in Section IV suggests that his primary concern is to determine whether any of the main kinds of empiricist philosophy—represented by the ancient schools—are compatible with experimental philosophy. His aim is to identify the epistemic standards—and thus the species of philosophy—that a consistent experimentalism will attribute to a subject who functions according to its principles. These standards, he argues, rule out all the dogmatic empiricist philosophies; and, where rationalist theses are in view, they too are clearly ruled out. Only ancient scepticism conforms to experimental principles: experimental philosophy is thus a form of scepticism. The implications of experimental philosophy for 'moral subjects'—for the world of human action and society—are, then, considerably more profound than has hitherto been imagined. By ruling out dogmatic philosophy, experimental philosophy calls into question all the certitudes based upon it, which is to say, all the certitudes of the old world: the traditions, orthodoxies, and authorities by which human beliefs and practices have been judged.

To put the point more sharply (and anachronistically): modern science, when applied to human knowledge and human affairs, shows human beings to be the victims of a grandiose (and aggrandizing) illusion: the illusion that they can cut nature at its joints, can discern 'what there is'. The chief fruit of this illusion, and built directly upon it, is religion. So the principles on which modern science rests call into question all traditional authorities, including, not least, religious authority. This is why the *Enquiry* moves so quickly from epistemological reflections to critique of religion: it is the advancement of the view, now so familiar, that science and religion are not harmonious, but fundamentally opposed; and that the defence of scientific principles requires the rejection of religion, and the structures of authority that derive from it. The *Enquiry* thus advances recognizable, if cautiously stated, Enlightenment themes. In this sense, then, Hume is an Enlightenment philosopher, and the *Enquiry* is an Enlightenment tract.

The point needs some clarification: it is no news to be told that Hume is a philosopher of the Enlightenment, if by that term we understand the intellectual flowering of the mid-eighteenth century. In this sense, he is of course *the* philosopher of the Scottish Enlightenment. But there is another, more popular sense of 'the Enlightenment', to refer to the anti-religious, anti-traditional, self-consciously secularizing mentality of the period, and exemplified by the French *philosophes*—in particular by Voltaire and the editors of the *Encyclopédie*, Diderot and d'Alembert. This sense of the term is better loved by popularizers than by professional historians, because it imposes a spurious uniformity on a complex and many-sided intellectual flowering. Thus, as one commentator on the period (and the term) observes:

The eighteenth-century Enlightenment is the only period of modern history described, most often by its detractors but sometimes also by its admirers, as a single intellectual movement or campaign, orchestrated around a common set of themes. Its leading thinkers, comprising Europe's first intelligentsia, are perceived as jointly committed to liberating mankind from the tyrannies of dead dogma and blind faith.[46]

It is true that neither the period, nor the intellectual flowering it witnessed, ever possessed such uniformity, and any employment of the term should keep this clearly in mind. Nevertheless, as Wokler's summary itself shows, the period was characterized, not least in the mouths of its more vigorous public figures, by sharp criticism of religion and other hallowed traditions, and by the sense that new forms of social order were both necessary and, because of the revolutionary developments in the understanding of the natural world, possible. In this sense, it is possible to speak of an 'Enlightenment Project': its *locus classicus* is d'Alembert's *Preliminary Discourse to the Encyclopedia*, which traces the rise of the new philosophical outlook, from scholastic ignorance to Baconian and Newtonian

---

[46] R. Wokler, 'Enlightenment, Continental', in E. Craig (ed.), *The Routledge Encyclopedia of Philosophy* (London: Routledge, 1998), iii. 315.

understanding, from religious prejudice and backwardness to secular, useful, freethinking.[47] In this sense, 'Enlightenment' refers only incidentally to a historical period, primarily to a cast of mind—and has attracted friends and foes accordingly.[48] It is in this sense that the *Enquiry* shows Hume to be an Enlightenment thinker: in its pages the Enlightenment Project—if in a more modest and sceptical garb than commonly to be found amongst its French enthusiasts—finds clear expression.

To hold Hume to be an Enlightenment thinker in this time-honoured sense is at once obvious and controversial. On the one hand, his criticism of religion, in particular, seems characteristic of the period, and it is perhaps for this reason that most studies of Enlightenment thought will find him a place amongst a familiar pantheon: the above-mentioned Frenchmen, together with the likes of Adam Smith, Gibbon, La Mettrie, Kant, Goethe, Jefferson, Thomas Paine, and of course that combustible mixture of pro- and anti-Enlightenment sentiments, Rousseau.[49] On the other hand, Hume seems at odds with these other thinkers: he cannot share in the enthusiastic endorsement of Reason in terms of which the attack on tradition was so often mounted; and his scepticism seems so thoroughgoing that it must rule out any optimistic hopes for social progress (or 'improvement').

To take these two points in turn. Hume is indeed no friend of Reason: his attack on empiricist dogmatism is, of course, to make space not for a rationalistic philosophy of human nature, but for a form of scepticism. In this respect he is far removed from the rationalistic *vocabulary* of many of the *philosophes*. But this vocabulary can too readily inspire the conclusion that Hume and the *philosophes* are divided by an intellectual gulf, for behind this difference there are surprising levels of agreement. For example, in d'Alembert's classic tract—and, indeed, in one of its principal sources, Voltaire's *Letters on England*[50]—it is the revolution in natural philosophy, beginning with Bacon and finding its greatest expression in Newton, that is picked out as the origin of the

[47] J. Le Rond d'Alembert, *Preliminary Discourse to the Encyclopedia of Diderot* (1751), trans. R. N. Schwab (Chicago: University of Chicago Press, 1995).
[48] The Frankfurt School in particular has organized its thought around the theme of Enlightenment, and has spawned its notable friends and foes. Jürgen Habermas and Axel Honneth are prominent defenders of the Enlightenment's 'unfinished project'—see e.g. Habermas, *The Philosophical Discourse of Modernity*, trans. F. G. Lawrence (Cambridge, Mass.: MIT Press, 1987)—while the bluntest critique remains T. Adorno and M. Horkheimer, *Dialectic of Enlightenment*, trans. J. Cumming (New York: Herder & Herder, 1972). Most notable of the recent critiques is A. MacIntyre, *After Virtue*, 2nd edn. (London: Duckworth, 1984), and *Whose Justice? Which Rationality?* (London: Duckworth, 1988).
[49] See e.g. D. Outram, *The Enlightenment* (Cambridge: Cambridge University Press, 1995).
[50] Voltaire, *Letters on England*, 59–91 (Letters 12–17).

46 *Approaching the Text*

mentality brought to fruition by the *Encyclopédie*. The social improvements for which the *philosophes* are staunch advocates have their beginnings traced to natural philosophy. 'Newtonian-ism' is thus one possible name for progressive-mindedness in the social sphere. The similarities with Hume's description of his project—as the extension of experimental, Newtonian, thought to 'moral subjects'—are plain.[51]

Moreover, d'Alembert's treatment of Descartes is very revealing. He is treated far more sympathetically than would any English account of this revolution, as we shall see below. However, it is striking that d'Alembert identifies Descartes's central error to lie in his divergence from empiricism—even if this central error had the serendipitous effect of revealing all the other mistakes of the Aris-totelians: 'No doubt he was mistaken in admitting the existence of innate ideas. But had he retained that single truth taught by the Aristotelians concerning the origin of ideas through the senses, perhaps it would have been more difficult to uproot the errors that debased this truth by being alloyed with it.'[52]

The point is clear: the revolution in natural philosophy has affirmed the truth of (some form of) empiricism, and for this reason Bacon and Newton are heroes of enlightenment. Descartes remains significant—because he taught to question authority[53]—but the fact remains that, for all the French Enlightenment's invo-cations of Reason, its principal spokesmen identify the source of their revolution as lying in the empirically minded philosophy of experiment, a philosophy most fully developed across the English Channel.

The second problem of thinking of Hume as an Enlightenment thinker is his scepticism. This sometimes seems so marked—espe-cially in the *Treatise*—that it is not clear how Hume could hold *any* constructive doctrines at all. This is one important reason why the suspicion addressed in the previous chapter—that he was just an opportunist who gave up philosophy when it failed to provide

---

[51] In fact, this sense of Enlightened thought as consisting in the application of new devel-opments in natural philosophy to human subjects—to develop a more-or-less Baconian 'natural history of man'—was widespread. See e.g. P. B. Wood, 'Science and the Aberdeen Enlightenment', in P. Jones (ed.), *Philosophy and Science in the Scottish Enlightenment* (Edin-burgh: John Donald Publishers, 1988), 39–66, and 'The Natural History of Man in the Scot-tish Enlightenment', *History of Science*, 27 (1989), 89–123. See also W. Clarke, J. Golinski, and S. Schaffer (eds.), *The Sciences in Enlightened Europe* (Chicago: University of Chicago Press, 1999).
[52] D'Alembert, *Preliminary Discourse*, 80.
[53] 'Descartes dared at least to show intelligent minds how to throw off the yoke of scholasticism, of opinion, of authority—in a word, of prejudices and barbarism. And by that revolt whose fruits we are reaping today, he rendered a service to philosophy perhaps more difficult to perform than all those contributed thereafter by his illustrious successors' (ibid).

him with the notoriety he craved—has been so durable. The issue cannot be addressed adequately at this point, for it is the purpose of this study to show why this doubt is misplaced. At this stage the following remarks will have to suffice. In the first place, it is the meaning of Hume's confessed scepticism that is crucial: if this can be understood as a constructive doctrine with intelligible connections to experimental philosophy, the problem will be overcome. Secondly, the suspicion that this cannot be done arises from certain sections of *Treatise* Book I, so it is necessary to explain those sections such that they need not clash with a moderate or constructive scepticism. One way of doing this would be by a synoptic interpretation of the *Treatise* as a whole, in which the Pyrrhonian moments are discovered to be youthful exaggerations, or are isolated as moments in a dialectic.[54] Another way is the course to be followed in this study: to take Hume at his word by devoting primary attention to the *Enquiry*, and to show thereby the coherence of his mature thought. To do so is to develop, among other things, an account of his mature scepticism; and so to deny priority to the *Treatise*'s more extreme pronouncements—whatever the final judgement on their meaning. The task of interpretation is, after all, the construction of that account that has the best overall fit, not the mere repetition of proof texts arbitrarily elected to authority, whatever their costs for making sense of an intellectual career.[55]

The New Philosophy and the Old

Hume's sense of the relationship of his work to his philosophical antecedents conforms to the requirements of the interpretation spelt out above. He accepts that the 'experimental philosophers',

[54] Much of the 'New Hume' literature is committed to some version of the former; for versions of the latter, see the Pyrrhonian interpretation of R. H. Popkin, 'Hume's Pyrrhonism and his Critique of Pyrrhonism', in V. C. Chappell (ed.), *Hume: A Collection of Critical Essays* (London: Macmillan, 1966), 53–98, repr. in Popkin, *The High Road to Pyrrhonism*, 103–32; and the more constructive versions of Penelhum, 'Hume's Skepticism and the *Dialogues*' in D. F. Norton, N. Capaldi, and W. L. Robison (eds.), *McGill Hume Studies* (San Diego: Austin Hill Press, 1979), 253–78; and A. Baier, *A Progress of Sentiments: Reflections on Hume's Treatise* (Cambridge, Mass.: Harvard University Press, 1991).

[55] One virtue of the more charitable approach to Hume's career offered here is that it makes plain why he turned to history. No reader of his *History of England* is left in any doubt that it is not antiquarianism: he has moral, political, and other philosophical lessons to teach. To write history for such purposes was, however, absolutely typical of the reforming Enlightenment thinker, for whom history was not a catalogue of facts about the past, but the opportunity for reflection on social experience, and to draw useful lessons therefrom. The point is pressed by C. L. Becker, *The Heavenly City of the Eighteenth-Century Philosophers* (New Haven: Yale University Press, 1932), ch. 3, 'The New History: Philosophy Teaching by Example'.

particularly the British natural philosophers who see themselves as descendants of Bacon, have sufficiently established that the natural world is to be understood according to broadly mechanical principles. The great culmination of this intellectual revolution in natural philosophy is Newton's *Principia*.[56] Subsequently, Newton and (especially) his followers have attempted to work out the implications of this revolution for the world of human affairs— for religious belief, in particular. Their endeavour is to be applauded, but they have not fully understood their own revolution. A broadly mechanical outlook, consistently applied, will include an account of the workings of the mind as it is affected by mechanical (that is, bodily) processes. This is the realm of the imagination, and includes all those mental events in which the mind is passive (for example, sensation), but also all mental events that, although forms of mental activity, are nevertheless attributable to mechanical processes (for example, the linking of ideas by association). Hume believes that, once the full extent of these mechanical processes is recognized—when they are seen to explain all our causal beliefs, and even the nature of belief and the very idea of causation itself—it will also be recognized that the full implications of the experimentalists' revolution are considerably more far-reaching for the world of human affairs than has been imagined. The casualties will include not merely the obvious candidates, the varieties of medieval Aristotelianism taught in the schools, and the religious forms ineluctably wedded to them, but also all forms of dogmatic philosophy, including dogmatic religious philosophy—and therefore all forms of Christianity.

The road Hume takes to his conclusions is shaped by this conception of the task and its goals. He signals to the reader that an enquiry inspired by the new philosophy associated with Newton will chase out school metaphysics and its accompanying supersti-

---

[56] In one respect, it could be (and was) argued that Newtonian philosophy was not the culmination of the mechanical philosophy, but its abandonment: that Newtonian gravitation reintroduced the occult powers and action at a distance that it was the aim of mechanical philosophy to eliminate. To a certain (limited) extent, the objection is sound, and for that reason I have spoken here of *broadly* mechanical principles. But it should be noted that Newton, for his part, did preserve the central mechanical doctrine of the passivity of matter by denying that gravity was a property of matter itself. In a much-quoted letter to Bentley he denied the doctrine of 'innate gravity': 'That gravity should be innate, inherent, and essential to matter, so that one body may act upon another at a distance through a *vacuum*, without the mediation of anything else, by and through which their action and force may be conveyed from one to another, is to me so great an absurdity that I believe that no man who has in philosophical matters a competent faculty of thinking can ever fall into it. Gravity must be caused by an agent acting constantly according to certain laws, but whether this agent be material or immaterial I have left to the consideration of my readers' (*Newton's Philosophy of Nature: Selections from his Writings*, ed. H. S. Thayer (New York: Hafner, 1974), 54).

tion. The pursuit of the enquiry, however, discovers the casualties to be greater than advertised, and that a form of scepticism is the necessary outcome. All forms of Christianity—even those varieties that understand themselves to be fully in accord with the new intellectual world, and indeed pride themselves on the fact—are revealed to be dependent on philosophical commitments that have been swept away by the revolution in philosophy. Christianity is, and always has been, a philosophical religion; therefore a fundamental revolution in philosophy cannot but be a disaster for it. The modern rationalist philosophies, despite their mechanical commitments, have failed properly to purge themselves of assumptions derived from discredited philosophy. They are, therefore, best regarded as philosophies in which the revolution has been left incomplete. Criticism of their doctrines is thus appropriate; but the best and, in any case, necessary response to them is simply to work out the broad implications of the new philosophy, and to let the conclusions speak for themselves.[57]

For this interpretation to be plausible, several things need to be established. First, if Hume is thinking in terms of a clash, not merely between particular philosophical schools, but between rival and incompatible *Weltanschauungen*, then evidence needs to be provided that he sees the contest to be of this scale. Secondly, if he thinks of Christianity as inextricably wedded to ancient philosophy, he must understand it as, in effect, a *species* of ancient philosophy.

Thirdly, if his background target is Aristotelianism in particular, then a concern to rebut it must be a credible ambition for an eighteenth-century thinker: it cannot be a hopelessly dead duck. And, finally, his relative lack of interest in distinctively rationalist theses is best explained if he sees the rationalists as misguided fellow-travellers, so it must be reasonable to attribute to him the view that modern rationalism is an incomplete revolution. These requirements can all be met. An exhaustive discussion of the issues is not appropriate here, but some main considerations can be sketched in. This section will consider the first three questions, leaving the fourth to the following section.

First, it is not difficult to see that Hume thinks of his work as the attempt to complete a philosophical revolution that will usher in a new world. It has already been noted that he describes the

---

[57] Of course, when this task is done, it will also be discovered that the Newtonians are themselves guilty of selling their revolution short: for the consistent application of their basic principles will undermine their attempts to defend Christianity—and, indeed, any religion worthy of the name. My aim at this point, however, is to catch the broader context within which Hume sets himself, before turning to attack his fellow Newtonians.

Treatise as the application of experimental philosophy to the 'moral subjects'. It is sufficient, for present purposes, to illustrate his sense of the revolution underway, but not complete, in his handling of the iconic figure of Newton. He clearly invokes Newton at particular points in his works, and always favourably. Moreover, these references are not to debate points of disagreement between rival modern views, or even in criticism of Newton's philosophical forerunners, whose works are now eclipsed by the Newtonian achievement. Rather, Hume invokes Newton either to commend a certain modestly sceptical attitude, or as the crowning achievement of the whole tradition of 'experimental philosophy' and its practitioners.[58]

Hume's explicit appeals to Newton are few, but revealing. He is explicitly mentioned only once in the first *Enquiry*, in a technical footnote.[59] In the second *Enquiry* there is also one mention, this time of more general significance: Hume defends his method of seeking general causes of diverse phenomena by pointing out that it conforms to 'Newton's chief rule of philosophizing'.[60] When compared to the *Treatise*, this may suggest a partial retreat from Newtonianism, since it is only in the *Treatise* that we see attempts at specific comparisons of Hume's doctrines with Newton's: for example, the famous description of association of ideas as comparable to gravitation, as 'a kind of ATTRACTION, which in the mental world will be found to have as extraordinary effects as in the natural, and to shew itself in as many and as various forms'.[61] Hume did abandon such specific claims in the later works, but this is not a retreat from a Newtonian spirit of a more general kind. The sentences immediately following the quoted analogy have a markedly Newtonian flavour, and indicate well the stance of the later work:

Its effects are every where conspicuous; but as to its causes, they are mostly unknown, and must be resolv'd into *original* qualities of human nature, which I pretend not to explain. Nothing is more requisite for a true philosopher, than to restrain the intemperate desire of searching into causes, and having establish'd any doctrine upon a sufficient number of experiments, rest contented with that, when he sees a farther examination would lead him into obscure and uncertain speculations. In that case his enquiry wou'd be much better employ'd in examining the effects than the causes of his principle.[62]

---

[58] A more complete treatment of these issues will be provided in the next chapter.
[59] *Enquiries*, 73 n. See Sir Isaac Newton, *Opticks, or A Treatise of the Reflections, Refractions, Inflections, & Colours of Light*, 4th edn. (1730) (New York: Dover, 1979), 401–2.
[60] *Enquiries*, 204.   [61] *Treatise*, 12–13.   [62] Ibid.

Compare this with Hume's remark, in the Appendix to the *Treatise*, that 'Nothing is more suitable to that [i.e. Newtonian] philosophy, than a modest scepticism to a certain degree, and a fair confession of ignorance in subjects, that exceed all human capacity'.[63] Newtonian philosophy is, for Hume, a form of modest scepticism that scrupulously resists knowledge claims about matters beyond our reach.

Newtonianism is also seen by Hume as the crowning achievement of the entire experimental tradition. The point is clearly illustrated by a passage in the opening section of the first *Enquiry*:

Astronomers had long contented themselves with proving, from the phænomena, the true motions, order, and magnitude of the heavenly bodies: Till a philosopher, at last, arose, who seems, from the happiest reasoning, to have also determined the laws and forces, by which the revolutions of the planets are governed and directed. The like has been performed with regard to other parts of nature. And there is no reason to despair of equal success in our enquiries concerning the mental powers and economy, if prosecuted with equal capacity and caution.[64]

Newton is presented here as having brought to triumphant completion a long-held ambition of the human intellect; in effect, to have ushered in a new age. He is also, therefore, a source of inspiration for those who seek comparable great breakthroughs in the study of other hitherto recalcitrant phenomena, including students of human nature. Of course, the inspiration can only bear further fruit amongst those who also see the model of sound philosophizing he provides: those who take to heart his 'happiest reasoning', and who learn to proceed with sufficient 'capacity and caution'. But for those who take this lesson to heart, his example shows that it would be 'precipitate', even 'dogmatical', to abandon the hope of breakthroughs 'in subjects of such unspeakable importance'.[65] In fact, Newton himself recommended the extension of experimental principles to moral subjects, in order to 'enlarge' moral philosophy.[66] Newton has, then, ushered in a new age; and, in hoping, at least, to be the Newton of the moral sciences, Hume likewise hopes to bring a revolution to fruition, and to sweep away the last obstacles to a new age in human affairs.

The second question to be considered here is Hume's conception of Christianity's relationship to ancient philosophy. He discusses the issue in one of his essays, 'Of Parties in General'. He there explicitly identifies Christianity not merely as a specific cluster of religious beliefs, but as a species of ancient philosophy. His implicit

[63] Ibid. 639.   [64] *Enquiries*, 14.   [65] Ibid. 15, 16.   [66] Newton, *Opticks*, 405.

view is that Christian theology, in its most sophisticated forms, is
a complex intellectual structure built from raw materials provided
by ancient philosophies. So it is dubitable that, for Hume, there
was a 'primitive' Christianity that was prior to, and subsequently
transformed into, a philosophical system. He holds that it was,
rather, from its inception a *philosophical* religion—even if it was
fashioned from components that were not exclusively philosophical. The point is made in response to the question, why has
Christianity been the scene of so much conflict? His answer is
this:

Religions, that arise in ages totally ignorant and barbarous, consist mostly of
traditional tales and fictions, which may be different in every sect, without
being contrary to each other; and even when they are contrary, every one
adheres to the tradition of his own sect, without much reasoning or disputation. But as philosophy was widely spread over the world, at the time when
Christianity arose, the teachers of the new sect were obliged to form a system
of speculative opinions; to divide, with some accuracy, their articles of faith;
and to explain, comment, confute, and defend with all the subtilty of argument and science.[67]

For Hume, then, Christianity was from its inception a philosophical endeavour. In marking itself off from its rivals it needed
to explain its points of convergence and divergence, and this
required it to make use of the available philosophical vocabulary—
and even to appeal to the dominant conceptions of reality and
cosmic order. Thus the Christian Church, from its earliest days—
shown first in the Epistles of Paul, and later in the Church Councils—defined its creeds in the philosophical terms of the day.[68]
The consequence is that Christianity is to be understood as a
version of ancient philosophy. So when, for example, Galileo fell
foul of the official Christian Aristotelianism of his day, this should
not be judged as a religious dispute tacked onto the clash of
ancient philosophy with the emerging new world view, but as part
and parcel of the clash between the ancient and the modern.
Christianity is not, for Hume, a religion that happens to express
itself in the terminology of an ancient philosophy, and from which
it can detach itself readily and without loss; it is, rather, a species
of ancient philosophy—and so confronts a serious threat in the
new natural philosophy. Hume's conclusion will be that this is a
threat it cannot survive: that the principles of experience implied

[67] 'Of Parties in General', in *Essays*, 62.
[68] See W. Pannenberg, 'The Appropriation of the Philosophical Concept of God as a
Dogmatic Problem of Early Christian Theology', in *Basic Questions in Theology* (London:
SCM Press, 1971), ii. 119–83.

by the new philosophy will deny its foundations, both its revealed and its natural theology. The argument of the *Enquiry* is directed at showing that to complete the revolution in philosophy—to extend mechanical principles to human functioning—spells the end for the Christian religion, the most complex achievement of the ancient philosophies.

We can now turn to the third issue. Since, as a species of ancient philosophy, Christianity was, from the High Middle Ages, primarily a species of Aristotelianism, then it is natural to conclude that the metaphysics to which Hume refers as 'a shelter for super stition' is Aristotelianism. However, this conclusion will not be credible if scholastic or other forms of Aristotelianism, no matter how broadly conceived, were completely dead ducks by the middle of the eighteenth century, and so just not worth the bother. But this was not so. Recent scholarship has done much to undermine the cheerful assumption that the seventeenth-century revolution in natural philosophy caused Aristotelian philosophy simply to wither away. It did not. In fact, there was no single unified Aristotelian position, so an attack thought to be successful against one version could leave others standing. No doubt partly for this reason, different strands of Aristotelian thought lingered long after Descartes. This is shown clearly in the work of Christia Mercer,[69] building on earlier studies by P. O. Kristeller, J. H. Randall, and Charles Schmitt.[70] Mercer is principally concerned with the seventeenth century, however—so is it also credible to attribute some lingering vitality to Aristotelianism into the middle of the eighteenth century? Without pretending to be thorough, it is possible to make three relevant observations.

The first is that Locke's *Essay* provoked several responses of an Aristotelian variety, most notably John Sergeant's *Method to Science* (1696) and *Solid Philosophy Asserted* (1697), so Aristotelian views found serious defenders at the turn of the century.[71] Further, it is well known that, throughout his intellectual career, Leibniz sought to accommodate the new philosophy to the old—to such an extent that Stuart Brown has questioned the value of calling him a 'rationalist' at all.[72] Leibniz died in 1716, so, up until this date at least, Aristotelian views found a champion in an intellectual figure of

---

[69] C. Mercer, 'The Vitality and Importance of Early Modern Aristotelianism', in T. Sorell (ed.), *The Rise of Modern Philosophy* (Oxford: Clarendon Press, 1993), 33–67.

[70] Ibid. 33. Mercer acknowledges, in particular, C. Schmitt, 'Towards a Reassessment of Renaissance Aristotelianism', *History of Science*, 2 (1973), 159–93.

[71] See e.g. P. Phemister, 'Locke, Sergeant, and Scientific Method', in Sorell (ed.), *The Rise of Modern Philosophy*, 231–49.

[72] S. Brown, *Leibniz* (Brighton: Harvester Press, 1984), ch. 1. Cf. Leibniz, *New Essays*, 71–3.

recognized substance. However, cases of this kind are really the tip of the iceberg. The continuing presence of Aristotelian styles of thought in the period is not reducible to a few isolated instances because accommodation of a Leibnizian kind was more typical than is usually recognized. As Thomas Lennon notes, even in Sergeant's case Aristotelianism was modified to incorporate mechanical elements, even where this caused serious strains in the theory.[73] In France, accommodation typically took a different form: 'If in England a tendency was to reshape Aristotle to the New Science, [there] it was to show that the New Science was not something new under the sun, that in fact it was saying nothing more than what had been said by the ancients, especially Aristotle.'[74] Even Descartes had adopted this strategy on occasions, particularly in the *Principles of Philosophy*. Such accommodation is not what Hume has in mind, so, even if it were the case that pure Aristotelianism was dead, Aristotelianized new philosophy would certainly fall within his critical purview. This applies most directly to those parts of Aristotelianism that were commonly thought to be compatible with the new philosophy. Aristotle's empiricism is a case in point. It has been noted above that d'Alembert specifically exempted its empiricism from his dismissal of Aristotelian thought. If this view was reasonably common, then an experimentalist attack on Aristotle's *interpretation* of empiricism—that is, of what could be gleaned from experience—would not be a remixing of bromides, but a distinctive and significant argument.

Secondly, in the realm of polite education, the status of the ancient world in England and France was not seriously challenged until the episode dubbed the 'Battel between the Antient and Modern Books' by Jonathan Swift.[75] This dispute, between the relative merits of the ancient and modern worlds, broke out in 1690, but did not subside until the 1730s. Even then, the issue was not resolved, but petered out in a draw.[76] The episode shows just how durable respect for the ancient world remained in educated society

---

[73] T. M. Lennon, *The Battle of the Gods and Giants: The Legacies of Descartes and Gassendi, 1655–1715* (Princeton: Princeton University Press, 1993), 53–4.

[74] Ibid. 55–6.

[75] Jonathan Swift, *A Tale of a Tub. Written for the Universal Improvement of Mankind. To which is added, An Account of a Battel between the Antient and Modern Books in* St James's Library (1704) (New York: Garland, 1972).

[76] For a full account, see J. M. Levine, *The Battle of the Books: History and Literature in the Augustan Age* (Ithaca, NY: Cornell University Press, 1991). Hume's views are modernist, but not exceptionlessly so. On natural philosophy, he sides with the moderns. On moral and social issues, however, his stance is more complex. He espouses the moral values of the ancients, especially Cicero; but also argues that a modern view (his own) is necessary properly to explain the foundations of those beliefs. See e.g. *A Letter from a Gentleman*, 30. (In this respect his view bears interesting similarities with, and differences from, the views of Alasdair MacIntyre and Bernard Williams.) On other 'moral subjects' he was sometimes unequiv-

at large, and, although Aristotle's philosophy was not an explicit part of this dispute, it is not unreasonable to conclude that the hostility towards Aristotle so frequently—and energetically— expressed by advocates of the new philosophy was not uniformly shared in polite circles; that accommodation of one kind or another was a more attractive option. Moreover, the humanist cur- riculum that had grown up in Europe in the wake of the Renais- sance meant that, for the politely educated, ancient examples, including the main schools of philosophical thought, provided the *currency*—the categories and concepts—of intellectual debate. Thus opponents of medieval scholastic thought did not, typically, reject it as antiquated, but as a corrupted version of the ancient heritage, to be contrasted with the pristine fruit of antiquity, whether Pla- tonism or one of the Hellenistic schools. Thus the very thought- world generated by the humanist curriculum helped to maintain a concern with Aristotelianism even when it was rejected, because it represented to the early modern mind a *type* of philosophical theory.[77]

Thirdly, and most importantly, on issues of religion and morals the survival of one specific form of Aristotelianism into the eigh- teenth century is the plainest of facts. The dominant Thomism of that most durable of institutions, the Catholic Church, shows that forms of Aristotelianism can be expected to flourish well into the twenty-first century, let alone the eighteenth. Thus any attempted critique, even today, of Catholic theology or morals, whether of hoary old issues like the 'real presence', or of highly topical practi- cal matters such as abortion or *in vitro* fertilization, will simply fail to address all the relevant issues if it ignores the broadly Aristotelian notions that underpin the concepts and conclusions of Catholic theology.[78] For the eighteenth-century British world, the reach of Catholic theology was considerably greater, in both depth and breadth. Not to mention in practical politics, as the Revolt of 1745 had shown: neither Hume nor his contemporaries, whether

ocally modern, such as in 'Of the Populousness of Ancient Nations', in *Essays*, 377–464, which would have been read as a defence of the modern period. Nevertheless, as is plain to the reader of the *Essays*, his modernism does not diminish his *esteem* for the ancients—except, of course, for those aspects of the ancient heritage that sheltered 'superstition'.

[77] See e.g. S. Gaukroger (ed.), *The Uses of Antiquity* (Dordrecht: Kluwer, 1992).

[78] The crucial role of Aristotelian conceptions in the Catholic position is sufficiently illus- trated by the determination to think in terms of organisms, and thus to resist the distin- guishing mark of modern liberal thought: the sharp distinction between *person* and *human being*. The failure to recognize the key significance of this issue vitiates both criticisms and defences of the Catholic view. See e.g. M. Tooley, *Abortion and Infanticide* (Oxford: Clarendon Press, 1983), 50–164; Sacred Congregation for the Doctrine of the Faith, *Instruction on Respect for Human Life in its Origin and on the Dignity of Procreation: Replies to Certain Questions of the Day* (Homebush, NSW: St Paul Publications, 1987), 19–22.

Catholic or Protestant, were in any position to tell that Culloden was the last hurrah of Catholic politics in Britain. So for this reason as well, he could not have considered an attack on the fundamentals of the Catholic position to be a waste of time. In fact, this provides all the more reason for presenting one's work as a Protestant attack on the baleful influences of Catholicism and its distinctive metaphysics. That this is a ruse on his part does not diminish, but reinforces, its explanatory value. This is because his understanding of Christianity as a philosophical religion—and therefore as all too inclined to foster political conflicts—gave him a reason to attack it; and he would have judged it a real achievement to show that the argument applied, in essentials, to Protestantism as well, even though the nature of his audience required this to be at least half hidden.[79] So it is reasonable to conclude that his self-described attempt to introduce the experimental method of reasoning into moral subjects includes in its purview just what the *Enquiry* suggests—the banishing of the lingering influences of Aristotelian (and related) concepts and categories on practical and especially religious beliefs—even though that purview would reveal itself to be considerably wider than his audience at first expected.

Rationalist Philosophy as an Incomplete Revolution

The remaining unsolved problem concerns the place of the modern rationalists in this scheme. If Hume is a campaigner for the new philosophy against the old, a campaign that will have profound practical implications, what then of the *other* new philosophy? The marginal role attributed to the rationalists in this interpretation will seem unconvincing if it is thought that they were major players in the intellectual debates to which Hume was a contributor. This section will offer some brief remarks on this question. It makes no pretence to thoroughness: what follows is intended as no more than an antidote to the impression established—by permeation if not promulgation—that eighteenth-century philosophy can be understood as a battle between 'warring schools' of rationalists and empiricists.

It has been mentioned above that one problem with thinking of the history of philosophy in terms of 'warring schools' is that it glosses over, even eclipses, doctrines that the contesting parties shared—not excluding those that the parties at the time recog-

[79] See Hume's treatment of the political excesses of Protestant 'enthusiasm' in *The History of England* (Indianapolis: Liberty Fund, 1983), v.

nized to be significant commonalities. One way in which this is achieved in the present case is through a variety of Whig historiography. That is, if we think of the history of philosophy as essentially a story of progress that culminates in the present, we thereby justify the imposition of present-day doctrines and—not least—categories on the past because these constitute the measuring stick of the most enlightened age. Whiggishness of this kind is very reassuring to the modern academic in his or her study: and so it has never wanted for adherents. However, a thumbnail sketch of the recent history of philosophy as a professional discipline within the modern university will show how distorting this view can be. The modern professionalization of the discipline called 'philosophy' has forced an emphasis on those areas of activity that *distinguish* the discipline from its neighbouring disciplines. The great growth in empirical disciplines in the modern university has thus forced philosophy towards identifying itself as essentially a non-empirical enterprise. 'Philosophy' has come to name a narrowed enterprise in which armchair methods dominate—and therefore also the divisions of the enterprise that are constituted by armchair methods. Logic and epistemology thus have come to loom increasingly large, to be seen as the core of the discipline. The consequence is that, once history of philosophy is conducted from this standpoint, the narrowed modern focus is read back into the past, as if this is to pick out what is philosophically relevant in the thought of past thinkers. It is not. The gentlemanly amateur of the past may have lacked the modern arsenal of symbolic logic, but he compensated for this by his freedom from disciplinary constraints, and the wider vision this allowed. We do not do a service to past philosophers by excluding the wider reaches in which they saw themselves to be engaged; rather, we simply fail to understand what philosophy was (and lose the opportunity for a critical perspective on our own situation).

This is relevant here. If we think of Descartes and Hume as essentially epistemologists, then their differences do loom large, and their commonalities are few and surprising. Thus, in sharp contrast to Hume's apparently complacent acceptance that all ideas arise ultimately from impressions, Descartes insists that the idea of God, and indeed everything knowable by the 'natural light', do not have sensory origins. He even introduces echoes of Plato's cave, when, against Hobbes's crabby complaints, he states that his aim in adopting the method of doubt was to encourage the reader to turn away from the senses: 'My aim was partly to accustom the reader's mind to consider intelligible objects and distinguish them from corporeal things.'[80] As long as we restrict our focus to such epistemological issues, then, the gulf between Descartes and Hume is considerable. However, if the focus is widened, they are revealed to be both on the same side—the side of the 'moderns' in the philosophical revolution—and in this light the significance of their differences diminishes.

John Wright provides a very apposite example, given Descartes's Platonic echoes, and given also the picture offered above of Hume's allegiances. He quotes a passage from a play, *Three Hours after Marriage*, by John Gay, Alexander Pope, and John Arbuthnot, in which a certain Dr Fossile aims to test the virginity of the local women. Along the way, he instructs his nephew on some key philosophical issues:

FOSSILE. My niece professes herself a Platonick. You are rather a Cartesian.
CLINK. Ah dear uncle! How do the Platonicks and Cartesians differ?
FOSSILE. The Platonicks are for idea's, the Cartesians for matter and motion.[81]

As Wright observes, this mechanical thesis is the prevailing conception of Cartesianism in eighteenth-century Britain. He adds: 'There is good reason to think that eighteenth-century English intellectuals did not interpret Cartesian philosophy through the abstruse metaphysics of the *Meditations*.'[82] The early modern philosophers now described as 'rationalists' were in their eyes moderns, philosophical revolutionaries who, like the British experimental philosophers, accepted the need for experiment to broaden and deepen knowledge of the natural world.[83] All opposed blind adherence to the authority of the ancients.[84] Their differences, over the foundations and extent of human knowledge, were real enough; but, considered in this broader context, rationalists

---

[80] First Reply, Third Set of Objections and Replies. This is the translation in *Descartes: Philosophical Writings*, trans. E. Anscombe and P. T. Geach (London: Thomas Nelson, 1954), 127. The Platonic air is somewhat reduced in *The Philosophical Writings of Descartes*, Cottingham *et al.*: 'Partly I wanted to prepare my readers' minds for the study of the things which are related to the intellect, and help them to distinguish these things from corporeal things' (ii. 121).

[81] Quoted in Wright, *The Sceptical Realism of David Hume*, 6.   [82] Ibid. 6 n. 23.

[83] See e.g. D. Clarke, *Descartes' Philosophy of Science* (Manchester: Manchester University Press, 1982).

[84] Indeed, Descartes's method of doubt (which ultimately led him to affirm the reality of innate ideas), and Locke's frontal assault on innateness, were *alike* commended by the French Enlightenment *philosophes*, because both were read as rejections of traditional authority. See d'Alembert, *Preliminary Discourse*, 78–85. Locke's anti-authoritarian motives are plain (see *Essay*, I. iv. 23–5), Descartes's less so; but the shared commitments to (what later came to be identified as) Enlightenment ideals are expounded in two works by P. A. Schouls, *Descartes and the Enlightenment* (Edinburgh: Edinburgh University Press, 1989), and *Reasoned Freedom: John Locke and Enlightenment* (Ithaca, NY: Cornell University Press, 1992).

could readily be seen by an experimentalist as fellow-travellers who had gone astray, in part by having wandered up a few blind alleys, but especially by having failed fully to extricate themselves from the beguiling inheritance of the past, scholastic philosophy in particular.

It is not implausible to suppose that Hume also thought something of this kind. Certainly, it makes sense of his practice of criticizing rationalist theses along the way, but not considering them appropriate targets of a sustained critique. It is also not difficult to show that the view has substance; that is, that it would *reasonably* have been held by Hume and others. This is most obviously true of Descartes himself; and especially of the central plank of his constructive epistemology, his cosmological argument for the existence of God in the third of the *Meditations*. Scholastic principles, most notably the idea that a cause must possess greater reality than its effect, are there introduced without warning, and play a key role in the development of the argument. A brief examination of the relevant part of the argument is useful here, both to illustrate Descartes's scholastic debts, and also to highlight the transformation of the conception of causation that was central to the philosophical revolution itself.

In the Third Meditation, Descartes inspects the ideas that comprise the contents of his consciousness. They fall, he suggests, into three groups: 'some appear to be innate, some to be adventitious, and some to have been invented by me.'[85] Since he is operating at this stage with how things appear, the lists he offers of each kind are unsurprising: the idea of truth seems to be innate, ideas of sensible objects seem adventitious, and ideas like those of sirens and hippogriffs appear to be invented. He then subjects these ideas to further scrutiny, to test whether a more penetrating analysis of ideas is possible. Considered purely as modes of thought, for example, it is clear that ideas are not separable into the three groups, since 'it is not reliable judgement but merely some blind impulse' that is responsible for classifying the ideas in this way. As modes of thought, ideas are not to be distinguished one from another: 'they all appear to come from within me in the same fashion.'[86]

This is not the end of the analysis, however, since it is also possible to consider ideas, not according to their status as modes of thought, but according to their kinds of content. He puts it this way:

---

[85] *The Philosophical Writings of Descartes*, ii. 26.   [86] Ibid. ii. 27–8.

in so far as different ideas <are considered as images which> represent
different things, it is clear that they differ widely. Undoubtedly, the ideas
which represent substances to me amount to something more and, so to
speak, contain within themselves more objective reality than the ideas
which merely represent modes or accidents. Again, the idea that gives me my
understanding of a supreme God, eternal, infinite, <immutable,> omniscient,
omnipotent and the creator of all things that exist apart from him, certainly
has in it more objective reality than the ideas that represent finite
substances.[87]

Here we see Descartes relying on a cluster of notions he has
imbibed from the scholastics—substance, mode, and accident,
and, most strikingly, the 'objective reality' of an idea[88]—and all at
a stage in the argument of the *Meditations* where no new foundation for genuine knowledge has yet been identified.

   The claim that causes must possess at least the reality of their
effects is next introduced, and applied to the 'objective reality' of
ideas to establish the raw materials of the cosmological proof:

Now it is manifest by the natural light that there must be at least as much
<reality> in the efficient and total cause as in the effect of that cause. For
where, I ask, could the effect get its reality from, if not from that cause? And
how could the cause give it to the effect unless it possessed it? It follows from
this both that something cannot arise from nothing, and also that what is
more perfect—that is, contains in itself more reality—cannot arise from what
is less perfect. And this is transparently true not only in the case of effects
which possess <what the philosophers call> actual or formal reality, but also
in the case of ideas, where one is considering only <what they call> objective
reality.[89]

---

[87] Ibid. ii. 28. Note the translators' remarks in their General Introduction: 'Our own translations of Descartes' works are made, in each case, from the original language in which they
were composed . . . Where subsequent translations approved by Descartes provide important
additional material, this has also been translated, but in footnotes or diamond brackets
<. . .>, to distinguish it from the original material' (ibid. ii, p. viii).

[88] In the words of the translators' editorial footnote: 'According to the scholastic distinction invoked in the paragraphs that follow, the "formal" reality of anything is its own intrinsic reality, while the "objective" reality of an idea is a function of its representational content'
(ibid. ii. 28 n.). According to Thomas Lennon, the truth is more complicated: these are
Descartes's own terms, but for a distinction that is indeed scholastic. In scholastic terminology, the formal/objective distinction is the distinction between what is *materially* in the mind,
and what is *immaterially* in it (see Lennon, *The Battle of the Gods and Giants*, 241). Either way,
the *distinction* is scholastic.

[89] *The Philosophical Writings of Descartes*, ii. 28. Note that in this passage Descartes affirms
just what Hume denies in his discussion of the possibility of a necessary being already referred
to: 'That impious maxim of the ancient philosophy, *Ex nihilo, nihil fit*, by which the creation
of matter was excluded, ceases to be a maxim, according to this [i.e. experimental] philosophy' (*Enquiries*, 164). The passage is mischievous, of course, since the medieval defenders of
this doctrine did not wish to exclude the creation of matter—and did not have to, given their
different notions of causation. The relevance of mentioning this here, however, is to point
out a clear case of Descartes affirming a notion, shared with the Scholastics and the ancients—
but Hume attacks it as an ancient, rather than a rationalist or otherwise modern doctrine.
The issue is complicated, however, by the extent of the mischievousness: Hume may be
enjoying himself at the expense of *pious* readers who accept the doctrine.

In this passage, we see Descartes's whole pattern of thought running counter to the general picture encouraged by the mechanical philosophy, despite the concern of the *Meditations* to defend mechanism, at least in its proper sphere. The problem is that the justification for talking of causation in this way, even with respect to minds, needs to be made out. With respect to the physical world, it is a way of talking that mechanical philosophy rules out, since a central plank of mechanism is a new conception of causation. The new conception can be outlined as follows. Events happen in the physical world because objects are pushed by other, moving, objects that impart motion to them, such that the total amount of motion is conserved.[90] The actual motions themselves reflect the specific mechanisms that make each object what it is. On this picture, there is no place for speaking of degrees of reality, no content to be given to the idea of perfection, and even no necessity to postulate an ultimate explanation.[91] Since Descartes's cosmological argument appeals precisely to these considerations, it is clear that it belongs to a thought-world that, in other domains, he means to root out completely. The conclusion must be, then, that Descartes's metaphysics remains indebted to the thought-world of scholasticism, and at precisely the point where he is putting in place the metaphysical foundations for his system. Why this should be so can provide scope for dispute, but the fact itself cannot seriously be contested.[92] Descartes's philosophical revolution shows, then, the marks of its own incompleteness.

[90] Thus Descartes: 'God . . . always preserves the same quantity of motion in the universe' (*Principles of Philosophy*, II. 36, in *The Philosophical Writings of Descartes*, i. 240).

[91] For an account of this transition, see e.g. E. A. Burtt, *The Metaphysical Foundations of Modern Physical Science* (Atlantic Highlands, NJ: Humanities Press, 1952): 'Different thinkers and ages have made widely different assumptions as to what constitutes a sound causal explanation of any event . . . One is the teleological position of Platonic and Aristotelian philosophy and expressed with meticulous precision in the scholastic dictum that the cause must be adequate to the effect 'either formally or eminently'. In simple language we may put it thus: the cause must be at least as perfect as the effect. When worked out in detail this means an essentially religious picture of the world, and a being not dissimilar to the scholastic deity (an *ens realissimum et perfectissimum*) must be postulated as the ultimate and all-embracing cause of events. The second is the mechanical position . . . Its fundamental assumptions are that all causes and effects are reducible to motions of bodies in time and space and are mathematically equivalent in terms of the forces expressed. From this standpoint the notion of perfection drops out of sight entirely . . . Here there is no such thing as an ultimate explanation except in the form of a most general law exemplified in the specific explanations' (307–8). Burtt's view that the differences between the two views reflect different *assumptions* is misleading, and has not gone uncriticized; see e.g. G. Hatfield, 'Metaphysics and the New Science', in D. C. Lindberg and R. S. Westman (eds.), *Reappraisals of the Scientific Revolution* (Cambridge: Cambridge University Press, 1990), 93–166. For a recent study focused directly on the transformation of the concept of causation, see K. Clatterbaugh, *The Causation Debate in Modern Philosophy 1637–1739* (London: Routledge, 1999). For the varieties of rationalist views, see Nadler (ed.), *Causation in Early Modern Philosophy*.

[92] Two contrasting views are provided by Stephen Gaukroger and Daniel Garber. Gaukroger, in his substantial study of Descartes's intellectual development, argues that the *Meditations* is not a self-contained work, that it should rather be read 'as one which prepares the way for

What is true of Descartes does not necessarily apply to other rationalists, of course. The point here, however, concerns not so much an accurate estimation of the rationalists themselves, but whether Hume could reasonably be thought to have regarded them as having failed to detach themselves sufficiently from the weight of the past. The case against Descartes is clear. Similar conclusions about other major rationalist philosophers can also be reached quite readily—for example, by noting the extensive role of the notion of perfection in the works of Leibniz and Male-branche.[93] Hume's practice thus plausibly reflects such a view; that is, his relative lack of interest in attacking distinctively rationalist doctrines is consistent with the thought that he saw them as having failed to effect the necessary break with the past. Strikingly, the clearest evidence of such incompleteness concerned religious questions, so it is perhaps no accident that he detected, at this same point, the Newtonians' own failure to break with the past. These possibilities fit well the task he set himself, to show that a properly understood, consistent Newtonianism had implications for the human condition that had not been accurately appreci-ated—and not least with respect to ultimate questions. To this extent, he can indeed be described as a critic of the 'speculative excesses of the Newtonians'.[94] However, that this is so should not blind us to the bigger picture: in offering his account of the impli-cations of experimental philosophy for moral subjects, Hume understands himself to be completing the philosophical revolu-tion—sweeping away the last, stubbornly resistant, productions of the medieval mind—by demolishing the ancient foundations of dogmatism.

In order to achieve this goal, he must examine the possibility of philosophical insight into the nature of the world—that is, of knowledge of causes. If we accept that mechanical philosophy rightly limits us to explanations only in terms of efficient causes,

a full presentation of Descartes' metaphysically grounded natural philosophy'. That full pre-sentation is in the *Principles*, where, says Gaukroger, the scholastic terminology is merely an 'overlay' (*Descartes: An Intellectual Biography* (Oxford: Clarendon Press, 1995), 362). Garber, in contrast, sees the scholastic past as a continuing living presence in Descartes's thought. He concludes his major study by observing that Descartes unwittingly spoke also of himself when, in the Introduction to the French edition of the *Principles*, he remarked: 'Those who have not followed Aristotle . . . have nevertheless been saturated with his opinions in their youth . . . and this has so dominated their outlook that they have been unable to arrive at knowledge of true principles' (quoted by Garber, *Descartes' Metaphysical Physics*, 308).

[93] G. W. Leibniz, *Discourse on Metaphysics and Related Writings*, trans. R. N. D. Martin and S. Brown (Manchester: Manchester University Press, 1988); Nicolas Malebranche, *The Search after Truth* and *Elucidations of the Search after Truth*, trans. T. M. Lennon and P. J. Olscamp, with Philosophical Commentary by T. M. Lennon (Columbus, Oh.: Ohio State University Press, 1980).

[94] Noxon, *Hume's Philosophical Development*, 77.

---

then the first task is to explain how knowledge of such causes is possible. For this reason Hume homes in on the new conception of causation and its implications in the central sections of the *Enquiry*. His argument is that the manner in which our idea of efficient causation arises shows that genuine knowledge of real causes, of causal powers, is impossible for us—and philosophical knowledge therefore lies beyond our reach. The faithful adherence to experimental philosophy thus has significant sceptical implications, as the *Enquiry* makes plain: three of its twelve sections are explicitly concerned with scepticism, and sceptical refrains are frequent in most of the others. Hume thus connects experimentalism to a form of scepticism, and thereby redraws the battle lines between the old and new philosophies as a battle between metaphysical dogmatists and metaphysical sceptics—with victory going to the latter. This is what woke Kant from his dogmatic slumbers; he read Hume aright when he formulated the alternatives to the Critical Philosophy in just those terms.[95] They share the view that dogmatism has had its day. They differ, of course, on the solution. But they also differ on the question of which forms of dogmatism are worth taking seriously. For Kant, rationalism in the form of the Leibniz–Wolffian philosophy could hardly be ignored; Hume, however, considers rationalistic thought only in passing, and directs his attack at the dogmatic empiricisms that he sees to offer specious but false interpretations of experimental philosophy.

Chauvinism, Progress, and Prudence

There is another possible source for Hume's disregard of the modern rationalists, and one that may be further evidence of his tayloring his message to fit his audience (and in the *Treatise* no less

[95] Kant's estimation of the philosophical legacy of Hume, and his own response to it, are summed up in the following passage: 'The first step in matters of pure reason, marking its infancy, is *dogmatic*. The second step is *sceptical*; and indicates that experience has rendered our judgment wiser and more circumspect. But a third step, such as can be taken only by fully matured judgment, based on assured principles of proved universality, is now necessary, namely, to subject to examination, not the facts of reason, but reason itself, in the whole extent of its powers, and as regards its aptitude for pure *a priori* modes of knowledge. This is not the censorship but the *criticism* of reason, whereby not its present *bounds* but its determinate [and necessary] *limits*, not its ignorance on this or that point but its ignorance in regard to all possible questions of a certain kind, are demonstrated from principles, and not merely arrived at by way of conjecture. Scepticism is thus a resting-place for human reason, where it can reflect upon its dogmatic wanderings and make survey of the region in which it finds itself, so that for the future it may be able to choose its path with more certainty. But it is no dwelling-place for permanent settlement. Such can be obtained only through perfect certainty in our knowledge, alike of the objects themselves and of the limits within which all of our knowledge of objects is enclosed' (Immanuel Kant, *Critique of Pure Reason*, trans. N. Kemp Smith (London: Macmillan, 1933), 607).

than in the *Enquiry*). This source is intellectual chauvinism. To
draw out this feature of the British, particularly English, public
mind in the first half of the eighteenth century will be to illuminate some further dimensions of Hume's situation and strategy:
the implicit connection between Englishness and progressive, or
enlightened, views; and the wider value of claiming Newtonian
debts, especially when advancing controversial theses.

Chauvinism is visible in Hume's tendency, already mentioned,
to equate Newtonianism with the new philosophy itself. In
England, Newton's great achievement was a source of immense
national pride,[96] and this pride exercised itself in dismissing
eclipsed foreign theories. So the view was quickly established there
that the works of Descartes and his followers, if they had ever been
significant, had now been consigned to the dustbin of history. To
the chauvinistic eyes of English public culture, Descartes and his
followers were not to be taken seriously. The widespread influence
of this attitude is indicated indirectly by the young Voltaire, in his
Letters on England, first published in 1734. Voltaire there praises
Newton, but also offers a qualified defence of Descartes. In the
process he gives the clear impression that the educated English
public were extremely ignorant of, and prejudiced against, the
intellectual achievement of the latter. His remarks, written shortly
after Newton's death in 1727, give a vivid picture of the English
attitude:

People here have eagerly read and translated into English the *Eulogy of Newton*
that M. de Fontenelle delivered in the Académie des Sciences. In England it
was expected that the verdict of M. de Fontenelle would be a solemn decla-
ration of the superiority of English natural science. But when it was realized
that he compared Descartes with Newton the whole Royal Society in London
rose up in arms. Far from agreeing with this judgement they criticized the
discourse. Several even (not the most scientific) were shocked by the comparison simply because Descartes was a Frenchman . . . In England, public
opinion of the two of them is that the first was a dreamer and the other a
sage.

Very few people in London read Descartes, whose works, practically speaking, have become out of date. Very few read Newton, either, because much
knowledge is necessary to understand him. However, everybody talks about
them, conceding nothing to the Frenchman and everything to the Englishman. There are people who think that if we are no longer content with the
abhorrence of a vacuum, if we know that the air has weight, if we use a tele-

---

[96] See e.g. D. Gjertsen, 'Newton's Success', and M. McNeill, 'Newton as National Hero',
both in J. Fauvel, R. Flood, M. Shortland, and R. Wilson (eds.), *Let Newton Be!* (Oxford: Oxford
University Press, 1988), 23–42, 223–40.

scope, it is all due to Newton. Here he is the Hercules of the fable, to whom the ignorant attributed all the deeds of the other heroes.[97]

These comments are all the more striking because, on the whole, Voltaire's little book is a comparison of English enlightenment with French intolerance and superstition. Compared to the rest of the work, they stand out for their contrasting tone—so there is no good reason for treating them other than as they appear, as an accurate report of English chauvinism and self-satisfaction in the wake of Newton's achievement. It is not hard to conclude that, in such a climate, serious engagement with Cartesian philosophy would have seemed like so much wasted effort.

Hume himself provides some indirect evidence for a lack of interest amongst the reading public for foreign ideas, in two different places. The first occurs in a letter, written to his friend Michael Ramsay, advising him on the books that would help him to understand the 'metaphysical Parts' of the *Treatise*:

to make you enter into them more easily, I desire of you, if you have Leizure, to read once over La Recherche de la Verité of Pere Malebranche, the Principles of Human Knowledge by Dr Berkeley, some of the more metaphysical Articles of Bailes Dictionary; such as those [. . . of] Zeno, & Spinoza. Des-Cartes Meditations would also be useful but don't know if you will find it easily among your Acquaintances . . .[98]

Hume's remark shows that Descartes's *Meditations* was not widely available, and (presumably) not widely read, in 1740s Scotland. This is striking, although the significance of the fact may be less than it seems. John Wright's view, that 'eighteenth-century English intellectuals did not interpret Cartesian philosophy through the abstruse metaphysics of the *Meditations*',[99] is sufficient to explain the fact without implying an absence of interest in Cartesian thought altogether. However, this explanation directly implies a relative lack of British interest in Cartesianism's 'abstruse' aspects— that is, in its rationalistic foundations.

The second piece of evidence is in his essay 'Of the Rise and Progress of the Arts and Sciences'. Hume offers there a number of observations on the background conditions most conducive to the

---

[97] Voltaire, *Letters on England*, 69, 70–1. At least some of Fontenelle's comparisons were entirely innocuous: for example, Newton was fortunate to achieve fame in his lifetime, whereas Descartes was unhonoured until well after his death. See Gjertsen, 'Newton's Success', in Fauvel *et al.* (eds.), *Let Newton Be!*, 24.

[98] Quoted by R. H. Popkin, 'So, Hume did Read Berkeley', in *The High Road to Pyrrhonism*, 291.

[99] Wright, *The Sceptical Realism of David Hume*, 6 n. 23.

development of artistic and scientific culture. The second of these
is as follows:

*That nothing is more favourable to the rise of politeness and learning, than a number
of neighbouring and independent states, connected together by commerce and policy.*
The emulation which naturally arises among those neighbouring states is an
obvious source of improvement. But what I would chiefly insist on is the stop
which such limited territories give both to *power* and *authority.*

One of the examples then adduced in favour of this general observation concerns the comparative international and intranational
fates of Descartes and Newton:

What checked the progress of the CARTESIAN philosophy, to which the FRENCH
nation showed such a strong propensity towards the end of the last century,
but the opposition made to it by the other nations of EUROPE, who soon discovered the weak sides of that philosophy? The severest scrutiny which
NEWTON'S theory has undergone proceeded not from his own countrymen,
but from foreigners; and if it can overcome the obstacles which it meets with
at present in all parts of EUROPE, it will probably go down triumphant to the
latest posterity.[100]

   Here we see an indication of the nationalistic determinants on
fame, and therefore on Descartes's cross-channel fate. The English,
amongst others, were not inclined to spare the Frenchman the
most searching criticism, and he was not able to survive the test.
Newton, in contrast, overcame all—or at least, sufficient[101]—objections. It does seem that the sense of national glory consequent
upon the Englishman Newton's achievement, made all the sweeter
by the overcoming of a cross-channel rival, reduced Descartes, in
English eyes, to the status of mere pretender.
   If a sense of English triumphalism was a prominent feature of
the intellectual culture to which Hume was contributing, then two
useful lessons can be drawn. The first is that Hume's presentation
of himself as contributing to an English intellectual tradition,
whether described as Newtonian, experimental, or as following
'some late philosophers in *England,* who have begun to put the
science of man on a new footing',[102] is simultaneously an appeal
to (what his audience will regard as) the most progressive principles. To place his work within the experimental tradition that
Newton had brought to such heights of achievement was to place
himself at the intellectual cutting edge of European culture. The

[100] 'Of the Rise and Progress of the Arts and Sciences', in *Essays,* 119, 121–2. For an account
of the fortunes of Cartesianism in France, see D. Clarke, *Occult Powers and Hypotheses:
Cartesian Natural Philosophy under Louis XIV* (Oxford: Clarendon Press, 1989).
[101] Cf. Geoffrey Cantor, 'Anti-Newton', in Fauvel *et al.* (eds.), *Let Newton Be!,* 203–21.
[102] *Treatise,* p. xvii.

very Englishness of Hume's project is, then, itself evidence of enlightened, if not quite of Enlightenment, principles. Secondly, there is also prudential value in thus marking himself out: it would clearly have been sound policy for a young British author in search of a readership to cloak himself in the Newtonian achievement, and to derive from it what shelter it could afford, should his ideas be met with hostility. This would have been no idle worry, given the author's conviction that it was precisely non-experimental premisses—not least in the hands of eminent experimentalists—that exercised a continuing influence on morals and religion, and thereby sustained an unsustainable Christian heritage. It would be wise indeed to emphasize the continuities between Newtonian principles and such unpopular conclusions. Certainly, such a strategy would be far more compelling to an educated, polite, and, not least, British readership than an attack on the intellectual descendents of a Frenchman who was not to be compared with the great Newton. Hume pays little explicit attention to philosophical rationalism primarily because it was an inferior brand of new philosophy; but, for many of his readers, it was misguided, outdated, and unfortunately foreign.

Chapter 3

Experimentalism and Scepticism

To cast Hume as a player in the major drama of the new philosophy against the old may appear to make him Newtonian to a degree no longer seriously defensible. To qualify this view by adding that he is seeking to purify the new philosophy, even against some of its most notable defenders and interpreters, may seem only to ease the problem, and not to remove it. This is because some significant modern studies have challenged the validity of Hume's Newtonian credentials. One such is James Noxon, who, in *Hume's Philosophical Development*, observes:

Taking up Hume's supposedly Newtonian *Treatise of Human Nature*, the reader finds neither of the chief methodological features of the *Principia* and the *Opticks*. There is not the slightest suggestion of any attempt to apply mathematics to the solution of the problems of the *Treatise*. The book is as unmathematical as Ovid's *Metamorphoses*. Nor is it experimental, except in an extremely attenuated sense, nor even observational except, at certain times, in a peculiar sense (in the sense of introspection) or, at other times, in a very loose sense (in the sense of attending to men's behaviour 'in the common course of the world').[1]

Approaching Hume from a different perspective, Peter Jones expresses reservations of a similar kind. In *Hume's Sentiments: Their Ciceronian and French Context*, he surveys the textbooks available to Hume in his student days, and other possible sources of ideas about Newton's work. He concludes that Hume knew (and needed) less than has often been thought:

---

[1] Noxon, *Hume's Philosophical Development*, 112. The absence of mathematics is a striking feature of Hume's works, given some earlier attempts to introduce mathematical methods into moral subjects. Before Newton, works inspired by the new philosophy had set out their views in geometrical format, even if it was little more than an imposition on an essentially discursive treatise. Samuel Pufendorf's early work, *Elementa Jurisprudentiae Universalis* (1660), is a case in point; Spinoza's *Ethics* the most convincing example of the genre. Newton shifted the focus away from geometry to arithmetical relations; and in this light Francis Hutcheson's *An Inquiry concerning Beauty and Virtue* (1725), which attempts to explain aesthetic responses with the help of the inverse square law, among other things, is notable.

we may surmise that Hume was familiar, at most, with the Prefaces, Definitions, and Axioms of *Principia*, together with the General Scholium, the Rules
of Reasoning in Book III and Cotes's famous Preface in the second edition. In
addition, Hume would have been familiar with parts of the *Opticks*, but especially with the Queries appended to Book III. There is no evidence that Hume
was competent to follow the mathematical core of *Principia*, and we may
infer that he understood the 'Newtonian method' in one or more of the
non-technical senses that became extremely popular in the first half of the
eighteenth century.[2]

Jones's conclusion here may seem a little too quick, since it implicitly rules out Hume furthering his education in mathematics and
natural philosophy after leaving university. This is an important
question, and will be returned to below.

However, the problem can be further sharpened. Michael Barfoot
has reinforced Jones's conclusion by comparing the first *Enquiry*
with other avowedly experimental contemporary literature. He
offers the following summary:

The textual evidence for Hume's so-called 'Newtonianism' has recently been
re-examined and found to be both limited and ambiguous. We can go further:
if Hume's explicit statements about Newton and scientific procedure in *An
enquiry concerning human understanding* are compared with the wider community of 18th-century texts which discussed such matters, it is clear that there is
nothing unusual about them. In fact, it can be argued that his rather brief and
undeveloped views were either commonplace or vicarious, and perhaps even
inconsistent. Hume's insistence upon the role of empirical experience and
facts in scientific discovery, together with the somewhat casual amalgamation
of Newton's method with Bacon's, can be found in Pemberton and MacLaurin.
His appeal to the rules of reasoning in philosophy (E. 204) was also standard.
Hume's related denial of men's perception of any necessary connection
between physical phenomena was also widely accepted, alongside a more
general nescience about the essence and process of nature. A version of the
well-known footnote about the ether (E. 73) can be found in Ramsay. On the
status of hypotheses, Hume displayed the same Janus-faced attitude evident in
the period at large: he simultaneously endorsed their elimination from
philosophy generally, while reserving a use for them in favoured instances.[3]

In this light, it seems that the absences and superficialities observed
by Noxon are no accident. It seems that Hume's knowledge of
Newtonian natural philosophy was nothing special (at best), and
that his work will not be illuminated by invoking any alleged
Newtonian connections.

---

[2] P. Jones, *Hume's Sentiments: Their Ciceronian and French Context* (Edinburgh: Edinburgh
University Press, 1982), 12–13.
[3] M. Barfoot, 'Hume and the Culture of Science', in Stewart (ed.), *Studies in the Philosophy
of the Scottish Enlightenment*, 161.

The conclusion is not, however, defensible. A necessary assumption of both Noxon's and Jones's arguments is that, for the eighteenth-century man of letters, especially for one interested in the criticism of religion, an interest in (what we now call) science and (what we now call) philosophy were separable, indeed separated; that the 'two cultures' were then, as now, largely independent. This is mistaken. The discussion, in Chapter 1, of the world of 'letters' in the early modern world suggests as much. The same point has been well made by James E. Force in a response to Jones. He details Hume's references to Newton, and argues to the conclusion that, just because 'Hume's sort of scientific interest (and his sort of science) bears no relationship to what an employee at the Cavendish Laboratory would call scientific is no reason to treat it as not truly scientific'. He further argues that 'Hume's interest in science cannot be separated from his epistemology or his religious scepticism', because 'the doing of science at this time is inextricably bound up with religious philosophizing'.[4]

Force's carefully documented argument effectively shows that Hume is not to be dismissed as a merely 'literary' figure, dabbling occasionally in what he does not properly understand. The following sections will provide support for this conclusion, by comparing relevant features in Newton's and Hume's works. This method is not beyond criticism, since no attempt will be made to prove that Hume did read carefully all the relevant Newtonian remarks. I think it more than likely that he was alert to most, if not all, of the passages quoted. However, nothing serious hangs on the issue, since, as Force and also Barfoot show, Hume moved in circles where there was a pronounced 'culture of science'—that is, of Newtonian science—where the lessons of Newtonian experimentalism were in the air. So we can be confident that the Newtonian connections are real, even if in some cases they may be less direct than the method of textual examination may suggest. Interestingly, the evidence for the connections stems, in part, from the apparently negative verdicts quoted above.

Mathematics and Experiment in Experimental Philosophy

Hume's Newton is the crowning achievement of the 'experimental' tradition in natural philosophy. As such, his position is

---

[4] Force, 'Hume's Interest in Newton and Science', 166–7.

Newtonian in a broad sense: he aims to conform his enquiries to the 'experimental' philosophy practised—or preached—by Newton. Newton's great success made him an inspiring figure, and gave hope to those who sought to emulate his achievements; further, for those capable of proceeding with 'equal capacity and caution', his methods and discipline were highly instructive. Hume plainly accepts this much—and this can be affirmed without holding, for example, that Hume was uniquely, or more deeply, Newtonian than other contemporaries.

In fact, to suppose that he was would mislead twice over, because, not only does he not make any such claims (in the Introduction to the *Treatise*, it will be remembered, he places himself amongst a new breed of philosophers who have appeared in Britain), the claim he *does* make is rather different, and these commonalities in no way undermine it. His claim is, of course, that he applies the experimental philosophy to *moral* subjects. So what is distinctive about Hume's stance is not the fact of its broadly Newtonian experimentalism, but the particular *uses* to which he puts the philosophy. Barfoot, for his part, recognizes that his list of Hume's commonalities does reveal this distinctiveness, if negatively. He observes: 'While it is right to revise the picture of Hume's "Newtonianism", this does not mean the wider culture of science was unimportant to him, or that he failed to incorporate features of it in a distinctive and innovative way.'[5] These distinctive and innovative features lie, for example, not in arguing that forces are beyond our sense perceptions, but that associative mechanisms provide the best explanation of how our notions of force arise in the first place, and that to recognize this is to see further implications: that our knowledge of the world, and even of our inner life, depends on habitual connections only; that the probabilism on which we are therefore reliant shows belief in miracles always to be misplaced; that the consequent limitations inherent in reasoning about effects and their causes undercuts the experimental philosophers' affection for the argument from design; and so on.[6]

This is to leap ahead: but it is useful at this point to provide a reminder of what Hume thought himself to be up to, especially as a closer acquaintance with the orthodoxies of the experimentalists so effectively brings his distinctive concerns into sharp relief.

---

[5] Barfoot, 'Hume and the Culture of Science'.

[6] As Hume says of himself in the *Abstract*, it is 'the *use* he makes of the principle of the association of ideas' that can entitle him 'to so glorious a name as that of an *inventor*' (*Treatise*, 661; first emphasis added).

It is also useful to bring such issues to the fore because it indicates a real misunderstanding on Noxon's part concerning experimentalism itself. He speaks, in the quotation above, as if experimental philosophy must be spending all its time doing experiments: but the orthodoxies listed by Barfoot serve to show that not only experimenting itself, but also what the young experimental tradition had been judged to establish, and what it had been thought to presuppose, were also key parts of the experimental programme. These issues are central to the overall thrust of this study, and will be considered in some detail below.

The more immediate question, however, is to determine whether Hume's apparent mathematical shortcomings disqualify him from serious consideration as a Newtonian. The problem has been put most sharply by Noxon, in his already quoted remark that the *Treatise* is 'as unmathematical as Ovid's *Metamorphoses*'. To be fair to Hume, this is rather less obvious than once it seemed. Although there is very little of a mathematical kind in the *Treatise*—and, if anything, somewhat less in the *Enquiry*—there are passages that discuss mathematical issues, or mathematical treatments of metaphysical issues, and these are not unsophisticated. The *Treatise* has sections on space and time, and on the possibility that they are infinitely divisible. Section XII of the *Enquiry* discusses some mathematical paradoxes, again concerned with infinities. And Hume continued to reflect on some mathematical issues, at least into the 1750s. He even considered including 'some Considerations previous to Geometry & Natural Philosophy' in the *Four Dissertations*, a collection that appeared in 1757 after several false starts. A casualty of the delays was the 'Considerations' itself, which was dropped after he became convinced that 'there was some Defect in the Argument or in its perspicuity'.[7] Further, Barfoot's thorough investigation of the scientific library available to Hume as a student in Edinburgh, and comparison of Hume's brief discussions of the vacuum and infinite divisibility with contemporary mathematical and scientific works, has led him to the conclusion that Hume was both mathematically able and scientifically literate—that is, by the relevant eighteenth-century standards. He sums up as follows: 'While science affords merely one of the intellectual cultures which impinged upon his development as a metaphysician, moralist, critic, and political theorist, its significance is more profound than most Hume scholars have previously recognized.'[8]

---

[7] See David Hume, *Four Dissertations* (1757) (Bristol: Thoemmes Press, 1995), Introduction by John Immerwahr, pp. vi–vii; cf. Barfoot, 'Hume and the Culture of Science', 168 n.

[8] Barfoot, 'Hume and the Culture of Science', 190. See also Frasca-Spada, *Space and the Self in Hume's* Treatise.

The conclusion is firmly based. However, it must still be admitted that it is not to say all that much. Most Hume scholars have thought Hume's mathematical and scientific remarks scarcely worthy of attention at all, so more than that may still be not much at all. And, even if Hume was considerably more mathematically sophisticated than has been assumed, it remains true that specifically mathematical issues play little more than a cameo role in his philosophy. Furthermore, some of the explicit remarks about mathematical issues are not what would be expected of a philosopher who saw himself to belong amongst the mathematical philosophers. Most strikingly, the main mathematical passage in the first *Enquiry* is anything but flattering to the mathematicians: 'No priestly *dogmas*, invented on purpose to tame and subdue the rebellious reason of mankind, ever shocked common sense more than the doctrine of the infinite divisibility of extension, with its consequences; as they are pompously displayed by all geometricians and metaphysicians, with a kind of triumph and exultation.'[9]

This is little more than a repetition of Berkeley's objections to the absurdities of infinite divisibility,[10] and, although Berkeley was not lacking in mathematical ability, his opposition to Newtonian philosophy makes him a strange ally at this point. For Hume to maintain or protect Newtonian credentials, it would seem more appropriate to cast himself in the role of a friend of mathematics, even if defending it required objecting to its misuse by ardent metaphysicians. In fact, even this might not be an available option, because, if the natural world is genuinely mathematical, then it is not at all clear how mathematics *can* be misused by metaphysicians. They might get it wrong, of course: but Hume's charge appears to be that philosophers have been led astray by thinking that whatever is capable of mathematical treatment is physically possible. Since this is, if anything, a *weaker* view about the relationship between the mathematical and the real than held by some of the new philosophers—Galileo, most notably—Hume seems here to be setting himself *against* the new natural philosophers. He seems to be so antipathetic to mathematics in this passage to preclude any Newtonian sympathies.

In fact, the tensions here are resolved fairly readily, if not unsurprisingly. Hume is here genuinely antipathetic to chains of unconstrained mathematical reasoning producing conclusions about the nature of reality—but Newton would have agreed entirely. The

---

[9] *Enquiries*, 156.
[10] G. Berkeley, *A Treatise Concerning the Principles of Human Knowledge*, ed. J. Dancy (Oxford: Oxford University Press, 1998), 149–53 (I, §§123–32).

problem detected by Noxon resides more in his conviction
(although not, of course, his alone) that Newton's natural philosophy is an attempt to show the fundamentally mathematical
character of the physical world, for, despite its title—*Mathematical
Principles of Natural Philosophy*—the *Principia* does not hold that all
of physical reality is explicable mathematically, nor even that
mathematics is the 'master discourse' of natural philosophy. He
does believe—although he knows that he cannot prove—that the
phenomena of the physical world reduce to matter in motion. He
also believes that, in so far as these motions are capable of exact
description, that description is mathematical. However, whether
natural motions are indeed capable of exact description is a matter
that cannot be assumed, but must always be subject to experimental testing. And, last but not least, to hold that *motions* are
capable of mathematical treatment is not at all to accept that
matter is amenable to mathematical elucidation. In fact, Newton
believes that the nature of matter is not, and cannot be, revealed
by this method. The physical world may be matter in motion, and
a mathematical treatment of those motions may be the only reliable path to follow: but at no stage can experimental testing be
left behind, and all the while such procedures must necessarily
leave the nature—and therefore the powers—of that matter, whose
motions are described, quite undiscovered.[11]

Newton is quite explicit on these issues, even though his remarks
on them are scattered throughout his work, and are not entirely
consistent. Although profoundly interested in the religious implications of his conclusions, he was, more so than Descartes, an
unwilling metaphysician, all too conscious of the distracting and
even dangerous controversies to which it could lead. For this
reason he avoided any systematic attempt at spelling out the implications of his views, restricting himself to brief philosophical
remarks in the Scholia of the *Principia* and the 'Queries' that close

[11] The acceptance of mechanical principles was not entirely without implications for the
nature of matter, however. Strictly speaking, mechanism required matter to be passive—to
move only by being moved around by other moving things, themselves so moved around—
and so denied that forces could be intrinsic to matter. Thus, as previously noted, Newton
denies that gravity is intrinsic to matter in his letter to Richard Bentley: 'That gravity should
be innate, inherent, and essential to matter, so that one body may act upon another at a distance through a *vacuum*, without the mediation of anything else, by and through which their
action and force may be conveyed from one to another, is to me so great an absurdity that
I believe that no man who has in philosophical matters a competent faculty of thinking can
ever fall into it. Gravity must be caused by an agent acting constantly according to certain
laws, but whether this agent be material or immaterial I have left to the consideration of my
readers' (*Newton's Philosophy of Nature*, ed. Thayer, 54). Newton's remarks serve to illustrate
that the mathematical and mechanical elements of the new philosophy were distinct, and
capable of coming into conflict. Cf. R. S. Westfall, *The Construction of Modern Science: Mechanisms and Mechanics* (Cambridge: Cambridge University Press, 1977).

the *Opticks*. This is never the best way to achieve consistency, and, when it is added that the various discussions are usually presented with an eye to meeting philosophical or religious objections—and different objections in different cases—it is no wonder that the end result is not a model of philosophical rigour. Burtt's conclusion is not uncommon: 'In scientific discovery and formulation Newton was a marvellous genius; as a philosopher he was uncritical, sketchy, inconsistent, even second-rate.'[12] This is probably not unfair, but it may be taken to mean that Newton's scattered remarks are of no value whatsoever, and provide no insight into his practices and their implications. In fact they do give quite a clear picture of his method and outlook, in part because his specifically methodological remarks are more cogent than his more general metaphysical pronouncements. And on the matter at issue, the meaning of his mathematical principles, he is quite clear enough. So we can turn to his remarks on the mathematical treatment of matter in motion with some confidence.

First, he explicitly states that a mathematical treatment of the physical world leaves the nature of matter, and of the forces associated with it, undisclosed. He says, introducing his non-technical exposition of his position, *The System of the World*, that his aim is to explain the force (that is, gravitational attraction) that produces the circular motions of the planets:

our purpose is only to trace out the quantity and properties of this force from the phenomena, and to apply what we discover in some simple cases as principles, by which, in a mathematical way, we may estimate the effects thereof in more involved cases; for it would be endless and impossible to bring every particular to direct and immediate observation.

We said, *in a mathematical way*, to avoid all questions about the nature or quality of this force, which we would not be understood to determine by any hypothesis; and therefore call it by the general name of a centripetal force, as it is a force which is directed towards some centre . . .[13]

A mathematical treatment, then, is a purely quantitative treatment, which in no way reveals the 'nature or quality' of the forces it investigates, because it is entirely limited to investigating

---

[12] Burtt, *Metaphysical Foundations of Modern Physical Science*, 208.

[13] *Sir Isaac Newton's Mathematical Principles of Natural Philosophy and his System of the World*, trans. A. Motte, rev. F. Cajori (Berkeley and Los Angeles: University of California Press, 1934) (hereafter referred to as Newton, *Principia*), 550. Cf. Newton's earlier remarks, in Book One, that 'I use the word *impulse*, not defining in this treatise the species or physical qualities of forces, but investigating the quantities or mathematical proportions of them; as I observed before in the Definitions. In mathematics we are to investigate the quantities of forces with their proportions consequent upon any conditions imposed; then, when we enter upon physics, we compare those proportions with the phenomena of Nature, that we may know what conditions of those forces answer to the several kinds of attractive bodies' (192).

phenomena, and not the matter or substance behind, or powers associated with, those phenomena. This distinction, between the mathematical and the real, is also attested to in another remark, in a Scholium at the beginning of Book Two. Newton remarks there that the conclusion just arrived at 'is more a mathematical hypothesis than a physical one'.[14]

This is not to say that there is a fundamental divide between the mathematical domain and the domain of physical objects. The point is, rather, that the mathematical must always be subordinated to experiment and to measured results. In the quotation above, the role of mathematical treatment of a topic is to avoid the necessity of endless, wearisome, measurement of every single case: 'it would be endless and impossible to bring every particular to direct and immediate observation'. Mathematics is thus a kind of labour-saving device, applicable where results can be measured exactly. As such it has no authority over results arduously attained through observation and experience. In fact, in the Preface to the first edition of the *Principia*, Newton restricts mathematics to a branch of mechanics—the branch that displays precise measuring. This is an important passage, and requires quoting at some length:

Since the ancients ... esteemed the science of mechanics of greatest importance in the investigation of natural things, and the moderns, rejecting substantial forms and occult qualities, have endeavoured to subject the phenomena of nature to the laws of mathematics, I have in this treatise cultivated mathematics as far as it relates to philosophy. The ancients considered mechanics in a twofold respect; as rational, which proceeds accurately by demonstration, and practical. To practical mechanics all the manual arts belong, from which mechanics took its name. But as artificers do not work with perfect accuracy, it comes to pass that mechanics is so distinguished from geometry that what is perfectly accurate is called geometrical; what is less so, is called mechanical. However, the errors are not in the art, but in the artificers. He that works with less accuracy is an imperfect mechanic; and if any could work with perfect accuracy, he would be the most perfect mechanic of all, for the description of right lines and circles, upon which geometry is founded, belongs to mechanics ... To describe right lines and circles are problems, but not geometrical problems. The solution of these problems is required from mechanics, and by geometry the use of them, when so solved, is shown; and it is the glory of geometry that from those few principles, brought from without, it is able to produce so many things. Therefore geometry is founded in mechanical practice, and is nothing but that part of universal mechanics which accurately proposes and demonstrates the art of

---

[14] Newton, *Principia*, 244.

measuring. But since the manual arts are chiefly employed in the moving of bodies, it happens that geometry is commonly referred to their magnitude, and mechanics to their motion. In this sense rational mechanics will be the science of motions resulting from any forces whatsoever, and of the forces required to produce any motions, accurately proposed and demonstrated . . . But I consider philosophy rather than arts and write not concerning manual but natural powers, and consider chiefly those things which relate to gravity, levity, elastic force, the resistance of fluids, and the like forces, whether attractive or impulsive; and therefore I offer this work as the mathematical principles of philosophy, for the whole burden of philosophy seems to consist in this—from the phenomena of motions to investigate the forces of nature, and then from these forces to demonstrate the other phenomena . . .[15]

Mathematics is thus that part of mechanics that possesses perfect accuracy. For this reason, the perfect mechanic will produce a product that is wholly mathematical, and so the extent to which a mathematical treatment of the world is possible shows the extent to which God is indeed a geometer. A universal mechanics will reveal the mathematical principles of all motions; the more limited horizons of natural philosophy, the mathematical principles of natural motions and the forces that operate to produce them. Mathematical reasoning can extend these horizons: results drawn directly from observation can be extended to further phenomena.

Newton does not doubt that the task remains incomplete; that there are further tasks to which this philosophic method can be applied. He holds out hopes for a grander synthesis that may even supplant his own:

I wish we could derive the rest of the phenomena of Nature by the same kind of reasoning from mechanical principles, for I am induced by many reasons to suspect that they may all depend upon certain forces by which the particles of bodies, by some causes hitherto unknown, are either mutually impelled towards one another, and cohere in regular figures, or are repelled and recede from one another. These forces being unknown, philosophers have hitherto attempted the search of Nature in vain; but I hope the principles here laid down will afford some light either to this or some truer method of philosophy.[16]

These hopes, however, are not to justify abandoning the careful testing of results, even of accurate deductions from results securely established. All results are to be subject to the tribunal of experience: mathematical demonstration can bestow no more than provisional acceptance. This is the point of Newton's fourth rule of reasoning in philosophy:

[15] Ibid., pp. xvii–xviii.   [16] Ibid., p. xviii.

In experimental philosophy we are to look upon propositions inferred by general induction from phenomena as accurately or very nearly true, notwithstanding any contrary hypotheses that may be imagined, till such time as other phenomena occur, by which they may either be made more accurate, or liable to exceptions.[17]

Newton remembers to insist on this rule in a significant passage in the *Opticks*, when he surveys some of his results:

And these Theorems being admitted into Opticks, there would be scope enough of handling that Science voluminously after a new manner, not only by teaching those things which tend to the perfection of Vision, but also by determining mathematically all kinds of Phænomena of Colours which could be produced by Refractions . . . By this way of arguing I invented almost all the Phænomena described in these Books, beside some others less necessary to the Argument; *and by the successes I met with in the Trials*, I dare promise, that to him who shall argue truly, *and then try all things with good Glasses and sufficient Circumspection*, the expected Event will not be wanting.[18]

Here we see mathematical reasonings commended for their key role in the discoveries of this treatise: nevertheless they are firmly subordinated to the authority of experiment. An author, then, seeking to follow in the footsteps of Newton, drawing inspiration not only from his achievement, but also from his example, would recognize the necessity of proceeding 'with equal . . . caution'. He would recognize that this required both the most accurate deductive reasonings possible, but also the subordination of all such reasonings to the test of experience.[19]

Furthermore, such an author, if he had reason to think that the most accurate deductive reasonings possible fell short of the precision of mathematics, would have no need to introduce mathematical reasonings to make good his Newtonian self-image—and in fact good reason to avoid doing so, since this would be to undermine careful reasonings by importing a spurious show of accuracy that the subject matter itself was not able to allow. And, unless Newtonian principles were thought to rule out any conceivable

[17] Newton, *Principia*, 400.
[18] Newton, *Opticks*, 131–2 (emphases added). The importance of the fourth rule is similarly emphasized by Force, 'Hume's Interest in Newton and Science', 178–87.
[19] Newton's famous remark in the General Scholium—'I frame no hypotheses' (*Principia*, 547)—is perhaps assimilable to this point. At least, it is if we can suppose him to be familiar with Socrates' discussion of 'hypotheses' in the *Phaedo*: for there Socrates contrasts investigation guided by 'hypotheses' with the empirical investigation of nature. In Socrates' account, 'hypotheses' are the mark of the true philosopher guided by the Forms, rather than of the merely empirical investigator guided only by sights and sounds. This is certainly the view Newton wants to oppose, and so may be his meaning. See e.g. *Plato's Phaedo*, ed. R. S. Bluck (London: Routledge & Kegan Paul, 1955), 105–17 (*Phaedo* 95e–102a). See also F. Cajori, 'An Explanatory and Historical Appendix', in *Principia*, 671–6.

dalliance with Aristotle, Hume had readily available a reason for thinking that mathematics was, in general, neither required nor even appropriate for his researches:

> Our discussion will be adequate if it has as much clearness as the subject-matter admits of; for precision is not to be sought for alike in all discussions, any more than in all the products of the crafts. Now fine and just actions, which political science investigates, exhibit much variety and fluctuation . . . We must be content, then, in speaking of such subjects and with such premisses to indicate the truth roughly and in outline, and in speaking about things which are only for the most part true and with premisses of the same kind to reach conclusions that are no better. In the same spirit, therefore, should each of our statements be *received*; for it is the mark of an educated man to look for precision in each class of things just so far as the nature of the subject admits: it is evidently equally foolish to accept probable reasoning from a mathematician and to demand from a rhetorician demonstrative proofs.[20]

In this famous passage, Aristotle himself provides the reason why the adoption of these remarks would not be inappropriate for an aspiring moral philosopher of a Newtonian stamp: for here Aristotle affirms that in his moral and political thought he rests content with probable reasons, and eschews the demonstrations attempted in those other works where accuracy is indeed to be expected. Thus Aristotle, of all unlikely allies, provides a case for thinking that the pursuit of mathematical certainty is inappropriate in moral subjects, no matter how impeccable one's method.

Hume effectively affirms as much in his own brief account of the difference between mathematical and moral sciences:

> The great advantage of the mathematical sciences above the moral consist in this, that the ideas of the former, being sensible, are always clear and determinate, the smallest distinction between them is always immediately perceptible, and the same terms are still expressive of the same ideas, without ambiguity or variation . . . But the finer sentiments of the mind, the operations of the understanding, the various agitations of the passions, though really in themselves distinct, easily escape us, when surveyed by reflection . . . Ambiguity, by this means, is gradually introduced into our reasonings: Similar objects are readily taken to be the same: And the conclusion becomes at last very wide of the premises.[21]

---

[20] Aristotle, *Nicomachean Ethics*, trans. W. D. Ross and J. O. Urmson, rev. J. Barnes, I. iii (1094^{b}12–27), in *A New Aristotle Reader*, ed. Ackrill, 364. It perhaps needs to be noted that Aristotle's point here *might* be a casualty along with his philosophical doctrines—but it is not obviously so. If Hume was alert to the significance of this remark, he need have felt no anxiety about calling on this piece of Aristotle while ditching the rest.

[21] *Enquiries*, 60.

Any attempt to import mathematical rigour into moral subjects
is thus a recipe for disaster: the ineradicable ambiguities of the fundamental terms, embedded in chains of mathematical deductions,
mean that errors will multiply, and confusion be the result. The
Newtonian moral philosopher, then, can be judged not guilty of
any impropriety by avoiding mathematics, except in those particular parts of the subject where accuracy may be expected. The
important thing for such a philosopher is constantly to submit his
researches to the authority of experience, remembering all the
while that any reasonings drawn from experience must themselves
be contained within a cautious empirical temper: 'We must therefore glean up our experiments in this science from a cautious
observation of human life, and take them as they appear in the
common course of the world, by men's behaviour in company, in
affairs, and in their pleasures.'[22]

Indeed, Newton himself suggests the possibility of such an
extension of his principles, in the final pages of the *Opticks*. It is
not difficult to imagine how Hume would have responded to these
lines, containing Newton's thoughts on the relevance of extending his philosophical principles to moral subjects:

> if natural Philosophy in all its Parts, by pursuing this Method, shall at length
> be perfected, the Bounds of Moral Philosophy will also be enlarged. For so far
> as we can know by natural Philosophy what is the first Cause, what Power he
> has over us, and what Benefits we receive from him, so far our Duty towards
> him, as well as that towards one another, will appear to us by the Light of
> Nature. And no doubt, if the Worship of false Gods had not blinded the
> Heathen, their moral Philosophy would have gone farther than to the four
> Cardinal Virtues; and . . . they would have taught us to worship our true
> Author and Benefactor . . .[23]

Hume would have agreed with Newton that the latter's natural
philosophy did pave the way for moral philosophy to be enlarged.
It is equally clear, however, that he would have agreed with little
else of Newton's substantive views in this passage. For Hume, a
properly experimental moral philosophy would make much of
Newton's insights, but employ them to ends almost diametrically
opposite.

---

[22] *Treatise*, p. xix. Hume continues: 'Where experiments of this kind are judiciously col-
lected and compared, we may hope to establish on them a science, which will not be inferior in certainty, and will be much superior in utility to any other of human comprehension.'
Plainly the *Treatise* itself does not match the accuracy of the natural sciences, so, on the interpretation offered here, this remark must be regarded as a promissory note for the future, and
not a claim about how much the *Treatise* delivers. But the whole cast of the Introduction is
to advertise a revolution in moral philosophy that has only recently got underway—not one
nearing completion—so this suggestion does not seem implausible.

[23] Newton, *Opticks*, 405–6.

This general picture of Hume's Newtonian outlook is, in fact, much what one should expect, given the broader movement into which Newton was usually fitted, especially by his British successors. Hume was not alone in thinking of him as the crowning glory of a broad movement. That movement was not so much the mathematical astronomy and physics of Copernicus, Galileo, and Descartes, but the British experimental tradition centred on the Royal Society. The great names of that tradition were those of Bacon and Boyle; and it is noteworthy in this connection that it is 'my Lord BACON' whom Hume picks out in the *Treatise* as the modern originator of the—distinctively English—movement in which he situates himself.[24] Boyle is not mentioned there—nor is Newton—but, since the point being made concerns not the new philosophy *per se*, but those adherents of it who are extending it to 'the science of man', the absence is explicable;[25] and other evidences of Boyle's importance are not hard to come by, some indirect, some direct. In the first place, in the Edinburgh University science library of which Hume was a student member, 'Boyle was singled out above all others as a practising experimental mechanical philosopher', whereas Newton 'appeared in more specialized parts of the catalogue dealing with mathematics and mathematical natural philosophy'.[26] Secondly, Hume's brief biographical note on Boyle in his *History of England*, which immediately precedes the much better-known entry on Newton, focuses on his famous inventions, but also on his experimental credentials:

Boyle improved the pneumatic engine invented by Otto Guericke, and was thereby enabled to make several new and curious experiments on the air, as well as on other bodies: His chemistry is much admired by those who are acquainted with that art: His hydrostatics contain a greater mixture of reasoning and invention with experiment than any other of his works; but his reasoning is still remote from that boldness and temerity which has led astray so many philosophers.[27]

In other words, Boyle, although tempted by the speculative path, managed to stay within the bounds of sober experimentalism. The eulogy of Newton that follows, and to which we shall return below, shows not the Newton of the narrow, specialist enclave to which he was consigned in the Edinburgh science

---

[24] *Treatise*, p. xvii.
[25] Hobbes's absence is more controversial. Although he certainly belongs among the philosophers indebted to Bacon, and also concerned to rewrite the science of human nature in the light of the new philosophy, he is inadequately experimental—too much the traditional dogmatist—to deserve a place. But cf. D. Forbes, *Hume's Philosophical Politics* (Cambridge: Cambridge University Press, 1975), 8–9.
[26] Barfoot, 'Hume and the Culture of Science', 160.   [27] Hume, *History*, vi. 541.

library in the 1720s, but the Newton of eighteenth-century public imagination. He is the great man; Boyle, in contrast, is little more than the link in the chain. There is honour in even this, however, since the chain stretches from Bacon to Newton. For the British mind, Boyle was the crucial link that held the tradition together. In this sense it is possible to agree with Moelwyn-Hughes's rather florid thumbnail biography:

He flourished in the seventeenth century, that turbulent time of pestilence and fire so amply described by Evelyn and Pepys . . . when Britain's monarch was overthrown and Cromwell made Protector. Throughout the storm Boyle kept the ship of science on an even keel, and assuming command after Francis Bacon, navigated her skilfully until Isaac Newton appeared on the bridge.[28]

Hume can be taken to be of similar mind. To be an experimental philosopher was to be in the tradition of Bacon, Boyle, and Newton, with the most significant lessons to be learnt from the principles and practices of the last and greatest of the three. The tradition itself was experimental rather than mathematical, and it was this aspect that an aspiring successor would need to keep uppermost in mind.

Admittedly, this leaves open the possibility that Hume's experimentalism is of inferior quality. This is effectively the charge Noxon brings: that Hume's philosophy is experimental only in an attenuated sense, and observational only in peculiar or loose senses—concerning introspection and observation of 'the common course of the world'. If we are looking for the full battery of modern social scientific techniques applied to broad questions of human behaviour, and the information then crunched through powerful computers, then Hume's approach is bound to disappoint. But this is to see it against the wrong background, and to fail to see that what counts as an experiment depends on what is being investigated. The important point, however, concerns what Hume is *not* doing: he is not appealing to any kind of 'occult' quality on which to hang his conclusions, nor is he building a deductive edifice on any axiomatic beginnings. At every point, he makes claims about the contents of experience that the reader can test directly against his or her personal experience, and develops arguments that depend on no privileged claims to esoteric knowledge. Besides, Noxon's contrast between the experimental and the observational is misplaced: Hume's experiments are observations, and their experimental—testing—character is a function of their being relevant and sufficiently precise to test the various claims in

---

[28] E. A. Moelwyn-Hughes, Introduction to Sir Robert Boyle, *The Sceptical Chymist* (London: Everyman, 1964), p. v.

question; and this level of functionality is for the reader to judge. It was just such considerations that led Edmund Husserl to judge Hume to be an important precursor, and it is in this respect, as engaging in disciplined phenomenological enquiries that are transparent to all reflective enquirers, that his experimentalism is revealed.[29] The point can be illustrated by comparing Hume's works with, for example, those of Aquinas or Spinoza.

A related objection can also be met. Hume's employment of introspection, it is said, shows an excessive attachment to Cartesian notions of self-transparency. In John Biro's words, he retains 'a deep commitment, inherited from the "way of ideas" tradition of both the Cartesians and his empiricist predecessors, to introspection as a way of finding epistemological bedrock'—a commitment that does not sit comfortably with the 'objective, third-person' methods more characteristic of the tradition of experimental science.[30] To take the latter half of the complaint first. It is certainly true that the tradition of experimental science has had great difficulties in knowing what to do with first-person subjectivity: Descartes's dualism was precisely the recognition of this problem, and the centrality of questions in the philosophy of mind for twentieth-century philosophy is a direct reflection of its continuing presence. However, the very fact that this problem is characteristic of modern philosophy means that it is no special problem of Hume's. The former half of the complaint can be met head on. Hume does indeed engage in introspective thought experiments, but not because of any commitment to Cartesian self-transparency. Rather, like Locke, he holds that the thoughts and feelings observable in reflection are just another form of sense perception, and so subject to limitations comparable to those that afflict the sensing of external objects. For this reason, Locke referred to reflection as 'internal Sense'.[31] Hume followed suit; and, indeed, thought this to be a central part of his Newtonianism.

Hume's Newton

To this point, it has been accepted that Hume's Newtonian experimentalism lies primarily, if not entirely, in his adoption of a

---

[29] See G. Davie, 'Edmund Husserl and "the as yet, in its most important respect, unrecognised greatness of Hume"', in G. P. Morice (ed.), *David Hume: Bicentenary Papers* (Edinburgh: Edinburgh University Press, 1977), 69–76.

[30] J. Biro, 'Hume's New Science of the Mind', in Norton (ed.), *The Cambridge Companion to Hume*, 56.

[31] Locke, *Essay*, II. i. 4. See M. R. Ayers, *Locke* (London: Routledge, 1991), i: Epistemology, chs. 3–5; and *Locke: Ideas and Things* (London: Phoenix, 1997), 6–7.

certain method. This has been a dominant assumption amongst
Hume's critics. It is implicit in Noxon's remarks quoted above; and
it is no accident that the section from which it has been extracted
is entitled 'Principles of Method, Newton's and Hume's'. The tendency is, if anything, even more strongly marked in John Passmore's *Hume's Intentions*: Hume's debt to Newton is there discussed
extensively in a chapter entitled 'The Methodologist', but in other
chapters Newton is mentioned only in passing.[32] Hume's Newtonianism does not, however, reduce to the adoption of experimental method, no matter how important his use of that method
might be. Obviously, experimental philosophy cannot be detached
from an acute concern for practising a properly experimental
method. Nonetheless, the identification of experimental philosophy with the employment of a particular method is significantly
overplayed.

The important further aspect of Hume's avowed experimentalism is often missed because of an excessive preoccupation with the
Treatise. In that work, the title page announces its concern as
the introduction of the experimental method into moral subjects;
and within the work itself we see the obvious parallels, in thought
experiments, and in the three principles of association being
described as 'a kind of ATTRACTION', a gravitational force by which
ideas are connected.[33] In the later work, these features, although
still present, are no longer stressed. Instead, such superficial parallels between Hume's philosophy and Newton's are replaced by a
stress on a deeper, and more abiding, feature: the necessary premiss
on which the argument for the experimental philosophy was built.
What is that premiss? Noxon, discussing Newton's Rules of Reasoning, suggests that 'Certain ontological and epistemological
presuppositions lay behind his recommendations: the simplicity
and uniformity of nature and the reliability of sensory evidence'.[34]
There is a measure of truth here, but only a measure. The simplicity and uniformity of nature, affirmed in Newton's first three
rules, are firmly limited by the priority of experimental evidence,
as affirmed in the fourth rule. That rule, and its significance for
Newton and Hume, have been stressed above. Supposed simplici-
ties and uniformities that fly in the face of contrary experience are
to be rejected. This is the central point of the attack on 'hypotheses'. And, on the second aspect, Noxon is no more than half-right.
Sensory evidence is reliable, yes—in the sense that, properly tested,

[32] J. Passmore, *Hume's Intentions*, 3rd edn. (London: Duckworth, 1980), ch. 3.
[33] *Treatise*, 12.   [34] Noxon, *Hume's Philosophical Development*, 82.

it is the best evidence there is. But it is equally a premiss of Newton's rules of philosophizing that sensory evidence reveals little if anything about the real nature of the world. For both Newton and Hume, the lesson taught by the history of philosophical enquiry into the nature of the world, and on which the experimental philosophy was therefore built, concerned the *limitations* of what experience revealed. The secure path to understanding the world depended, therefore, on understanding those limits, and so avoiding the errors attendant on straying beyond them.[35]

Hume presses the point even in the early work. The limitations of experience are insisted on in the *Treatise*'s Introduction, where the nature of the work's experimentalism is most fully described. The best-known passage is probably the following:

For to me it seems evident, that the essence of the mind being equally unknown to us with that of external bodies, it must be equally impossible to form any notion of its powers and qualities otherwise than from careful and exact experiments, and the observation of those particular effects, which result from its different circumstances and situations. And tho' we must endeavour to render all our principles as universal as possible, by tracing up our experiments to the utmost, and explaining all effects from the simplest and fewest causes, 'tis still certain we cannot go beyond experience; and any hypothesis, that pretends to discover the ultimate original qualities of human nature, ought at first to be rejected as presumptuous and chimerical.[36]

This passage shows a twin commitment to the experimental philosophy *and* to the idea that experiential knowledge is inherently imperfect. In fact, it clearly connects the necessity for very careful and exact experiments precisely to this imperfection: it is because the essence of body is unknown to the natural philosopher that he must pursue his enquiries by means of careful experiments; and the moral philosopher, having likewise no knowledge of the essence of mind, has no option but to proceed in the same manner. Experience imposes limits that we cannot go beyond. It gives us no access to the 'ultimate original qualities', whether of physical or of human nature. Experimental philosophy does not overcome these barriers—it cannot, since it is no more than experience itself, subjected to a severe discipline—but it enables us to make the best of a bad job, by learning how to discern the orderliness that lies

---

[35] Thus Locke, a faithful ally of the experimental natural philosophers, Boyle and (later) Newton included, wrote his massive enquiry into 'the Original, Certainty, and Extent of humane Knowledge; together, with the Grounds and Degrees of Belief, Opinion, and Assent' (*Essay*, I. i. 2).

[36] *Treatise*, p. xvii.

in experience itself. The beginning of wisdom lies in the recognition of the limits of experience.

It is this connection that Hume discerns in Newton, especially in his more methodological, and therefore more theoretically cautious, moments. In Hume's eyes, Newton in these passages stands out for what I shall call his sceptical interpretation of experience; and Newton and, especially, his eighteenth-century successors come in for sharp criticism when they retreat from this austere standard. For retreat they do—and just when the stakes are at their highest, in the discussion of the religious implications of the Newtonian revolution. They are not alone in this failure, however, so Hume's attempt at a consistent application of Newtonian principles in the *Enquiry* will show that the crucial shortcomings of the Newtonians and of the rationalists alike are due to their failure properly to detach themselves from the medieval past. This section will therefore show the extent to which Newton insists on the imperfections of experience, and of the science built on it, and that it is for this reason that Hume picks him out for special commendation; and why it is appropriate to describe this, as I have done, as a sceptical interpretation of experience. The subsequent sections of this chapter will then show how this way of looking at things explains the *Enquiry*'s main argumentative strategies.

The limits of experience insisted on by Hume in the *Treatise* passage quoted above depend on the claim that the essences of mind and body are unknown to us, and are so because experience does not penetrate into such 'ultimate original qualities'. These are just the sorts of claims that Newton makes in the philosophical parts of both the *Principia* and the *Opticks*. Thus, for example, in the General Scholium added at the end of the *Principia* (in the second edition of 1713) he remarks that 'In bodies, we see only their figures and colors, we hear only the sounds, we touch only their outward surfaces, we smell only the smells, and taste the savors; but their inward substances are not to be known either by our senses, or by any reflex act of our minds . . .'.[37]

It is because 'inward substances' remain hidden that enquiries in natural philosophy are restricted to phenomena, and that the causes of the phenomena remain unknown. This is why he pronounces his famous ban on 'hypotheses': although his use of this term is notoriously flexible, the basic point is that, because we are in no position to explain why a particular thing has the proper-

---

[37] *Principia*, 546. See also Locke, *Essay*, II. xxiii.

ties it has, we cannot set up fundamental principles that can be used to infer what other properties it must have. The Aristotelians are the famous villains on this issue, and so Newton singles them out for specific criticism when he allows himself to indulge in some qualified speculations in the 'Queries' at the end of the *Opticks*. He says there that his three laws of motion, and principle of gravity, are considered

not as occult Qualities, supposed to result from the specifick Forms of Things, but as general Laws of Nature, by which the Things themselves are form'd; their Truth appearing to us by Phænomena, though their Causes be not yet discover'd. For these are manifest Qualities, and their Causes only are occult. And the *Aristotelians* gave the Name of occult Qualities, not to manifest Qualities, but to such Qualities only as they supposed to lie hid in Bodies, and to be the unknown Causes of manifest Effects . . . Such occult Qualities put a stop to the Improvement of natural Philosophy, and therefore of late Years have been rejected . . . But to derive two or three general Principles of Motion from Phænomena, and afterwards to tell us how the Properties and Actions of all corporeal Things follow from those manifest Principles, would be a very great step in Philosophy, though the Causes of those Principles were not yet discover'd: And therefore I scruple not to propose the Principles of Motion above-mention'd, they being of very general Extent, and leave their Causes to be found out.[38]

Here we see the same basic point being put. The problem with the Aristotelians is that they claim to have discovered the 'occult' (hidden) qualities of things, meaning by this their fundamental natures: 'the specifick Forms of Things'. They thus lay claim to knowledge of the underlying causes of natural processes. This 'put a stop to the Improvement of natural Philosophy' because there is in fact no access to such ultimate principles. Experience cannot penetrate to the ultimate causes of natural processes, and so the proper task of natural philosophy is to restrict itself to what can be found out, the 'manifest Qualities', and, by careful experiments and cautious deductions from these experiments, to formulate 'general Laws of Nature' that express the regularities manifested by the phenomena. This cautious procedure is 'a very great step in Philosophy', precisely because it jettisons the search for what cannot be found.

Newton does not always keep strictly to this position. He clearly entertains the hope, at least, that ignorance of ultimate causes is not final, but merely our *present* condition. Thus in another passage from the 'Queries' he asserts that 'the main Business of

[38] Newton, *Opticks*, Query 31, 401–2.

natural Philosophy is to argue from Phænomena without feigning
hypotheses, and to deduce Causes from Effects, till we come to the
very first Cause . . .'.[39] The same thought underlies his firm avowal
of the Argument from Design in the General Scholium. So it is necessary to conclude that Newton is inconsistent, sticking to a much
stricter line when criticizing his opponents than when defending
his own positive views. However, this need not trouble us over-
much. The important point is that, in his more careful moments,
Newton does disavow knowledge of ultimate principles, and
defends his strict adherence to experimental results on just this
disavowal; and that it is this feature that Hume picks out and
commends.

Hume frequently signals that he understands the key element of
Newtonianism to be the consistent denial that experience gives us
access to the inward natures of things. The Introduction to the
Treatise has already been quoted; another clear instance occurs in
the Appendix later added to the work:

As long as we confine our speculations to *the appearances* of objects to our
senses, without entering into disquisitions concerning their real nature and
operations, we are safe from all difficulties, and can never be enbarrass'd by
any question . . . If we carry our enquiry beyond the appearances of objects
to the senses, I am afraid, that most of our conclusions will be full of scepticism and uncertainty . . . Nothing is more suitable to that [i.e. Newtonian]
philosophy, than a modest scepticism to a certain degree, and a fair confession of ignorance in subjects, that exceed all human capacity.[40]

In the *Enquiry*, the background presence of Newton is sometimes
very marked, and precisely in passages that deny knowledge of the
ultimate causes of natural phenomena. The following is strongly
reminiscent of the passage from the *Opticks* quoted above, and
implicitly eulogizes Newton along the way:

no philosopher, who is rational and modest, has ever pretended to assign the
ultimate cause of any natural operation, or to show distinctly the action of
that power, which produces any single effect in the universe. It is confessed,
that the utmost effort of human reason is to reduce the principles, productive of natural phenomena, to a greater simplicity, and to resolve the many
particular effects into a few general causes . . . But as to the causes of these
general causes, we should in vain attempt their discovery . . . These ultimate
springs and principles are totally shut up from human curiosity and enquiry.
Elasticity, gravity, cohesion of parts, communication of motion by impulse;
these are probably the ultimate causes and principles we shall ever discover
in nature; and we may esteem ourselves sufficiently happy, if, by accurate

---

[39] Newton, *Opticks*, Query 28, 369.   [40] *Treatise*, 638–9.

enquiry and reasoning, we can trace up the particular phenomena to, or near to, these general principles.[41]

Nor do Newtonian echoes stop there, for in the succeeding paragraph Hume goes on to subordinate geometry to the operations of nature, and thus to mechanics, just as Newton had done in the Preface to the *Principia*.[42]

For a final example of Hume connecting Newtonianism to the preservation of nature's secrets, we can turn to the famous eulogy in the *History of England*. Newton's achievement is there described in glowing terms, but the nature of that achievement is not quite what one might expect:

In Newton this island may boast of having produced the greatest and rarest genius that ever arose for the ornament and instruction of the species. Cautious in admitting no principles but such as were founded on experiment; but resolute to adopt every such principle, however new or unusual: from modesty, ignorant of his superiority above the rest of mankind; and thence, less careful to accommodate his reasonings to common apprehensions: More anxious to merit than acquire fame: He was from these causes long unknown to the world; but his reputation at last broke out with a lustre, which scarcely any writer, during his own lifetime, had ever before attained. While Newton *seemed* to draw off the veil from some of the mysteries of nature, he shewed at the same time the imperfections of the mechanical philosophy; and thereby restored her ultimate secrets to that obscurity, in which they ever did and ever will remain.[43]

Hume's Newton is thus sharply distinct from the figure of popular acclaim, the man who revealed the truth about the world's workings. In the words of Pope's famous 'epitaph':

> Nature and Nature's Laws lay hid in Night.
> GOD said, *Let Newton be!* and all was Light.[44]

Pope's image of the revelatory prophet captures the common eighteenth-century understanding of Newton's achievement; but Hume's Newton is the man who restored nature's ultimate secrets to their inevitable obscurity. Newton's own self-understanding is certainly closer to Hume's than to Pope's; even if, as has been noted, he is not entirely consistent. He certainly believes he has identified genuine laws of natural phenomena, but precisely because these are laws of *phenomena*, he does not believe he has

---

[41] *Enquiries*, 30–1.
[42] Compare *Enquiries*, 31, with *Principia*, pp. xvii–xviii (quoted above, n. 15).
[43] Hume, *History*, vi. 542 (emphasis added).
[44] Alexander Pope, Epitaph 'Intended for Sir ISAAC NEWTON, in Westminster-Abbey', in *Alexander Pope*, ed. Rogers, 242.

brought anything *hidden* into the light. The central place accorded
to experiment in his rules of philosophical reasoning attests to
just this difference. For Newton, experiment is necessary precisely
because the long history of error that is the only fruit of the philosophical dogmatists shows us what we do not—and possibly
cannot—know. He thus connects experimentalism to 'a modest
scepticism to a certain degree'.[45] This is the Newton Hume eulogizes, and whose lessons he remembers, and extends, in his own
philosophy.

Mechanism and Scepticism

To deny that we can know more than the manifest principles of
natural phenomena is to accept a modest scepticism to a certain
degree. In this section it will be argued that this modest scepticism
derives directly from mechanical philosophy itself. Newton
himself gives one reason why this might be so. In a passage from
the 'Queries' to the *Opticks*, in which he attempts explanations of
a wide variety of experimental phenomena, he concludes that corpuscularianism seems the best answer:

it seems probable to me, that God in the Beginning form'd Matter in solid,
massy, hard, impenetrable, moveable Particles, of such Sizes and Figures,
and with such other Properties, and in such Proportion to Space, as most
conduced to the End for which he form'd them; and that these primitive
Particles being Solids, are incomparably harder than any porous Bodies
compounded of them; even so very hard, as never to wear or break in pieces;
no ordinary Power being able to divide what God himself made one in the
first Creation.

He then points out a further implication:

While the Particles continue entire, they may compose Bodies of one and the
same Nature and Texture in all Ages: But should they wear away, or break in
pieces, the Nature of Things depending on them, would be changed. Water
and Earth, composed of old worn Particles and Fragments of Particles, would
not be of the same Nature and Texture now, with Water and Earth composed
of entire Particles in the Beginning.[46]

Changes to the 'Nature and Texture' of things will cause changes
in the course of events, and thus in the laws of nature themselves.
So Newton affirms that our ignorance of the ultimate secrets of
nature extends to our not being able to rule out changes to the

---

[45] *Treatise*, 639.   [46] Newton, *Opticks*, Query 31, 400.

course of nature itself. Hume's famous sceptical doctrine is thus affirmed by Newton, and, strikingly, in a passage where he discusses the implications of corpuscularianism, one version of the new mechanical philosophy. The sceptical result is not, however, restricted to corpuscularianism. Newton's point here is a particular instance of the more general problem of ignorance of nature's secrets; and it is mechanical philosophy itself, not merely its corpuscularian version, that denies us access to these secrets. To see why, we need to ask why belief in access to ultimate principles is worth denying. This brings us back, once again, to Aristotle and the Aristotelians.

Aristotle held that, through experience, we *can* arrive at knowledge of nature's inner secrets; in fact, his theory aims precisely at establishing that knowledge of the essences of things does arise through a process that begins from sense perception. A brief sketch of his account will bring this out. In the first place, Aristotle argues that perception is the reception of the form, but not the matter, of the object perceived: 'In general, with regard to all sense-perception, we must take it that the sense is that which can receive perceptible forms without their matter, as wax receives the imprint of the ring without the iron or gold, and it takes the imprint which is of gold or bronze, but not *qua* gold or bronze.'[47] The qualification—'not *qua* gold or bronze'—indicates that there must be a second step before the essence of the object can be grasped. To know the essence of a thing is to know not its *perceptible* form, received by the faculty of sense, but its *intelligible* form; and this intelligible form, the 'form of the form', is grasped by the highest cognitive faculty, active mind or *noûs*. The difference between the two forms is the difference between 'a magnitude and *what it is to be* a magnitude', between 'water and *what it is to be* water'.[48]

The path from receiving the perceptible form to grasping the intelligible form depends on memory and thus experience, in the everyday sense of the accumulation of many similar perceptions. *Noûs* then is able to take hold of the form of these different instances, and thereby to grasp the essence of the thing: to understand. Aristotle sums up the whole process in this way:

from perception there comes memory . . . and from memory (when it occurs often in connection with the same thing) experience; for memories that are many in number form a single experience. And from experience, or from the whole universal that has come to rest in the soul (the one apart from the

---

[47] Aristotle, *On the Soul*, II. xii, in *A New Aristotle Reader*, ed. Ackrill, 186.
[48] *On the Soul*, III. iv, in ibid. 195 (emphasis added).

many, whatever is one and the same in all those things), there comes a principle of skill and of understanding—of skill if it deals with how things come about, of understanding if it deals with what is the case.[49]

Aristotle holds, then, that, by beginning from sense perception, creatures possessed of memory and of active mind can grasp the essences of things, and thereby come to know nature's secrets. The whole process is guaranteed by the important claim that, in knowing, the mind becomes identical with that which is known: 'in the case of those things which have no matter [i.e. minds and essences], that which thinks and that which is thought are the same; for contemplative knowledge and that which is known in that way are the same.'[50] Aristotelian *noûs* can know the object truly because, in knowing, it *conforms* itself to the object. The scholastic account, although differing in detail, especially with respect to the account of substantial forms, affirms the same positive outcome: experience delivers knowledge of essences to the attentive mind, and does so because the mind can make itself identical with the object *qua* intelligible object.

The mechanical hypothesis, in contrast, makes any such optimistic story impossible. Perception is reduced to the communications of motion by impulse—of external bodies impressing themselves on sense organs, themselves being conduits that transmit further motions to the brain, 'the mind's Presence-room'.[51] On this picture, perception is a function of contact between different physical *surfaces*, and the fruit of such contact is motions that are then transmitted to more remote receivers. The whole story, moreover, is one of efficient causation, so perception is the end point of a chain in which the links are all distinct events.[52] So there is no possibility of affirming Aristotle's claim that the mind is able to grasp the essence of the object by becoming identical to the form of its form. Even if an Aristotelian division of an object into formal and material aspects were accepted, there is no place within

---

[49] *Posterior Analytics*, II. xix, in ibid. 58.

[50] *On the Soul*, III. iv, in ibid. 196.

[51] Locke, *Essay*, II. iii. 1. (The image employed here is of the mind as a monarch who receives visitors in a special reception hall. It is a limited monarchy, however, since the monarch has no choice but to receive any visitor admitted—the mind is passive with respect to sense perception—and also cannot receive visitors anywhere else.)

[52] It is the triumph of efficient causation over its rivals that explains why Hume does not tire of reminding us that causes are distinct from their effects; e.g. *Enquiries*, 29. See also Descartes: 'When dealing with natural things we will, then, never derive any explanations from the purposes which God or nature may have had in view when creating them <and we shall entirely banish from our philosophy the search for final causes>. For we should not be so arrogant as to suppose that we can share in God's plans. We should, instead, consider him as the efficient cause of all things . . .' (*Principles of Philosophy*, I. 27, in *The Philosophical Writings of Descartes*, i. 202).

the mechanical account of perception for forms or natures to be communicated. Everything the senses receive is due merely to surface features of the object, and the effects those features efficiently cause: the senses receive only *appearances*. And, even if it were allowed that we have an active mind that grasps the form of the percept delivered to it by the senses, that form would not be the essence, the form of the form, but the form of the appearance. The perception is wholly distinct from the object that causes it.[53] Thus mechanical philosophy, by reducing perceptions to (mere) appearances, commits itself to an interpretation of experience with a distinctly sceptical air.[54]

The point is clearly brought out by Descartes in his *Optics*. He illustrates the mechanical account of perception by analogy with the manner of perceiving of a blind man with a stick:

I would have you consider the light in bodies we call 'luminous' to be nothing other than a certain movement, or very rapid and lively action, which passes to our eyes through the medium of the air and other transparent bodies, just as the movement or resistance of the bodies encountered by a blind man passes to his hand by means of his stick . . . Nor will you find it strange that by means of this action we can see all sorts of colours . . . You have only to consider that the differences a blind man notes between trees, rocks, water and similar things by means of his stick do not seem any less to him than the differences between red, yellow, green and all the other colours seems to us. And yet in all those bodies the differences are nothing other than the various ways of moving the stick or of resisting its movements. Hence you will have reason to conclude that there is no need to suppose that something material passes from objects to our eyes to make us see colours and light, or even that there is something in the objects which resembles the ideas or sensations that we have of them. In just the same way, when a blind man feels bodies, nothing has to issue from the bodies and pass along his stick to his hand; and the resistance or movement of the bodies, which is the sole cause of the sensations he has of them, is nothing like the ideas he forms of them. By this means, your mind will be delivered from all those little images flitting through the air, called 'intentional forms', which so exercise the imagination of the philosophers.[55]

Here we see both perception on the mechanical model being explained by means of an analogy with the limited perceptions

[53] The best that can be hoped for on the mechanical account is that the effect (the perception) *resembles* the cause (the object). This issue will be addressed further below.
[54] Thus Pierre Bayle argues that Cartesianism 'put the final touches' to the revival of scepticism, since 'now no good philosopher any longer doubts that the skeptics were right to maintain that the qualities of bodies that strike our senses are only appearances' (Pierre Bayle, *Historical and Critical Dictionary: Selections*, trans. R. H. Popkin and C. Brush (Indianapolis: Hackett, 1991), 197).
[55] Descartes, *Optics* (*Discourse and Essays*, First Essay), in *The Philosophical Writings of Descartes*, i. 153–4.

available to a blind man—a remarkable feature in its own right—
and also the analogy being employed to rule out the scholastic
account, by ruling out any communication from the object to the
perceiver other than the communication of motion by impulse.
Communication of forms is explicitly ruled out. It is little wonder,
then, that, with such an understanding of sense perception,
Descartes should have chosen to go down a quasi-Platonist road
in order to render knowledge of essences possible. Mechanism
rules out sense perception as a source of knowledge of the essences
of objects; so, if such knowledge is to be possible, it has to arise
quite independently of sensation. The famous example of the wax
in the Second Meditation is to show that knowledge of essences
depends on the intellect alone.[56] Thus the importance of his reply
to Hobbes's allegation that he was just recycling tired old stuff in
the First Meditation: 'I wanted to prepare my readers' minds for
the study of the things which are related to the intellect, and help
them to distinguish such things from corporeal things.'[57] Only by
turning away from corporeal things, and the blind mechanical
means by which such things are apprehended, is knowledge of
essences possible.

In this light, it is plain why Locke and his successors continued
to hold that the mind knows only its own ideas, and why their
rejection of Cartesian rationalism had an air of ruling out entirely
any knowledge of the way things really are. This was no surprise
to them, Locke included. His denial that we can have knowledge
of real essences—of the 'very being' or 'real constitution' of
things[58]—and must instead make do with nominal essences—the
complex ideas we construct from our perceptions—is precisely the
denial that we have access to the form of the form, and must settle
for the form of the appearance instead. It is on this premiss that
he builds his enquiry into the extent of human knowledge, with
its characteristic emphasis on human limitations, and it is with an
eye to what appearances do and do not deliver to us that he makes
many of his more famous claims. To take one example:

'Tis of great use to the Sailor to know the length of his Line, though he cannot
with it fathom all the depths of the Ocean. 'Tis well he knows, that it is long
enough to reach the bottom, at such Places, as are necessary to direct his
Voyage, or caution him against running upon Shoals, that may ruin him.
Our Business here is not to know all things, but those which concern our
Conduct.[59]

[56] *Meditations on First Philosophy*, in ibid. ii. 20–2.
[57] Third Set of Objections with the Author's Replies, in ibid. ii. 121.
[58] Locke, *Essay*, III. iii. 15; III. vi. 6.   [59] Ibid. I. i. 6.

It is the inadequacy of our perceptual capabilities that is the problem here, and the mechanical theory explains why that inadequacy is not superficial but deep.

So those critics who have attributed the sceptical tendencies of the 'way of ideas' to the simple failure of early modern philosophers to detach themselves from a misleading vocabulary have themselves failed to see what drives these views. It is not the new theory of ideas *simpliciter* that generates the problem—such that a conceptual revision will save the day—but the mechanical account of perception on which the new theory is built. On that account, causes and their effects are distinct existences. This applies to the causes of perceptions themselves, and so experience, built as it must be on the perceptions (the effects), cannot deliver insight into the essence or nature of the object. Experience, the effects of real things on the soul, is forever cut off from the causes of those effects, the real things themselves; and, in particular, it is cut off from the essences or natures that explain what those things are, and that the mind seeks to grasp. Experimental philosophy, built on mechanical principles—and thus on the elevation of efficient causes (mere motions) to the primary, and indeed the only reliable, explanatory principles—is, for precisely this reason, committed to what I have called a sceptical interpretation of experience.[60]

The point can be illustrated by reference to familiar arguments surrounding a central doctrine of the new philosophy: the doctrine of primary and secondary qualities. From Galileo on, mechanical philosophers argued that, while some of our ideas *resemble* the properties of the objects that caused them, others do not.[61] This concern, for whether effects resemble their causes, clearly grows up as a replacement for the lost guarantee of the identity of object and perception. The sense that guarantees had

[60] Margaret J. Osler has shown how Galileo's own development illustrates the issue nicely, in his shift from essentialist explanations in *De Motu* (1590) to their abandonment in *Il Saggiatore* (1623). In the early work, the sound produced by a struck bell is attributed to a 'sonorous quality' in the bell. In the later work, such identity between perceptible quality and real qualities disappears: 'Sounds are created and are heard by us when—without any "sonorous" or "transonorous" property—a rapid tremor of the air, ruffled into very minute waves, moves certain cartilages of a tympanum within our ear.' The relevant point here is that, in the second explanation, no longer is anything communicated from the bell to the hearer: intrinsic properties have been replaced by motions. The example here concerns a secondary quality, but it is not obviously restricted to secondary properties only. Osler concludes: 'No longer is sonority a real quality that somehow modifies, if only temporarily, the naturally silent essence of the bell; it is the result of the impact . . . on our sense organs. No longer can the essential nature of the object be determined from its phenomenal attributes. Qualities . . . no longer reveal anything of the real essences of bodies' ('Galileo, Motion, and Essences', *Isis*, 64 (1973), 507, 509).

[61] This is how Locke distinguishes the primary from the secondary (*Essay*, II. viii. 7, 15–22).

indeed been lost is shown by the drift of the objections to the distinction. The recurring objection brought against this mechanical orthodoxy, by several generations of critics, was not the absurdity of such claims about secondary qualities, but that the conclusion must inevitably extend to include the primary qualities as well.[62] No less than for the secondary qualities, the perceptions of primary qualities are distinct from their causes. The raising of doubts about the primary qualities shows not merely an alertness to the wider application of the arguments employed against the reality of secondary qualities, but an awareness of the inner logic of the mechanical philosophy itself, of its inherently sceptical tendencies.

At this point, some qualms may be felt, for, by and large, this is a familiar story about the rejection of Aristotelian physics, and about the unresolved problems that rapidly rose up to plague modern philosophy. It is about the triumph of sober, fallible scientific knowledge over the reckless claims of the metaphysicians. The problems have not been solved, true enough—and, indeed, the sceptical genie has not been wholly contained. But why describe the limitations of the mechanical account of experience as a *sceptical* interpretation of experience?[63]

The key issue here is, of course, what counts as scepticism, and why; and so the next section will be devoted to providing an answer. Before doing so, however, it will be useful to recognize that the question of the sceptical tendencies of the new philosophy was very much in the air in the controversies of the time. The point is not that all the mechanical philosophers identified themselves as sceptics. Many of them firmly rejected any such implication.[64]

[62] Berkeley's objections to Locke on this point are the stuff of the Anglophone curriculum, but the objection had been made thirty years earlier against the Cartesians—Malebranche in particular—by Simon Foucher: 'You recognize that these colors are in us! But where is the shape of these colors, the extension of these colors, if not in the place where the colors are?' (*Nouvelle Dissertation sur la Recherche de la verité* (1679), quoted by R. H. Popkin, 'The High Road to Pyrrhonism', in *The High Road to Pyrrhonism*, 19).

[63] The problem is felt particularly acutely if scepticism is thought to consist in doubts concerning the existence of the external world. It needs to be recognized, however, that this sense of 'scepticism' is itself a product of the sceptical tendency in mechanical philosophy set out above. This is because this doubt arises precisely because of the distinctness of the perception and its efficient cause in the mechanical model. If the perception is a distinct existence, then the supposition that it is the effect of an external cause is itself beyond empirical proof; the possibility that the perception is completely uncaused cannot be ruled out. In this way mechanical philosophy gave the sceptical outlook a very modern twist, by generating the problem of the 'external world'—a problem so acutely felt in modern epistemology that 'scepticism' is now commonly taken to *mean* the entertainment of such doubts. This is regrettable, because it systematically obscures the nature of early modern (and indeed ancient) scepticism; among other things, it renders unintelligible Hume's moderate scepticism in the *Enquiry*.

[64] Hobbes is one example of contested territory. Richard Tuck has argued, in *Hobbes* (Oxford: Oxford University Press, 1989), and more specifically in 'Hobbes and Descartes', in

Their critics, however, frequently alleged a connection between scepticism and the new scientific philosophies. Thus, for example, Edward Stillingfleet, in his controversies with Locke in the 1690s, discerned scepticism at the heart of Locke's philosophy;[65] and the title of Henry Lee's critique of Locke, *Anti-Scepticism* (1702), needs no elaboration. These critiques attribute sceptical tendencies not to idiosyncratic aspects of Locke's philosophy, but to the central doctrines that distinguish it as a flag-bearer of the new philosophy: not least, the theory of ideas. The best-known case, of course, is Berkeley's charge that Locke and the Newtonians purvey a form of scepticism. Thus the subtitle of the *Principles of Human Knowledge* (1710), which runs: *wherein the Chief Causes of Error and Difficulty in the Sciences, with the Grounds of Scepticism, Atheism, and Irreligion, are inquired into.*[66]

In fact, the charge of scepticism is so commonly brought against the new philosophy that modern readers, perhaps excessively attuned to the dangers of early modern religious politics, have sometimes been tempted to dismiss such charges as absurd—as nonsense propagated from the pulpit by ignorant and alarmist divines to their ignorant and alarmed congregations. This would be a mistake, for, even in cases where scepticism was not ultimately affirmed, mechanical philosophers frequently made use of

G. A. J. Rogers and A. Ryan (eds.), *Perspectives on Thomas Hobbes* (Oxford: Clarendon Press, 1988), 11–41, that Hobbes survived a 'sceptical crisis', before going on to try to outdo Descartes in the refutation of hyperbolic doubt. Tuck's views have been vigorously contested by Tom Sorell, in 'Hobbes without Doubt', *History of Philosophy Quarterly*, 10 (1993) 121–35, and 'Hobbes's Objections and Hobbes's System', in R. Ariew and M. Grene (eds.), *Descartes and his Contemporaries* (Chicago: University of Chicago Press, 1995), 83–96. The same question can also be addressed to Descartes: it has often been assumed that he suffered a 'sceptical crisis', but this has been contested, most recently by Gaukroger, in *Descartes: An Intellectual Biography*. There is little doubt that Descartes's arguments are designed to meet sceptical positions, but this does not mean he himself ever flirted with the scepticisms he entertains. The whole strategy of the hyperbolic doubt is readily explicable as the attempt to give the sceptics enough rope to hang themselves—and thus as the strategy of an individual exceedingly confident of his opinions. Both these controversies, however, lead somewhat away from the main point, since the claim that mechanical philosophy has an ineradicable sceptical thrust is not to say that it is implicitly Pyrrhonian, nor that it ushers in hyperbolic doubt, nor even that to affirm a sceptical view is to be plunged into a 'crisis'. It will be shown below how inappropriate such assumptions are for handling the scepticisms of the early modern world.

[65] See R. H. Popkin, 'The Philosophy of Bishop Stillingfleet', *Journal of the History of Philosophy*, 9 (1971), 303–19. Popkin summarizes: 'As the modern age of empiricism dawned, Stillingfleet diagnosed some of its major tendencies. While Locke was being applauded by the Newtonians in England, France and Holland, the Bishop saw the direction this new empiricism was going to take. Without having to wait until Berkeley and Hume pushed Locke's theory to its logical conclusion, Stillingfleet perceived that a kind of scepticism was already involved. Locke could insist that he did *really* believe in substances, and that all men had to believe in them. But . . . [he] had undermined any possibility of knowing anything about them . . . Locke's world was reduced to Hume's at the very outset, without any further intellectual development being involved' (316).

[66] Berkeley, *Principles*, 85 (title page).

sceptical devices and themes, and in that way invited the criticisms they in fact received. Thus, for example, Joseph Glanville, a prominent member of the Royal Society, indicated sceptical affinities in the title of his defence of experimental philosophy and of true religion: the work was entitled *Scepsis Scientifica or, Confest Ignorance, The Way to Science; in an Essay of the Vanity of Dogmatizing and Confident Opinion* (1665). The title indicates that scepticism is here understood more to be a beginning than an end of the experimental philosophy. If this seems puzzling, it needs to be remembered that here 'science' means *scientia*—that is, systematic knowledge of causes. The point is that to doubt of certain and complete knowledge opens up a space for experimental investigations. The project implied is, then, somewhat in the manner of Descartes's radical doubt.

A similar position is taken by Robert Boyle. He explicitly employs sceptical devices in his polemical work against the Aristotelians and chemical philosophers, *The Sceptical Chymist*. Boyle's spokesman in the work is Carneades, one of the leading figures of the sceptical later Academy. However, like Glanville, Boyle's method is to make use of sceptical arguments to raise doubts about established views, and not ultimately to affirm scepticism. In the Preface he distinguishes himself from Carneades, and allows Carneades to defend himself against possible objections by affirming that it is his particular role in the work 'to play the antagonist and the sceptic'.[67] Carneades is, in other words, presented as a *persona* whose task is to draw out the flaws in the established views; he is not the official representative of Boyle's own considered conclusion. For Boyle, as for Glanville and Descartes, scepticism is a device adopted for the particular purpose of exposing unthinking prejudice, and therefore of clearing the decks for a fresh approach to entrenched problems.

Nevertheless, the very willingness to employ the device suggests that the sceptic was not a wholly uncongenial figure for many of the new philosophers. As noted above, for several of their critics— especially of Locke—the association was all too close and too real, reflecting what I have called the sceptical interpretation of experience at the heart of mechanical philosophy. To resolve these issues, a fresh look at what counts as scepticism, and why, is needed. The conclusion will be that experimentalism, mechanism,

---

[67] Boyle, *The Sceptical Chymist*, 4.

and (moderate) scepticism can be considered as different aspects of the same basic viewpoint.[68]

Scepticisms New and (Especially) Old

The modern reader, confronting early modern philosophy, is met by two barriers to understanding claims concerning scepticism. In the first place, he or she is not always alert to the variety of ancient opinions that identified themselves as sceptical, nor, therefore, to what might qualify as a feature common to those different opinions. The early modern world, however, understanding itself as the intellectual flowering engendered by the 'revival of letters'—or, as we would put it, as the culmination of the Renaissance—rather than as a complete break with the past, remained powerfully influenced by ancient models.[69] Secondly, the special form of scepticism introduced by Descartes in the *Meditations*, which hinges on the method of doubt, has occluded other forms of sceptical thought. It has done so in two ways: by encouraging the equation of scepticism with a priori forms of doubt; and, by its very extremism, of encouraging the equation of scepticism with the most extreme of ancient forms of scepticism: Pyrrhonism. It is this set of associations that is mainly responsible for the idea that the achievements of modern science can be justified only if the

[68] Cf. an observation by Tom Beauchamp and Alexander Rosenberg, in *Hume and the Problem of Causation* (New York: Oxford University Press, 1981), 45 n.: 'An important linguistic point about eighteenth-century usage of "scepticism" has been made by Mary Shaw Kuypers, in *Studies in the Eighteenth Century Background of Hume's Empiricism*... She offers evidence that there is "a curious identification of scientific method with scepticism" as early as Locke and that "Hume subscribed to it". She also *suggests* that Hume's full acceptance of empiricism and rejection of rationalism is closely tied to the usage of "scepticism" in his philosophy.' This is (roughly) right, and reflects the limitations on knowledge implied by mechanical accounts of perception. What remains to be shown is that it is this feature that explains the application of the term, and that the application is not improper.

[69] There is no shortage of rhetoric that claims a complete break with the past, of course—here Descartes's *Discourse* is exemplary—but a closer examination will reveal that the past being sloughed off, whether successfully or not, is the medieval past of scholastic thought. (The case of Descartes's argument for God's existence, considered above, is a clear instance.) Further, in order to aid that sloughing off, other, putatively more genuinely ancient, philosophies do yeoman service. Thus Descartes's epistemological strategies have a strong Platonic flavour, albeit percolated through Augustine; and the dispute between Arnauld and Malebranche turns on whether the Augustinian element should be removed. In other respects, Descartes's views have a Stoic air; and against these views Gassendi developed a self-consciously Epicurean position. On the differences between Descartes and Gassendi, and their significance, see Lennon, *The Battle of the Gods and Giants*; and M. J. Osler, *Divine Will and the Mechanical Philosophy: Gassendi and Descartes on Contingency and Necessity in the Created World* (Cambridge: Cambridge University Press, 1994).

'sceptical challenge' can be met; and, for this reason, modern philosophers sympathetic to the cause of modern science frequently understand the key task of philosophy to be to answer, once and for all, the sceptic's doubts.

Considered on its own terms, this is a worthwhile endeavour. As a standpoint from which to approach the early modern world, however, it cannot but lead astray. In the first place, it accords excessive significance to Descartes's solutions to his problems, not least because it supposes too widespread a concern for those problems themselves. Descartes's philosophical contemporaries were not without programmes of their own, and so were not anxiously waiting for him to invent 'modern philosophy' in order to provide them with a set of issues to discuss; nor were subsequent philosophers all reduced to following in his footsteps—even if it is thought that they *should* have been. Like philosophers today, they located themselves in various traditions, and felt no burning need to solve the self-inflicted problems of other schools, even of fellow-travelling other schools. Hobbes's complete indifference to Descartes's problems, as shown in his set of objections to the *Meditations*, is one clear illustration; Hume's self-location within the 'experimental' tradition of Bacon, Boyle, Newton, and Locke is another.

Secondly, too much emphasis has been placed on the extreme, Pyrrhonian, forms of scepticism. There is no doubt that Pyrrhonism in its purest form is incompatible with the new natural philosophy, because it seeks merely to oppose different views to one another, thereby cancelling each other out through a kind of mutual opposition of forces. By this method, the Pyrrhonian sought to suspend judgement, and thereby to reach a state of tranquillity—*ataraxia* or *apatheia*. Exactly what was meant by the attempt to suspend judgement is a subject of dispute. There are conflicting accounts of just how far Pyrrho himself was prepared to go in this regard. Diogenes Laertius, in his *Lives of Eminent Philosophers*, summarizes Pyrrho's main claims, and also records the differing reports of his actual practice:

he would maintain that nothing is honourable or base, or just or unjust, and that likewise in all cases nothing exists in truth; and that convention and habit are the basis of everything that men do; for each thing is no more this than this. He followed these principles in his actual way of life, avoiding nothing and taking no precautions, facing everything as it came, wagons, precipices, dogs, and entrusting nothing whatsoever to his sensations. But he was looked after, as Antigonus of Carystus reports, by his disciples who accompanied him. Aenesidemus, however, says that although he practised philosophy on the principles of suspension of judgement, he did not act carelessly in the details of daily life.[70]

Even allowing for a degree of uncertainty in the meaning of the key notion, suspension of judgement, it is plain that this philosophy is at odds with the outlook of the new philosophy. The new philosophers did not, in their experimental endeavours, aim at tranquillity, nor at any form of suspension of judgement strong enough to result in 'entrusting nothing whatsoever to . . . sensations'. Descartes adopts this stance in the First Meditation, of course, but does not tarry there; and Newton's ban on 'hypotheses', while it is an attempt to suspend judgement, is limited to conclusions about hidden realities—and precisely in order to keep within the limits of experience. This is to propose only a guarded trust in sensations, but it is not to deny experience itself by entrusting nothing at all to them. So it can be concluded that Pyrrhonism is a philosophy at odds with the experimental philosophy of the early modern period.

It cannot be concluded, however, that *scepticism* is therefore opposed to the new philosophy, for neither Cartesian nor Pyrrhonist sceptical strategies exhaust the meaning of the term. Boyle's choice of Carneades to serve as the sceptical critic of the Aristotelian and Neoplatonist chemists of his day is evidence enough. Carneades was a major figure of the later Academy and its brand of scepticism. To Sextus Empiricus, the most extensive early modern source on ancient sceptical thought, the Academics were not properly to be regarded as sceptics: he refers to them as a third school of thought, alongside dogmatists and sceptics (Pyrrhonians).[71] The issue, however, is whether the early modern philosophers accepted his view. Boyle's example suggests not. The various charges of scepticism made against Locke also indicate that there was an understanding of sceptical philosophy that did not reduce to Pyrrhonism. So Hume's description of the Academic philosophy—when he adopts it in the *Enquiry*—as a form of 'mitigated' scepticism seems not to be eccentric. It is reasonable to conclude that it was not uncommon for early modern thinkers to

[70] Diogenes Laertius, *Lives of Eminent Philosophers*, IX, 61–2, in Long and Sedley (eds.), *The Hellenistic Philosophers*, i. 13. (The paragraph concludes: 'He lived to be nearly ninety.' We may take this to offer some support to Aenesidemus' version!)
[71] Sextus Empiricus, *Outlines of Scepticism*, trans. J. Annas and J. Barnes (Cambridge: Cambridge University Press, 1994), I. 3–4: 'Those who are called Dogmatists in the proper sense of the word think that they have disocovered the truth . . . The schools of Clitomachus and Carneades, and other Academics, have asserted that things cannot be apprehended. And the Sceptics are still investigating. Hence the most fundamental kinds of philosophy are reasonably thought to be three: the Dogmatic, the Academic, and the Sceptical.'

understand 'scepticism' to embrace Academic philosophy as well
as Pyrrhonism.

Why is this alternative so frequently overlooked? One reason is
because it is sometimes thought not to be *real* scepticism. This
is simply to beg the question—but it does provide a clue to the
answer. The oversight occurs, I suggest, because, to the modern
reader, Academic philosophy may not look like scepticism *at all*.
One of Cicero's examples of the Academic attitude will illustrate
the problem:

the wise man will make use of whatever apparently probable presentation he
encounters, if nothing presents itself that is contrary to that probability, and
his whole plan of life will be charted out in this manner . . . when a wise man
is going on board a ship surely he has not got the knowledge already grasped
in his mind and perceived that he will make the voyage as he intends? how
can he have it? But if for instance he were setting out from here to Puteoli,
a distance of four miles, with a reliable crew and a good helmsman and in
the present calm weather, it would appear probable that he would get there
safe. He will therefore be guided by presentations of this sort to adopt plans
of action and of inaction . . . and whatever object comes in contact with him
in such a way that the presentation is probable, and unhindered by anything,
he will be set in motion. For he is not a statue carved out of stone or hewn
out of timber; he has a body and a mind, a mobile intellect and mobile senses,
so that many things seem to him to be true . . .[72]

Where is the scepticism here? For the Academics themselves, the
key feature was the stress on probability. To be guided by the
probable was to recognize uncertainty, and this provides a link to
Pyrrhonism because it can be understood as a form of suspension of
judgement. This is not as strange as it may seem: 'judgement' here
means not any mental activity, but a definitive assessment of a state
of affairs. (Judging is what judges do.) Thus the quoted passage continues: 'although nevertheless they do not seem to him to possess
that distinct and peculiar mark leading to perception, and hence
the doctrine that the wise man does not assent . . .'.[73] For the
Academic, then, probability is understood as an alternative to
judging, and judgement is withheld because the whole cannot be
definitively assessed: uncertainty cannot be removed.

[72] Cicero, *Academica*, II. xxxi, in *De Natura Deorum* and *Academica*, trans. H. Rackham
(Cambridge, Mass.: Harvard University Press, 1951), 595–7.
[73] Ibid. 597. Notice that 'perception' is here understood to mean the successful reception
of the object sensed, and that successful reception itself is indicated by the sensation bearing
the mark of truthfulness—the *criterion*. The Academic denies that perception in any proper
sense occurs, because the appearances delivered to the senses are merely appearances because
they lack any mark of truthfulness. For example, they deny the Stoic view that perceptions
can be clear and distinct, and thus be cognitive impressions.

The similarities to, and differences from, the Pyrrhonists thus begin to emerge. The key differences can be brought out by turning to Sextus Empiricus's *Outlines of Pyrrhonism*. He discusses the Academics in a number of passages, and in the relevant case of the later (or New) Academy under Carneades, the role of probability looms large. He regards the Academics' acceptance of probability as a departure from scepticism proper, the latter seeking a thoroughgoing suspension of judgement that dictates a practical conformism. The difference is brought out nicely in the following passage:

The members of the New Academy, if they say that everything is inapprehensible, no doubt differ from the Sceptics precisely in saying that everything is inapprehensible. For they make affirmations about this, while the Sceptic expects it to be possible for some things actually to be apprehended. And they differ from us clearly in their judgements of good and bad. For the Academics say that things are good and bad not in the way we do, but with the conviction that it is plausible that what they call good rather than its contrary really is good (and similarly with bad), whereas we do not call anything good or bad with the thought that what we say is plausible—rather, without holding opinions we follow ordinary life in order not to be inactive.

Further, we say that appearances are equal in convincingness or lack of convincingness (as far as the argument goes), while they say that some are plausible and others implausible. Even among the plausible ones they say there are differences: some, they think, really are just plausible, others plausible and inspected, others plausible and scrutinized and undistractable . . . The members of the New Academy, then, prefer plausible and scrutinized appearances to those which are merely plausible and to both they prefer appearances which are plausible and scrutinized and undistractable.[74]

The Academics, like the Pyrrhonians, thus agree that there is no certain knowledge to be had, but they disagree about where this leaves us. For the Pyrrhonian, all that remains are appearances, and all appearances are equal. But appearances are also contradictory, and, because there can be no higher court of appeal by which to resolve the contradictions, there remains no alternative but to eschew even opinion, and so to live according to established customs. For the Academic, in contrast, appearances can be clustered into groups or kinds that can be ranked according to their degree of plausibility. This opens up the possibility of a life lived *without* knowledge, but *according to* opinion. In this vein, Sextus concludes his account of the differences: 'those who profess to belong to the Academy make use of the plausible in their lives,

---

[74] Sextus Empiricus, *Outlines of Scepticism*, I. 226–9.

while we follow laws and customs and natural feelings, and so live without holding opinions.'[75]

With the acceptance of opinion, and its organization according to the degrees of plausibility, it comes as no surprise that the Academics focus less attention on immediate sense experience, concentrating instead on philosophical theories about the world—and therefore on the output of the other philosophical schools. In particular, they opposed the Stoic idea that there could be a criterion of certainty in sense perception. A criterion—a marker of truthfulness—would enable us to distinguish true and adequate ideas of the world from false and inadequate ones. If there is no such marker, we must remain uncertain about the truthfulness and reliability of our perceptions—that is, of signs of anything beyond themselves. This is not, for the Academic, a counsel of despair, but the invitation to scrutinize appearances themselves, and to be guided by the appearances thus scrutinized—as does Cicero's wise man. A. A. Long explains Carneades' concerns accordingly:

> The scepticism of the Academics is not focused upon everyday judgments but upon philosophical theories which seek a criterion of certainty in sense-perception. In more modern terminology, Carneades is saying that the truth of empirical judgments is always contingent and never necessary. The world might, as a matter of fact, be quite different from our perception of it; but our empirical judgments can be true or false, provided that we refer truth or falsity to the world as we observe it and do not claim that our statements are true or false about the world in itself.[76]

Thus defined, Academic scepticism has obvious affinities with the experimental outlook. Hume's own endorsement of both Newtonian experimentalism and Academic scepticism in the *Enquiry* thus falls into place. The principal barriers to accepting these twin endorsements, then, are the twin failures to see the sceptical edge to the mechanical account of perception, and the tendency to think of scepticism in only the more extreme senses. Two examples will bring out the influence of these factors.

John Biro, in 'Hume's New Science of the Mind', offers an account of Hume's position that is fully consonant with Academic scepticism; but, unwilling to accept weaker forms of scepticism as worthy of the name, and simultaneously offering an anachronistic term for the products of experimental enquiry ('scientific knowledge'), he carefully skirts around the vantage point from which Hume's views and self-descriptions all fall into place:

---

[75] *Outlines of Scepticism*, 1. 231.   [76] Long, *Hellenistic Philosophy*, 99.

while there is a sense in which Hume can be said, as he so often is, to be a sceptic, his scepticism is better understood as one about pretended supra-scientific metaphysical knowledge, rather than about scientific knowledge itself. It is this kind of scepticism that separates him most sharply from other philosophers of his day, who conceived of philosophy as going beyond mere scientific knowledge to disclose a deeper and more certain knowledge of reality.[77]

A comparison of this passage with Long's account of the Academic position above shows the two to be practically indistinguishable. But, without a better sense of the variety within the sceptical tradition, or of the sceptical air of what we *now* call 'science', Biro fails to see that he has shown Hume's position to be perfectly intelligible as a form of scepticism. Related problems afflict Robert Fogelin's essay in the same volume. He describes a form of 'empiricism' (another anachronistic term) that insists that empirical claims that go beyond immediate reports are not certain, that knowledge implies certainty, and therefore that such claims are not knowledge. He allows that this might be described as a form of scepticism, but then denies that it is 'really' so: 'Scepticism of this kind might better be called *fallibilism*, not scepticism.'[78] Well, it might, but not without removing the requirement that knowledge implies certainty. Since it is the very denial of certain knowledge that is the core of the Academics' sceptical self-understanding—in both the ancient world, *and* in the antiquity-soaked world of early modernity—then, whatever the merits this proposal may have for us and our own self-understanding, we are nevertheless much better off without it if our aim is to understand the philosophical past.

This brings us to the heart of the issue. The Academics propounded a view that, by denying certainty and replacing it with standards based on degrees of probability, saw them classed as sceptics. This is odd to the modern philosopher, who has come to identify scepticism with the much stronger position of denying even reasonable belief. The literal meaning of 'sceptic', however, is 'enquirer', so, in its original ancient setting, the scepticism of the Academic required no special hedging of terms, despite Sextus' desire to distinguish them from Pyrrhonism. The sceptics were enquirers, and were opposed, as already pointed out, to the dogmatists. The dogmatists, themselves, whether Aristotelian,

---

[77] Biro, 'Hume's New Science of the Mind', 38. Biro adds, significantly in this context: 'An example of this more ambitious expectation is the common refusal of Leibniz and the Cartesians to admit that Newton had really *explained* anything.'

[78] Robert Fogelin, 'Hume's Scepticism', in Norton (ed.), *The Cambridge Companion to Hume*, 91.

Neoplatonist, Stoic, or Epicurean, claimed certain knowledge of things, and did so because, in one way or another, they confidently believed that the human mind could come to grasp the essences or natures of real things. This confidence meant that difficulties in their views were no cause for doubt, nor for trimming their ambitions by pinning their doctrines on appearances rather than realities, or on probabilities—of whatever degree of reliability—rather than certainties. To entertain doubts about the one implied doubts about the other; and to entertain such doubts was to embrace scepticism.[79] This remained true, in both the ancient and early modern worlds, even if one doubted only in the very weak sense of affirming preferred views cautiously and undogmatically, where 'to doubt' means simply to possess an undogmatic disposition.[80] The dogmatist, in short, believed in the attainability of genuine, certain knowledge of the world as it is in itself. The sceptics denied knowledge in order to make room for enquiry; and the Academic understanding of the life of enquiry corresponds closely to the attitude of undogmatic experimentation, of resisting 'hypotheses'— that is, of the new philosophy.

Scepticism as the Denial of *Scientia*

The ancient distinction between the dogmatist and sceptic survived into the early modern world, and did so because that world shared, with antiquity, the same notion of genuine knowledge. However, that specific notion of genuine knowledge goes, in the early modern world, by a word that now has rather different connotations; and for this reason the significance of the term is often missed. That word is 'science'. It is a translation of the Latin *scientia*, a word that expresses, in the Latinate intellectual world of the medieval period, the ideal of certain and rationally justified knowledge: knowledge of the essences of real things themselves, and therefore of their necessary connections with other real objects. These connections survive when the word is translated into English in early modern Anglophone philosophy. This is well illustrated by Hobbes's definition of 'science' in *Leviathan*:

[79] See Sextus Empiricus: 'But nature, someone will say, has made the senses commensurate with their objects. What nature? . . . if the senses do not apprehend external objects, the intellect is not able to apprehend them either (since its guides fail it), so by means of this argument too we shall be brought to suspension of judgement about external existing objects' (*Outlines of Scepticism*, I. 98–9).
[80] See Norton, *David Hume*, 279–90.

Whereas Sense and Memory are but knowledge of Fact . . . *Science* is the knowledge of Consequences, and dependance of one fact upon another: by which, out of that we can presently do, we know how to do something else when we will, or the like, another time: Because when we see how any thing comes about, upon what causes, and by what manner; when the like causes come into our power, wee see how to make it produce the like effects.[81]

In the following paragraph, Hobbes adds that 'science' means a set of 'certain rules'. So, although he allows that the deliverances of sense and memory can be called 'knowledge', such knowledge is to be distinguished from theoretical, or 'scientific', knowledge, because the latter possesses a logical structure, and gives certainty. It is this knowledge—scientific knowledge or *scientia*—that the sceptic denies. The Academic, no less than the Pyrrhonian, denies the possibility of such certainty, and so also denies knowledge of this kind. The experimental philosopher, committed to the necessity of careful experiment because his mechanical account of experience denies the possibility of penetrating beyond phenomena, denies knowledge in precisely the same respect, and can therefore rightly be described as a philosophical sceptic. However, he also believes that experiment provides a basis for sorting doctrines into the more and less probable, and so the experimental philosopher is for this reason an Academic, rather than a Pyrrhonian, sceptic.

Locke fits this picture. His definitions closely conform to Hobbes's, and he accepts the implications for his own experimental endeavours. He initially defines knowledge in broad terms as *'the perception of the connexion and agreement, or disagreement and repugnancy of any of our Ideas'*;[82] but 'philosophical' knowledge—science (*scientia*)—is the perception of connections between ideas of a special kind—ideas of the real natures of things, and thus also of the *necessary* connections between them. Experience, however, does not provide such ideas or such insights. It gives us access only to the *'nominal Essence'* of an object, not to the underlying 'real Constitution of Substances', the *'real Essence'* on which 'philosophical' knowledge depends.[83] Since the *'Connexions* and *Dependancies'* between objects are 'not discoverable in our *Ideas'*, we are reduced to mere 'experimental Knowledge'—a condition of 'darkness'. Locke puts it as follows:

The Things that, as far as our Observation reaches, we constantly find to proceed regularly, we may conclude, do act by a Law set them; but yet by a

---

[81] Thomas Hobbes, *Leviathan*, ed. R. Tuck (Cambridge: Cambridge University Press, 1991), ch. V, 35–6.
[82] Locke, *Essay*, IV. i. 1.   [83] Ibid. III. vi. 2.

Law, that we know not: whereby, though Causes work steadily, and Effects constantly flow from them, yet their *Connexions* and *Dependancies* being not discoverable in our *Ideas*, we can have but an experimental Knowledge of them. From all which 'tis easy to perceive, what a darkness we are involved in, how little 'tis of Being, and the things that are, that we are capable to know. And therefore we shall do no injury to our Knowledge when we modestly think with our selves, that we are so far from being able to comprehend the whole nature of the Universe, and all the things contained in it, that we are not capable of a philosophical *Knowledge* of the Bodies that are about us, and make a part of us . . . as to a perfect *Science* of natural Bodies, (not to mention spiritual Beings,) we are, I think, so far from being capable of any such thing, that I conclude it lost labour to seek after it.[84]

The 'science' Locke rejects here is *scientia*, knowledge of the essences of things. Another way of putting it is to say that he is denying *philosophy*, in the ordinary seventeenth-century sense of the term. As he puts it himself in the Epistle to the Reader with which the *Essay* begins, 'Philosophy . . . is nothing but the true Knowledge of Things.'[85] His own ambition in the *Essay* is not to provide such knowledge; it is, rather, 'to be employed as an Under-Labourer in clearing Ground a little, and removing some of the Rubbish, that lies in the way to Knowledge', and thereby to support the experimental endeavours of the great natural philosophers of the day—not least, 'the incomparable Mr. Newton'.[86] Thus Locke denies 'science' in order to make room for experimental philosophy; and, because the denial of *scientia* was a mark of scepticism, for this reason he was criticized by both the old and the new schools in dogmatic philosophy—the Aristotelians and the modern rationalists—for propounding scepticism. These critiques included not only the works of Stillingfleet, Lee, and Berkeley already mentioned, but also John Sergeant's *Method to Science* and *Solid Philosophy Asserted*, and Leibniz's *New Essays*.[87]

It will be helpful at this point to consider an objection. A not uncommon complaint about Locke's account of knowledge and its limits in Book IV of the *Essay* is that he there abandons the empiricism spelt out in Books I and II, and reverts to a rationalist standard of knowledge. This complaint is, however, no more than 'the expression of bafflement in a learned way';[88] and removing the baffles will reveal how Locke's philosophy looked to his dogmatic critics. In the *Essay*, Locke denies philosophical knowledge of nature—that is, knowledge of causes, powers, natures, essences, or

---

[84] Locke, *Essay*, IV. iii. 29.   [85] Ibid., Epistle to the Reader, 10.   [86] Ibid.
[87] For a brief discussion of the critiques of Locke by Lee, Sergeant, and Leibniz, see J. W. Yolton, *John Locke and the Way of Ideas* (Oxford: Clarendon Press, 1956), ch. 3.
[88] In Mary Douglas's happy phrase (*Purity and Danger* (London: Routledge, 1991), 45–6).

substances. The so-called empiricist and rationalist strands in his thought are unified into a single viewpoint when this claim—much emphasized—is given centre stage. In fact, it is only in this way that the 'empiricism' of Books I and II is properly understood. Locke is not there introducing a positive programme for an alternatively founded system of knowledge to rival the rationalists. Rather, his emphasis on experience is in order to *limit* the reach of our understanding, and thereby to rule out the possibility of systematic certain knowledge.[89] Thus he denies innate principles in Book I in order to rule out all knowledge claims allegedly exempt from the tribunal of experience, and in Book II founds the contents of our minds on 'simple ideas': sights, sounds, feels, and so on—but not ideas of substances and their essences. Book III investigates the deceptive role of words, arguing that they only ever succeed in picking out 'nominal essences', while obscuring from us this limitation. Book IV then addresses the question of what, in the light of these conclusions, we can reasonably claim to know. His answer is that we know enough for the purposes of life; but of the real natures of things we must remain forever ignorant. *Scientia* is beyond us. In this sense, then, Locke's philosophy is indeed a form of scepticism—as his critics claimed.

Of course, Locke was not unperturbed by the charge, so, if the above account is sound, this fact requires explanation. The task is less difficult than might be imagined. In the first place, Locke's message is not sceptical across the board: he affirms that we do have genuine, if not comprehensive, knowledge, of morals and the cornerstones of religion, and he had good reason to be anxious that the sceptical message about natural philosophy not be confused with moral and religious scepticism. The controversies over innate knowledge indicate just how delicate the issue could be.[90] The problem was exacerbated by the fact that, then as now, the varieties of scepticism were not clearly distinguished in the public mind. So, although for (British) experimental philosophers the rejection of metaphysical speculations could be understood as an antidote to 'superstition' and 'idolatry' (that is, Catholicism), and a reliable road to 'true religion' (that is, Protestantism), scepticism

[89] Cf. Aristotle, *Metaphysics*, I. i, in *A New Aristotle Reader*, ed. Ackrill, 256–7.
[90] Cf. Yolton, *John Locke and the Way of Ideas*, chs. 1–2. Cf. also the third Earl of Shaftesbury, who attacked his former tutor in these terms: 'It was Mr. Locke that struck the home blow: for Mr. Hobbes's character and base slavish principles in government took off the poison of his philosophy. 'Twas Mr. Locke that struck at all fundamentals, threw all order and virtue out of the world and made the very idea of these . . . unnatural and without foundation in our minds' (*Letters of the Earl of Shaftesbury to a Student at the University* (1716), in B. Rand (ed.), *The Life, Unpublished Letters, and Philosophical Regimen of Anthony Ashley Cooper, Earl of Shaftesbury* (London and New York: Sonnenschein, 1900), 403).

was nevertheless a label that had to be handled with care. It is reasonable to suppose that this was especially so in the fickle tides of
religious politics in the uncertain years following the Glorious
Revolution—the years in which the *Essay* was making its way in
the world.

Secondly, Locke signals that he accepts the view, stemming from
Gassendi, that Academic philosophy can provide a constructive
alternative to dogmatism or despair—a new middle way for epistemology. This is particularly apparent from his employment of
the notion of 'nominal essence'. His pronounced nominalism and
particularism would have led his readers to expect him to hold
that through experience we were acquainted with names *merely*.
Galileo and Hobbes, although they pressed the point to different
ends, had both held that, where we did not have access to real
qualities of objects, only names remained. Locke's terminology, in
contrast—by applying the term 'essence' to regularities in experience—draws attention to the regularities evinced by sensible
qualities, whatever their underlying foundations. From a more traditional viewpoint, this probably seemed no more than a muddy-
ing of the waters. Locke's terminology, however, deliberately
dignifies those regularities, and affirms a constructive role for
appearances. Despite not contributing to genuinely philosophical
insight—to *scientia*—appearances can be understood to possess
knowledge-like characteristics. In fact, through this affirmation,
Locke gave a significant impetus to the modern redefinition of the
concept of knowledge itself.[91]

These two factors help to show why Hume, in contrast, felt no
qualms about wearing the sceptical label. First, he accepted that
the sceptical denial of knowledge of causal powers, and the probabilistic conclusions to be drawn from it, did have sceptical implications for both religion and morals—although the implications
for the latter were considerably less drastic than for the former.[92]
Thus he had a positive motive that Locke lacked. And, living in
less turbulent political times, he had less cause to worry about

---

[91] On this issue, see Osler, 'John Locke and the Changing Ideal of Scientific Knowledge'
Journal of the History of Ideas, 31 (1970), 3–16. (Note that the shift in the meaning of 'scepticism'—as the rejection of this ideal of knowledge—is also implied by this change.)

[92] David Fate Norton's division of Hume's philosophy into a sceptical metaphysics and
common-sense morals—revealed in the very title of his book, *David Hume: Common-Sense
Moralist, Sceptical Metaphysician*—overlooks the means for uniting these under a single
conception: if understood, not as unreflective adherence to the views of the vulgar, but as a
moral outlook that eschews metaphysics for the ordinary moral reasonings of common life—
and does so because the former can be grounded only in unattainable knowledge of
essences—then 'common-sense' morality is wholly conformable to the Academic sceptic's
outlook.

getting into trouble.[93] Thus he also lacked the negative motive that Locke possessed. Secondly, although he stressed regularities even more than Locke had done, the idea of a nominal essence makes no appearance in his writings. This may have been because he did *not* want the waters muddied: too great an emphasis on a middle way that seemed to hold out some hope of leaving things as they are (suitably redefined) would not have served his purposes, since it could have blunted the critical edge of his arguments; and, perhaps, have shifted attention away from his claim that an ancient sceptical outlook—even if of a moderate kind—was the inner meaning of the new philosophy.

Whatever the best explanation here, one thing is clear and important: in labelling himself a sceptic, Hume accepts the very same standard for philosophical knowledge—the so-called rationalist standard—maintained by Locke and his critics, and, for that matter, by just about everybody else. That is, Hume is a sceptic because he believes that the systematic knowledge of necessary connections—philosophical knowledge or *scientia*—is the standard at which philosophy aims, and by which philosophies are judged; and that such knowledge is beyond us, because we must rely on experience, but experience cannot deliver it. Scepticism begins with the denial that we human beings, with our limited capacities, can attain to such insight into reality: its identifying characteristic is therefore lost if that standard is not preserved. The sceptic accepts that *scientia* is the only proper standard of philosophical knowledge—but denies that its attainment is possible for beings like us.[94]

Sceptical Realism and Anti-Sceptical Anti-Realism

There is an important implication of recognizing that, even for the sceptic, *scientia* is the standard for philosophical knowledge. Plainly, to deny such knowledge does not rule out fruitful investigation of the orderliness manifested by natural phenomena. Nor does it render indefensible all *opinion* concerning the real structure of the world. The Pyrrhonian, of course, will not be assuaged by this thought: but, in attempting to avoid opinion because knowledge cannot be had, Pyrrhonism reveals itself as Platonism

[93] Consider, in this light, the Latin Epigraph to the *Treatise*, taken from Tacitus: 'Rara temporum felicitas, ubi sentire, quæ velis; & quæ sentias, dicere licet' ('Rare the happy times when we can think what we like; and are allowed to say what we think') (*Treatise*, p. xi).

[94] Cf. J. P. Wright, 'Hume's Rejection of the Theory of Ideas', *History of Philosophy Quarterly*, 8 (1991), 160.

Disappointed. It should be noted, however, that, in thus seeking
to avoid even opinion, the Pyrrhonian does not—at least, not in
the active sense entertained by Descartes[95]—*doubt* the existence of
an underlying real order. The Pyrrhonist seeks to live without opinions, and this means not only to live without the opinion that
there is a real world beyond our comprehension, but also the contrary opinion that there is *not*. Pyrrhonism, it might be said, leaves
everything as it is.

The Academic is not so uncommitted. He or she aims to live and
judge precisely according to opinion, and to this end scrutinizes
competing opinions in order to settle on that which is most probable. So if we ask, Is there a real order of independent objects
underlying experience, an order of necessary relations that explains
the undeniable regularities of experience?, the Academic will not
hope for a definitive answer, but will seek out the most probable
opinion. Although it can be doubted whether all Academics were of
one mind on the question, the stress on probabilities provides a
powerful tendency towards an affirmative answer. This is because
to deny insight into essences, and to seek instead the most probable
opinion, is most readily, if not necessarily, interpreted as testing for
the relative verisimilitude of different beliefs—that is, their degree
of approximation to real states of affairs. This is to be committed to
a realist interpretation of the world, and so Academic scepticism is
naturally interpreted as sceptical realism.[96]

Hume, for his part, gives the whole issue a surprising twist. He
argues that belief in the external world is a natural belief, something 'which we must take for granted in all our reasonings'.[97] This
may seem like an evasion, but is not. The doctrine of natural belief
is not a shelter against scepticism, but part of a sceptical account
of human functioning: an account that stresses that human reason
is of very narrow extent, and that, in consequence, 'the whole
conduct of life' depends on 'a species of instinct or mechanical
power'.[98] This instinctive power governs belief formation itself,
and, most importantly, does so according to probabilistic principles. This means that the natural belief in the reality of the
external world is, *ipso facto*, the most probable opinion. So the
probabilism of Hume's position displays its Academic credentials,
and his account of belief in the external world established by the
operations of instinctive probabilistic mechanisms shows him to
be a sceptical realist.

[95] Cf. Norton, *David Hume*, 279–95.
[96] The term is Wright's: see *The Sceptical Realism of David Hume*, 1–7.
[97] *Treatise*, 187.   [98] *Enquiries*, 108.

Scepticism characteristically holds that there is something fundamental about the world that we do not know, and in this respect is committed to the view that there is more to the world than we are able to perceive. This shows that realism can be thought of as a natural support of scepticism, rather than its enemy. Thus the *denial* of realism about physical bodies could be thought of as an antidote to scepticism. It is in this respect, I suggest, that Berkeley thought of himself as defeating scepticism. In affirming that *esse* is *percipi*, he denied that there is any unknowable *something* beyond our perceptions, any substratum 'we know not what'.[99] And, if there is no unknowable, hidden reality underpinning our perceptions of objects, then there is nothing we need to discover. Real essences are not distinct from the nominal essences that experience reliably delivers. Nothing is hidden. It is only philosophers misguided by their own assumptions who have failed to see this, and so have raised the spectre of scepticism quite unnecessarily: 'we have first raised a dust, and then complain, we cannot see.'[100] Scepticism is defeated, concludes Berkeley, by removing its realist foundation: anti-realism is anti-scepticism.

Scepticism in the *Enquiry*

Scepticism, in the ancient and the early modern worlds, is characterized by the denial that we are in possession of genuinely philosophical knowledge, or *scientia*. This means that, to persuade others that their confidence is misguided, the sceptic must argue that the supposed sources of such knowledge either do not exist, or do not deliver the goods. What are those sources? They are *intuition* and *demonstration*, the sure foundation and equally certain reasonings that alone can build an indubitable and systematic epistemic structure.[101] If, then, it can be shown that we are able neither to intuit, nor rationally to deduce, any knowledge of the essential natures of things, then it will have been shown that, whatever we may previously have believed, we do not and cannot possess any genuinely philosophical knowledge. We would then have no option but to accept the sceptical interpretation of the human situation.

---

[99] Locke, *Essay*, II. xxiii. 2, 3.

[100] Berkeley, *Principles*, 90 (Introduction, §3).

[101] Cf. Descartes's statement of these two principles in the *Regulae*: 'By "intuition" I do not mean the fluctuating testimony of the senses or the deceptive judgement of the imagination as it botches things together, but the conception of a clear and attentive mind . . . [and] deduction . . . the inference of something as following necessarily from some other propositions which are known with certainty' (in *The Philosophical Writings of Descartes*, i. 14–15). See also *Enquiries*, 37.

This is precisely the strategy Hume adopts in the first *Enquiry*. The opening sections assert that our ideas derive from impressions, and that the mind is capable of connecting ideas through association. This is implicitly to accept that ideas arise from a mechanical process (impressing or stamping) and can also be connected by mechanical motions (associations). In both origin and manner of composition or change, then, our ideas reflect non-rational processes. Further, the principles of association imply that there is no *criterion* by which we can accurately distinguish true ideas from false, adequate from inadequate. Hume is setting out the germ of the Academic outlook as summed up, very neatly, by Cicero: 'Our position is not that we hold that nothing is true, but that we assert that all true sensations are associated with false ones so closely resembling them that they contain no infallible mark to guide our judgment and assent.'[102]

One virtue of understanding Hume in these terms is that it explains his remarkably relaxed attitude towards innate ideas.[103] If we have no criterion for distinguishing the true from the false, and therefore cannot accurately distinguish innate ideas from closely resembling adventitious ideas, the question of innate ideas is drained of all significance. Certainly Hume does not bother to offer detailed arguments for his starting points. He briefly outlines his position, and in terms that are sufficient to indicate his broad sympathies with the mechanical picture of human perception and mental functioning. He then passes directly to the central argument.

Section IV, 'Sceptical Doubts concerning the Operations of the Understanding', and Section V, 'Sceptical Solution of these Doubts', are the heart of the work, building a specific sceptical argument onto the starting points already laid down. The sceptical doubts consist in showing, in Section IV Part I, that our factual beliefs depend on prior causal beliefs. These are then shown to depend neither on a priori reasoning nor on direct perception, but entirely on 'experience'—here meaning not the discrete perceptual building blocks of twentieth-century empiricism, but, as in Aristotle, the temporally extended encounter with the world. The argument is against the possibility of rational insight into the real being of things from rational reflection on the deliverances of sense perception. The central target here is the Stoic philosophy

---

[102] Cicero, *De Natura Deorum*, I. v, in *De Natura Deorum* and *Academica*, 15. See also Long, *Hellenistic Philosophy*, 99; and Hume, *Treatise*, 60–1.
[103] *Enquiries*, 22 n.

of the genesis of knowledge through cognitive impressions,[104] and the point of the argument is to show that, as Aristotle had held, there is no knowledge of 'ultimate causes' independently of 'connected experience' of the world.[105]

This leaves open the Aristotelian (and Epicurean) possibility that, *through* connected experience of the world, reason may be able to discover the nature of the ultimate causes. The second part of Section IV is concerned to rule out this prospect, by showing that conclusions drawn from experience—from temporally extended contact with the world—do not depend on reason in any way. Neither intuition, nor demonstrative, nor probable reasoning play any part. The recognition that there is a difference between *having found* the world a certain way, and *expecting* that it will continue in that way—and that this difference requires explaining— is itself to deny that there is any intuitive insight. Moreover, formal demonstrations like those of geometry cannot provide the desired result, because they work by ruling out logical impossibilities, and there is nothing self-contradictory in natural occurrences being other than they are. Nor can factual reasoning do the job, because it is based on cause and effect, and thus on experience, and so must *assume* the uniformity of nature, when it is the very constitution of nature that is at issue. So experience cannot provide us with the rational insight into ultimate principles that rational reflection on perceptible properties failed to provide. Therefore the mind can in no way come to grasp the real being of things. The sceptical doubts concerning the operations of the understanding thus consist in showing that the understanding, the rational faculty of the human mind, is not able to provide us with genuinely philosophical knowledge of the world.

The sceptical solution of these doubts is sceptical because it accepts that there is indeed no rational insight. Instead, our basic beliefs about the world, the beliefs by which we live, arise through a non-rational process: custom or habit. This is no more than an observable propensity of human beings, and so is not itself a form of insight into essential natures. Hume is explicit on the point: 'wherever the repetition of any particular act or operation produces a propensity to renew the same act or operation, without being impelled by any reasoning or process of the understanding, we always say, that this propensity is the effect of *Custom*. By employing that word, we pretend not to have given the ultimate

---

[104] Although perhaps Hume intends it also to cover Platonic and Cartesian views. The question will be considered more fully in Part Two.
[105] Aristotle, *Metaphysics*, I. i, in *A New Aristotle Reader*, ed. Ackrill, 255.

reason of such a propensity.'[106] Custom is, then, a purely manifest principle, a propensity of human beings that is readily observable, but perhaps not capable of further explanation. It is also, happily, a propensity that we have found to be pretty reliable, at least as far as our preservation is concerned. It can, therefore, properly be called an instinct, and so the conclusion to be drawn is that we are creatures of instinct rather than rational insight.

This conclusion, so far from being, as is sometimes thought, a retreat from the sceptical impulse of Hume's philosophy, is in fact its central point. The philosophical tradition stemming from Plato and Aristotle had conceived of human beings as rational animals— that is, distinguished from animals by their capacity to con- template the ultimate principles of reality. The fruits of such contemplation, systematic knowledge or *scientia*, thus became the highest goal of human activity. Hume argues that *scientia* is impossible for creatures like us, and therefore that we are not to be distinguished from animals by any capacity for rational insight into nature's secrets. We do have rational powers, but in this we differ from animals in degree, not kind—just as human beings themselves have different degrees of this capacity. The point is not pressed until later, in the short section entitled 'Of the Reason of Animals'—but it is already implicit. The 'sceptical solution' under- mines the status and distinctiveness of the understanding itself.

This becomes clear if we turn back to Locke. He had opened the *Essay* with the observation that 'it is the *Understanding* that sets Man above the rest of sensible Beings, and gives him all the Advantage and Dominion, which he has over them'.[107] Later on in the same work, reason is picked out as the capacity that distin- guishes Man from the beasts: it is 'that Faculty, whereby Man is supposed to be distinguished from Beasts, and wherein it is evident he much surpasses them'.[108] Reason is the proper activity of the understanding, and as such is that which distinguishes human beings from animals. Hume's sceptical doubts arrive, first, at the conclusion that the human understanding is incapable of that which philosophers since Thales have dreamed, rational insight into the real; and then, further, that human beings occupy no special, semi-divine, place within the wider world of animals and things.[109]

---

[106] *Enquiries*, 43.   [107] Locke, *Essay*, I. i. 1.   [108] Ibid. IV. xvii. 1.

[109] This is a characteristic conclusion of the sceptical tradition, especially the Pyrrhonian. It is implicit in the Ten Modes (Sextus Empiricus, *Outlines of Scepticism*, I. 35–163), and pressed by Montaigne in 'An Apology for Raymond Sebond': 'The natural, original distemper of Man is presumption. Man is the most blighted and frail of all creatures and, moreover, the most given to pride. This creature knows and sees that he is lodged down here, among the mire

The unifying thread running through these arguments is that the human ability to comprehend the world is considerably more limited than philosophers have tended to suppose. They have sought a comprehensive and systematic knowledge of the essential properties of the world; indeed, they have identified philosophy with the search for such knowledge, and not untypically have claimed to possess it. Hume's argument is that such knowledge is not possible, and in denying the possibility identifies himself as a sceptic. The self-identification thus presupposes that such knowledge is an appropriate standard for our enquiries, even though we inevitably fall far short of its requirements. It is an appropriate standard because we cannot but believe that there is a world independent of our conceptions of it, but at the same time we cannot provide any guarantees that our conceptions—including that belief in the real—are adequate to it. We are reduced to careful investigations to help us settle on the more plausible of our alternative accounts. This is Hume's experimental philosophy, a reinvigorated version of the scepticism of the later Academy.

In accepting that experimental enquiry can identify the more probable opinion, the Academic sceptic is naturally led to suppose a hidden standard against which the probabilities are, ultimately, to be measured. In this way, it naturally inclines towards 'sceptical realism'; and Hume clearly signals, in a well-known passage in his essay 'The Sceptic', that this is just how he sees the issue:

If I examine the PTOLOMAIC and COPERNICAN systems, I endeavour only, by my enquiries, to know the real situation of the planets; that is in other words, I endeavour to give them, in my conception, the same relations, that they bear towards each other in the heavens. To this operation of the mind, therefore, there seems to be always a real, though often an unknown standard, in the nature of things; nor is truth or falsehood variable by the various apprehensions of mankind. Though all human race should for ever conclude, that the sun moves, and the earth remains at rest, the sun stirs not an inch from his place for all these reasonings; and such conclusions are eternally false and erroneous.[110]

and shit of the world, bound and nailed to the deadest, most stagnant part of the universe, in the lowest storey of the building, the farthest from the vault of heaven . . . yet, in thought, he sets himself above the circle of the Moon, bringing the very heavens under his feet. The vanity of this same thought makes him equal himself to God; attribute to himself God's mode of being; pick himself out and set himself apart from the mass of other creatures; and (although they are his fellows and his brothers) carve out for them such helpings of force or faculties as he thinks fit' (in *The Complete Essays*, trans. Screech, 505).

[110] 'The Sceptic', in *Essays*, 164. This passage, and its 'sceptical realist' commitments, are discussed in J. P. Wright, 'Hume's Academic Scepticism: A Reappraisal of his Philosophy of Human Understanding', *Canadian Journal of Philosophy*, 16 (1986), 407–35.

The opponents of this carefully qualified, undeniably realist outlook are the Pyrrhonians and the philosophical dogmatists. Of these alternatives, the latter is the more important, at least in terms of cultural impact. So the task of the *Enquiry* is to show that the experimental philosophy, properly understood, has sceptical implications that undercut all the dogmatists—old and new, secular and (not least) religious—and the body of the work is structured accordingly. The Pyrrhonian challenge is not forgotten, however, so the work concludes with a final section that defends the Academic's position against the self-defeating extremism of Pyrrhonism. A suitably moderated scepticism, as the Academic philosophy is, can avoid the absurdities into which the Pyrrhonian is thrown, and at the same time provides standards for intellectual enquiry that can separate genuine enquiries from (as we would say) pseudo-sciences, and thereby promises to free human life from the burdens of metaphysical fantasy and superstition. The critical arguments of *An Enquiry concerning Human Understanding* underpin an ambitious Enlightenment dream.

PART TWO

The Argument

Section I

Of the different Species of Philosophy

The opening section of the first *Enquiry* has two main tasks. The first is pre-emptive damage control, the second to signal the work's critical purpose. The damage control is the task of encouraging the polite reader not to be disheartened when the subsequent chapters become harder going; that the effort required will not be unreasonable. To this end, Hume contrasts an 'easy' philosophy with 'abstruse' philosophy in order to show to the uncertain reader that he is alert to the merits of the former, and sensitive to the failings of the latter. He nevertheless insists that the latter is both necessary and advantageous. The way forward, then, will be to attempt to combine the accessibility of the 'easy' philosophy with the depth and profundity of 'abstruse' philosophy. The second task, to signal the work's critical purpose, is also part of this persuasive endeavour, because it aims to show that the effort will be worthwhile. The argument of the book will show important matters in a new light: in particular, it will 'undermine the foundations of an abstruse philosophy, which seems to have hitherto served only as a shelter to superstition, and a cover to absurdity and error!' (16).[1] Since this section is so often skipped over entirely, and (as has been shown in Chapter 1) one particular remark in it is so often misread, it will be useful to provide a short summary of what Hume actually says.

He begins by observing that moral philosophy—or 'the science of human nature'—can be treated in two ways, each of which has value. The first considers man as an *active* being, directed by feelings and by the immediate appearances of things. This form of philosophy proceeds by pointing out the attractions of moral virtue in an uncomplicated way. By careful selection of examples, and judicious contrasts between types of character, it shapes our desires and actions by making us feel the difference between good and evil. In contrast, the other kind of philosophy considers man

---

[1] Throughout Part Two, all page references in the text will be to Hume's *Enquiries*.

as a *reasoning* being, and so attempts to shape his beliefs. This philosophy aims to understand human nature itself, by identifying the basic principles that regulate thought, feeling and action. So it is not satisfied with determining what is good and what is not, but seeks to explain 'the source of these distinctions' (6): *why* we draw the distinctions we do between good and evil, beauty and ugliness, and so on. To most people, this latter kind of enquiry seems dry as dust, and for good reason: it can be very hard going; and, typically, the intellectuals who engage in it are not interested in communicating with a large audience, but only with those who understand their concerns.

The first kind, the 'easy' or uncomplicated philosophy, will always be more popular, and will usually be thought more useful because of its immediate practical value in shaping action. It has also achieved the greater fame, because, while abstract thinkers may briefly come to prominence, they are quickly forgotten. Their very method almost guarantees as much, with its reliance on long chains of reasoning. Further, this method is justifiably regarded with suspicion, because a single error in a long chain of reasoning will infect all the conclusions drawn; and, since these intellectuals are not sensitive to public opinion, they are also not likely to be corrected by public opposition, which could rescue them from their own blunders. In contrast, the accessible philosopher, who merely paints a picture drawn from common sense, is also corrected by common sense, and so is protected from falling into dangerous illusions.

In fact, Hume continues, the dedicated philosopher enjoys only low public esteem precisely because his concerns are so remote from the ordinary concerns of society. Although no one admires ignorance, the dedicated philosopher is thought to lack the balanced views (and activities) that make for a good life. The established view is that the best life is a mean between extremes: the well-developed person is versatile, able to appreciate fine literature and to understand the world of public affairs. This well-rounded character seems to be best developed by the 'easy' style of writing—it is neither too remote nor too demanding, and provides inspiration for meeting life's difficulties. The established view is not unattractive, and can be summarized in the following way: man has intellectual needs, but the limitations on human capacities mean that there are no secure achievements or lasting satisfactions to be had through intellectual enquiry; man is a social creature, but company can pall; man is also active, and seeks employment, but relaxation is no less important. So nature itself seems to teach us that the best life is a mixture containing each of these capabilities and needs in due measure. Further, it also seems to teach that the pursuit of knowledge is genuinely part of the best life only when directed to useful enquiries: for study of abstract problems produces only unhappiness and uncertainty in oneself, and a cold reception from others. Philosophy is all right in its proper place, but must not be allowed to dominate one's life: 'Be a philosopher; but, amidst all your philosophy, be still a man' (9).

Hume immediately distances himself from this *apparently* natural conclusion. He is not without sympathy for it: he regards it as a reasonable attitude to be held by the person of limited philosophical interests, *provided that* no criticism is implied of those differently inclined. Since, however, this condition is not always satisfied, it is necessary to investigate what can be said on behalf of 'profound reasonings, or what is commonly called *metaphysics*' (9). There are two related advantages. In the first place, abstract philosophy underpins the easy philosophy by giving it the accuracy it needs to be convincing. For example, the anatomist shows the underlying structures of the body, and, despite the ugliness of these structures, there is no depiction of beauty without knowledge of them: 'The anatomist presents to the eye the most hideous and disagreeable objects; but his science is useful to the painter in delineating even a Venus or a Helen' (10).[2] To oppose accuracy to beauty, or clear thinking to fine feeling, is to generate false dichotomies. Secondly, accuracy has practical value. The researches of an abstract thinker may have positive effects, by developing the politician's foresight, the lawyer's discernment, the general's system in controlling his troops or directing his operations. Similarly, the stability of government and the accuracy of philosophy have developed in tandem; in all probability, they will continue to do so.

There is, however, a problem with abstract philosophy that cannot be ignored: it generates error. The mind, overstretched, produces pseudo-science; and, even worse, the obscurity of such philosophy makes it a haven for superstition. The unwary, who would readily recognize nonsense if it were presented in plain words, are taken in by it when it is decked out in obscure jargon. In this way abstract philosophy protects all sorts of rubbish: 'The stoutest antagonist, if he remit his watch a moment, is oppressed. And

---

[2] Hume's attraction for this analogy is shown by his use of it in the *Treatise*, 620–1, and also in the letter to Francis Hutcheson, prior to the publication of *Treatise* Book III, replying to Hutcheson's complaint that it lacked 'a certain warmth in the cause of virtue' (*Letters*, ed. Greig, i. 34).

many, through cowardice or stupidity, open the gates to the enemies, and willingly receive them with reverence and submission, as their legal sovereigns' (11). Obscure philosophy protects oppressive politics and religion.

Hume accepts the relevance of the objection—indeed, it is an aim of the *Enquiry* to show it to be so—but denies that the cure lies in abandoning abstract philosophy itself. He repeats the Lockean dictum that the only way to overcome the shortcomings of abstract philosophies is through a careful examination of the capacities of the human mind. This enquiry, carefully conducted, will reveal what lies beyond human capacity, and thereby reveal the philosophies that are 'false and adulterate'. Although demanding, the task will be worth it, for only in this way will false philosophy be overcome: 'Accurate and just reasoning is the only catholic remedy, fitted for all persons and dispositions; and is alone able to subvert that abstruse philosophy and metaphysical jargon, which, being mixed up with popular superstition, renders it in a manner impenetrable to careless reasoners, and gives it the air of science and wisdom' (12–13).

Moreover, Hume adds, there is an intrinsic value in accurate philosophy when its object is human nature, or the workings of the human mind. The human mind, because it is so intimate to us, is all the more difficult to examine, and so it is a real achievement, and a real satisfaction, to be able to produce a 'mental geography', a 'delineation of the distinct parts and powers of the mind'. Nor can its possibility be dismissed, short of an extravagant scepticism: it is plain that the mind has distinct powers and faculties, and so this kind of enquiry does not drag us 'beyond the compass of human understanding'. We are all able to distinguish between the will and the understanding, for example, and a more accurate account of mental parts and functions is similarly within human competence.

In fact, recent progress in just such enquiries encourages the hope that it may be possible to go beyond mental geography, 'and discover, at least in some degree, the secret springs and principles, by which the human mind is actuated in its operations' (14). Astronomers used to rest content with identifying the movements, order, and sizes of the heavenly bodies; but Newton has discovered the laws and forces that govern the movements of the planets. It is probable that the mind works along the same lines as the rest of nature, in the sense that its surface variety can be resolved into general principles, so, if such enquiries are 'prosecuted with equal capacity and caution', there is reason to hope for real progress. The example of successes already enjoyed in this endeavour—by moralists, and, to a lesser degree, critics, logicians, and political thinkers—shows that to abandon the attempt in advance would be indefensibly hasty and dogmatic.

Nevertheless, Hume concludes, the attempt has previously proved difficult, and should not now be thought easy. If the difficulties can be overcome, and breakthroughs achieved, the satisfactions will be all the greater. But difficulty itself is no recommendation. So we should seek to avoid unnecessary difficulties, by means of an accessible style, while aiming for outcomes of real significance:

> Happy, if we can unite the boundaries of the different species of philosophy, by reconciling profound enquiry with clearness, and truth with novelty! And still more happy, if, reasoning in this easy manner, we can undermine the foundations of an abstruse philosophy, which seems to have hitherto served only as a shelter to superstition, and a cover to absurdity and error! (16)

This is the message of the opening section. It is not an exercise in the 'easy' philosophy that appeals primarily to the feelings, nor does it embrace the common conclusion of such philosophy against serious pursuit of intellectual goals: to 'be a philosopher; but . . . be still a man'. It aims, rather, to take from this easy philosophy its accessible style, and to combine that style with a serious and, indeed, difficult enquiry into the workings of the human mind—especially as it concerns moral subjects—to arrive at a damaging critique of an established philosophy, and of its unfortunate public effects. The *Enquiry* signals, from the beginning, that it is at times hard going; but that the difficulty is never more than the subject matter requires (it is never wilfully obscure); and that the purpose of the work is philosophically serious and practically significant. It is not mere essaying, but a sustained argument to an important conclusion.

This conclusion has been reached solely on the evidence of the text itself. Attention to the personal and ideological circumstances of the work—some of which have been sketched above in Part One Chapter 2—only serves to reinforce the essential point. In fact, it suggests that, if the conclusion errs, it errs by excessive charity towards the 'easy' philosophy. The ruling idea of the 'easy' philosophy, that philosophy should concern itself less with technical systems or arguments, and more with the rhetorical praise of virtue, stems from the sixteenth-century humanist critique of scholastic learning. It reflects the humanist conviction that the intellectual tradition of the medieval period was barren, and that this barrenness stemmed from rendering wisdom (*sapientia*) subservient to—dependent on—systematic philosophy (*scientia*).[3] The way forward, therefore, was to break this link, to free up moral thought and reflection from the constraints imposed by the Schools, by cultivating a more direct praise of virtue: to *paint* virtue in all her true *beauty*.

The 'painterly' philosophers were those who displayed more of the virtues of the poet, and who did so by giving the poet's ruling faculty—the imagination—free rein. To defenders of the intellectual virtues—if not necessarily the doctrines—of the tradition of the Schools, this project, and its products, were, whatever their popularity, ultimately a false trail. Thus Nicolas Malebranche, in his great doorstopper, *The Search after Truth*, devotes several chapters to the obvious attractions but hidden flaws of a representative sample of such writers and writings. The natural interpretation is that his specific targets—Tertullian, Seneca, and Montaigne—are chosen precisely because of their widespread popularity in later seventeenth-century France. They are also chosen in order to illustrate the strength of the imagination, and the mistake of relying upon it.[4] The latter point, in particular, is one to which we will return in the following sections.

To turn to the English literary scene in the eighteenth century. The great champion of the 'easy' philosophy, and accordingly in the best-seller lists, was the third Earl of Shaftesbury. Shaftesbury attacked the narrowness and coldness of school learning, attributing it, in part, to the cloistered lives of its practitioners. His effect, not merely on the reading public, but on the professional intellectuals, was considerable, and found several significant supporters in the Scottish universities of Hume's day: not least, Francis Hutcheson. So, when Hutcheson criticized Hume for showing, in the *Treatise*, insufficient warmth in the cause of virtue, he was invoking the well-established stance of Shaftesburian humanism. Hume's reply shows him to belong to the opposing camp. His distinction between the anatomist and the painter, and his defence of the independent value—and even foundational role—of the anatomist is a defence of 'abstruse' or 'accurate' philosophy. The point is underlined by the well-known fact that it was the favourable opinion of Joseph Butler, above all, that Hume had sought on the publication of the *Treatise*: and Butler was an

[3] Cf. Menn, *Descartes and Augustine*, 20–1.
[4] Malebranche, *The Search after Truth*, 173–90.

explicit defender of the importance of 'accurate' or 'metaphysical' reasonings.

The *Enquiry*'s ambition to unite the virtues of the two species of philosophy is, up to a point, a softening of the line in the *Treatise*. But only up to a point. Any thought that the painterly style can *replace* metaphysics is very firmly rejected. It is only the agreeable, engaging style of the 'easy' philosophy that is to be accepted, by being married to the accurate reasonings on which the *Enquiry* will rely. Hume sticks to his guns, if in as reconciling a manner as he can muster. It is unlikely to be mere coincidence that the Scottish advocates of painterly or poetic warmth—Hutcheson and his associates—had played a significant role in blocking his appointment to the Edinburgh Chair. His adherence to abstruse philosophy, modified only in its style, is the continuation of his resistance to a prevailing view—the view of a prevailing faction that had blocked his academic career. Moreover, the promised result of the investigation—the refutation of a competing abstruse philosophy, 'a shelter to superstition and a cover to absurdity and error' (16)—will apply not only to the obvious target of Catholicism, but also to the Christian Stoicism of Hutcheson and his allies. It is difficult to resist the thought that the outcome was one in which Hume found some private satisfaction.[5]

It would be unduly limiting, however, to place Hume's marriage of 'easy' style with 'abstruse' philosophy too firmly within a Scottish context; or, indeed, to think of him as alone pursuing this goal. In fact, the attempt to make philosophy relevant by breaking it free of the bonds of scholastic terminology was part and parcel of the Enlightenment's attack on the scholastic heritage. Thus Diderot had proclaimed: 'Let us hasten to make philosophy popular. If we want the philosophers to march on before, let us approach the people at the point where the philosophers are.'[6] Hume's remarks in the early essay 'Of Essay Writing' have a similar flavour: if philosophy is to improve the people, then it must be rescued from the barbaric style and doctrines that make it so unattractive to the people.[7] It should hardly need emphasizing that this is a position that the advocates of a philosophical revolution must take: the new philosophy's message, if it is to be communicated

[5] In these several paragraphs I have drawn heavily on M. A. Stewart, 'Two Species of Philosophy: The Historical Significance of the First *Enquiry*', in P. J. R. Millican (ed.), *Reading Hume on Human Understanding: Essays on the First* Enquiry (Oxford: Oxford University Press, 2000).

[6] Denis Diderot, *De l'interprétation de la Nature*, sect. xi, quoted by E. Cassirer, *The Philosophy of the Enlightenment*, trans. F. C. A. Koelln and J. P. Pettegrove (Princeton: Princeton University Press, 1979), 268.

[7] 'Of Essay Writing', in *Essays*, 534–5.

to the people, must speak in an idiom they can readily comprehend. Hume's marriage of 'easy' and 'abstruse' philosophy is an essential part of his ambition to teach a new philosophy with civilizing consequences.[8]

[8] Donald Livingston has emphasized the importance, in Hume's thought, of the contrast between 'true' philosophy and civilization, on the one hand, and 'false' philosophy and barbarism, on the other—and on the consequent necessity of true philosophy making itself 'popular' ('easy'). See his 'Hume on the Natural History of Philosophical Consciousness', in P. Jones (ed.), *The 'Science of Man' in the Scottish Enlightenment* (Edinburgh: Edinburgh University Press, 1989), 68–84; and *Philosophical Melancholy and Delirium: Hume's Pathology of Philosophy* (Chicago: University of Chicago Press, 1998).

Section II

Of the Origin of Ideas

Hume begins with a distinction that 'every one will readily allow': that there is a difference of intensity between feelings and sensations on the one hand, and the deliverances of memory and imagination on the other. The latter may 'mimic or copy' the former, but, unless we are 'disordered by disease or madness', they never reach 'such a pitch of vivacity' to rival them. In all non-extreme cases, he concludes, 'the most lively thought is still inferior to the dullest sensation' (17). The former, original, perception he denominates *impressions*, the latter, copies, are *ideas*. In drawing this distinction, Hume's aim seems to be to identify the mental standard by which we distinguish thoughts from sensations. However, it is not infrequently held that his reason for doing so is to call into doubt our grounds for belief in an external world. The point is that, while we take our thoughts to be wholly mental events, whereas we take our sensations to be *of* external objects, our means of distinguishing the two is wholly in terms of the vividness of our different perceptions, and vividness *per se* justifies no external reference. Therefore we have no reason to suppose that our sensations are of external objects after all: phenomenalism stands at the door.

It is true that Hume is aware of this possibility, and in Section XII will address it directly. However, there are several reasons for thinking that, in making the distinction in this way, his *purpose* is not to raise the spectre of phenomenalism (or solipsism, or any other radical scepticism). In the first place, the distinction is introduced as if uncontroversial; as if the reality of the external world is not immediately at issue. In fact, the passage unfolds in a manner that supposes some sort of commonsensical realism. Thus the distinction between thoughts and sensations comes first: the degrees of vivacity is then offered as a way of marking the difference. Its role is not to undermine the significance normally attached to the distinction; if anything, it aims to build on that normal significance. It is introduced to prepare the way, first, for

the general claim that ideas are copies of impressions, and, secondly, for the principle that the meaningfulness of an idea can
be tested by hunting down the originating impression. The distinction is, therefore, introduced for a critical purpose. This means
that the 'copy principle', which serves that purpose, must be
understood accordingly—and this implies a realist picture in the
background.

Hume has already indicated, in Section I, that his critical
purpose is to demolish a philosophy that has been a shelter for
superstition. In order to do so, the work will aim to produce a
science that is not 'uncertain and chimerical' (13). It is not impossible that that science will turn out to be some kind of extreme
scepticism, of course—but it would then be very hard indeed to
see what the *point* of the *Enquiry*'s critique could be. If a radical
scepticism is the only defensible view, then not only would the
shelter for superstition be false: so would almost every other cher-
ished belief. To single one philosophy out for criticism would then
be wholly arbitrary. Hume's critical aims, announced at both the
beginning and the end of the work, would be hopelessly undermined unless extreme doubts concerning, in particular, the reality
of the external world can be contained. So the possibility of being
caught in a phenomenalist web is not the point of the distinction
between impressions and ideas.

A second reason for thinking this is to recognize that Hume's
distinction is only partly an innovation, and that its innovative
aspect seems to contain a realist, but sceptically realist, moral. The
distinction itself is, of course, meant, in part, to avoid the ambiguities and uncertainties that arise from Locke's very broad definition of 'Idea': 'whatsoever is the Object of the Understanding
when a Man thinks.'[1] But the precise nature of Hume's account
can be explained as a modest modification of Locke's remarks on
the clarity or obscurity of our ideas:

The Perception of the Mind, being most aptly explained by Words relating to
the Sight, we shall best understand what is meant by *Clear*, and *Obscure* in
our *Ideas*, by reflecting on what we call *Clear* and *Obscure* in the Objects of
Sight. Light being that which discovers to us visible Objects, we give the name
of *Obscure*, to that, which is not placed in a Light sufficient to discover
minutely to us the Figure and Colours, which are observable in it, and which,
in a better light, would be discernable. In like manner, our *simple Ideas* are
clear, when they are such as the Objects themselves, from whence they were
taken, did or might, in a well-ordered Sensation or Perception, present them.
Whilst the Memory retains them thus, and can produce them to the Mind,

[1] Locke, *Essay*, I. i. 8.

when-ever it has occasion to consider them, they are *clear Ideas*. So long as they either want any thing of that original Exactness, or have lost any of their first Freshness, and are, as it were, faded or tarnished by Time, so far are they obscure. *Complex Ideas*, as they are made up of Simple ones; so they are *clear*, when the *Ideas* that go to their Composition, are clear . . .[2]

This particular passage is notable, first, as a possible source of Hume's distinction: the products of the memory, says Locke, are often faded or tarnished by time. Hume relies on this claim in order to make his own point: we identify memories and comparable mental phenomena by the fact that they *are* faded or tarnished by time. He thus implies that our human capacities are inherently flawed; that the human mind necessarily fails to preserve its objects truly; that we are, as Locke puts it, 'like Wax of a temper too soft, which will not hold [its impressions] well, when well imprinted'.[3]

That this is indeed Hume's point is supported by the second notable feature of Locke's passage: that the differing degrees of vividness correspond to the relative clarity or obscurity of our ideas. Hume dispenses with Locke's (Stoic and Cartesian) language of clarity and obscurity—and with its baggage—but his point has a similar *practical* purpose. The fainter the copy, the more obscure, the less reliable, the idea. It is for this reason that we must refer our fainter ideas to originating vivid impressions. If we cannot do so, we cannot show our thoughts to be *adequate* to the world to which they refer,[4] so Hume's requirement that ideas be traced to impressions is pointless unless it is implicitly realist. However, his claim that all ideas are fainter copies of impressions is the sceptical claim that all our ideas *fail* adequately to represent the world to which they refer. Hume's 'copy principle' is sceptical realism.

This conclusion has been reached rather suddenly. So it will be useful to indicate other ways in which Hume can be seen to be hinting at a philosophy that is realist, but sceptically so. First, Hume's implicit realism is confirmed by his terminology itself: thoughts or ideas are distinguished from *impressions*. The new term is needed, because there is no single term to denote the two kinds of experience from which thoughts flow: (external) sensations and (internal) feelings. The term itself, however, is not new. Hume's immediate source was probably Locke himself, but it has a long philosophical history, with antecedents stretching back to Aristotle. Locke's official position, as already noted, is that all objects of

---

[2] Ibid. II. xxix. 2.   [3] Ibid. II. xxix. 3.
[4] See Locke's treatment of the adequacy of our ideas (ibid. II. xxxi).

the mind are to be called 'ideas'—but he does not always keep to his own script. He refers to sensations as 'impressions', or as 'impressed' or 'imprinted', and even as 'stamped'. Thus the thesis of innate principles is described as the view 'that Men have native *Ideas*, and original Characters *stamped* upon their Minds, in their very first Being'.[5] The progress of children's ideas begins with ideas of physical objects, because 'all that are born into the World being surrounded with Bodies, that perpetually and diversly affect them, variety of *Ideas*, whether care be taken about it or no, are *imprinted* on the Minds of Children'.[6] In contrast, they arrive at ideas of their own mental operations only later, because, 'though they pass here continually; yet like floating Visions, they make not deep *Impressions* enough, to leave in the Mind clear distinct lasting *Ideas*, till the Understanding . . . makes them the Object of its own Contemplation'.[7]

This way of describing perceptions derives originally from Aristotle, who had explained perception as analogous to the making of impressions in wax.[8] Locke exploits just this analogy in the passage quoted above: that ideas become obscure because our memory is like wax that is too soft.[9] In both Aristotle and in Locke, it has the plain sense of external objects pressing on the body's sense organs. In some cases, Locke makes this quite explicit ('the impression of outward Objects on the Senses').[10] Furthermore, impressions made on the bodily senses cannot give rise to ideas unless those impressions are communicated to the brain, 'the mind's Presence-room'.[11] So, if the realist picture is of a world of mechanical processes, impressions must be (or become) motions. This is just what Locke says: '*Sensation* . . . is . . . an *Impression or Motion*, made in some part of the Body, as produces some perception in the Understanding.'[12] The terminology of perceptions as impressions is realist terminology; and is so, for Locke, because it is part and parcel of a mechanical picture of the world.

He is not alone. In fact, in the new natural philosophy, the term 'impression' carried a precise meaning. Newton defines an *impressed force*, as '*an action exerted upon a body, in order to change its state, either of rest, or of uniform motion in a right line*. This force consists in the action only, and remains no longer in the body when the action is over.' It does not remain in the body because

---

[5] Locke, *Essay*, II. i. 1 (second emphasis added).
[6] Ibid. II. i. 6 (second emphasis added).
[7] Ibid. II. i. 8 (first emphasis added).
[8] *On the Soul*, II, xii, in *A New Aristotle Reader*, ed. Ackvill, 186.
[9] *Essay*, II. xxix. 3.   [10] Ibid. II. xxi. 1; cf. II. i. 23.   [11] Ibid. II. iii. 1.
[12] Ibid. II. i. 23 (second emphasis added).

it arises from origins external to the body, including, among other things, 'percussion' and 'pressure'.[13] A very similar picture can be found in Hobbes's *De Corpore*, where 'pressing' is defined as the operation of one body (its 'endeavour') to make another body 'go out of its place'. Hobbes goes on to describe the effects of pressing in the following terms:

a body which is pressed and not wholly removed is said to RESTORE *itself, when, the pressing body being taken away, the parts which were moved do, by reason of the internal constitution of the pressed body, return every one into its own place.* And this we may observe in springs, in blown bladders, and in many other bodies, whose parts yield more or less to the endeavour which the pressing body makes at the first arrival; but afterwards, when the pressing body is removed, they do, by some force within them, *restore* themselves, and give their whole body the same figure it had before.[14]

Pressing, then, causes a deformation of some kind in an object, but objects with the appropriate internal constitution recover their shape when the pressing ceases. This is the situation Newton describes as remaining in the body only as long as the external force is applied.

The sense organs can be understood as structures that have the internal constitution necessary to respond to pressing in this way. Sensations can be understood as impressed forces. A perception lasts as long as the relevant force (the perceptual stimulus) is applied, and is replaced by a new perception once a new force is applied. The rapid succession of a series of perceptions thus provides, in the case of sight, a moving image; or, in the case of sounds, music or speech. These perceptions are possible only because one sight or sound is rapidly replaced by another, resulting in a sequence, or a succession of distinct perceptions. The senses are not perfect, however, and their limits are discernible by this means. Thus, in the case of sound, too intense a noise produces ringing in the ears; in the case of sight, too rapid a succession produces a blur; and too slow a succession produces fading of colour, and, subsequently, an after-image. These phenomena do not undermine the general picture of physical pressing; in fact, they support it, by indicating the limits of the sense organs' capacity to restore themselves. Physical bodies are finite, and phenomena like after-images help to show as much.

Hume's adoption of the term 'impression' is thus strong, if circumstantial, support for his accepting a background picture that

[13] Newton, *Principia*, Definition IV, 2.
[14] Thomas Hobbes, *De Corpore* III. 2, in *Metaphysical Writings*, ed. M. W. Calkins (La Salle, Ill.: Open Court, 1989), 100.

is not only realist, but mechanical. His further description of ideas as copies of impressions is also readily conformable to this picture. Copies *resemble*, of course; and that is his main point. He says that 'when we reflect on our past sentiments and affections, our thought is a faithful mirror, and copies its objects truly' (17–18). But the evidence for this claim cannot be compelling. In certain cases we can check our idea against an impression that is reasonably taken to be phenomenally identical to the impression that gave rise to the idea. In many cases, however, such checking reveals error: we discover that memory has deceived us. And, in a wide range of other cases, checking simply is not possible. In such cases, all we can check our memory against is that memory itself. So Hume's sanguine view that ideas are faithful, if fainter, copies of impressions is rather surprising, and not obviously comfortable with his penchant for sceptical conclusions. The explanation, I suggest, is precisely the background influence of the mechanical picture, with its emphasis on stamping and impressing.

The picture of perception being presented is this: external objects or other forces press on our sense organs, and set up internal motions within the perceiver. The impression perceived by the mind depends on these motions being communicated to the brain, whereupon it is received by the mind. The impression is transferred by the transference of motion. Original motions produce other motions of the same kind, motions that are therefore faithful copies of the original but for a steady decrease in energy, and thus in perceived vivacity—like the steady diminution of the ripples from a stone dropped in a pond. Similarly, a stamp forcibly impressed on a layer of paper will leave a deep imprint or impression on the top sheet, but increasingly fainter marks on the lower sheets. Violent motions will cause initially violent motions, whereas gentle motions will cause only gentle motions; but all communications of motion involve some net loss of motion, and so the copies, although faithful reproductions, necessarily lose vivacity. It is this background picture that explains both Hume's terminology—impressing and copying—and also his uncharacteristic confidence in the basic accuracy of a mere bodily process.[15]

[15] The origins of the passions—the impressions of reflection—is not explained by this account. The vivacity of a given passion will, presumably, reflect the vivacity of the corresponding idea (and of its relation to the self—see *Treatise*, 277), but, although we can observe the factors that make for the most violent of passions, these do not seem readily reducible to initially violent motions that then decay. Rather, since passions arise from reflection, and therefore from ideas, it looks as if violent motions might have to be attributed to weaker ones. See *Treatise*, 421–2, for an account of the causes of violent passions.

A basically accurate process would seem to be at odds with scepticism, but this is not so. In the first place, the accuracy is limited, preserving the basic relations but not the vividness itself, and in any case doing so only as long as the preserved image remains distinct. Secondly, the accuracy in question is merely physical, not intellectual. This is indicated again by the terminology: ideas, like impressions, are more or less *vivid*, a quality that Descartes had identified as revealing a sensory, and thus bodily, provenance.[16] The relative vivacity of an idea is not a marker of truthfulness or of any intellectual significance. But scepticism is the denial of *knowledge*, and, for Hume's contemporaries no less than for the ancients, knowledge is an intellectual act: the intellectual *grasping* of the essence, or the intelligible form, of the thing. On Aristotle's account, this grasping is performed by the active intellectual part of the soul, active *noûs*.[17] In contrast, Hume's account of ideas as copies of impressions leaves active intellectual grasping entirely out of the picture. For an idea to arise through a copying process is for it to arise through a mechanical process in which the mind plays no active role. If this is the whole of Hume's story, then, it is indeed sceptical, because it implicitly denies that the human mind exercises any active grip on its own contents.[18] My own view is that this is not the whole of Hume's story, because, like Locke in Book II of the *Essay*, his concern at this point is not with knowledge, but merely with mental contents. Nevertheless, by limiting the contents of the mind to what impressions deliver, he is, like Locke, ruling out the possession of ideas that are free of the imperfections of bodily processes. He thus rules out the possession of any idea that can function as a *criterion* of truth, and thereby denies the possibility of certain knowledge. Experience is all; but experience is not wisdom or knowledge. This sceptical tendency is already present in Locke. Hume sharpens its edge by the prominent place he accords to the principles of association.

[16] Descartes, Sixth Meditation, in *Philosophical Writings*, ii. 52.
[17] Aristotle, *On the Soul*, III. iv, in *A New Aristotle Reader*, ed. Ackrill, 195.
[18] Cf. Zeno's simile of the hand: 'Zeno used to clinch the wise man's sole possession of knowledge with a gesture. He would spread out the fingers of one hand and display its open palm, saying "An impression is like this." Next he clenched his fingers a little and said "Assent is like this." Then, pressing his fingers quite together, he made a fist, and said that this was cognition (and from this illustration he gave that mental state the name of *katalepsis*, which it had not had before). Then he brought his left hand against his right fist and gripped it tightly and forcefully, and said that scientific knowledge [*scientia*] was like this and possessed by none except the wise man' (Cicero, *Academica*, in Long and Sedley (eds.), *Hellenistic Philosophers*, i. 253–4). Hume offers nothing remotely resembling this story, and so it should be presumed that his impressions are mere impressed forces, not the cognitive impressions of the Stoic. This presumption will be shown correct in the argument of Section IV Part I.

(The sceptical implications of those principles will be shown in Section III.)[19]

The general view outlined here owes much to John P. Wright, who has offered a detailed defence of Hume as a sceptical realist in *The Sceptical Realism of David Hume*.[20] The account here has placed more emphasis on the Lockean connections, thereby indicating the affinity of Hume's basic terms and distinctions with a philosophy that is avowedly realist and mechanical. However, where possible, Locke, like Hume, avoids physical speculations,[21] so it might be objected that the dependencies and similarities pointed out are merely superficial—simply a shared technical language—and do not indicate an implicitly mechanical outlook. This seems to me unconvincing; but I have brought Wright into the picture at this point because the further evidence he provides shows the objection to be wholly implausible.

Wright accepts that the way to read Hume is to take him at his word: to read the 'metaphysical Parts' of the *Treatise* against the background of Malebranche's *Search after Truth*, as he had himself suggested to his friend Michael Ramsay.[22] One of the many tasks Malebranche takes on in that massive work is to trace the contents of the mind to the physical motions that occasion them, and Wright shows the extent to which Hume's method and terminology reveals broad agreement with the Frenchman's project. In fact, in the *Treatise* he says as much. In the closing pages of his discussion of the immateriality of the soul, he responds to a possible objection in these terms:

you reason too hastily, when from the mere consideration of the ideas, you conclude that 'tis impossible motion can ever produce thought, or a different position of parts give rise to a different passion or reflexion. Nay 'tis not only possible we may have such an experience, but 'tis certain we have it; since everyone may perceive, that the different dispositions of his body change his thoughts and sentiments. And shou'd it be said, that this depends on the union of soul and body; I wou'd answer, that we must separate the question concerning the substance of the mind from that concerning the cause of its thought; and that confining ourselves to the latter question we find by the comparing their ideas, that thought and motion are different from

---

[19] See also S. Buckle, 'British Sceptical Realism: A Fresh Look at the British Tradition', *European Journal of Philosophy*, 7 (1999), 1–29.

[20] Wright, *The Sceptical Realism of David Hume*, ch. 5, esp. 209–21.

[21] Locke, *Essay*, I. i. 2: 'I shall not at present meddle with the Physical Consideration of the Mind . . . These are Speculations, which, however curious and entertaining, I shall decline, as lying out of my Way, in the Design I am now upon.'

[22] Of the metaphysical arguments, Hume says: 'to make you enter into them more easily, I desire of you, if you have Leizure, to read once over La Recherche de la Verité of Pere Malebranche . . .' (quoted by R. H. Popkin, 'So, Hume did Read Berkeley', in *The High Road to Pyrrhonism*, 291).

each other, and by experience, that they are constantly united; which being all the circumstances, that enter into the idea of cause and effect, when apply'd to the operations of matter, we may certainly conclude, that motion may be, and actually is, the cause of thought and perception.[23]

The point could not be more clearly made. Motions in the body (caused by motions in the world) cause thought in the mind. Hume's view is premised on a broadly mechanical account of the world. At no point does he claim it to be certainly true; but he does accept it as the best working model of the nature of the world and of ourselves, in so far as we are material beings.[24] This is just what we should expect of someone who claims to be *applying* the experimental philosophy to moral subjects, and therefore to the operations of the mind. His terminological starting points reveal it: in the mechanical world, ideas are copies of impressions produced by impressed forces.

The second task Hume sets himself in this section—to limit the mind's power to create new ideas to the *compounding* of the simple raw materials into new and diverse forms—also conforms to this picture. He observes that the mind's powers *seem* unbounded, because it can 'transport us into the most distant regions of the universe . . . What never was seen, or heard of, may yet be conceived' (18). But this appearance of unboundedness is illusory. In the first place, we cannot conceive anything that 'implies an absolute contradiction'. Neither is the vast scope of our thoughts, when more closely examined, anything more than the power 'of compounding, transposing, augmenting, or diminishing the materials afforded us by the senses or experience' (19). Thus Hume follows Locke in limiting the sources of even our most sublime ideas to original *impressions*, whether of sensation or reflection. He is, like Locke, therefore also guilty of Leibniz's charge of lowering 'not only the condition of man but also that of the universe'.[25]

Hume offers two arguments in support of his claim. The first is that all ideas, 'however compounded or sublime', can be analysed into 'such simple ideas as were copied from a precedent feeling or sentiment'. The appearance at this point of the Lockean terminology of simple ideas—even if adapted to a Humean classificatory scheme—prepares us for an example lifted straight from Locke: 'The idea of God, as meaning an infinitely intelligent, wise,

---

[23] *Treatise*, 247–8.
[24] Moreover, the more adequate the explanations thereby provided, the more reason for thinking that we might be *wholly* material beings—a possibility Locke had raised himself (*Essay*, IV. iii. 6).
[25] Leibniz, *New Essays*, 73.

and good Being, arises from reflecting on the operations of our own mind, and augmenting, without limit, those qualities of goodness and wisdom' (19).[26] The striking thing about this claim is that it is introduced as if it is very largely uncontroversial. The Lockean provenance could hardly have been missed by the eighteenth-century reader; and no attempt is made to argue against Cartesian views to the contrary. The conclusion therefore seems irresistible: Hume is presenting himself as a follower of Locke and kindred philosophers, and understands himself to be preaching to the converted. The contrary views of the philosophical rationalists are not to be seriously considered.

   Much the same impression is given by Hume's second reason for tracing all ideas to impressions. It too is put very succinctly. He claims that the dependence of ideas on impressions can be shown by the fact that, where there are defects in the relevant sense organ, there are also defects in, or absences of, 'the correspondent ideas': 'A blind man can form no notion of colours; a deaf man of sounds' (20). Even the discovery of a counter-example causes no serious rethinking. The case of the missing shade of blue—also discussed in the *Treatise*[27]—is treated as no more than the exception that proves the rule. The example is of a person who has never experienced a certain shade of blue, and who is then provided with a colour chart in which all the shades of blue, other than the one he has not seen, are 'placed before him, descending gradually from the deepest to the lightest'. In such a case, will the person be able to call up the missing idea? Hume concludes in the affirmative, and thereby shows his own account not to be exception free. However, his confidence in his account is quite unshaken: 'this instance is so singular, that it is scarcely worth our observing, and does not merit that for it alone we should alter our general maxim' (21).

   Hume's confidence at this point suggests that there is more here than meets the eye, for the counter-example *could* be taken to be an instance of a more common case, at least wherever experiences of a similar kind are presented in a uniform pattern of variation. Admittedly, such occurrences would not be the kinds of innate ideas or principles that the modern rationalists typically sought in order securely to ground human intellectual capacities. Nevertheless, why should Hume be so untroubled? I suggest it is because the example in fact serves a positive role in Hume's account: it provides him with a first, and striking, instance of the mind generating new

---

[26] Cf. Locke, *Essay*, II. xxiii. 15, 18–21, 31–6.   [27] *Treatise*, 5–6.

ideas through *habituation*—in this case, through becoming accustomed to a series of *resembling* impressions. So, while the example does undercut the 'no ideas without a precedent impression' story, for Hume there are more benefits than costs in the case. The 'one contradictory phenomenon' illustrates the fundamental significance of the principle of custom or habit in human life.

Hume does not pursue the point, for he has other fish to fry. He emphasizes the *general* reliability of the account of the origins of ideas in more vivid impressions in order to reaffirm his critical purpose. The account of the origins of ideas, he concludes, provides us with a standard for assessing metaphysical reasonings.

all impressions . . . either outward or inward, are strong and vivid: the limits between them are more exactly determined: nor is it easy to fall into error or mistake with regard to them. When we entertain, therefore, any suspicion that a philosophical term is employed without any meaning or idea (as is but too frequent), we need but enquire, *from what impression is that supposed idea derived?* And if it be impossible to assign any, this will serve to confirm our suspicion. By bringing ideas into so clear a light we may reasonably hope to remove all dispute, which may arise, concerning their nature and reality. (22)

The natural interpretation of these remarks is of a piece with his critical remarks in Section I. The standard targets of unclarity in thought, and of concepts that had lost all grip on reality, were the schoolmen; the typically assigned cause of the disease was their blind adherence to authority, rather than referring their claims to the test of reality.[28] Hume signals a familar style of attack on a familiar target—even if, in the end, there will be unexpected levels of collateral damage. The enterprise is not to advance an extreme scepticism, but it is to employ some form of sceptical thought to sort philosophical views about the world into the wheat and the chaff.

Needless to say, the conclusion has been reached remarkably swiftly, and potential problems with the enterprise are passed over. But what is particularly striking about the project thus introduced is that almost no role has been allocated to reason. The standard against which ideas are to be measured, although a product of (experimental) reasoning about the source of the mind's contents,

[28] Thus, for example, Hobbes: 'if it be a false affirmation to say *a quadrangle is round*, the word *round quadrangle* signifies nothing; but is a meere sound. So likewise if it be false, to say that vertue can be powred, or blown up and down; the words *In-powred vertue, In-blown vertue*, are as absurd and insignificant, as a *round quadrangle* . . . words are wise mens counters, they do but reckon by them: but they are the mony of fooles, that value them by the authority of an *Aristotle*, a *Cicero*, or a *Thomas*, or any other Doctor whatsoever, if but a man' (*Leviathan*, ch. IV, 30, 28–9).

is not itself a rational standard, but the mere matching of pale and vivid perceptions. Pure reason is acknowledged only implicitly, in the concession that we cannot imagine what implies a contradiction. But beyond this, reason is left aside. Hume presents a picture in which the primary processes of the mind consist in the origin of ideas from impressions, and their multiplication by mere agglomeration. Reason is implicitly denied the dominant role in human mental life.

This is why Hume is so relaxed about questions of innateness, as the footnote that concludes this section shows. He can cheerfully suggest that impressions are innate, because on his model nothing hangs on the issue. He reduces the question of innateness merely to the task of identifying the first link in a causal chain: it is 'what is original or copied from no precedent impression'. This is what innateness reduces to on a mechanical account of the mind; and, thus shorn of any claims to immutable truth, it is indeed deserving of no more than a footnote. This is also why Hume can say of Locke, in the same place, that he 'was betrayed into this question by the schoolmen, who, making use of undefined terms, draw out their disputes to a tedious length, without ever touching the point in question' (22 n.). Locke attacked innateness because he wished to deny that we possess any infallible truths independently of experience;[29] Hume, in contrast, allows innateness—but his implicitly mechanical story denies the connection presumed to hold between innateness and truth.

To deny that the human mind is governed by reason—in particular, to deny reason's power to direct the mind by knowledge of the nature of things—is to affirm a form of scepticism. Hume has not yet gone so far, but the hints contained in this first section are sufficent to alert the attentive reader that a sceptical philosophy is in the offing. In the next section, any doubts about the matter will be removed, for there Hume will propose a principle by which our thoughts are unified: a principle of a non-rational—indeed mechanical—kind.

---

[29] This is why Locke connects belief in innate ideas with mental laziness and dogmatism (*Essay*, I. ii–iv *passim*), and also why he is uninterested in innate *dispositions*. Innate human capacities *per se* are not his concern.

Section III

Of the Association of Ideas

'It is evident that there is a principle of connexion between the different thoughts or ideas of the mind, and that, in their appearance to the memory or imagination, they introduce each other with a certain degree of method and regularity' (21). Hume opens the section with a claim he treats as unproblematic. He simply offers a few supporting reminders: at one extreme, errant thoughts are immediately ejected when they intrude into disciplined thinking; at the other, even in the 'wildest and most wandering reveries', a closer scrutiny will reveal that 'the imagination ran not altogether at adventures', but that principles of connection were in play. No philosopher has yet sought to classify these principles of association, so Hume volunteers to fill the gap: there are three, and they are resemblance, contiguity, and cause and effect. Nothing much is said of these principles here: their importance lies in the work they will be made to do in later sections. Nor does he attempt to prove that there are no more than these three. However, he is sufficiently confident that the list is complete to invite the reader, after examples of each kind have been provided, to try to think of others that do not reduce to his trio.

One striking feature of this section is its brevity. This is most pronounced in the standard (1777) edition. For that edition, Hume removed the further illustrations of the principles, which were mainly literary in character.[1] Why is the section so short? Terence Penelhum proposes one explanation: 'This progressive abridgment of Hume's account is a clear sign that he came to lose interest in the details of his Newtonian psychology, even though he has singled it out for special commendation in the *Abstract*.'[2] This may be so, but it is not the only possible answer. It seems no less likely

---

[1] The standard Selby-Bigge–Nidditch edition is based on the 1777 edition. Much of the literary material is reincluded in T. Penelhum, *David Hume: An Introduction to his Philosophical System* (West Lafayette, Ind.: Purdue University Press, 1992), 44–5. It has also been reincluded in the new Oxford student edition of *An Enquiry concerning Human Understanding*, ed. T. L. Beauchamp (Oxford: Oxford University Press, 1999), which is based on the 1772 edition.
[2] Penelhum, *David Hume*, 57.

that Hume did not want to distract attention from the main point of the psychology, to provide an account of basic mental functioning in line with mechanical principles, and, in particular, of its implications. This view would be confirmed if Hume thought, by the 1770s, that associationism had become rather old hat to his readers, such that space devoted to its exposition and defence was a waste. The reason for thinking this likely is that David Hartley's *Observations on Man*, a major work on human nature erected on the foundation of associationism, was published in 1749, the year after the *Enquiry* first appeared. It seems reasonable to suppose, then, that what may have been fresh and original in 1748 was looking a little tired and obvious by 1776, when Hume was completing his revisions. If this seems plausible, then the brevity of the section indicates not a decline of interest in associationist principles, but evidence of its wider intellectual successes. Hume's cuts thus would indicate only that he did not want to bore his readers by labouring what they took to be obvious. And, because it was obvious, it freed him from the dull exposition of his basic principles, enabling him to move quickly on to his distinctive contribution to associationist theory—to show what its principles implied for human practical life. As he had said in the *Abstract*, the original feature of his philosophy is the *use* it makes of the association of ideas.[3] Abridging the description of those principles does not detract from putting them to use, but, by quickly bringing the reader's attention to the implications of the principles—in the succeeding sections—Hume brings the distinctive features of his thought to the fore.[4]

The second striking feature is that an account of the connections of ideas has been proposed, but reason is once again notable by its absence. Hume does not even bother to argue that the discernible principles of mental functioning are not principles of reason or of the understanding, even though they are principles that *regulate* the free play of the imagination. Ideas are connected by the imagination, and the principles that order the imagination are principles of association, not of reason. The general picture is

---

[3] *Treatise*, 661.

[4] The virtue of this angle is that it provides a firm reminder that Hume's associationism places him within a school of thought, and identifies his philosophy as a particular application of the principles of that school. By thus placing himself, he also invites us to see his arguments as *contributions* to the basic commitments of that school. What are those commitments? They are, at bottom, materialist. This is well illustrated by Coleridge's division, forty years later, of philosophies into two main camps: the Idealists, and the associationist materialists—the latter stemming from Aristotle, passing through Hume, and culminating in Hartley. See Samuel Taylor Coleridge, *Biographia Literaria; or, Biographical Sketches of my Literary Life and Opinions* (1817) (Menston, UK: Scolar Press, 1971), i, chs. 5–9.

the same as that given in the *Abstract*, where 'the empire of the imagination' is regulated by 'a secret tie or union among particular ideas, which causes the mind to conjoin them more frequently together, and makes the one, upon its appearance, introduce the other'.[5]

Why should it matter if the mind is under the sway of the imagination, and the processes by which it works? Why should it matter if the understanding is not the dominant faculty? The answer to these questions is, at bottom, the same: the imagination is that faculty of the mind that is the reception in consciousness of the effects of bodily processes. To give it priority—to place human beings under 'the empire of the imagination'—is to treat the mind as dominated by bodily—and thus material—processes. It is not to be *committed* to materialism, but it is to attenuate the reach of those human powers thought to lie beyond materialist explanation. Similarly, it is not to deny human rationality, but it is to undermine its claims to distinctiveness. It is to attenuate Reason, in the sense of a power possessed by human beings that orientates them towards truth. To cast human beings as creatures governed by their faculty of imagination, as Hume does, is thus evidence of a sceptical and naturalistic project.

The connections will stand out more if we turn to some other accounts of the imagination, from both materialist and anti-materialist philosophers. For the materialist Hobbes, the imagination is the repository of images because these are effects of bodily motions:

When a Body is once in motion, it moveth (unless something els hinder it) eternally; and whatsoever hindreth it, cannot in an instant, but in time, and by degrees quite extinguish it: And as wee see in the water, though the wind cease, the waves give not over rowling for a long time after; so also it happeneth in that motion, which is made in the internall parts of a man, then, when he Sees, Dreams, &c. For after the object is removed, or the eye shut, wee still retain an image of the thing seen, though more obscure than when we see it. And this is it, the Latines call *Imagination*, from the image made in seeing; and apply the same, though improperly, to all the other senses.[6]

The imagination is thus that power of the mind to receive impressions, motions in the sense organs; and because, as Hume also accepts, what remains in the imagination is 'more obscure than when we see it', 'IMAGINATION therefore is nothing but *decaying sense*'.[7] Moreover, Hobbes also subordinates the ordinary capacity to understand to the imagination: 'The Imagination that is

---

[5] *Treatise*, 662.　　[6] Hobbes, *Leviathan*, ch. II, 15.　　[7] Ibid.

raysed in man (or any other creature indued with the faculty of imagining) by words, is that we generally call *Understanding*; and is common to Man and Beast. For a dogge by custome will understand the call, or the rating of his Master; and so will many other Beasts.'[8] Hobbes distinguishes understanding in this sense from rational powers, so reasoning is not itself under the sway of the imagination. The will, however, is: 'the Imagination is the first internall beginning of all Voluntary Motion.'[9]

Hobbes thus provides a clear account of the nature of the imagination, and of its bodily basis. He thereby indicates that the more extensive the role attributed to the imagination by any account of mental functioning, the more congenial that account is to mechanical (and indeed materialist) views. In fact, it is impossible not to be struck by the similarities between Hobbes's and Hume's accounts, and even of their larger projects.[10] A cursory reading of the opening chapters of *Leviathan* will show the very themes canvassed by Hume in his opening sections: sensations as impressions, imagination as the repository of decaying sense (memory), and even of connection by association, in the discussion of the 'TRAYNE of Thoughts', including those that proceed *'Unguided, without Designe'*.[11] The similarities are sufficient to invite the conclusion that Hume's opening sections are an anti-dogmatic rewriting of Hobbes's psychology.[12]

Hobbes's account of the imagination is entirely typical, however, so it is not necessary to rely on detailing similarities between his account and Hume's to establish the meaning of placing priority on the imagination. The significance of the claim can be established by considering other influential definitions of 'imagination'. Thus Descartes refers to the activity of imagining as 'simply contemplating the shape or image of a corporeal thing', and identifies the imagination itself with the operation of bodily processes, specifically, the 'common sense', the faculty that integrates the data from the five senses, seated in the pineal gland.[13] Male-

---

[8] Ibid., ch. II, 19.   [9] Ibid., ch. VI, 38.

[10] See P. Russell, 'Hume's *Treatise* and Hobbes's *The Elements of Law*', *Journal of the History of Ideas*, 46 (1985), 51–64.

[11] Hobbes, *Leviathan*, ch. III, 20.

[12] Note also that Hume's assessment of Hobbes's philosophy in *The History of England* is critical of its dogmatism: 'Though an enemy of religion, he partakes nothing of the spirit of scepticism; but is as positive and dogmatical as if human reason, and his reason in particular, could attain a thorough conviction in these subjects' (*History*, vi. 153). Although the specific subject matter here is religion, Hume's objection can be thought to catch the chief difference between their philosophical foundations.

[13] Descartes, Second and Sixth Meditations, in *Philosophical Writings*, ii. 19, 22, 51, 59. Note also that, in the 'Rules for the Direction of the Mind', Descartes links the operation of the imagination with error: in Rule 3, he speaks of 'the deceptive judgement of the imagination as it botches things together' (i. 14). He does not mean that it is *essentially* error-prone, however: see Rule 12 (i. 39 ff).

branche, in *The Search after Truth*, offers a comparable account: 'the *senses* and the *imagination* are nothing but the understanding perceiving objects through the organs of the body.'[14] The Cartesian and Malebranchean physiological account, in terms of animal spirits and impressions, is echoed in Chambers's *Cyclopaedia* (1728), a standard reference work of Hume's day. One reads, under 'Imagination': 'A Power or Faculty of the Soul, by which it conceives, and forms Ideas of Things, by means of certain Traces and Impressions that had been before made in the Fibres of the Brain by Sensation.'[15] Once again, the imagination is defined in terms of the mental effects of bodily processes. The empire of the imagination affirmed in Hume's philosophy is thus, in the terms of its day, the domination of the mental life of human beings by the effects of bodily (material) processes. If the best account of those material processes is mechanical in kind, then the mind's workings have been, in large part, subordinated to the imperatives of mechanical operations. Ideas are formed in the mind through mechanical processes, and *associations* of ideas are further effects of these processes—including, not least, collateral effects.

Hume puts things in just this way in a striking passage in the *Treatise*. Like Locke, he typically avoids physiological issues, not least because they are inevitably speculative. However, he considers it necessary to call in physiology at one point. Significantly, this is in order to show why the principles of association play a role in explaining mental malfunction:

When I receiv'd the relations of *resemblance, contiguity* and *causation*, as principles of union among ideas, without examining into their causes, 'twas more in prosecution of my first maxim, that we must in the end rest contented with experience, than for want of something specious and plausible, which I might have display'd on that subject. 'Twou'd have been easy to have made an imaginary dissection of the brain, and have shewn, why upon our conception of any idea, the animal spirits run into all the contiguous traces, and rouze up the other ideas, that are related to it. But tho' I have neglected any advantage, which I might have drawn from this topic in explaining the relations of ideas, I am afraid I must here have recourse to it, in order to account for the mistakes that arise from these relations. I shall therefore observe, that as the mind is endow'd with a power of exciting any idea it pleases; whenever it dispatches the spirits into that region of the brain, in which the idea is plac'd; these spirits always excite the idea, when they run precisely into the proper traces, and rummage that cell, which belongs to the idea. But as their motion is seldom direct, and naturally turns a little to one side or the other;

---

[14] Malebranche, *The Search after Truth*, 3.
[15] Ephraim Chambers, *Cyclopaedia: or, an Universal Dictionary of Arts and Sciences* (London: 1728), ii. 375, quoted in Wright, *The Sceptical Realism of David Hume*, 189, 189 n. 4 (235).

for this reason the animal spirits, falling into the contiguous traces, present other related ideas in lieu of that which the mind desir'd at first to survey. This change we are not always sensible of; but continuing still the same train of thought, make use of the related idea, which is presented to us, and employ it in our reasoning, as if it were the same with what we demanded. This is the cause of many mistakes and sophisms in philosophy; as will naturally be imagin'd, and as it wou'd be easy to show, if there was occasion.[16]

This passage is important not merely because it gives such a graphic indication of the physiological picture that Hume acknowledges, but also because of the special use to which he puts the point: to explain error in reasoning. Human rationality is undermined not simply because of the *power* of the imagination, which is able to receive, and to connect and disconnect almost any ideas; and not merely because ideas are associated by the mind according to some hidden mechanical cause; but because its power is of imperial extent, as evidenced in the fact that the associative mechanisms, grounded in brain physiology, even contaminate the operations of the understanding itself. The implications are profound: human rationality, whatever its capacity and extent, cannot insulate itself against the corrupting effects of associative mechanical processes. The human mind *inevitably* falls into error.[17]

The connection between associations and error, including failures of rationality itself, are at the heart of Hume's use of the principles of association, and an integral part of his scepticism. They are not, however, his own discovery. They had been recognized by Locke in the *Essay*, in the chapter on the association of ideas— added to the end of Book Two in the Fourth Edition of 1700. He introduces the discussion of associations to rectify an important oversight in his treatment of the mind: associative processes are undeniable, and evidence of serious limitations on human rationality. They explain the unreasonableness shown by people due to the blind spots in their beliefs and behaviour, blindnesses they are

---

[16] *Treatise*, 60–1. Note that here 'specious' does not mean, as might be supposed, *merely* plausible, but attractive, reasonable. Cf. Hume's use of 'specious' in this sense in Section I of *An Enquiry concerning the Principles of Morals* (*Enquiries*, 171).

[17] When set against the Malebranchean background Hume had recommended as preparation for reading the *Treatise*, the human predicament, according to Hume's philosophy, becomes clear. Malebranche held that 'we have such a close tie with our body and depend on it so much that we do well to be apprehensive about not always having distinguished *the cacophony with which the body fills the imagination* from the pure voice of the truth that speaks to the mind' (*The Search after Truth*, p. xxviii; emphasis added). The *Search* then proceeds to show, in considerable detail, how the senses, the imagination, and the passions are obstacles to the attainment of truth, before proposing the Cartesian discipline of reason as the antidote. Hume's philosophical beginnings are, roughly speaking, Malebranche without the antidote.

quick to notice in others; they are even akin to that most serious
human mental malfunction, madness. (The mad, he observes,
do not fail to reason, but 'by the violence of their Imaginations,
having taken their Fancies for Realities . . . make right deductions
from them'.[18]) They are the principal explanation of human error,
being a mental force operating alongside reason, and even capable
of undermining it by supplying it with false starting points:

Some of our *Ideas* have a natural Correspondence and Connexion one with
another; It is the Office and Excellency of our Reason to trace these, and hold
them together in that Union and Correspondence which is founded in their
peculiar Beings. Besides this there is another Connexion of *Ideas* wholly owing
to Chance or Custom; *Ideas* that in themselves are not at all of kin, come
to be so united in Mens Minds, that 'tis very hard to separate them, they
always keep in company, and the one no sooner at any time comes into the
Understanding but its Associate appears with it; and if they are more
than two which are thus united, the whole gang always inseparable shew
themselves together.

This strong Combination of *Ideas*, not ally'd by Nature, the Mind makes in
it self either voluntarily, or by chance, and hence it comes in different Men
to be very different, according to their different Inclinations, Education, Interests, *etc.* Custom settles habits of Thinking in the Understanding, as well as
of Determining in the Will, and of Motions in the Body; all which seems to
be but Trains of Motion in the Animal Spirits, which once set a going continue on in the same steps they have been used to, which by often treading
are worn into a smooth path, and the Motion in it becomes easy and as it
were Natural. As far as we can comprehend Thinking, thus *Ideas* seem to be
produced in our Minds; or if they are not, this may serve to explain their
following one another in an habitual train, when once they are put into that
tract, as well as it does to explain such Motions of the Body . . .

This wrong Connexion in our Minds of *Ideas* in themselves, loose and
independent one of another, has such an influence, and is of so great force
to set us awry in our Actions, as well Moral as Natural, Passions, Reasonings,
and Notions themselves, that, perhaps, there is not any one thing which
deserves more to be looked after.[19]

This is a cameo of Hume's basic principles. The passage brings
sharply into focus that, for a philosopher to make the principles
of the association of ideas the centrepiece of his philosophy, is to
bring non-rational mental processes, and therefore the capacity for
error, to the centre of his philosophical anthropology. It is to sup
with the sceptic. Hume's position is close to Cicero's moderate
scepticism: 'Our position is not that we hold that nothing is true,
but that we assert that all true sensations are associated with false

<hr />

[18] Locke, *Essay*, II. xi. 13.   [19] Ibid. II. xxxiii. 5, 6, 9.

ones so closely resembling them that they contain no infallible mark to guide our judgment and assent.'[20]

In summary: a philosophy that makes the associations of ideas the fundamental principles of connection of the human mind is a philosophy that stresses both mechanical background processes, and the non-rational elements in human thought and behaviour that flow from them. An experimental philosophy of moral subjects, thus conceived, will be a philosophy alert to the implications of mechanical models, even though nothing will be *pinned* on principles so speculative in character. (Some brief introductory sections indicating the plausibility of the general picture should be enough.) Such a philosophy will emphasize the non-rational element in human functioning—including the hidden effect on many apparently rational mental operations—and will seek to bring out the consequences for everyday belief, thought, and action. It will entertain, not least, sceptical doubts about the operations of the rational faculty: the understanding. Hume has packed a good deal into his beginnings.

[20] Cicero, *De Natura Deorum*, I. v, in *De Natura Deorum* and *Academica*, 15.

Section IV

Sceptical Doubts concerning the Operations of the Understanding

Locke opens the *Essay* by observing that 'it is the *Understanding* that sets Man above the rest of sensible Beings, and gives him all the Advantage and Dominion, which he has over them'.[1] In Book IV, this faculty is identified with reason.[2] From this perspective, then, to have sceptical doubts about the operations of the understanding is to have doubts about the efficacy or extent of human rational powers; and, implicitly, to raise the question of the distinctiveness of being human. Thus the ancient sceptics were led from a critique of the dogmatic philosophies of antiquity to criticisms of the alleged specialness of human beings; and early modern followers like Montaigne followed suit.[3] Locke, for his part, is certainly interested in the question, and rejects the Aristotelian definition of the human being as a rational animal.[4] Nevertheless, his main concern is to deny rational insight into the real essences of things.

In this section, at least, Hume's concern is much the same. His argument is the thoroughly Lockean argument that a properly experimental philosophy undermines the dogmatists' belief in the capacities of human reason to discern the underlying nature of reality. Thus, in Part I, he rejects the dogmatic claims of philosophies that seek to ground the rational grasp of essences of things in conclusions drawn from immediate acquaintance with the object's perceptible properties. Without experience of the object's behaviour in the world—that is, without connected experience in the Aristotelian sense—rational comprehension of the object is impossible. To this point the argument could be defending an

---

[1] Locke, *Essay*, I. i. 1.　　[2] Ibid. IV. xvii. 1. Cf. above, Ch. 3.

[3] Montaigne, 'An Apology for Raymond Sebond', in *The Complete Essays*, ed. Screech, 502 ff. Cf. above, Ch. 3.

[4] His distinction between 'Man' (the biological species) and 'Person' (the conscious, moral being) does complicate the issue; but he discusses the tale of the chicken-minding rational parrot precisely in order to conclude that such a rational animal is not, for all that, a 'Man' (Locke, *Essay*, II. xxvii. 8–9).

Aristotelian position. In Part II, however, the Aristotelian alternative is rejected: Hume denies that experience provides any further information about the world, and so leaves us no better off than in the first case. Dogmatic philosophies, whether of an a priori or a posteriori cast,[5] alike fail to make good their promise to reveal the natures or essences of things. In this way they open the door to sceptical philosophy of some form. To this extent, Hume's argument differs little from Locke's. In Section V, however, Hume will firmly take hold of what Locke noted only in passing—the important role of custom in human life—and will on that basis argue that a positive scepticism, a sceptical *solution*, is at hand: that a non-rational, and thus sceptical, principle is sufficient to explain human functioning in the world.

It seems to me that the basic strategy of this section is often missed. It is setting up a problem that will be resolved in the following section, by, so to speak, abandoning all metaphysical hopes. The reality of that problem—that reason does not and cannot provide access to 'ultimate principles'—is the cornerstone of scepticism, because to deny reason such a capacity is to deny the possibility of *scientia*, philosophical knowledge of the essential structures of reality. This is why, in both Part I and Part II, the issue concerns the role of reason. Hume takes it for granted that it is reason that is the faculty capable of knowledge of essences, because it is the faculty by which anything is *understood*. So he tackles a priori reason in Part I, and a posteriori reason in Part II, to show that the required understanding can arise in neither case.

Importantly, he is not proposing experience as an alternative *foundation* of knowledge in Part I, and then undermining it in Part II (as, for example, Russell's view of Hume as the destroyer of empiricism might lead one to think).[6] It would be closer to the truth to suppose him to be arguing, in Part I, that experience is necessary for knowledge, and then, in Part II, that it is not sufficient. But even this is misleading, because he does not—nor does his audience—suppose that experience *could be* sufficient for knowledge. Rather, knowledge is a rational affair, and the argument is built on this supposition. Part I argues that a priori reason is not sufficient to understand the nature of the world. Part II

---

[5] Cf. Ch. 2, where Hume's use of these terms is explained by reference to experience in the Aristotelian sense.

[6] B. Russell, *History of Western Philosophy*, 2nd edn. (London: George Allen & Unwin, 1961), 634. The very idea that he could be trying to do this also depends on misunderstanding what 'experience' means in his hands. The Aristotelian distinction explains the very divisions of the argument both here and in Section VII: in each case, Part I considers the single case, Part II the case of multiple instances.

argues that experience does not help; that a posteriori reason is likewise unable to draw conclusions about the nature of the world from what experience provides. The conclusion is not that experience somehow fails to measure up, but that rational insight is not possible for creatures like us who have only experience as our guide.

Part I

Hume begins with his famous division of human enquiries into those concerning *Relations of Ideas*, and those concerning *Matters of Fact*: 'Hume's Fork', as it has been called. The first kind of enquiry—such as geometry, algebra, and arithmetic—is known either by intuition or by demonstration (deductive arguments). They are enquiries that deal in certainties: but they do not concern real things. Euclid's theorems are certain, and known to be so, whether or not there are any circles or triangles in nature. Enquiries concerning matter of fact, on the other hand, follow different methods, and cannot claim such certainty. Since the opposite of any factual state of affairs is not self-contradictory, we cannot rule out any such possibility in advance. Thus, he observes, it would be foolish to attempt to settle, by purely logical means, whether or not the sun will rise tomorrow. Of course, we are all confident that it *will*. But, Hume asks, why do we think so? On what basis do we believe this and other like convictions—that is, all factual beliefs that go 'beyond the present testimony of our senses, or the records of our memory' (26)?[7]

Hume's question arises naturally from reflections on Lockean philosophy. Locke had defined knowledge as the perception of the relations between ideas: '*the perception of the connexion and agreement, or disagreement and repugnancy of any of our Ideas*'.[8] Thus, strictly speaking, *all* knowledge concerns relations of ideas. These relations are perceived either directly (intuition), or indirectly through reasoning (demonstration). What then of sense perception? Can it provide knowledge? Locke's answer is in two steps: in one sense, sense perception gives us intuitive knowledge, because we are aware of the ideas it provides us: 'There can be nothing more certain, than that the *Idea* we receive from an external Object

---

[7] Note that this question could be put another way: 'How do the non-rational components of the imagination give rise to rational conclusions about the nature of reality?'

[8] Locke, *Essay*, IV. i. 2. Cf. Descartes, *Regulae*, in *The Philosophical Writings of Descartes*, i. 14.

is in our Minds. This is intuitive knowledge.' But does this knowledge embrace not only the idea itself, but also the object that is
its cause? At this point, Locke weakens his definition to allow that
we do have such knowledge: '*the particular existence of finite Beings
without us*', although 'not reaching perfectly to either of the foregoing degrees of certainty', nevertheless 'passes under the name of
Knowledge'.[9] His reason for this concession is that perceptions of
external objects, while we are having them, *do* convince us of the
reality of the objects. We are as certain of this relation—between
idea and the object that causes it—as we are of the relations of
ideas we perceive by intuition or demonstration. Thus there is '*Sensitive Knowledge*' of existing things. This is knowledge of fact, but
is of very narrow extent: it reaches 'no farther than the Existence
of Things actually present to our Senses'.[10] So, for Locke, factual
beliefs about whatever is actually present to the mind cannot effectively be called into question, and in this sense deserve to be called
knowledge.[11] Hume is less accommodating than Locke at this
point: what is present to the senses cannot be doubted, and is,
therefore, necessarily or naturally believed; but it is not, for that
reason, to be honoured as knowledge.[12] Nevertheless, against this
Lockean background, Hume's question follows naturally: What of
all those beliefs that concern what is *not* actually present?

Thinking of the issue in this way is useful, because it suggests
that 'Hume's Fork' is itself not meant to be anything more than
the restatement of a distinction, and its significance, well known
from Locke (and others),[13] and is introduced at this point primarily in order to introduce discussion of a question Locke had left
undiscussed. It is, in other words, Hume flagging his experimental starting points: the 'Fork' is not, and is not meant to be, a great
novelty. This is important, not so much because it undermines
Hume's originality, but because it provides him with a defence
against unfair dealing. The point is that the 'Fork' is *obviously* ten-
dentious. To deny that matters of fact can ever be necessary is
immediately to rule out the Cartesian and scholastic view that God

---

[9] Locke, *Essay*, IV. ii. 14.   [10] Ibid. IV. iii. 5.

[11] Cf. Aristotle: 'we think that *knowledge* and *understanding* belong to art rather than to
experience, and we suppose artists to be wiser than men of experience . . . because the former
know the cause, and the latter do not . . . Again, we do not regard any of the senses as wisdom;
yet surely these give the most authoritative knowledge of particulars. But they do not tell us
the "why" of anything—e.g. why fire is hot; they only say that it is hot' (*Metaphysics*, I. i, in
A New Aristotle Reader, ed. Ackrill, 256).

[12] See *Treatise*, 187.

[13] See e.g. A. Arnauld and P. Nicole, *Logic or the Art of Thinking*, ed. J. V. Buroker (Cambridge: Cambridge University Press, 1996), IV. xiii (263); G. W. Leibniz, *Monadology*, in *Philosophical Texts*, trans. and ed. R. S. Woolhouse and R. Francks (Oxford: Oxford University
Press, 1998), §33 (272).

exists necessarily, or that the idea of God can have ontological implications. Hume is not, in other words, presenting himself as a solitary critic of rival views, but as a member of an intellectual tradition, engaged in working out its ramifications for human affairs.

We are now in a position to summarize the argument. What is the source of those factual beliefs not contained in present sense and memory? They depend, says Hume, on the relation of *Cause and Effect*. If a man is asked to provide a reason for his belief about some factual matter that does not concern something immediately at hand, his reply will concern some other fact that is present, and that is causally connected to, the fact or thing under considera-tion. Thus a letter is evidence of a friend's whereabouts, and a watch on a desert island is evidence of a previous human presence. Unless a causal connection is supposed between the present fact and the absent one, the present fact has no value as evidence.

It follows that our evidence for our factual beliefs is as solid as our knowledge of cause and effect. So what is the foundation of our knowledge of this relation? It is not, says Hume, 'attained by reasonings a priori, but arises entirely from experience, when we find that any particular objects are constantly conjoined with each other' (27). No matter how perfect one's rational faculties, it is impossible to deduce the causes or effects of an entirely unfamiliar object, despite the most careful examination of its perceptible properties. The perceptible properties of an object do not reveal its causal powers; nor, from these perceptible properties, is it possible for reason to draw any conclusions about those powers. From the perception of an unfamiliar object, we can neither intuit nor demonstrate its nature or its powers.

This conclusion will seem obvious enough, if, in the first place, we think of our first experience of effects that were previously quite unknown to us. In such cases we are perfectly aware of our inabil-ity to predict what will occur. Thus it is not predictable, but a genuine surprise, to discover that 'two smooth pieces of marble ... will adhere together in such a manner as to require great force to separate them in a direct line, while they make so small a resis-tance to a lateral pressure' (28).[14] Secondly, when we believe a par-ticular effect is due to the microstructure, or some other hidden feature, of an object, we also readily admit that our knowledge of these effects is known only by experience. But we tend not to see that the same truth also applies to humdrum, everyday events as

---

[14] Cf. Locke, *Essay*, II. xxiii. 24.

well: events that are thoroughly *familiar* because we learnt them when very young; events that are *typical* sorts of occurrences; and events that we judge to be due to the *directly perceptible* properties of objects. In cases like these, we tend to believe that we know, or can work out, why they happen entirely by means of reasoning. We imagine, for example, that we could predict the effect of one billiard ball striking another even if we had no experience of such occurrences. But this confidence of ours is entirely misplaced, and only shows just how powerful—and deceptive—custom is in human affairs: 'Such is the influence of custom, that, where it is strongest, it not only covers our natural ignorance, but even conceals itself, and seems not to take place, merely because it is found in the highest degree' (28–9).[15]

To establish that in these—and, indeed, all—natural processes, our knowledge of natural laws and powers is due wholly to experience, Hume throws down a challenge: if we were asked to discover, by reason alone, the powers of a particular object, how would we do it? Any conclusion we reach must be entirely arbitrary, since the only avenue open to us is to inspect the object (the cause) in order to find the clue to its possible effects. But, since causes and effects are wholly distinct, the attempt cannot hope to succeed. The same problem of arbitrariness must also defeat the attempt to discover, by purely rational means, the necessary connection between the cause and its effect (29). Every effect is an occurrence distinct from its cause, and so cannot be discovered by an examination of the cause alone. It is therefore impossible to determine causes and effects 'without the assistance of observation and experience' (30).

'Hence,' concludes Hume, 'we . . . discover the reason why no philosopher, who is rational and modest, has ever pretended to assign the ultimate cause of any natural operation, or to show distinctly the action of that power, which produces any single effect in the universe' (30). Human reason cannot achieve more than to bring simplicity and uniformity into our understanding of nature, by resolving nature's great diversity into the operations of a few general causes. But we cannot hope to discover the causes of these general causes: 'These ultimate springs and principles are totally shut up from human nature and enquiry.' The best natural philosophy really only shifts our ignorance, it does not overcome it; and the best moral or metaphysical philosophy actually enlarges our awareness of our ignorance. Thus the outcome of all intellec-

[15] Cf. Locke, *Essay*, II. ix. 10.

tual endeavour is to teach us our ignorance—precisely the opposite of what we hope to achieve.[16] This remains true even when science takes advantage of the precision of geometrical methods. Precise reasoning like applied mathematics works on the assumption that nature works according to established laws. The role of such reasoning in science is either to assist experience in discovering the laws, or to give a precise account of their effects in particular circumstances. Through experience we discover the laws of nature, and then reason teaches us their implications.

This is the argument of Part I. The question is, at whom is it aimed? The critique of reason's powers, and the emphasis placed on experience as the true source of factual judgements, has encouraged the supposition that the modern rationalists are being subjected to an empiricist critique. This view immediately runs into trouble, however, first because the critique of reason's powers is no less a concern of Part II, which plainly is not aimed at rationalism, but at a form of empiricism. If the case is amended by distinguishing the critique of a priori reason in Part I from the critique of a posteriori reason in Part II, problems do not disappear because of Hume's distinctive use of a priori to include sense perceptions. So are we being presented with a critique of rationalism at all? Or of a different but not entirely dissimilar view? Or of some broader cluster of views? It will be best to begin by looking at some Cartesian claims.

Descartes seems, no less than Hume, to deny that reason can discover the causal powers of an object through the scrutiny of its perceptible properties. His characteristic emphasis is on the *deceptiveness* of sense perception, and the need to turn away from its misleading influence. Thus he replies to Hobbes's objection to the doubts of the First Meditation by describing his enterprise there as preparing his readers' minds 'for the study of the things which are related to the intellect, and help them to *distinguish* these things from corporeal things'.[17] Secondly, the discussion of the wax and its properties at the end of the Second Meditation concludes: 'I now know that even bodies are not strictly perceived by the senses or the faculty of imagination but by the intellect alone, and that this perception derives not from their being touched or seen but from their being understood.'[18] These passages suggest that the perceptible properties of an object provide no basis for

---

[16] Cf. ibid. IV. iii. 22–31.
[17] Third Set of Objections and Replies, in *The Philosophical Writings of Descartes*, ii. 121 (emphasis added).
[18] *Meditations on First Philosophy*, Second Meditation, in ibid. ii. 22.

understanding it; that the rational activity that gives rise to understanding must begin by turning away from the deceptive deliverances of sense.

The *Principles* follow a similarly strong line against sense perception. Thus Descartes says, for example, that

sensory perception does not show us what really exists in things, but merely shows us what is beneficial or harmful to man's composite nature . . . If we bear this in mind we will easily lay aside the preconceived opinions acquired from the senses, and in this connection make use of the intellect alone, carefully attending to the ideas implanted in it by nature.[19]

The reasons Descartes offers for these claims are mechanical: sensations are not reliable guides to the real natures of objects because 'the nature of the mind is such that various sensations can be produced in it simply by motions in the body', and that the thoughts 'excited' in the mind 'have no likeness to the movements in question'. He uses a striking example to underline the distinctness and dissimilarities:

we see that spoken or written words excite all sorts of thoughts and emotions in our minds. With the same paper, pen and ink, if the tip of the pen is pushed across the paper in a certain way it will form letters which excite in the mind of the reader thoughts of battles, storms and violence, and emotions of indignation and sorrow; but if the movements of the pen are just slightly different they will produce quite different thoughts of tranquillity, peace and pleasure, and quite opposite emotions of love and joy.[20]

The motions of the pen thus produce in the mind phenomena that in no way resemble those motions. Similarly, perceptible properties of objects cause motions in the body of the perceiver that stimulate the mind to ideas that do not resemble their causes. Descartes's mechanical philosophy, no less than Hume's, leads to sceptical conclusions about the veracity of sense experience. So it would seem that, on the question of what reason can discover from the perceptible properties of an object, Descartes and Hume are actually on the same side.

Some further remarks of Descartes's may appear to undermine this conclusion, for, although he does not hold precisely the view that an object's nature can come to be known 'by the most accurate examination of its sensible qualities' (as Hume puts it), he nevertheless indicates that the operations of the intellect do depend on prior sensory acquaintance in order to discover the essences of material things:

[19] *The Principles of Philosophy*, II. 3, in ibid. i. 224.   [20] Ibid. IV. 197, in ibid. i. 284.

all our sensations undoubtedly come to us from something that is distinct from our mind . . . we have sensory awareness of, or rather *as a result of sensory stimulation we have a clear and distinct perception* of, some kind of matter, which is extended in length, breadth and depth, and has variously shaped and variously moving parts which give rise to our various sensations of colours, smells, pain and so on.[21]

It is not immediately obvious in just what way sensory stimulation underlies clear and distinct perceptions. However, if we turn to Descartes's famous example of the wax, we can see that he is not affirming the view that Hume is attacking. He says there that the mind alone can understand the wax's nature as extended stuff, but cannot do so without first being stimulated by sense perception of the wax. This *seems* to be the view Hume has in his sights, but it is not. There are two reasons for this. First, Descartes does not mean, as Hume's critique requires, that the mind can arrive at comprehension of the wax through rational scrutiny of a *single* perception. Rather, rational insight depends on the perception of the *changes* the wax undergoes when heated. This is not the scrutiny of perceptible properties *per se*, it is *experience* in Aristotle's sense, the target of Part II of Hume's argument. Secondly, the role of experience here is in any case wholly negative: what it teaches is simply that the perceptible properties of the wax *cannot be* its essential properties. The changes that the perceptible properties of the wax undergo are so drastic that they force the attentive mind seeking the wax's essence *away from* the perceptible properties:

Let us take . . . this piece of wax. It has just been taken from the honeycomb; it has not yet quite lost the taste of the honey; it retains some of the scent of the flowers from which it was gathered; its colour, shape and size are plain to see; it is hard, cold, and can be handled without difficulty; if you rap it with your knuckle it makes a sound. In short, it has everything which appears necessary to enable a body to be known as distinctly as possible. But even as I speak, I put the wax by the fire, and look: the residual taste is eliminated, the smell goes away, the colour changes, the shape is lost, the size increases; it becomes liquid and hot; you can hardly touch it, and if you strike it, it no longer makes a sound. But does the same wax remain? It must be admitted that it does; no one denies it, no one thinks otherwise. So what was it in the wax that I understood with such distinctness? Evidently none of the features which I arrived at by means of the senses; for whatever came under taste, smell, sight, touch or hearing has now altered—yet the wax remains.[22]

Descartes's point here is, then, just what he had said it was when replying to Hobbes: to stimulate the mind, so that it can discover

---

[21] Ibid. II. 1, in ibid. i. 223.   [22] Second Meditation, in ibid. ii. 20.

that comprehension of an object—the intellectual grasp of its essence—is distinct from perception of its sensible properties. Sense perception plays a role in coming to understand the thing, but that role is not to provide raw materials that reason then scrutinizes to discover the essence. Rather, sense perceptions—in this case, by their changeability[23]—confront the mind with *problems* that the intellect alone must solve. Descartes's view is more Platonic than not: like Meno's slave boy and the inhabitants of the cave, one must learn to turn the soul around, away from the senses, in order to arrive at rational insight into how things are.

Hume's argument thus does not fit at all comfortably onto Descartes's views. It is possible, of course, that he had some other modern philosopher of a rationalist cast in mind—but the possibility is not compelling. This is because, first, the view he has in mind looks far more like some optimistic form of empiricism than of rationalism; secondly, it looks very much indeed like Stoicism. The Stoics had argued that all knowledge arises from sense perceptions, which they called *phantasia*, or impressions. Of course, some impressions are misleading, and so cannot be foundations for genuine knowledge of the world. These they called 'incognitive' impressions. The other kind of impressions, which do provide sound foundations for knowledge, they called 'cognitive' impressions, because the mind, in having such a perception, *grasps* what it is that it perceives.[24] The distinction is described by Sextus Empiricus as follows:

Of true impressions, some are cognitive, others not. Non-cognitive are ones people experience when they are in abnormal states . . . A cognitive impression is one which arises from what is and is stamped and impressed exactly in accordance with what is, of such a kind as could not arise from what is not. Since they [the Stoics] hold that this impression is capable of precisely grasping objects, and is stamped with all their peculiarities in a craftsmanlike way, they say that it has each one of these as an attribute . . . the Stoics say that one who has the cognitive impression fastens on the objective difference of things in a craftsmanlike way, since this kind of impression has a peculiarity which differentiates it from other impressions, just as horned snakes are different from others.[25]

---

[23] Changeability itself is a popular topic for those philosophers seeking a distinction between primary and secondary qualities of things. Cf. Lucretius, *On the Nature of the Universe*, trans. R. E. Latham, rev. J. Godwin (Harmondsworth: Penguin Books, 1994), ii. 748–841 (56–8); and Locke, *Essay*, II. viii. 19–20.

[24] Cf. Ayers's summary: 'cognitive impressions are the foundation of all knowledge, and sense-perception in ascertainably normal conditions, on the part of someone with the appropriate discriminatory skill, is the ultimate arbiter of truth' (*Locke*, i. 82).

[25] Sextus Empiricus, *Against the Professors*, VII. 247–52, in Long and Sedley (eds.), *The Hellenistic Philosophers*, i. 243.

We see in this passage several features that fit it immediately for Hume's account. The first and most obvious to the modern reader, the similar terminology of the modern translation, may indicate only a superficial resemblance—but the basic conception of sense perception is itself sufficiently similar to the Humean position, as argued in the preceding sections, to suggest a deeper connection. However, nothing will be pinned on this similarity. More important is the fact that Hume's argument concerns a view that founds knowledge on veridical perceptions from which reason establishes a system of knowledge. The cognitive impression is 'impressed exactly in accordance with what is'; and, because this means that the differences between things are preserved in different cognitive impressions, these differences are grasped 'in a craftsmanlike way', enabling a systematic account of their relations.

These features are brought out more sharply in Cicero's exposition of Stoicism:

The mind itself, which is the source of the senses and even identical with the senses, has a natural force which it applies to the things by which it is activated. So it seizes some impressions in order to make immediate use of them, others, which are the source of memory, it stores away so to speak, while all the rest it arranges by their likenesses, and thereby conceptions of things are produced . . . With the addition of reason, logical proof and a multitude of innumerable facts, cognition of all those things manifests itself and reason, having been perfected by these stages, arrives at wisdom. Since then the human mind is completely suited to the scientific knowledge of things and to consistency of life, it embraces cognition above all, and it loves that *katalepsis* [cognition or grasping] . . . both for its own sake and also for its utility.[26]

Hume's target, an account of knowledge that reasons from veridical perceptions, is here clearly displayed. From an Aristotelian point of view, it is a position that places too much hope in a priori reason, in the sense of hoping for rational insight independently of 'connected experience'—that is, of extended acquaintance with the *patterns of interactions* between objects—of the world.[27] This is how Hume describes the view he has in his sights; and it is reasonable to suppose that he described it from an Aristotelian perspective precisely because Aristotelianism (and the related view of the Epicureans) will be the target of Part II. The role of Part I is partly to criticize a very optimistic form of empiricist dogmatism; partly a set-up for the main argument, against the more widely supported forms of empiricism.

[26] Cicero, *Academica*, II. 30–1, in Long and Sedley (eds.), *The Hellenistic Philosophers*, i. 247. See also Long, *Hellenistic Philosophy*, 123–31.
[27] Aristotle, *Metaphysics*, I. i, in *A New Aristotle Reader*, ed. Ackrill, 255.

Hume's conclusion to Part I suggests an additional, more immediate, reason for attacking ancient Stoic views and their modern
relatives. Since Descartes and many of his followers could be
thought to belong to this latter group, it also provides one way of
enlarging the group of *intended* targets of the argument. The clue
here is that Hume's concluding paragraphs indicate a concern to
subordinate reason to experience in order to rein in the ambitions
of geometry. It thus appears that he has in mind all those modern
philosophers who are too inclined to release geometry from the
constraints of experiment. So, although the argument is aimed
directly at Stoic views, Hume appears to have meant it to apply
more widely. A sketch of those paragraphs will bring this out.

Hume first of all reruns the argument already set out to show its
application not only to single objects but also to *pairs* of perceptions—that is, to causes and effects. The argument turns on the
key mechanist principle that only efficient causes are genuine
causes; that, therefore, 'every effect is a distinct event from its
cause' (30). The striking thing about this claim is that Hume sees
no need to defend it. The natural interpretation, then, is that his
targets share the view, and that he is compelling them to accept
a conclusion implied by a principle they accept. His targets are,
then, mechanical philosophers—but those mechanical philosophers who misconstrue the relationship of reason and experience
in properly experimental philosophy. The correct understanding
of that relationship is that of the philosopher who is 'rational and
modest'. This philosopher's outlook is summarized in a passage
that is a sketch of Newtonian experimental philosophy and its
characteristic denials:

the utmost effort of human reason is to reduce the principles, productive of
natural phenomena, to a greater simplicity, and to resolve the many particular effects into a few general causes, by means of reasonings from analogy,
experience, and observation. But as to the causes of these general causes, we
should in vain attempt their discovery . . . These ultimate springs and principles are totally shut up from human curiosity and enquiry. Elasticity, gravity,
cohesion of parts, communication of motion by impulse; these are probably
the ultimate causes and principles which we shall ever discover in nature; and
we may esteem ourselves sufficiently happy, if, by accurate enquiry and reasoning, we can trace up the particular phenomena to, or near to, these general
principles.   (30)[28]

[28] Several passages from Newton are echoed here. They include, from the *Principia*, the
Rules of Reasoning in Philosophy, with their insistence on simplicity and experimental
authority, and, more particularly, the General Scholium added to the Second Edition. Thus
Newton observes, in the closing paragraphs of the latter, that 'we have explained the phenomena of the heavens and of our sea by the power of gravity . . . But hitherto I have not

In the following, and final paragraph, Hume goes on to insist that the properly experimental philosopher also recognizes that geometry does not 'remedy this defect' (31): its accuracy of reasoning does not serve to reveal the hidden powers. He here affirms the Newtonian subordination of mathematics to experimental authority, and thereby rules out speculative 'hypotheses' built up from mathematical considerations.[29]

The argument is thus specifically directed against the alternative camp of modern philosophers, who follow too whole-heartedly the 'geometrical' path. The geometrical method begins by establishing starting points with the indubitability of Euclidian axioms, and then proceeds by showing how, from these starting points, the states of affairs to be explained *could* arise. Thus the Stoics and their followers begin by identifying cognitive impressions, and draw their conclusions accordingly. Other modern philosophers, however, try to establish indubitable starting points by the method of doubt. Thus Descartes begins with the method of doubt in order to arrive at indubitable starting points, and from these starting points derives an account of 'how all the things in nature could have arisen'.[30] Even modern philosophers of a more

been able to discover the cause . . . of gravity from phenomena, and I frame no hypotheses; for whatever is not deduced from the phenomena is to be called an hypothesis; and hypotheses, whether metaphysical or physical, whether of occult qualities or mechanical, have no place in experimental philosophy. In this philosophy, particular propositions are inferred from the phenomena, and afterwards rendered general by induction. Thus it was that the impenetrability, the mobility, and the impulsive force of bodies, and the laws of motion and of gravitation, were discovered' (*Principia*, 546–7). Query 31 of the *Opticks*—while making clear that, if in the end corpuscularian mechanism is to be regarded as a hypothesis, nevertheless it is the best available—covers similar territory. Newton insists there that his laws of motion, gravity, and cohesion are not dependent on any hypothesis, since they concern only manifest qualities, and concludes, with respect to the laws of motion, in the following vein: 'to derive two or three general Principles of Motion from Phænomena, and afterwards to tell us how the Properties and Actions of all corporeal Things follow from those manifest Principles, would be a very great step in Philosophy, though the Causes of those Principles were not yet discover'd: And therefore I scruple not to propose the Principles of Motion abovemention'd, they being of very general Extent, and leave their Causes to be found out' (*Opticks*, 402).

[29] He also appears to be following the Newtonian order of exposition, since both the *Principia* and the *Opticks* present bans on hypotheses at this point. The *Opticks* makes the application to mathematically inspired conjectures particularly clear: 'As in Mathematicks, so in Natural Philosophy, the Investigation of difficult Things by the Method of Analysis, ought ever to precede the Method of Composition. This Analysis consists in making Experiments and Observations, and in drawing general Conclusions from them by Induction, and admitting of no Objections against the Conclusions, but such as are taken from Experiments, or other certain Truths. For Hypotheses are not to be regarded in experimental Philosophy' (*Opticks*, 404).

[30] Descartes, *Principles*, IV. 204, in *Philosophical Writings*, i. 289; cf. *Discourse on Method*, Part Five, in ibid. i. 132ff. Note that Hobbes also instructs the intending philosopher to adopt the method that resembles 'that of the creation'; to explain things by their method of generation, 'though perhaps not that by which it was made, yet that by which it might have been made' (Hobbes, *De Corpore*, in *Metaphysical Writings*, 3, 10). The significance, for Hobbes's political thought, of understanding geometrical method as a method of

thoroughly experimental bent are tempted by this approach, as the cases of Boyle and Glanville show. Properly understood, however, experimental philosophy requires that laws, arrived at through experience, remain subject to the authority of experience alone. Geometry can do no more than apply those laws with accuracy:

Geometry assists us in the application of [a] law, by giving us the just dimensions of all the parts and figures which can enter into any species of machine; but still the discovery of the law itself is owing merely to experience, and all the abstract reasonings in the world could never lead us one step towards the knowledge of it.   (31)

Thus any suggestion that the geometrical method can possess any authority independent of experience is dismissed.

The argument of Part I is designed to clip the wings of reason—to show that it cannot provide us with insight into the real constitution of the world, merely by reflecting on the objects with which sense perception acquaints it—and of its methodological ally, the geometrical method. Reason cannot hope to build with the confidence of geometrical method because the raw materials on which it must ultimately rely, the perceptions themselves, are not up to the task. As Locke had insisted, the ideas with which reason must work do not provide access to the real natures of objects.[31] Impressions are never cognitive. However, it is one thing to accept that many philosophers place too whole-hearted a trust in reason's powers, and so have erred in trusting in geometrical method; it is quite another to conclude that rational insight cannot be achieved through some more cautious empirical route. Is it possible, as Aristotle had supposed, for reason to discover, *through* experience, the real natures of things? Or does experience, as Locke had also argued, itself constitute a barrier that reason cannot surmount? This is the question Hume now addresses.

hypothetical generation is pointed out by M. M. Goldsmith, 'Hobbes: Ancient and Modern', in Sorell (ed.), *The Rise of Modern Philosophy*, 334, and pursued in more detail in R. E. Ewin, *The Moral Philosophy of Thomas Hobbes* (Boulder, Colo.: Westview Press, 1991).

[31] See Locke, *Essay*, IV. iii. 26: 'By the Colour, Figure, Taste, and Smell, and other sensible qualities, we have as clear, and distinct *Ideas* of Sage and Hemlock, as we have of a Circle and a Triangle: But having no *Ideas* of the particular primary Qualities of the minute parts of either of these Plants, nor of other Bodies which we would apply them to, we cannot tell what effects they will produce; Nor when we see those Effects, can we so much as guess, much less know, their manner of production. Thus having no *Ideas* of the particular mechanical Affections of the minute parts of Bodies, that are within our view and reach, we are ignorant of their Constitutions, Powers, and Operations . . .'

Part II

Hume begins Part II by stressing the limits of what has so far been achieved. To establish that all our conclusions about factual matters depend on the relation of cause and effect, and that causal judgements depend, in turn, on experience, is not to have settled the question, because it is not to have discovered on what experience itself depends. To see the force of his point, it is necessary to keep in mind two things. In the first place, by 'experience' he means, not sense perception *per se*, but the connected pattern into which perceptions fall over time, and in which memory plays a crucial role. Only creatures capable of *learning* are capable of experience in this sense; through experience they come to learn 'the way of the world'. Secondly, Aristotle had argued that, through experience (understood in this sense), the rational mind comes to understand the world by grasping the 'form of the form' of the objects it encounters. Through experience, reason is able to extract the intelligible core not revealed in the sights and sounds of sense perception itself. Experience enables reason to comprehend the natures or essences or causal powers of things, and thus to understand the necessary relations that hold between different things and different events: the 'why' of the world.[32]

Against this background, Hume's aim becomes clear. Part I has argued that the experimental philosopher must reject the optimistic interpretation of sense perception implied by those modern mechanical philosophers who trust in the geometrical method. All that we can discover about the way the world works depends on experience. The question then is, does experience itself provide the way to certain knowledge of what is? This view, in different forms, had been held by Aristotle and the Epicureans, and so also by their modern followers. Can the consistent modern experimentalist accept such a view? Or must it be rejected as well? Hume's argument is that it must indeed be rejected. He states that his conclusion will be that 'even after we have experience of the operations of cause and effect, our conclusions from that experience are *not* founded on reasoning, or on any process of the understanding' (32). So, just as Part I has ruled out the a priori route to *scientia*, so Part II rules out the optimistic a posteriori route of the

[32] See Aristotle, *Metaphysics*, I. i; *Posterior Analytics*, II. xix; in *A New Aristotle Reader*, ed. Ackrill, 255–7, 57–9. See also the discussion in Ch. 3 above.

Aristotelians and Epicureans.[33] Only through experience can we
come to interpret the world, but experience gives us no insight
into why the world works the way it does. The sceptical doubts
concerning the operations of the understanding deny the understanding any fundamental role in our relationship to the world we
encounter. Thus the possibility of *scientia* is denied, and a sceptical conclusion inevitable. But this is to leap ahead.

Hume begins his argument by pressing the point insisted on in
Part I, that sense perception does not reveal the natures of objects:
'nature has kept us at a great distance from all her secrets, and has
afforded us only the knowledge of a few superficial qualities of
objects; while she conceals from us those powers and principles
on which the influence of these objects entirely depends' (32–3).
Thus, for example, the perceptible qualities of bread—its colour,
weight, texture, and so on—give us no clue to why it nourishes
us. But, Hume points out, despite our ignorance of the underlying
powers, we always presume that whenever we come across *similar*
perceptible properties, there we will also find *similar* underlying
powers. So whenever we come across an object that *looks like* bread,
we expect it to nourish us. On what basis do we form this expectation? Since the perceptible qualities of objects are quite distinct
from—and so tell us nothing about—the underlying powers, conclusions drawn from the regular conjunction of perceptible qualities and underlying powers are not based on knowledge of those
powers. Past experience gives precise knowledge only of the particular past events of which it is made up. How then can it give
us knowledge of future events, or other objects, when for all we
know these may bear only a superficial similarity to our past experience? There is, Hume insists, a real problem here: the mind typically makes a connection that is not logically necessary. There is
a real difference between the experience of an object (with particular perceptible properties) and of its effects, and the belief that
whenever we meet with the same set of perceptible qualities, there
we *will* also see the same effects.

The mind, however, connects the two. On what basis does it do
so? Hume points out that the very fact that we can detect that
there is a gap between what we have experienced, and what we
expect on the basis of that experience, is sufficient to show that
the connection is not intuitive. Intuition is the mind's ability to

---

[33] In this way the argument of Part II can be understood as an extension of the Lockean
argument against Aristotelian claims to clear and distinct ideas of substances and thus of real
essences. See Locke, *Essay*, II. xxiii. 1. See also Ayers, 'The Foundations of Knowledge and the
Logic of Substance', 60–71; and above, Ch. 3.

perceive the 'agreement' or 'disagreement' of ideas. Our ability to see that there is a gap is to see that the two ideas *disagree*; so the mind's tendency to connect them—to treat them as agreeing—is necessarily not guided by intuition. If the connection is grounded in the realities of things, there must then be a process of reasoning by which the step is made. This requires a 'medium'—a linking premiss—to bridge the gap between the premiss (what experience delivers) and the conclusion (what we expect on that basis).

To show that there cannot be any premiss capable of performing the task, Hume once again appeals to the 'Fork'. Reasonings are either *demonstrative* (concerning relations of ideas) or *moral* or *probable* (concerning matter of fact). There cannot be a demonstrative argument, because demonstrations can succeed only in ruling out what is self-contradictory, and there is no contradiction involved in imagining circumstances at odds with the expectation that nature will continue in the same way. The reversal of the seasons, for example, involves no contradiction, and so cannot be ruled out by arguments that concern only the relations of ideas.[34] So, if it is reasoning that leads us to use past experience as the foundation of judgements about the future, it must be probable reasoning. But if the foregoing arguments are sound, it cannot do the job. The point can be succinctly stated: all arguments about factual matters depend on cause and effect; our knowledge of causes and effects depends entirely on experience; and reasoning based on experience works on the assumption that the future will resemble the past. So we cannot hope to prove that this assumption is true by means of reasoning based on experience, since such reasoning *assumes* exactly what it is we are trying to establish: the argument is circular.

Another way of putting Hume's point is as follows. What is needed to fill the gap between what we have experienced, and what we expect to experience, is a premiss to the effect that nature is uniform. The problem is that this premiss cannot itself be established by experience. Experience—including all the conclusions we draw from it (that is, probable reasoning concerning matters of fact)—depends on *assuming* that nature is uniform. It is quite useless without the assumption. So it cannot help us when what we are trying to determine is whether our expectation that nature is uniform is justified. The fundamental problem, as Hume stresses

[34] Hume has already done enough at this point to justify a sceptical conclusion, since he has thus ruled out intuitive and demonstrative knowledge of matters of fact, and therefore has denied philosophical knowledge, or *scientia*, of real objects themselves. (He has not, however, ruled out *scientia* of the relations between objects, or of certain abstract properties of them. See Hatfield, 'Metaphysics and the New Science', 128–33.)

in his recapitulation of the argument, is that experience does not teach us the 'secret nature' of bodies (38). This underlying, real constitution of things remains beyond our reach: all that experience can deliver is the perceptible qualities of objects, but we cannot discover the real powers of objects on the basis of those perceptible qualities. *Scientia* is beyond us. Experience is not a foundation on which certain knowledge of the world can be built, but, as Locke had insisted, a *limitation* on our capacities. Hume's argument is the application, to the factual beliefs that underpin everyday judgement and action, of Locke's argument that knowledge of real essences is beyond us. In so doing, he draws out an implication that Locke had not seen. Nevertheless, like Locke—and, indeed, Aristotle—he will argue, in Section V, that experience is a foundation that, although fallible, is sufficient for action in the world.[35]

The point is worth pressing, because Hume's argument here, that probable reasoning is founded not on reason but on the untestable assumption of the uniformity of nature, is commonly termed his 'scepticism about induction'—where this is not infrequently taken to mean that induction is unjustified or irrational in any normative or otherwise action-guiding sense. However, Hume's point is not at all that we should *refrain* from induction. One way of putting this is to deny that he holds that reasoning is 'deductive or defective'.[36] The problem with putting things in this way is that it supposes that there are forms of reasoning that are not deductive, and that Hume aims to reject them. This is beside his point. He takes it that reason is the power by which understanding or knowledge is achieved or extended. It is manifested in three ways: intuition, demonstration, and probable reasoning. The first of these is not *reasoning* at all, but the mind's ability to grasp truths. The latter two are both reasoning, and are both deductive in form. One proceeds from intuited (for example, axiomatic) premises, the other from empirical premises. The fallibility of the latter means that only demonstrative reasoning delivers certain conclusions—so even probable reasoning can be said to be 'defective', in the sense that it can deliver false conclusions. Probable reasonings are, because deductive, truth-preserving; but they are

---

[35] Locke, *Essay*, I. i. 6; II. xxiii. 12; IV. iii. 6, 18; IV. xxi. 3; etc. Cf. Aristotle, *Metaphysics*, I. i: 'With a view to action experience seems in no respect inferior to art' (*A New Aristotle Reader*, ed. Ackrill, 256).

[36] Karl Popper, for one, understands Hume this way: see *The Logic of Scientific Discovery* (London: Hutchinson, 1959), ch. 1; *Objective Knowledge: An Evolutionary Approach* (Oxford: Clarendon Press, 1972), ch. 1. For a discussion of the varieties of responses to Hume's argument, see Flew, *Hume's Philosophy of Belief*, ch. 4.

not an infallible source of true conclusions. Hume's insistence that experience is not based on reasoning is not, then, a roundabout way of saying that induction can arrive at false conclusions. In this respect, it may be no more defective than are probable reasonings themselves.

Misinterpretations arise because of hasty conclusions about Hume's aims. He is not trying to show that human beings are *irrational* in the broad, normative sense in which that term is now used. He is not trying to dissuade us from engaging in inductive practices. Indeed, the whole thrust of his argument in Section V is that we cannot help ourselves doing so. Nor has he any objection whatever to the development of standards for best inductive practices. In fact, he is committed to a standard of probability that is a standard of best practice (even if he also insists that it is not an infallible standard), and that he will explain and deploy in subsequent sections of the *Enquiry*. The central point of his scepticism is to deny that we can discover the ultimate constituents of the world, and to show how this conclusion implies that we are, in the conduct of life—including the principles we generate through careful empirical investigation of our world—hostages to fortune. But no modern fallibilist thinks any differently, nor perceives a 'sceptical crisis' in the conclusion. The basic trouble is the shifts of meaning that 'reason' and its cognates have undergone, precisely in response to (as we would say) the very *reasonableness* of fallibilist conclusions. Hume is attacking dogmatic philosophers who believe that certainty is possible; no small number of them even believe it to be in their possession. Modern philosophers typically deny such pretensions, and as a result have produced new standards for evaluating competing views. Thus armed—with notions of inductive logic, probabilistic justification, argument to the best explanation, and so on—they have adapted 'reason' and 'rationality' to standards and procedures so different from Hume's that misunderstandings are inevitable.

To reiterate: his point is that our inductive practices, in the narrow sense of inductive generalization, proceed on the assumption of the uniformity of nature; that this assumption does not arise as the result of any intuitive insight or deductive reasoning; nor can it arise from any empirical basis—that is, through an inductive procedure—since that would require presupposing just what is to be established. This simply means that, in the absence of an independent argument to establish that the uniformity of nature is a necessary truth, inductive generalization depends on an untested and untestable assumption, and is therefore inherently fallible. But to be fallible is not to be defective, unless what is at stake is certainty. For any modern philosopher of science, this is to raise the stakes absurdly high. Hume would agree; what he could not do was assume a consensus on the matter. The Aristotelians *did* hold that through experience certain knowledge could be achieved. Some experimentalists thought the same. His aim is, like Locke's, to puncture that ambitious view: he aims to show that certainty is an excessive demand, and that philosophy—and, indeed, human society—is the winner when it is given up. The 'problem of induction' is intended precisely to show the dogmatists that, in all empirical reasonings, certainty is an impossible ideal.

Newton had said the same. He had pointed out that, since the laws of nature reflect the real constitution of its fundamental parts, those laws would change if the parts themselves underwent change. In corpuscularian terms, this is to say that, if the corpuscles, subjected to collisions beyond their limit, 'wear away, or break in pieces, the Nature of Things depending on them, would be changed'.[37] Hume's point reflects this Newtonian view, and, as such, helps to keep in focus the nature of Hume's originality: in the *application* of experimental philosophy to the functioning of the human mind in 'the common course of the world'.[38] In this section, Hume has argued that experimental principles, applied to our fundamental convictions about this 'common course', reveal that those convictions are not based in any form of reason, and therefore do not comprehend the principles by which the world works. The hopes of all dogmatic philosophers have been met with sceptical doubts. Does this mean, then, that the application of experimental philosophy to common life generates a sceptical crisis?

[37] *Opticks*, 400.   [38] *Treatise*, p. xix.

Section V

Sceptical Solution of these Doubts

Part I

Sceptical doubts require an answer, or scepticism will be the result. Indeed, scepticism will also be the result if the answer given affirms sceptical themes; and the 'sceptical solution' provided in this section is a case in point. However, if to affirm scepticism is, as it is not infrequently said to be, to expose philosophy to a 'sceptical crisis', then this section opens on a surprising note. The tone of worldly-wise moderation that informs it does not indicate that the doubts expressed in the preceding section have plunged the philosopher into a crisis. Nonetheless, the mood is characteristic of the sceptical philosophers: it reflects both the ideal of *ataraxia*, and also its conscious realization in the tranquil, reflective mode of sceptical literature, of Montaigne in particular. Hume is here presenting his own positive picture of the sceptical attitude. This can be confirmed by comparing the long opening paragraph of this section with the opening pages of his essay 'The Sceptic'. That essay aims not only to present a case for scepticism, but to do so from the sceptic's point of view, so it is significant that the two passages are so similar.[1] Both the essay and this opening paragraph show (as much as say) that sceptical philosophy, although inspired by 'sceptical doubts', is not thereby a crisis for philosophy, because scepticism goes beyond mere doubts to offer a sceptical solution.

[1] 'The Sceptic', in *Essays*, 159–60. This essay concludes a set of four literary exercises designed to illustrate types of outlook from the inside. As he puts it in a footnote to the first of these (ibid. 138 n.), 'The intention of this and the three following essays is not so much to explain accurately the sentiments of the ancient sects of philosophy, as to deliver the sentiments of sects, that naturally form themselves in the world, and entertain different ideas of human life and happiness. I have given each of them the name of the philosophical sect, to which it bears the greatest affinity.' The other three are, in order, 'The Epicurean', 'The Stoic', and 'The Platonist'. The four together comprise Hume's conception of the main philosophical options—that is, those philosophical viewpoints capable of functioning as philosophies of life, because in one way or another they give expression to main lineaments of human nature. (This is, of course, a sceptic's sense of what makes a philosophy a viable option.)

It is a solution that is sceptical because it denies certainties; and it is genuinely a solution because it is the enunciation of a philosophical viewpoint that is 'durable and useful' (161).

Hume even argues at this point that scepticism is more stable and useful than competing philosophies because it appeals to no weakness in human nature. It is likely that his specific target, Stoicism, is chosen not merely because it can lead us to 'reason ourselves out of all virtue as well as social enjoyment', but also because, in its Christian version, it was the dominant view amongst the philosophers—as distinct from Church authorities— who had opposed Hume's appointment to the Edinburgh Chair. There is thus, in all probability, a deliberate barb in the conclusion that it may flatter 'our natural indolence . . . [seeking] a pretence of reason to give itself a full and uncontrolled indulgence' (40).[2] Scepticism, in contrast, is free of these vices: it flatters neither the intellect, since it confines the 'enquiries of the understanding' to 'very narrow bounds', nor the passions, since it mortifies every passion except the love of truth, a passion that 'never is, nor can be, carried to too high a degree'. In fact, he continues, scepticism's unpopularity as philosophy may be due precisely to its failure to flatter the human spirit: 'By flattering no irregular passion, it gains few partizans: By opposing so many vices and follies, it raises to itself abundance of enemies, who stigmatize it as libertine, profane, and irreligious' (41).

Nor does Academic scepticism undermine our capacity for action. It does not generate the kind of practical paralysis so well exemplified by Pyrrho—and which has often been brought against scepticism as evidence of its inadequacy. Rather, by leaving in place the genuine principles of human nature, it affirms ordinary life, including its diverse springs of action: 'Nor need we fear that this philosophy, while it endeavours to limit our enquiries to common life, should ever undermine the reasonings of common life, and carry its doubts so far as to destroy all action, as well as speculation. Nature will always maintain her rights, and prevail in the end over any abstract reasoning whatsoever' (41).

It is not reasoning *per se* that is rejected here, but the forms of 'abstract reasoning' that aim to rule over the diverse springs of

---

[2] Cf. Stewart, 'Two Species of Philosophy'. Note also that Hume's decision to illustrate scepticism's virtues by contrasting it with another ancient philosophy, and its probable target in Hutcheson and his allies, shows both the vitality of ancient philosophical categories in the contemporary intellectual environment, and also that his references to scepticism are self-consciously references to an ancient school of thought. Christian versions of Stoicism and Epicureanism were well established by Hume's day: the former stemming from Justus Lipsius, the latter from Pierre Gassendi.

everyday action: the *hubristic* reason generated by flattering its powers. To deny to reason—or, indeed, to any other faculty—hegemony in the soul is to preserve philosophy from the damaging indulgences already mentioned. It is also to affirm the traditional sceptical insistence on the diversity of the principles of human nature, and on the sceptic's capacity and willingness to live the customary life. Thus, as Sextus puts it:

We say, then, that the standard of the Sceptical persuasion is what is apparent ... [and] attending to what is apparent, we live in accordance with everyday observances ... These everyday observances seem to be fourfold, and to consist in guidance by nature, necessitation by feelings, handing down of laws and customs, and teaching of kinds of expertise. By nature's guidance we are naturally capable of perceiving and thinking. By the necessitation of feelings, hunger conducts us to food and thirst to drink. By the handing down of customs and laws, we accept, from an everyday point of view, that piety is good and impiety is bad. By teaching kinds of expertise we are not inactive in those which we accept.[3]

Sextus' commitment to ordinary life is not identical to Hume's, and the difference stems directly from his Pyrrhonism. Thus he adds that the Pyrrhonian follows everyday observances 'without holding any opinions': and for this reason he does not propose, as does Hume, standards for *assessing* ordinary life. Hume's standards of assessment will be examined below; here it suffices to note that they are wholly in accord with Academic scepticism, since they reflect not the avoidance of opinion, but the probabilistic standards derived from an accurate experimental philosophy.[4]

Moreover, once reason is situated as one faculty amongst others, rather than as the divine spark that judges the other, 'lower' capacities, Hume's practical-minded response to the excesses of Pyrrhonian doubt is seen to be quite appropriate.[5] The sceptical philosopher denies reason's claim to discover the ultimate principles, and thereby simultaneously undercuts its claim to privileged status. Further, experimental philosophy serves the sceptic's end by providing an explanation for why reason is unable to make such discoveries: if all intuition and demonstrative reasonings

---

[3] Sextus Empiricus, *Outlines of Scepticism*, I. 22–3.

[4] This provides him with standards for testing moral and religious principles, of course—but also for political principles. The affirmation of ordinary life does not imply conservatism. Hume is no advocate of wholesale social reconstruction, but neither is it convincing to think of him as Burke before his time. He is a (qualified) defender of liberty, and so better understood as a cautious proto-liberal. See Forbes, *Hume's Philosophical Politics*; and J. B. Stewart, *Opinion and Reform in Hume's Political Philosophy* (Princeton: Princeton University Press, 1992). See Livingston, *Hume's Philosophy of Common Life*, for a defence of the conservative interpretation.

[5] Hume gives a more detailed version of this response to Pyrrhonism in Section XII.

concern relations of ideas, and yet all ideas come from impressions, then the fruits of reason can only ever be as true to the real nature of the world as those impressions themselves. But impressions are no more than the mechanical effects of the world on our sense organs; every effect is distinct from its (efficient) cause; so reason is reduced to working with materials that do not and cannot reveal the true nature of the world. So our ideas, no matter how accurately perceived, or manipulated in our reasonings concerning them, do not reveal to us how the world is: they are not, in short, 'adequate' to reality.[6] In fact, the presumed independence of reason is thereby undermined. Thus Hume concludes, in a long footnote (43 n.), that reason is not a principle wholly separable from experience, but merely reflection on experience, reflection that can work only with the raw materials experience provides. According to the sceptical philosophy of experimentalism, then, reason can claim no authority over experience, nor over other principles of human nature.

This helps to explain Hume's next step, the claim that a solution to the sceptical problem that is itself sceptical is not, for that reason, to be rejected. The sceptical solution appeals to a non-rational principle of human nature; but the sceptic's displacement of reason means that there is no longer any standard by which non-rational principles are to be classed as inferior. No one doubts that non-rational principles can be efficacious, and, given the common objection concerning the 'impracticality' of Pyrrhonism, Hume's sceptical principle will have slain one dragon if its practical efficacy is not to be faulted. So it is just this point that Hume emphasizes:

Though we should conclude, for instance, as in the foregoing section, that, in all reasonings from experience, there is a step taken by the mind which is not supported by any argument or process of the understanding; there is no danger that these reasonings, on which almost all knowledge depends, will ever be affected by such a discovery. If the mind be not engaged by argument to make this step, it must be induced by some other principle of equal weight and authority; and that principle will preserve its influence as long as human nature remains the same.   (41–2)

He adds, 'what that principle is may well be worth the pains of enquiry'; but these pains are quickly brought to an end. He reit-

---

[6] This point, and its importance in Hume's philosophy, has been stressed by John Wright, especially in 'Hume's Rejection of the Theory of Ideas'. Cf. also Locke's denial of the 'adequacy' of our ideas of substances, *Essay*, II. xxxi. 6–12.

erates the argument of Section IV Part II, that the needed principle cannot be 'reason and reflection', because the 'particular
powers, by which all natural operations are performed, never
appear to the senses'; and that neither can experience fill the gap,
since repeated acquaintance with objects gets us no closer to those
hidden powers. So it must be 'some other principle' that produces
the mind's 'inference'. The identity of the principle is then simply
announced: it is 'Custom or Habit' (43).

This solution is quickly achieved because it affirms so little. It
simply transforms into a principle of human behaviour what
has already been observed to be the case: 'For wherever the
repetition of any particular act or operation produces a propensity
to renew the same act or operation, without being impelled by
any reasoning or process of the understanding, we always say, that
this propensity is the effect of *Custom*' (43). Note that this principle has been reached by inferring from observed to unobserved
cases, and so depends on precisely the step taken by the mind
that it explains. This should be sufficient to show that—unless
he is exceedingly foolish—Hume does not aim to reject our
inductive practices. Note also that the solution is sceptical for
the same reason that Newton's principles can be considered so:
custom is *nothing but* a manifest principle. Hume emphasizes
that his principle of custom makes no appeal to any hidden,
fundamental causes, which explain *why* we function as we do:

By employing that word [i.e. 'custom'], we pretend not to have given the ultimate reason of such a propensity. We only point out a principle of human
nature, which is universally acknowledged, and which is well known by its
effects. Perhaps we can push our enquiries no farther, or pretend to give the
cause of this cause; but must rest contented with it as the ultimate principle,
which we can assign, of all our conclusions from experience. It is sufficient
satisfaction, that we can go so far, without repining at the narrowness of our
faculties because they will carry us no farther.   (43)

Custom is, then, a manifest, or descriptive, principle, which
reminds us that human beings establish patterns of behaviour
through repeating them in everyday life. It does not explain why
human nature is influenced in this way, but its importance is not
thereby compromised. It is observable that human beings have a
propensity to treat nature as uniform, and so form expectations
about the unobserved and unobservable on the basis of past observations. This propensity is not based in any power of reason, nor
are its causes explicable. It is, nevertheless, the foundation on

which human practical activity is built. Custom is, therefore, 'the great guide of human life' (44).

It is possible to think of custom as a law of motion of human society; and there are also explanatory benefits in doing so. Human individuals and human societies can be thought of as being subject to two forces: an inertial principle and impressed forces. They continue in a state of rest, or of uniform motion in a specific direction, unless they are compelled to change by forces impressed upon them.[7] Where forces continue unchanged, ways of living become firmly entrenched; where contrary forces are introduced, these ways become weakened, and may change altogether. Once changed, inertia maintains them in the new form. Custom—the 'propensity to renew the same act or operation, without being impelled by any reasoning'—is the *vis inertiae* of human society. All this can be recognized without knowing what are the underlying principles of human nature that explain these tendencies, any more than describing the laws of motions of bodies informs us of the ultimate causes of those motions. However, just as in the case of natural bodies, it is possible to suppose what might best explain these tendencies; and, similarly, mechanical explanations are inviting. The vital role of customary connections in human life can be explained on the supposition that human beings are mechanical devices that are 'cranked up' by experience itself. Moreover, this 'cranking up' is itself possible because there is 'a kind of pre-established harmony between the course of nature and the succession of our ideas' (54): a harmony that reflects that human beings and external nature are both governed by the same—mechanical—principles.

This general relation can be made more specific by noting that Hume's initial account of the propensity, in Section IV, signals its associative character. The 'inference' that needs explaining is that 'from causes which appear *similar* we expect similar effects' (36). That is, resemblances repeated activate the mind: the principle of custom is a species of association, and so can readily be fitted to the mechanical account of neural function preferred by the experimentalists, and endorsed by Hume in the *Treatise*.[8] Resembling ideas have resembling (or contiguous) locations in the brain—or, more accurately, they are the products of contiguous locations— and the regularly repeated passage of the animal spirits in those parts of the brain wears those channels smooth, and encourages the animal spirits to move down them with ease. Customary con-

---

[7] Cf. Newton, *Principia*, 13 (First Law of Motion).   [8] *Treatise*, 60–1.

nections can, then, be supposed to correspond to physical features in the brain.[9] Hume does not imagine for a minute that he can show this to be so, but it is what he thinks; and, like a good Academic, he thinks it because, although it cannot be demonstrated, it is the most probable of the available explanations.

Hume concludes Part I with a brief account of the necessary conditions for factual beliefs. The brevity is because he wants to relegate the more technical issues concerned with belief formation to a separate discussion, in Part II—complete with the warning that discussion is not intended for all readers, but only for those who 'love the abstract sciences' (47). These closing paragraphs, then, are meant merely to provide the basics for an understanding of the phenomenon of belief. His aim is, first, to show that customary connections alone are not sufficient to produce beliefs. The customary associations of ordinary experience so far described relate ideas together, but these ideas would be 'merely hypothetical', simply entertained by the mind, unless some fact is present to the memory or senses, and from which we draw our conclusions. Belief formation thus depends on the joint operation of two factors: 'All belief of matter of fact or real existence is derived merely from some object, present to the memory or senses, and a customary conjunction between that and some other object.' The formation of factual beliefs is thus wholly independent of reason. It is a customary connection driven by a present perception—an impression.

Secondly, belief formation is wholly *involuntary* and *necessary*.[10] When an object is presented to the senses, customary connections will be made on the basis of past experience, and belief is the inevitable outcome: 'belief is . . . an operation of the soul, when we are so situated, as unavoidable as to feel the passion of love, when we receive benefits; or hatred, when we meet with injuries' (46). But a non-rational process that is involuntary and necessary can be described as an *instinct*, and this is just how Hume describes it: 'All these operations are a species of natural instincts, which no reasoning or process of the thought and understanding is able either to produce or to prevent' (46–7). And, like all instincts, its

---

[9] Although no modern neurologist would ever be tempted to talk of 'animal spirits', it is nevertheless worth pointing out that this picture of the brain—as developing a structure that reflects its past history of neuronal activity—is much the picture contained in the evolutionary theory of neuronal development of Gerard Edelmann, in *Bright Air, Brilliant Fire: On the Matter of the Mind* (New York: Basic Books, 1992).

[10] The involuntariness of belief in Hume puts him sharply at odds with Descartes, who, in the Fourth Meditation, adapted Augustinian free-will theodicy to explain false belief as a free choice. See Menn, 'Descartes, Augustine, and the Status of Faith', and *Descartes and Augustine*.

operation is a mystery to us. Hume brings the point out most clearly in his conclusion to Section V, at the end of Part II:

As nature has taught us the use of our limbs, without giving us the knowledge of the muscles and nerves, by which they are actuated; so has she implanted in us an instinct, which carries forward the thought in a correspondent course to that which she has established among external objects; though we are ignorant of those powers and forces, on which this regular course and succession of objects totally depends. (55)

To conclude, then: Hume's sceptical solution is *sceptical* because it denies any fundamental role to the understanding, to rational principles, and thereby denies any insight into the ultimate principles of nature on which philosophical knowledge depends. Custom is not an ultimate but a manifest cause. It is a nonrational principle, an 'instinct or mechanical tendency'. It is a *solution* because it is a principle of 'equal weight and authority' to reason, because it provides a reliable foundation for everyday human life. In fact, despite its limitations, it can be supposed of greater utility than reason itself: 'It is more conformable to the ordinary wisdom of nature to secure so necessary an act of the mind, by some instinct or mechanical tendency, which may be infallible in its operations, may discover itself at the first appearance of life and thought, and may be independent of all the laboured deductions of the understanding' (55). Custom is a purely manifest principle, which operates without any understanding of the 'why' of the world. Nevertheless, it is a principle of human nature that is 'durable and useful'. It is the foundation of our capacity to act in the world. As such, two issues are worth noting.

In the first place, by portraying human beings, in their everyday manner of engagement with the world, as creatures of habit and instinct, Hume has interpreted human nature in terms closely akin to animal natures. (The point will be pressed further, if implicitly, in Sections VIII and IX.) Here we see, then, Hume's sceptical solution opening the door to philosophical naturalism, in the sense of casting human beings as just one more kind of natural animal, rather than the semi-divine hybrid of the Graeco-Christian metaphysical tradition.[11] Hume's scepticism and naturalism are not opposing tendencies, not evidence of an unresolved tension in his thought: they are different sides of the same coin. Secondly, if custom is the basis of our everyday practice, it must provide us with standards of practical judgement. It is one thing to discover that we are naturally inclined to expect what we have become

---

[11] For a clear (and brief) expression of the metaphysical view, see Leibniz, *New Essays*, 50–1.

accustomed to; but how are we to act when different and incompatible experiences come into conflict? How are we to judge in such circumstances? Hume has given no answer to this question. However, he is alert to the issue: he will explain how we arrive at standards of practical judgement in Section VI.

Part II

Hume's concerns in Part II are reserved for those who 'love the abstract sciences', and who therefore appreciate accurate (and thus 'difficult') reasonings, even if such reasonings still 'retain a degree of doubt and uncertainty' (47). For the contents of this part, then, Hume claims neither certainty in his conclusions, nor their necessity for his larger argument in the *Enquiry*. The content is, to a significant degree, concerned with the details of an associationist account of belief, so Hume is, once again, shielding the polite reader from speculations in associationist psychology. In this case, though—unlike the drastically cut-down Section III—he aims not so much to set aside what may seem old hat, but to spare the reader dry detail that may have little intrinsic interest—and which, besides, leads astray of the main thread of the argument.

The content can be outlined quite briefly. Hume's aim is to throw light on the nature of belief, and he approaches the question by identifying the factor that separates 'fiction and belief' (47)—that is, the factor that distinguishes merely entertaining a thought from actually believing it. His answer to this question is already implicit in his remarks at the end of Part I, since there a belief is distinguished from a merely hypothetical state of affairs by a fact being present to sense or memory. Such a fact is, in the first case, an impression, and, in the second, a relatively vivid idea. To claim this is therefore implicitly to accept that it is the vivacity, or other comparable phenomenal properties, of the perception that provide the clue to the nature of belief.

This is Hume's point. He denies that belief can be constituted by the addition of another idea to a thought, because the capacity of the imagination to break up and recombine ideas knows no limits. If belief were constituted by an idea, then it would be possible for us to believe what we like. It is manifest that this we cannot do. Therefore belief 'lies not merely in any peculiar idea, which is annexed to such a conception as commands our assent' (47). It must, instead, depend on 'some sentiment or feeling ... which depends not on the will, nor can be commanded at pleasure'. This sentiment is distinguished from 'the loose reveries of the fancy' by a difference that is clearly felt, and familiar to all. He concludes: 'In this consists the whole nature of belief' (48).

If this seems less than expected or hoped for, he immediately compounds the difficulty: 'Were we to attempt a *definition* of this sentiment, we should, perhaps, find it a very difficult, if not an impossible task; in the same manner as if we should endeavour to define the feeling of cold or passion of anger, to a creature who never had any experience of these sentiments.' The structure of Hume's sentence is puzzling, as if he means to say that all of us are in the position of not having had the relevant feeling. The context makes it clear, however, that his point is the more general claim that the term refers to the feeling itself, and so its meaning cannot be made clear and distinct to one who lacks the relevant feeling. He is, in other words, following the Lockean account of words as names of ideas or impressions, so that to define a term is to point out the idea or impression that it names.[12] This is, obviously, a particularly difficult task where what is being defined is an idea or impression of reflection, and therefore essentially private.[13] We depend, in such circumstances, on being able to identify our own idea or impression which corresponds to the other's idea or impression, despite not being able to bring anything into the common space available in sense perception. In this way alone can we define belief: 'Belief is the true and proper name of this feeling; and no one is ever at a loss to know the meaning of that term; because every man is every moment conscious of the sentiment represented by it' (48–9). I have dwelt on this point partly in order to bring out the Lockean background, but also to draw attention to the fact that Hume's use of 'definition' can be misleading to the unwary reader. (The fact is of particular relevance when considering Hume's definitions of 'cause' in Section VII.)

Belief, although not readily, if at all, definable to those who have no experience of it, can nonetheless be described. It is 'nothing but a more vivid, lively, forcible, firm, steady conception of an object, than what the imagination alone is ever able to attain'. The piling-up of adjectives here is enough to reveal that this cannot be a definition: instead of discovering what belief *is*, we are being told what it is *like*. The felt quality that defines belief cannot be made an object of joint inspection, but it is something with which we

---

[12] Locke, *Essay*, III. i. 2.
[13] Thus, as Locke points out, terms for such ideas often derive from the analogical use of terms for 'common sensible *Ideas*' (ibid. III. i. 5).

are all acquainted, and Hume's description is a set of road signs for introspectively picking out the relevant characteristic:

This variety of terms, which may seem so unphilosophical, is intended only to express that act of the mind, which renders realities, or what is taken for such, more present to us than fictions, causes them to weigh more in the thought, and gives them a superior influence on the passions and imagination . . . belief consists not in the peculiar nature or order of ideas, but in the *manner* of their conception, and in their *feeling* to the mind. (49)[14]

As such, belief is not something rational added to thoughts; reveries of the fancy and firm beliefs are not distinguished by the absence or presence of any form of rational insight. Belief is neither generated, nor characterized, by any perception of the real nature of things. In this sense Hume's account is thoroughly sceptical. A belief is distinguished merely by its phenomenal quality. Moreover, this quality is the effect of some efficient cause, and so distinct from the cause. Beliefs are thus in no way self-guaranteeing. They are not intuitions, even when concerned with matters as fundamental as one's own existence.[15] Hume accepts, of course, that some beliefs are instinctive, or natural, and so cannot be resisted. But this is not, as it had been for Locke, evidence of their truth.[16] Nor can the universality of a belief show it to be true.[17] Hume does not spell out all these implications, but the later sections indicate—not least by their omissions—the impact of this conclusion. One important implication should be noted at this point: Hume's account of the nature of belief rules out Pyrrhonism. If belief consists in nothing more than a manner of perceiving ideas, and arises independently of rationality and will, then the Pyrrhonian ambition to live without holding opinions is an impossible dream. Belief is not under our control, and so cannot be suspended when the conditions for its genesis obtain. The Pyrrhonian, no less than the rest, will form 'a conception more intense and steady' whenever there occurs 'a customary conjunction of the object with something present to the memory or

[14] Cf. Locke's appeal to the qualitative difference in any perception 'that puts us past doubting', which is apparent to a man 'when he looks on the Sun by day, and thinks on it by night' (ibid. IV. ii. 14).
[15] The Cartesians held this, and Locke followed them: 'we have the Knowledge of *our own Existence* by Intuition' (ibid. IV. ix. 2).
[16] Ibid. IV. ii. 14; IV. xi.
[17] Hugo Grotius, amongst others, held that the universal, or near universal, agreement of the best men of widely differing backgrounds and periods amounted to an a posteriori proof (if not a demonstration) of such fundamental matters as the existence of a natural moral law. See Grotius, *De Jure Belli ac Pacis Libri Tres* (1625), trans. F. W. Kelsey (New York: Oceana Publications, 1964), I. I. xii. 1. For contemporary criticisms of this Grotian view, see Forbes, *Hume's Philosophical Politics*, 18.

senses'; and this is 'the whole nature of belief' (50, 48). Hume's account of belief is sceptical, but it is not Pyrrhonian.

The remainder of Part II is devoted to showing the influence of the principles of association in rendering conceptions more vivid, lively, and steady, and therefore on belief formation. Drawing out these influences, he suggests, will 'trace up' the phenomena of belief 'to principles still more general'. His point is that belief formation will then plausibly be regarded as an effect of the operation of associative mechanisms. (The obvious exception is that of belief in the existence of what is immediately present to the senses.) So he offers examples to show how the operation of each of the principles of association can make ideas reach 'a steadier and stronger conception': resemblance between ideas produces a steadier conception when, for example, the picture of an absent friend enlivens our thought of him (51); contiguity has the same effect, because 'when I am a few miles from home, whatever relates to it touches me more nearly than when I am two hundred leagues distant' (52); and causation also produces these effects, as the effects of the relics of saints on the superstitious sufficiently confirms (53). These associations do not, in these cases, establish belief, because, in each of them belief is presupposed—and 'without which the relation could have no effect' (53).

Hume argues, however, that they do provide analogies that serve to justify his claim that belief arises in the same way. The enlivening of beliefs, as in these examples, and belief formation itself, are not essentially different. In both cases, ideas are made more steady and lively through the effect of associative mechanisms. In both cases, the associations are triggered by a present perception, and the associated ideas themselves are selected on the basis of past experience—that is, through customary conjunctions:

what is there in this whole matter to cause such a strong conception, except only a present object and a customary transition to the idea of another object, which we have been accustomed to conjoin with the former? This is the whole operation of the mind, in all our conclusions concerning matter of fact and existence . . . The transition from a present object does in all cases give strength and solidity to the related idea.   (54)

Hume's point here involves more than meets the eye. In offering this account, and above all in insisting that it is the 'whole matter', he is, I believe, relying on his own preferred model of the workings of the brain. That model can be brought out, and his message made more sharp, by invoking his Lockean debts.

Locke had offered a neurophysiology of the association of ideas, in the following terms:

Custom settles habits of Thinking in the Understanding, as well as of Determining in the Will, and of Motions in the Body; all which seems to be but Trains of Motion in the Animal Spirits, which once set a going continue on in the same steps they have been used to, which by often treading are worn into a smooth path, and the Motion in it becomes easy and as it were Natural.[18]

If, to this account of the human mind coming to function in a predictable fashion because of the effect on brain structure of motions of animal spirits, we add Hume's affirmation, in the *Treatise*, that 'motion may be, and actually is, the cause of thought and perception',[19] the model of human functioning Hume has in the back of his mind can be brought out. It is this. Motions in the external world impinge on the sense organs, and set up motions (of animal spirits) in the brain. These motions have an effect on the brain, such that the most common motions wear 'smooth paths' in it. The motions that cause thoughts thus follow some paths more readily than others. The cause of belief, and its dependence on present perceptions, can thus be made clear. A belief is just a more vivid and steady idea, so it will be caused by strong motions in the pathways of the brain. It is sense impressions that produce these strong motions, so beliefs arise when present perceptions cause strong motions in the brain, and the smooth pathways in the brain—pathways created by the individual's past experience—convey those strong motions to the various corners of the brain. The difference between the reveries of the fancy, and actual beliefs, is due to the differences of motion of animal spirits along pathways in the brain. Experience gives the brain a structure, and thus a tendency to be moved in specific ways; and present impressions are the energy source—the impressed force—that kicks the system into vigorous life.

Hume is not a neurophysiologist, and would not claim to know that this picture is the ultimate truth about the causes of the phenomena of the human mind. It is, however, the model he has in the back of his mind; what he would take to be the most probable explanation. It is a mechanical model, and, no less importantly, it is a model of a mechanism that owes its structure to the effects of the mechanical processes of the natural world itself. It is thus orderly in a way that reflects the natural order, and Hume delights in pointing out the ironical implication:

[18] Locke, *Essay*, II. xxxiii. 6.   [19] *Treatise*, 248.

Here, then, is a kind of pre-established harmony between the course of nature
and the succession of our ideas; and though the powers and forces, by which
the former is governed, be wholly unknown to us; yet our thoughts and conceptions have still, we find, gone on in the same train with the other works
of nature . . . Those who delight in the discovery and contemplation of *final
causes*, have here ample subject to employ their wonder and admiration.
(54–5)

The orderly mechanical processes of nature operate on a body
and brain that similarly work according to mechanical principles,
and in this sense there is a pre-established harmony between the
course of the world and the course of our ideas. The irony is that
there is no need to appeal to forethought or design—or any operation of reason—to explain this harmony; it is all the fruit of the
correspondence between natural mechanisms and the 'instinct or
mechanical tendency' that governs the operations of the human
mind. The human mind goes on 'in the same train with the other
works of nature'; but the best explanation for why it does so is
because, like those works of nature, it is entirely governed by
mechanical principles, and by effects wrought by natural mechanisms themselves. Those who delight in final causes do indeed
have 'ample subject' for their 'wonder and admiration'; but they
have it for reasons that are entirely at odds with their own
favoured opinions.

Section VI

Of Probability

Probability, says Locke, is 'to supply the defect of our Knowledge',[1] and it is for this purpose that Hume now turns his attention to probabilities. He has argued that our beliefs about matters of fact are based not in reason, but in merely habitual connections. They are therefore not certain knowledge. On what basis, then, are we to judge between alternatives in order to act effectively in the world? Hume's answer is that experience itself provides the standards, in the sense that the relative frequencies of particular occurrences produces degrees of belief or expectation that correspond to those relative frequencies. The more commonly something has happened in the past, the more firmly we expect it in the future—the more firmly we believe it to be a 'fact of life'. It is custom, then, that is the real measure of all things: 'of things that are that they are, and of things that are not that they are not'[2]—and, it must be added, of things that are more or less, that they are more or less. That is, it is not a simple bivalent standard—of true or false, right or wrong. Rather, custom generates standards of judgement that are as subtle and nuanced as our experience itself.

This section, by bringing out these nuances in the operations of custom, is thus considerably more important than its size might suggest. It can even be described as the linchpin of the whole book, for here Hume's project, which to this point has been largely negative, takes a constructive turn. This section shows how creatures ruled by custom or habit become able to discriminate between the more and the less probable, and so are enabled to judge and act in the light of evidence. The story remains a sceptical one, however, because Hume's argument implies that, in establishing, and judging and acting, by these standards, we act well; but in so judging and acting we fail to see that the standards in which we repose our confidence are not infallible.

[1] Locke, *Essay*, IV. xv. 4.
[2] Diogenes Laertius, *Lives of Eminent Philosophers*, trans. R. D. Hicks (Cambridge, Mass.: Harvard University Press, 1925), 'Protagoras', ii. 463–5.

Hume begins by observing that there is no such thing as a chance or uncaused event: the naive belief that there is springs from ignorance of the real, hidden causes.[3] Nevertheless, our ignorance of the hidden causes means that we act *as if* things happen by chance: the mind draws conclusions about events according to the differential impact on the imagination of the different frequencies of relevant past experiences. Hume offers an illustration of how the mind might do this, by considering how we form expectations concerning the outcome when a die is thrown. Normally, we expect that the different values on the sides of the die are all equally likely. Hume points out that this is because we suppose an equal likelihood of each side coming to be face up: 'this is the very nature of chance, to render all the particular events, comprehended in it, entirely equal' (57). So it is because a normal die has different values on each side that we consider each of these values to be equally likely outcomes of throwing it. If, instead, we marked four sides with one value only, and the other two sides with one other value only, we would suppose that the first value would be twice as likely to come up as the second. So, when the die was rolled, we would *expect* the former value to come up, but that expectation would not amount to absolute assurance. However, if we had a die with a thousand sides marked with the same value, and with a different value on its only other side, our belief or expectation in this case would be markedly 'more steady and secure' (56).

Hume's point is that the confidence we place in a specific outcome is the result of comparing all the possible alternatives in our mind, and giving each alternative an equal weight. By combining the different alternatives, the mind then arrives at an overall judgement of the probability of each kind of outcome. In the case of the die this seems obvious; but note that to give each alternative an equal chance is to treat the die as *uniform* in its nature. Our expectation in this case is, as in other everyday cases, based on an assumption of uniformity. So, with this uncontroversial example to guide our thinking, Hume generalizes the point, and argues that the mind handles all events in just the same way.

---

[3] *Enquiries*, 56. This is as clear a statement of the 'sceptical realist' position as one could hope for, and would seem to be sufficient to settle disputes on this issue. It may be thought, however, that Hume only says this here because he has not yet shown that the idea of necessary connection depends entirely on the experience of constant conjunctions: the task performed in the next section. However, the very same point is twice made in subsequent parts of the text: 'It is universally allowed that matter, in all its operations, is actuated by a necessary force . . .' (82); and 'It is universally allowed that nothing exists without a cause of its existence, and that chance, when strictly examined, is a mere negative word, and means not any real power which has anywhere a being in nature' (95).

Each past experience of a particular event or occurrence is treated by the mind as of equal weight, and so we come to form beliefs and expectations based solely on the frequencies of the different alternatives in our past experience. The most frequent past occurrence—the one of which the mind has the most 'views or glimpses'—is the outcome most expected, what we believe *will* happen: 'The concurrence of these several views or glimpses imprints the idea more strongly on the imagination; gives it superior force and vigour; renders its influence on the passions more sensible; and in a word, begets that reliance or security, which constitutes the nature of belief and opinion' (57). Thus the different relative frequencies of different events cause patterns of expectations distinguished by degrees of assurance. The whole process depends, at bottom, not on reasoning, but on the series of perceptions 'imprinting' or 'begetting' degrees of belief in the mind. Like belief itself, probability depends not on the understanding, but on the relative vivacity—the relative strength of imprinting— of the various alternatives lodged in the imagination.

As for the frequencies of distinct events, so also for causes and their effects. They show variation in much the same way as do particular events. Some causes always produce the same effect: for example, fire always burns a human being. In other cases, however, the connection is not invariant: rhubarb purges and opium induces sleep, but they do not affect all human beings uniformly.[4] In these cases, where the cause is not uniformly connected with its effect, we judge the relationship between cause and effect to be merely probable, the probability varying according to the experienced frequency. This is not, Hume adds, because there is any genuine variation in the causal power of the causal agent itself (for example, of the rhubarb or opium). The best explanation is that there are other hidden conflicting causes that hinder the operation of the cause under consideration. However, the normal functioning of our mind is not built on such theoretical considerations: it works entirely according to appearances and their relative past frequencies:

Being determined by custom to transfer the past to the future, in all our inferences; where the past has been entirely regular and uniform, we expect the event with the greatest assurance, and leave no room for any contrary supposition. But where different effects have been found to follow from causes, which are to *appearance* exactly similar, all these various effects must occur to the mind in transferring the past to the future, and enter into our

[4] The examples—if not the use to which they are put—are Locke's: *Essay*, IV. iii. 25.

consideration, when we determine the probability of the event. Though we give the preference to that which has been found most usual, and believe that this effect will exist, we must not overlook the other effects, but must assign to each of them a particular weight and authority, in proportion as we have found it to be more or less frequent.   (58)

In some cases, the comparative frequencies may be such that one possible outcome 'approaches to a certainty'. Thus the very simple—'mechanical' in the popular sense of the term—process of transferring past experience to the future can produce degrees of belief or assurance that vary from equality of probability ('chance') to the conviction that a particular outcome is certain.

Convictions of this latter kind play a central role in Hume's subsequent argument, so it is worth drawing out how they present themselves to the mind. Where we believe, from past experience, that a particular outcome could not be imagined otherwise, we say, for example, that it is *bound* to happen; after the event, we say that it *had* to happen. These and similar expressions show that such occurrences are, for us, *necessary*; and, where they involve, not single events only, but conjunctions of events, they are, for us, *necessarily connected*. This is not logical necessity, of course; but Hume holds that it *feels* the same. Past experience, where it is wholly uniform, produces the same felt conviction as does a demonstrative argument: both, in their different ways, 'leave no room for doubt or opposition' (56n.).

For this reason, Hume introduces a special term to refer to convictions of necessity that arise from experience: *proof*. He divides arguments into demonstrations, proofs, and probabilities, defining 'proofs' as 'arguments from experience as leave no room for doubt or opposition'.[5] The definition shows proof to be an unusual, hybrid category. It is important to recognize that it is quite distinct from what would now be called a proof. The theorems and deductions of Euclid's geometry are, in Hume's terminology, demonstrations, not proofs. A proof is an argument from experience, and so, in one sense of the term, a probable argument: in contrast to a demonstration, its conclusion is not necessary, but

---

[5] Hume introduces the notion as an amendment to Locke, in order the better to reflect common use. Locke had, he says, divided all arguments into 'demonstrative' and 'probable'. But it is worth noting, first, that Locke does employ the term 'proof', if in a different way (*Essay*, IV. xv. 1); and, secondly, that he also appeals, in his account of 'sensitive' knowledge, to the impossibility of doubting certain deliverances of experience—and for this reason dignifies such deliverances *as* knowledge (IV. ii. 14). Hume's amendment is, then, constructed largely from materials Locke had already provided—and, in fact, to create room for scepticism. Against Locke, Hume denies that what we *take to be* knowledge is to be dignified *as* knowledge: the task of the concept of proof is precisely to pick out this particular form of human epistemic fallibility. (Because the notion is both distinctive and important, it will typically be italicized, in order to remind that this is the sense intended.)

probable. (It can be denied without contradiction.) In another sense, it is not a probable argument, because its conclusions are not probable *for us*: it is an argument that leaves 'no room for doubt or opposition'. This is a feature also true of demonstrative arguments—at least for the attentive mind—but a proof achieves this result without showing the agreement or disagreement of ideas, as does a demonstration.[6] The difference here reflects the fact that demonstrative arguments concern relations of ideas, whereas proofs, like ordinary probable arguments, concern matters of fact. Furthermore, a proof achieves (subjective) certainty both for attentive and for inattentive minds, since it arises through a natural process in any normally functioning mind.

Proof in this sense can be divided into two kinds. Although Hume is explicitly concerned only with the second, it is arguable that he recognizes both. The first is exemplified by G. E. Moore's proof of the external world: there is an external world, because, for example, we cannot doubt the existence of our hands—or of any other familiar objects—when we perceive them under unproblematic conditions. Seeing is believing, as we say; in Humean terms, seeing 'leaves no room for doubt or opposition'.[7] The second sense of the term—the sense with which Hume is explicitly concerned—can be described as the limit case of probable argument, since it is the conclusion drawn from experience where the uniformity of experience is unalloyed. This is the probability argument where—as we would now put it—the probability is 100 per cent. It may be described as that species of probability that is not, for us, *merely* probable: its conclusion is not necessarily true, but it is, for us, certain.[8]

The important things to notice are that Hume holds that uniform experience generates the conviction of necessity, and that he employs a familiar term in (what is for us) a distinctive fashion

[6] This is Locke's characterization of demonstrative argument, which lies in the background of Hume's account. See Locke, *Essay*, IV. xv. 1.

[7] G. E. Moore, 'Proof of an External World', in his *Philosophical Papers* (London: Allen & Unwin, 1959). Hume's account of belief implies the acceptance of proof in this sense: a present impression possesses the vivacity and steadiness that compels belief, and so leaves 'no room for doubt or opposition'. A first-hand experience of a miraculous event therefore can be, for us, a proof of miracles. This is, presumably, why Hume restricts his argument in Section X to *testimony* concerning miracles.

[8] I have put it this way, with what might seem clumsy repetitions of what something is *for us*—rather than talking more directly of indubitability (or incredibility)—because this is how Hume tends to put it, and because, by doing so, he lapses into modes of expression that can mislead. Something proven false by uniform past experience is incredible; that is, it is, *for us*, impossible. Hume's preference for this latter way of putting things results, on occasions, in claims that some state of affairs is impossible *simpliciter*. This is particularly marked in Section X, with the result that key arguments there are mistakenly read as if concerned with objective impossibilities, rather than as proofs.

in order to indicate that relation. Experience *proves* to us the necessity or impossibility of events, despite our having no knowledge of why things happen as they do, and, a fortiori, despite our possessing no rational or otherwise infallible grounds on which to base such judgements. Experience leads us to convictions that we cannot know, but cannot doubt. Hume's concept of proof, designed to capture just this feature of human functioning, is thus specifically adapted to the purposes of a sceptical philosophy. It is an appeal to the *authority* of experience, despite providing no adequate basis for such authority: past uniformities do not logically determine future possibilities. Proof is thus inherently deceitful, in that it hides its fallibility from us. Nevertheless, we cannot—and should not—avoid relying on it. We are so constituted that we do and therefore must rely on past regularities when making judgements: it is the only standard we possess, and in this negative sense, our rightful standard.[9] Human beings cannot but function according to mechanical principles, and the mechanical principle operative here is inertial force. The inertial transference to future experience of past regularities is the creation of the natural (inductive) standard by which human beings do and must measure all that they encounter. This process is sensitive to all the nuances and variety of our experience. In its strongest form, it constitutes proof, the natural and rightful—if fallible—measuring stick of the human mind in its practical employment.

To bring out the meaning and significance of Hume's notion of proof is also to recognize that this section is the linchpin of the *Enquiry*, because it is to reveal that Hume turns, in the succeeding sections, to put proof to work. Thus in the next section, he investigates the origin of our idea of necessary connection, and finds it in the experience of uniform conjunctions of events. Uniform experience generates the feeling of expectation that is the (inadequate) impression of necessity, and thus *proves* to us that constantly conjoined events are necessarily connected. Hume says so explicitly: 'When we say . . . that one object is connected to another, we mean only that they have acquired a connexion in our thought, and give rise to this inference, by which they become *proofs* of each other's existence' (76; emphasis added).

The subsequent arguments for the compatibility of liberty and necessity, and against belief in miracles, also pivot on proofs. In the former case, Hume argues that experience *proves* that human

---

[9] Cf. C. M. Korsgaard, *The Sources of Normativity* (Cambridge: Cambridge University Press, 1996), 66: for Hume, '*human nature* . . . is intrinsically normative, in a negative [sense] . . . there is *no intelligible challenge* that can be made to its claims'.

beings are subject to necessity, and that this proof is revealed in our behaviour. The only obstacle is our inability to recognize on what that necessity depends. In the latter case, Hume argues that experience *proves* to us that miracles cannot occur. If a uniform experience generates in us the conviction that things occur necessarily after a certain pattern—a conviction we express by denominating those patterns as laws of nature—then a violation of the pattern will be incredible; that is, we will judge it to be impossible. We will therefore reject it, as long as we function in our normal manner. Belief in miracles therefore depends on failing to function according to the principles of experience, and so demands a special explanation. Hume's explanation is this: when we confront the most abnormal occurrences we tend to lose our normal bearings, not least when powerful hopes and fears are involved, and especially when they are subject to unscrupulous manipulation.

Sketching in these arguments shows how, at their core, they all depend on the account of involuntary belief and involuntary probable judgement completed in this section; and, in particular, on the special notion of proof that depends on it. The arguments are, as Hume frequently says they are, proofs in this specific sense.[10] This short section is pregnant with all these conclusions. In this respect it represents a turning point in the *Enquiry*'s overall argument. It completes Hume's account of the basic principles of mental functioning, but it also indicates how those principles are not merely destructive of dogmatic orthodoxies, but can have a constructive purpose. It shows a way ahead. Much of the rest of the book is simply the application of the essentially mechanical principles of human functioning that have now been put in place.

---

[10] Cf. *Enquiries*, 76, 95 ('to prove, that all mankind have ever agreed'), 98, 99 ('proofs of criminal principles in the mind'), 110 ('a full *proof* of the future existence of that event'), 112, 114 ('proof against proof'), 115 ('a direct and full *proof*... against the existence of any miracle'), 127 ('no human testimony can have such force as to prove a miracle').

Section VII

Of the Idea of necessary Connexion

Hume has argued that the contents of our minds depend wholly on experience, and that through experience we gain no insight into the natures or essences or powers of objects. We are able to function effectively in the world only because we are creatures of habit: we are so geared that, without understanding why things occur as they do, we just *expect* the world to go on in the way that it has. Human beings are crude inductivists, and cannot but be so. However, we are not hopelessly crude, because our expectations are themselves capable of nuance: the more or less frequently something has occurred, the more or less confidently we expect it. Where experience has been entirely uniform, there our expectations are unshakeable: in such cases, (past) experience is for us a proof of how things must be, of what is, for us, *necessarily* the case.

Hume now turns to a direct consideration of the idea of necessary connection. His account of proof already implies that the idea of necessity *can* arise through experience, without the mind actually grasping real necessary connections; in this section he argues that it is only in this way—in what is *proven* to us by experience—that the idea of necessity *does* arise. The issue is important because it meets a possible objection to the argument so far, and in so doing affirms the sceptical position. The objection is that, if our ideas all arise from experience, and since we do possess the idea of power or cause or necessary connection, then Hume's analysis of experience must be wrong: it must be that we do perceive powers in nature. Hume's task is to meet this objection, and thereby to rule out this route to dogmatic empiricist philosophy. His argument is that we do have an idea of power or necessary connection, but that this idea does not arise from the successful perception of powers in nature—it originates merely in custom. The dogmatists' ambition to cut nature at the joints—to arrive at philosophical knowledge or *scientia* by discovering the necessary connections between things—can thus be nothing but a wild goose chase.

Two specific features of this section deserve noting. First, the section is structured similarly to Section IV, in that Part I considers 'single instances of the operations of bodies' (73), and Part II multiple instances. In another respect, however, its structure is better thought of as equivalent to Sections IV and V together, because in it a sceptical problem and its solution are compressed into one section. Thus Part I introduces sceptical doubts about the origin of the idea of necessary connection; and Part II provides a sceptical solution to those doubts, by tracing the origin of the idea to an internal impression of a very special kind, which arises independently of singular perceptions, and indeed of any operation of the understanding. The solution is that the idea of necessary connection does arise through an impression, but one generated by the instinctual force of habit: after being confronted with repeated instances of conjoined events, we judge the conjunctions necessary, because we '*feel* a new sentiment or impression . . . and this sentiment is the original of that idea which we seek for' (78).

Secondly, the arguments of Part I are not original. Both the formulation of the problem of causal power in terms of necessary connection, and the detail of the arguments themselves, reveal a profound debt to Malebranche's *Search after Truth*: so profound, in fact, that, if Hume were a modern academic, he would not escape the charge of plagiarism. The parallels are so striking that Charles McCracken, after comparing several passages, concludes that 'Hume not only kept the *Search* in mind, as he wrote on causality, but . . . he even had it open for consultation while writing'.[1] As McCracken points out, it is in Malebranche, rather than Descartes, Locke, or Berkeley, that the idea of causation is shown to rest on necessary connection. Further, Hume's arguments that we do not have any direct impression of necessary connection are obviously modified from Malebranche. This includes the introspective extension of the argument to apply to volitions: to the will's power to move the body, and to manipulate ideas in the mind. Hume here recycles a Malebranchean argument to reject Locke's view that, although sense perception of bodies does not deliver (in Hume's terms) any impression of power, reflective perception of volitions *does*.[2] The Malebranchean connection should not surprise: as noted

---

[1] C. J. McCracken, *Malebranche and British Philosophy* (Oxford: Clarendon Press, 1983), 258.

[2] Locke's position is this: 'if we will consider it attentively, Bodies, by our Senses, do not afford us so clear and distinct an *Idea* of active *Power*, as we have from reflection on the Operations of our Minds . . . The *Idea* of the beginning of motion, we have only from reflection on what passes in our selves, where we find by Experience, that barely by willing it, barely by a thought of the Mind, we can move the parts of our Bodies, which were before at rest

above, Hume had recommended Malebranche as preparation for reading his own work. Furthermore, despite pronounced differences of viewpoint, there is much in Malebranche's work that would have recommended itself to Hume. As McCracken observes:

Malebranche's visionary outlook was, of course, far removed from Hume's sceptical one. Yet in many ways the *Search* was a good textbook for a sceptic. Malebranche had, after all, passed each faculty in review—sense, imagination, intellect, volition, passion—and tried to show how pervasive was the tendency of each to lead us into error . . . That was a message welcome to a sceptic's ears . . .[3]

Bringing this dependence into plain view shows once again wherein Hume's originality actually lies: in the *use* he makes of experimental, and especially of associative, principles.[4] In fact, recognizing Hume's dependence on Malebranche's arguments both clarifies the structure of the section, and sharpens the edge of his particular conclusion. The structure is clarified because the reliance on Malebranche's negative arguments makes it obvious why Part I should conclude with a critique of occasionalism, Malebranche's positive doctrine about causation. To follow Malebranche's arguments, as Hume does, is to lead the reader to expect that a Malebranchean conclusion is in the offing: that we are about to be told that, since we perceive no power in objects, and not even in our own volitions, then all power must instead reside in God, who alone makes all things happen.[5] However, instead of offering an occasionalist resolution, Hume objects that this doctrine is too strange to be credible, and both theologically and philosophically self-undermining. His alternative, sceptical, solution, is the by-now familar pathway of customary connection: reason, including theology, is usurped by the non-rational processes of the imagination.[6]

It has been argued above that Hume's appeal to associative

. . . it seems to me, we have from the observation of the operation of Bodies by our Senses, but a very imperfect obscure *Idea* of *active Power*, since they afford us not any *Idea* in themselves of the *Power* to begin any Action, either motion or thought . . . we find in our selves a *Power* to begin or forbear, continue or end several actions of our minds, and motions of our Bodies, barely by a thought or preference of our mind ordering, or as it were commanding the doing or not doing such or such a particular action. This *Power* which the mind has . . . is that which we call the *Will*' (*Essay*, II. xxi. 4, 5).

[3] McCracken, *Malebranche and British Philosophy*, 254–5.   [4] *Abstract*, in *Treatise*, 661–2.
[5] As Hume summarizes: 'according to these philosophers, every thing is full of God' (*Enquiries*, 71).
[6] McCracken concludes: 'Malebranche had given a theological foundation to this doctrine; Hume gave a psychological one' (*Malebranche and British Philosophy*, 263). This is right, but it does need to be emphasized that the psychology in question consists of non-rational processes, explicable in terms of the effects of bodily mechanisms. Hume's psychologism and his scepticism are all of a piece.

processes reflects an attraction to mechanical models. In this light, it is striking that Hume signals this attraction by appealing to mechanical analogies in his specific arguments. 'Is there not,' he asks, concerning the human power of volition, 'either in a spiritual or material substance, or both, *some secret mechanism or structure of parts*, upon which the effect depends, and which [is] entirely unknown to us . . . ?' (68; emphasis added.) I suggest that, if we take such mechanical analogies seriously, we will arrive at the best interpretation of Hume's meaning in this section.

The starting point is to remember that the mechanical explanation of perception implies that the sensible contents of our minds are the mechanical effects of an external world on our sense organs, effects that are distinct from, and may not even resemble, their causes. The mind, furthermore, has no prior contents by which the effects of mechanical sensing can be assessed, so the inadequacies of our sensible ideas cannot be surmounted. The consequence is that our human capacities are insufficient to penetrate to the real nature of things—including, of course, the incapacity to determine the truth or otherwise of the mechanical model, our best explanation (our best *supposition*) of the nature of that world. We can only *suppose* operations—secret powers—in the world by which things happen; operations of which we are, and must remain, in ignorance. So we cannot claim to know that there *are* secret powers in objects, still less that these powers are mechanical in kind.

What is clear, however, is that mechanical philosophy holds that there is a real world independent of us, a world of matter in motion. This world works in the specific way that it does because of the different mechanisms that make each thing what it is, and so the different mechanisms constitute the distinguishing powers of different objects. Thus the power of the clock to keep time, or of the pulley to lift weights, is constituted by their different mechanisms. The mechanical model of the world proposes the same type of explanation for the natural powers of objects, whether the power of bread to nourish, or of rhubarb to purge, or of opium to induce sleep: powers are at bottom mechanisms.[7] Since the mechanisms are inaccessible to perceivers like us, the powers of the

---

[7] Strictly, it is motions applied to mechanisms that make these powers actual rather than potential, so it could be said that motion is, on this model, the ultimate (natural) cause—the general power on which the distinctive powers of objects rely. This is worth noting, partly because of its affinities with some modern quantum-physical views of a similar kind, but especially because it indicates that it would not be plausible for a mechanist—even for a sceptical (non-dogmatic) mechanist—to hold that causation might be regularity 'all the way down'.

objects must remain hidden: all that we can observe are their effects in the world, including their effects on us.[8] Nevertheless, there is some room for optimism, since if the mind is, like the world, mechanical in its main operations, there is a basis for a 'pre-established harmony' between the operations of our minds and the course of nature—even though this harmony should not (as it frequently is) be taken to indicate that we have access to the hidden structure of the world.

Mechanical philosophy therefore licenses a way of talking about our relationship to the world that can be described as sceptical realism: it is realist in that it affirms that we live in a world that exists independently of us, and that has real powers that reflect its specific constitution. It is sceptical because of its sceptical interpretation of experience: it implies that we are not able to penetrate beyond appearances—the mechanical effects of that world on us—to discover the essential nature of the world. We cannot *know*, but can only *suppose*, that that world conforms to our best explanation (our best hypothesis). This scepticism is, moreover, constructive, because it recognizes that, even if essences cannot be discovered, we can conduct careful observations of the appearances, and that these observations can be reliable and useful if we proceed with caution and with intellectual modesty. It thus affirms experiment. The upshot is that Hume's mechanical, experimental, and sceptical themes can all be expressed in a sceptical realist interpretation of his thought.[9]

The justification for this conclusion lies in its ability to unify the various strands in Hume's thought. In this section, then, I will seek to show how well the sceptical realist view fits what Hume actually says here in the *Enquiry*. There is, of course, a vast quantity of literature on Hume's account of causation, but, since much of it consists of minute examination of the relevant sections in the *Treatise* as well as the *Enquiry*, to that extent it falls outside the scope of this study. The narrowed focus here is not necessarily a

---

[8] Locke implicitly accepts the mechanical view as described above, by insisting that ideas are distinct from objects; but he also argues, in more optimistic vein, that with better eyes we could see the real mechanisms, not merely their effects on us. The problem, however, is that they're just too small. See *Essay*, IV. iii. 25.

[9] The principal sceptical realist interpretations of Hume's position are Craig, *The Mind of God and the Works of Man*, Livingston, *Hume's Philosophy of Common Life*, Kemp Smith, *The Philosophy of David Hume*, Strawson, *The Secret Connexion*, and Wright, *The Sceptical Realism of David Hume*. See also J. Broughton, 'Hume's Ideas about Necessary Connexion', *Hume Studies*, 13 (1987), 217–44, and M. J. Costa, 'Hume and Causal Realism', *Australasian Journal of Philosophy*, 67 (1989), 172–90. For the opposition, see S. Blackburn, 'Hume and Thick Connexions', *Philosophy and Phenomenological Research*, 50 (supp.) (1990), 237–50, Waxman, *Hume's Theory of Consciousness*, and K. P. Winkler, 'The New Hume', *Philosophical Review*, 100 (1991), 541–79.

disadvantage, though, because it is genuinely valuable to see just how thoroughly Hume's discussion in the *Enquiry* fits the sceptical realist view. It is the *Treatise* that is the primary source of the common view that he *reduces* causal power to mere regularity—constant conjunctions of objects.[10] Bringing this out shows that the relationship between the two works cannot be taken for granted: Hume's arguments in the two works need to be kept more separate than is often the case.[11]

Part I

The argument of Part I is not complex. After an initial *apologia* for what is to follow—a short defence of the importance of conceptual clarification in philosophy—Hume proposes to explain the important terms '*power, force, energy* or *necessary connexion*' (62). Their importance resides in the fact that they are terms 'of which it is every moment necessary for us to treat in all our disquisitions'; and, because, even though simple notions, they are obscure in meaning, so the appropriate method is to seek out the impression(s) from which they derive. Hume accepts, without arguing the point, that the idea of necessary connection is the fundamental notion, and so begins a search for the impression from which this idea arises. His first step is to reaffirm a conclusion stressed in Section IV, that no singular perception of any external objects related as cause and effect can reveal the causal power that is responsible for the effect: 'external objects as they appear to the senses, give us no idea of power or necessary connexion, by their operation in particular instances' (64).

What then of (singular) internal processes? Do our inner acts of volition provide us with the impression we seek? No they do not. Although we are well aware of our power to move our bodies, and to generate thoughts, inspecting individual instances of these processes shows that we do not, in fact cannot, find an impression of power or necessary connection. Our belief in this power stems entirely from experience—that is, from repeated conjoined perceptions. Hume twice deploys three arguments to show that,

[10] Kenneth Winkler, in 'The New Hume', defends a weaker version of the common view: that Hume's position is 'a *refusal to affirm* the existence of real powers' (567). The case for this view will be considered below.

[11] It is not uncommon for sceptical realist interpreters of Hume to blame positivism for the more common view. Winkler, in 'The New Hume', shows this to be mistaken, because pre-positivist readers typically held the common view (570-3). If instead the cause is the *Treatise*'s more colourful passages—passages that engraved themselves deeply in the minds of the positivists—the difficulty is overcome.

neither from our volitions concerning our body, nor from those concerning our mind, do we gain the relevant impression.

We have no immediate awareness of the power we have over our body because, first, if we were aware of this power, we would know how it operates, and thus how soul and body are related. But we do not have this knowledge: there is no principle in nature 'more mysterious than the union of soul with body' (65). Secondly, if we were acquainted with the power by which the will operates, we would know why the will can move the tongue and fingers, but not the heart or liver. But we do not know why this is so, as we can see from the cases of those who have suddenly been paralysed, or have newly lost a limb: they try to move the member, and so do not recognize introspectively that the power is lost. Rather, 'experience only teaches us, how one event constantly follows another; without instructing us in the secret connexion, which binds them together, and renders them inseparable' (66). Thirdly, the science of anatomy shows that the immediate effect of willing is to move muscles, nerves, and animal spirits, by which the bodily part is then moved. So what the mind wills (for example, moving an arm) is not the event it immediately causes (for example, activating the animal spirits to contract a muscle). So, since in acting we are not aware that this is so, we cannot be aware of the power by which we produce the action: 'That . . . motion follows the command of the will is a matter of common experience, like other natural events: But the power or energy by which this is effected, like that in other natural events, is unknown and inconceivable' (67).[12] The conclusion must be, then, that we have no inward impression of power attending bodily actions. We are well aware that we can direct our bodies, but how we do so is a mystery.

Much the same three arguments show that we are not aware of any power when we produce a new idea in the mind. First, to know a power is to know cause and effect, and the relevant relation between them. But we do not know the nature of the soul, nor the nature of an idea, nor the power of the first to produce the second.

---

[12] Hume says that the power is 'inconceivable'. This is not to claim that there is no such power. To suppose that it is would be to ignore the role—central to the argument of this section—of the doctrine that ideas arise from impressions. An idea is inconceivable if there is no impression from which it can arise. Since no impression of power can be found in singular perceptions of natural events, it is thus inconceivable that the idea of power can arise from any such source. This is the sum of Hume's point here—and also when he says, in the corresponding argument below, that the power of the will is 'incomprehensible' (69). Ideas come from impressions, so, *ex hypothesi*, it is 'inconceivable' or 'incomprehensible' or 'beyond our comprehension' (68) that an idea should arise where no originating impression can be found.

We know only that, following a command of the will, an idea arises: 'the manner, in which this operation is performed, the power by which it is produced, is entirely beyond our comprehension' (68). Secondly, the mind's power over itself has limits, but we don't know by reason or acquaintance why these limits are as they are. We recognize, for example, that 'our authority over our sentiments and passions is much weaker than that over our ideas', but we cannot say why. We simply discover it to be so through experience. Thirdly, the mind's power over itself varies according to circumstances: thus we have greater self-command when well than ill, in the morning than the evening, when fasting than after a full meal. We cannot explain why these variations are as they are, except by appealing to our experience of the fact. We can only suppose that there must be some underlying mechanical process that explains these variations; but this process, being beyond the reach of our perceptions, leaves the actual power of the will entirely beyond our reach: it 'renders the power or energy of the will equally unknown and incomprehensible' (68–9). So, Hume concludes, it must be that, although volition is an act of mind with which we are well acquainted, we do not perceive the power or energy by which the will acts: 'So far from being conscious of this energy in the will, it requires as certain experience as that of which we are possessed, to convince us that such extraordinary effects do ever result from a simple act of volition' (69).

With the conclusion in place, Hume turns to a discussion of the views of the occasionalists. The important point to recognize is that the nature of his criticisms are powerful counter-indicators to the common interpretation that he denies the existence of causal powers. This is because, in terms of the philosophical views spawned by the revolution in natural philosophy, that interpretation makes Hume's own view equivalent to occasionalism without God; equivalent to rendering all things in the world *really*, not merely apparently, 'loose and separate' (74). If this were his view, then we would expect him to argue, against the occasionalists, that they saw the truth, only to flee it and to seek refuge in theological excess. However, the natural interpretation of his actual objections to them is that their error lies precisely in concluding that there are no natural powers. He objects, in short, to the very view he is alleged to affirm.

He begins by pointing out that most people do not recognize that they are not acquainted, through either perception or reason, with the power an object has to bring about the effects it is judged to bring about. It is only when they are confronted with remarkable events that they are aware of their inability to explain why the effects occurred. Finding themselves at a loss, they resolve the problem by means of a *deus ex machina*:[13] 'It is usual for men, in such difficulties, to have recourse to some invisible intelligent principle as the immediate cause of that event which surprises them, and which, they think, cannot be accounted for from the common powers of nature' (69). In contrast, he continues, the more careful philosophers recognize that we never discern the causal powers in any event, no matter how familiar. However, this recognition has led many of them astray, because they then conclude that, because we perceive no power in the objects, there is no power there: that *all* events, not just miraculous ones, are produced directly by a divine intervention. They thus convert the occasional error of the masses into a central doctrine:

many philosophers think themselves obliged by reason to have recourse, on all occasions, to the same principle, which the vulgar never appeal to but in cases that appear miraculous and supernatural. They acknowledge mind and intelligence to be, not only the ultimate and original cause of all things, but the immediate and sole cause of every event which appears in nature. They pretend that those objects which are commonly denominated *causes*, are in reality nothing but *occasions*; and that the true and direct principle of every effect is not any power or force in nature, but a volition of the Supreme Being, who wills that such particular objects should for ever be conjoined with each other. (70)

Hume adds that these philosophers do not rest content with this, but even extend the argument to the operations of our minds. He concludes: 'Thus, according to these philosophers, every thing is full of God. Not content with the principle, that nothing exists but by his will, that nothing possesses any power but by his concession: *They rob nature, and all created beings, of every power*, in order to render their dependence on the Deity still more sensible and immediate' (71; emphasis added). Hume's protest is that the occasionalists remove all powers from objects. If he himself believes that there are no natural powers, this is, to say the least, a surprising complaint.

It would be hasty, however, to draw a firm conclusion at this point, because Hume is mainly concerned here to press an issue that is internal to the occasionalists' project. In so maximizing our dependence on the deity, he argues, they do not see that their argument is in an important respect self-defeating: it robs the

---

[13] Hume uses the original Greek term, *theos apo mēchanēs* (69 n.). His claim has implications for the unsophisticated response to miraculous events, although he does not press the point at this stage.

deity of the very grandeur they seek to attribute to him. It does so because

It argues surely more power in the Deity to delegate a certain degree of power to inferior creatures than to produce every thing by his own immediate volition. It argues more wisdom to contrive at first the fabric of the world with such perfect foresight that, of itself, and by its proper operation, it may serve all the purposes of providence, than if the great Creator were obliged every moment to adjust its parts, and animate by his breath all the wheels of that stupendous machine. (71)

Here we see Hume relying on a mechanical model to make his point. Admittedly, his aim with this argument is not to state his own beliefs, but to point out the—theologically speaking—self-undermining character of the occasionalist argument. Since the occasionalists are themselves mechanists, to appeal to mechanical principles at this point may be to do no more than the argument requires. This does not seem entirely convincing. Hume does not distance himself from these considerations—he does not 'quarantine' the machine metaphor in any way—so the natural interpretation is that he is appealing to a belief that he shares with those philosophers; and, indeed, with all well-educated individuals. That is, his objection is most naturally read as the complaint that they are drawing the wrong conclusions from the right—mechanical—conception of the world. So it seems that it *is* his view that the occasionalists go astray because 'they rob nature, and all created beings, of every power'.

Hume proceeds to offer 'a more philosophical confutation of this theory'. At this point we should expect him to reveal his points of agreement and disagreement with his targets. So if he does agree with the spirit of the occasionalist drive to 'rob nature . . . of every power', this would be the place to do it. He does not do so. Instead, he produces two objections, both moderately sceptical in character, but neither of which gives any comfort to the common interpretation. The first simply points out that, whatever the internal coherence of the argument, it is just too strange to compel belief: 'We are got into fairyland, long ere we have reached the last steps of our theory' (72). This complaint is close to the objection that Hume brings against Pyrrhonian scepticism, and as such implicitly suggests that his own views are closer to common sense. The second pushes more firmly in the same direction: it implicitly affirms the sceptical realist interpretation, that what he wants to deny is not natural powers, but merely our knowledge of them. He points out that the argument turns on our ignorance of any powers in bodies, but we cannot pretend to any greater assurance about the powers of the divinity: 'are we not equally ignorant of the manner or force by which a mind, even the supreme mind, operates either on itself or on body?' The argument here entirely concerns what we can know, not what there is. Hume's conclusion is simply that ignorance is ignorance, and as such cannot be the foundation of a positive system:

Were our ignorance, therefore, a good reason for rejecting any thing, we should be led into that principle of denying all energy in the Supreme Being as much as in the grossest matter. We surely comprehend as little the operations of the one as of the other. Is it more difficult to conceive that motion may arise from impulse than that it may arise from volition? All we know is our profound ignorance in both cases.   (72–3)

If this is all we know, then one thing we do not and cannot know is that there are no powers in nature.

Equally, we do not and cannot know that there are, so Hume concludes with a footnote to remind the reader that Newtonian principles do not depend on, or even appeal to, any insight into the real natures of objects. Newton's best-known forces are merely manifest principles, not the hidden, ultimate powers of objects:

We find by experience, that a body at rest or in motion continues for ever in its present state, till put from it by some new cause; and that a body impelled takes as much motion from the impelling body as it acquires itself. These are facts. When we call this a *vis inertiae* [inertial force], we only mark these facts, without pretending to have any idea of the inert power; in the same manner as, when we talk of gravity, we mean certain effects, without comprehending that active power. It was never the meaning of Sir ISAAC NEWTON to rob second causes of all force or energy; though some of his followers have endeavoured to establish that theory upon his authority.   (73 n.)

Thus Hume winds up his discussion of the occasionalists with the reminder that the manifest principles of Newton do not depend on claims about what is beyond experience, as Newton himself was so keen to point out. Nevertheless, Newton did not seek to deny that there are hidden powers in nature, and Hume appends this note precisely in order to side with Newton, against the occasionalists, on just this question. The sceptical doubt expressed in Part I is not that there are no powers in nature, but that we do not directly perceive them. Our idea of power does not arise from any impression of power in any *singular* perception, whether of external bodies or of internal acts of volition. Hume does not conclude that this requires denying real natural powers. That particular conclusion is the error of the occasionalists, most notably of Malebranche, since—imitation being the sincerest form of flattery—his negative *epistemological* arguments are so solid.

Part II

The sceptical solution is quickly reached. In *single* instances of the operations of bodies, of the operations of the mind on the body, and also on the will's authority 'over its own faculties and ideas', the conclusion is the same:

All events seem entirely loose and separate. One event follows another; but we never can observe any tie between them. They seem *conjoined*, but never *connected* . . . the necessary conclusion *seems* to be that we have no idea of connexion or power at all, and that these words are absolutely without any meaning, when employed either in philosophical reasonings or common life. (74)

Seems, but not *is*. Hume does not accept the conclusion that our idea of power has no foundation, and is therefore meaningless. For there is, he adds, 'one method of avoiding this conclusion'. Although it is true that, when confronted with single cases, we cannot discover causes and effects, the same is not true of repeated instances: 'when one particular species of event has always, in all instances, been conjoined with another, we make no longer any scruple of foretelling one upon the appearance of the other, and of employing that reasoning, which can alone assure us of any matter of fact or existence. We then call the one object, *Cause*; the other, *Effect*' (74–5).

So our (practical) difficulties disappear. The question is, why? Hume's answer is that we make a supposition concerning how the world must be: 'We *suppose* that that there is some connexion between them; some power in the one, by which it infallibly produces the other, and *operates with the greatest certainty and strongest necessity*' (75; emphases added). We come to accept that there is a connection between the two events, that the first has a power that produces the second: 'It appears, then, that this idea of a necessary connexion among events arises from a number of similar instances which occur of the constant conjunction of these events' (75).

How can this be so? Section IV Part II has argued that repetition of events does not reveal anything new about the relation between the events: the powers remain inaccessible no matter how many times a perception is repeated. Section V Part I, however, has drawn

attention to the mind's propensity to make customary connections: where sequences of events regularly recur, 'the mind is
carried by habit . . . to expect its usual attendant, and to believe
that it will exist'. That is, 'This connexion . . . which we *feel* in the
mind, this customary transition of the imagination from one
object to its usual attendant, is the *sentiment or impression* from
which we form the idea of power or necessary connexion. Nothing
farther is in the case' (75; emphasis added).

The impression from which the idea stems has been found.
There is no denying, however, that what has been discovered is
a very imperfect impression on which to found the idea. The
problem is not simply that the impression does not reveal the
underlying nature of the world, for no impression does that. It
is, rather, that the impression does not derive directly from the
impressions of the objects to which the idea is attached. The idea
of necessary connection between objects derives from an impression that is distinct from the perceptions of the objects themselves.
This impression is no more than the felt quality of the customary—involuntary—transition of the mind when confronted by
repetitions of similar events. (It can, perhaps, be called a *concomitant* impression, because it is an impression that comes to attend
another impression.[14]) The idea of cause—of power or necessary
connection—is an idea generated *through* experience of the world
around us, but it is specifically derived *from* an impression that
reflects not any feature of the external world—not any powers of
objects—but the instinctive tendencies of the human mind itself.
The idea of necessary connection arises in response to the observed
orderliness of the world, but not through any rational insight into
the sources of that order. Rather, that orderliness of experience
proves to us that there are causal powers. As Hume puts it, we
connect objects as cause and effect through 'this inference, by
which they become proofs of each other's existence' (that is, their
existence *as* cause and effect) (76). Proofs are not insights into how
nature really is; they are simply part of the instinctive processes
of the human mind. They are, however, beliefs that are, for us,
irresistible and thus normative—even if fallible. Experience thus
leads us, independently of any rational insight—any genuine
knowledge—to conclusions about the constitution of the world.
This is Hume's sceptical solution.

The human mind's tendency to function by habitual associa-

---

[14] Cf. Francis Hutcheson's doctrine of concomitant ideas, *An Essay on the Nature and
Conduct of the Passions and Affections. With Illustrations on the Moral Sense* (1728) (Hildesheim:
Georg Olms, 1969), I. 1.

tions is shown here at its most profound, since the idea of necessary connection embodies a special deceit: despite being so fundamental to so much of our reasoning—the foundation of 'all our
reasonings concerning matter of fact and existence'—and despite
being the idea of a relation that, *par excellence*, is to be contrasted
with merely habitual associations, it is itself founded on just such
an association. Once again we see the profound deceptiveness
of custom: 'Such is the influence of custom, that, where it is
strongest, it not only covers our natural ignorance, but even conceals itself, and seems not to take place, merely because it is found
in the highest degree' (28–9). In all factual reasonings that go
beyond immediate sense perceptions, then, the human mind is
both dependent on a purely instinctual tendency, and also systematically misled—by this very tendency—over the nature of its
operations. 'No conclusions can be more agreeable to scepticism
than such as make discoveries concerning the weakness and
narrow limits of human reasoning and capacity,' remarks Hume
(76), and here the limits of human rational powers are plainly
revealed.

Hume's conclusion is sceptical; but it will be misunderstood if
that scepticism is itself misunderstood. His scepticism is the denial
that we have access to the essences of things on which rational knowledge of the world—*scientia* or dogmatic philosophy—is
built. A key part of that denial is that reason cannot give us any
such access because it has no access independently of what is given
in perception, and perception itself provides no building blocks for
insightful rational construction. Since philosophical knowledge or
scientia is the knowledge of causes, then any such project will be
doomed from the start if we have no adequate idea of a cause—
that is, no idea of cause that accurately reflects real causes in the
world. So, if our idea of causal power arises through an indirect,
instinctive process that, however harmonious with the observed
orderliness of the world, occurs entirely independently of perception of the real powers in the world, then philosophical knowledge is indeed impossible. We will continue to think and reason
and believe, but we will do so not because we are rational beings
who act on the basis of discovering the way the world is, but
because we are instinctive beings for whom experience cranks our
mind into action, and does so such that we function *in parallel to*
the way the world is.

Hume said that what was original about his philosophy was the
use he made of the principle of the association of ideas. Those principles—causation included—are, he said, '*to us* the cement of the

universe'.[15] Hume's message can here be turned against the
common view, that he denies the existence of real causal powers.
On that view, things not only *seem* 'loose and separate': they *are*.
They are because the analysis of our sense impressions fails utterly
to detect powers. But to conclude this is to mistake Hume's use of
the 'theory of ideas'. Hume's target is dogmatism of all kinds, and
to this end he adapts the language of ideas. The theory of ideas is
reshaped to fit his own sceptical philosophy. Ideas are reduced to
copies of physical effects of the outer world on our minds, and so
lose all claim to clarity and distinctness in the Cartesian sense. No
ideas are markers of truth, *criteria* of reality in the sense employed
by the ancients; all ideas, true or false, adequate or inadequate,
vary merely in vivacity. To this sceptical idea is added another: the
analysis of our perceptions shows that the impressions from which
our ideas arise are not all directly produced by the world imping-
ing on us. Some are, instead, due to the influence of *human nature*
operating on our original perceptions: the associative powers of
the mind cause resembling but different ideas to become mixed
up; and they cause (uniformly) temporally contiguous perceptions
to be cemented together by the tie of necessity. Experience delivers vivid perceptions that, as Locke had emphasized, suffice
for our practical purposes; but they are merely the effects of impressed forces and associative mechanisms, and do not disclose
the natures of their causes. The theory of ideas is not, for Hume,
a means to the discovery of the true nature of the world, or of its
parts.[16]

A view of this kind will find support by discovering those ideas
that are *manifestly* inadequate, or obscure, or confused: ideas that,
so to speak, bear their falsehood on their face.[17] One such example
is those relative ideas where one of the relata is defined *only* rela-
tionally. The idea of the cause of my perceptions, for example, is

[15] *Abstract*, in *Treatise*, 662.
[16] John Wright has argued that Hume *rejects* the theory of ideas. See, in particular, 'Hume's
Rejection of the Theory of Ideas'. Edward Craig and Galen Strawson similarly raise questions
over its suitability for his project. See Craig, *The Mind of God and the Works of Man*, ch. 2;
Strawson, *The Secret Connexion*, 49–58. Kenneth Winkler has objected that Hume stays within
the bounds of ideas even when he is alleged to be rejecting them. See 'The New Hume',
552–61. My suggestion here recommends a middle course, but one sanctioned, I believe, by
Hume himself. The tensions discerned by Wright and his fellow-travellers are real, but their
interpretations are perhaps overly strong. Hume wants to keep the theory as a critical weapon,
especially for use against scholasticism. This is a well-trodden path, a part of the overtly anti-
Catholic air of the work. (Cf. Hobbes on Suarez's scholastic jargon: 'When men write whole
volumes of such stuffe, are they not Mad, or intend to make others so?' (*Leviathan*, ch. VIII,
59).) But his own version of the 'way of ideas', like Locke's, sharply distinguishes what can
be meaningfully said about the world from the way the world is. This is a sceptical feature
they share: see my 'British Sceptical Realism'.
[17] Cf. Locke's discussion of these different features of ideas (*Essay*, II. xxix–xxii). Note also
that they are followed immediately by a later addition, 'Of the Association of *Ideas*' (II. xxiii).

such an idea, because the object that is the cause of my perceptions is itself unperceived; it can be thought only in terms of its
place in the relation, not according to its own properties. Ideas like
this are obviously inadequate to the real state of affairs that they
attempt to capture.[18] So Hume sometimes refers to such inadequate
ideas as 'suppositions' or 'notions'. They are ideas, in the sense of
mental contents traceable to impressions; but they are not wholly
reducible to impressions, and so are manifestly incomplete or of
otherwise inferior stock.[19] This is also the case with the idea of necessary connection. It is another idea that is manifestly inadequate
to the reality for which it stands. We do find an impression from
which the idea arises, so it satisfies the meaning conditions of the
theory of ideas: to employ it is not to lapse into the drivel of the
scholastics, language that is unintelligible because it fails the test
of experience. But the investigation of the idea reveals it to be obviously flawed, quite inadequate for capturing the nature of the
world we inhabit.

In fact, the investigation teaches not only the inadequacy of the
idea itself, but, because of its importance for us, and because of
its manner of arising through a fundamental process of human
nature, it also reveals just what imperfect creatures we are, how far
human nature falls short of the task set for it by the dogmatic
philosophers. Hume had said, in the Introduction to the *Treatise*,
that 'the science of man is the only solid foundation for the other
sciences'.[20] What he meant, as we can now see, is that the science
of man is the only foundation for the sciences, but it is not solid,
and so there can in the end *be* no science—that is, no *scientia*—
after all. This does not, however, mean all is lost. Although
nature's depths cannot be plumbed, we do not thereby lose all our

---

[18] See Locke's discussion of the idea of substance ('Substance in general'), which is a
relative idea of this kind (*Essay*, II. xxiii. 1–3).

[19] It is well-formed (vivid) ideas that faithfully reveal their origins in impressions, and it
is such ideas that are the stock of accurate reasoning and experiment. Such ideas are para-
digm case ideas—capable of accurate definition—and so are sometimes referred to by Hume
as ideas, *in contrast to*, suppositions and notions and 'merely relative' ideas (although this
last term is employed only in the *Treatise*). Edward Craig picks up this difference, but somewhat overstates the case when he claims that ideas only cover 'that area of thought which
is susceptible of reasoning, experiment, clarity, knowledge of truth and falsehood' (*The Mind
of God and the Works of Man*, 126). In fact, *no* ideas are genuinely susceptible of clarity or of
knowledge of truth or falsehood (i.e. of real natures): there are no *criteria* given in experience. But it is only such stable and vivid, accurately definable ideas that can play a role in
accurate reasonings from experience, i.e. in accurate experimental philosophy. Only such
ideas, in short, have a role in what we *now* call the 'empirical sciences'. Cf. Hume's comments on 'the great advantage of the mathematical sciences above the moral' with which
Section VII begins, with what we 'suppose' when our clear ideas fall short (*Enquiries*, 60–2,
75). See also Strawson's discussion of Hume's use of 'relative idea', and of notions and suppositions, in *The Secret Connexion*.

[20] *Treatise*, p. xvi.

standards for judging the world and its effects. Experience remains our practical guide. The customary processes of the imagination operate on our perceptions, forging them into connected experience, and thereby manufactures a point of view that accords with—even if it does not comprehend—the course of the world itself. Scepticism thus arrives at a viewpoint that is 'durable and useful' (161), and does so even though it drastically confines the reach of our perceptions, and insists on profound limits to our rationality.

The starkness of these limits will be reproduced, not overcome, by any attempt to *define* necessary connection. A definition, by fixing the referent(s) of the idea, cannot escape the limitations discovered in the investigation; it cannot but faithfully reproduce them. Why is this so? It stems from the requirement, explicit in Locke but implicit in the sceptical interpretation of experience at the heart of experimental philosophy, that a definition of any real existence can pick out only the originating impressions, not the substance or real qualities that underlie them. A definition is therefore limited by the adequacy of the relevant idea. Ideas that are not adequate to the reality they represent will result in definitions in which that inadequacy is preserved. The problem is illustrated by Edmund Burke, writing shortly after the *Enquiry* was composed:

when we define, we seem in danger of circumscribing nature within the bounds of our own notions, which we often . . . form out of a limited and partial consideration of the object before us, instead of extending our ideas to take in all that nature comprehends, according to her manner of combining . . . A definition may be very exact, and yet go but a very little way towards informing us of the nature of the thing defined . . .[21]

There is no reason, then, to suppose that a definition will solve the difficulties encountered in explaining the relations of our ideas to the world. Since a definition does no more than connect an idea to its originating impression, it can be called upon to settle questions about the nature of the reality the idea represents only if we can be confident that the idea in question adequately represents that reality. If it does not, then the definition will simply reproduce the gap between the idea and the world. The moral is that homing in on definitions is not the way to determine what Hume believes about the real nature of the world.

---

[21] Edmund Burke, *A Philosophical Enquiry into the Origin of our Ideas of the Sublime and Beautiful* (1757), ed. J. T. Boulton (Notre Dame, Ind.: University of Notre Dame Press, 1958), 12. (My thanks to Galen Strawson for drawing this passage to my attention).

The problem is particularly acute with respect to the idea of necessary connection, for two reasons. In the first place, the idea being named is, on Hume's account, an idea that arises from an impression of reflection. It therefore cannot be defined ostensively as can our ideas of external objects. The problem here is the same as that already indicated by Hume in his discussion of belief: belief is a feeling, so 'belief' cannot be defined to anyone who is unacquainted with the feeling. One cannot directly introduce someone to a feeling, as one can introduce someone to a kind of object (to an impression of sensation), by pointing out the object. The problem is the same as that encountered in learning to understand what one is experiencing when encountering an emotion for the first time. The best examples of this are those emotions that reflect the peculiar tortures of encroaching adulthood, such as romantic love, or humiliation.

Secondly, in the case of the idea of necessary connection, the originating impression from which the idea arises—the felt quality of the instinctive tendency—is 'extraneous and foreign' to the real power, the *intended* referent of the idea. That is, what is being named is *in intention* a real power in the world, a relation between perceptible objects. In the normal case, relations are as readily definable by ostensive means as are the objects themselves: for example, 'above', 'below', 'beside', 'larger than', 'taller than', and so on present no special difficulties for ostensive definition. In the case of power, cause, or necessary connection, the idea appears to be ostensively definable in the same way, but is not. The definition can only point out the perceptible relations from which the idea arises, but to which it does not intend to refer. Offering a definition in that way does enable each individual to learn to fix the name to the corresponding idea—provided, of course, that, as in the case of belief, the relevant internal phenomena can be identified—and so the definition does serve a practical purpose. Nevertheless, the definition is, and must remain, very 'imperfect'. It can do no more than connect the idea either to the external circumstances that generate it—the *observed* conjunctions of events—or to the actual tendency of human nature by which it is produced—the *experienced* feeling of necessity occasioned by a present impression. Both of these foci are 'extraneous and foreign' to the intended referents, the real powers in the world, whatever they might happen to be. So the definition must be imperfect: it must fail to pick out the relevant real feature of the world.

Hume emphasizes the point when introducing his own definitions: 'so imperfect are the ideas which we form concerning it, that it is impossible to give any just definition of cause, except what is drawn from something extraneous and foreign to it' (76). It is part and parcel of the necessary imperfection of a definition of necessity that there are two equally good (or bad) ways of defining. The process by which the idea arises is indirect, so we can define the idea by focusing either on the unprocessed raw data (the observations of conjoined events), or on the product of the processing by the customary mechanisms of human nature (the impression of expectation). In the *Treatise*, Hume had called the first of these the 'philosophical' relation, because it depends on 'a comparison of two ideas': that is, it follows the typical use of the theory of ideas by analysing the distinct ideas (in his language, 'impressions') given to sense. This first definable relation also deserves to be called 'philosophical' because it acknowledges the insight of the philosophers, that powers are not directly perceived. The second relation he had called the 'natural' relation, because it depends on an operation of human nature, the 'association betwixt them [the "ideas"]'.[22] The fact of the two definitions is itself evidence of the unavoidable imperfection of definition in this case (just as multiplicity had indicated imperfection in the various 'descriptions' offered of belief in Section V). The further fact that they are not equivalent underlines the point. The moral is that close scrutiny of the definitions, conducted independently of an understanding of Hume's larger theory of human nature and its implications, is not the key to understanding his commitments. The definitions are not the high road to Hume's views of the nature of the world itself.[23]

The two definitions are as follows:

Similar objects are always conjoined with similar. Of this we have experience. Suitably to this experience, therefore, we may define a cause to be *an object,*

[22] *Treatise*, 170. See also Hume's discussion of 'philosophical' and 'natural' relations (ibid. 13–15).
[23] Thus it is not surprising that the vast literature on the definitions, in both their *Treatise* and *Enquiry* forms, is not always rewarding. As Alexander Rosenberg observes, 'rendering a single interpretation that does justice to . . . these explicit definitions has kept many philosophers occupied for a fair portion of the twentieth century' ('Hume and the Philosophy of Science', in Norton (ed.) *The Cambridge Companion to Hume*, 71). A widely read article, if too stipulative about what 'define' can mean, is J. A. Robinson, 'Hume's Two Definitions of "Cause"', in Chappell (ed.), *Hume*, 129–47. Cf. B. Stroud, *Hume* (London: Routledge, 1977), 88 ff., and Beauchamp and Rosenberg, *Hume and the Problem of Causation*, 13 ff. See also Craig, *The Mind of God and the Works of Man*, 102–11, and Strawson, *The Secret Connexion*, 208–13, for pertinent discussions of what Hume intends. A thorough recent discussion is D. Garrett, *Cognition and Commitment in Hume's Philosophy* (New York: Oxford University Press, 1997). Garrett divides views of the definitions into those that consider Hume to 'endorse' them, and those that do not. On the interpretation offered, Hume gives two answers to this question. He endorses *both* definitions *as definitions* (as determinations of the impressions from which the idea arises); but he endorses *neither* definition, if they are taken as telling us what powers exist in the world.

followed by another, and where all the objects similar to the first are followed by objects similar to the second. Or in other words *where, if the first object had not been, the second never had existed.* The appearance of a cause always conveys the mind, by a customary transition, to the idea of the effect. Of this we also have experience. We may, therefore, suitably to this experience, form another definition of cause, and call it, *an object followed by another, and whose appearance always conveys the thought to that other.* But though both these definitions be drawn from circumstances foreign to the cause, we cannot remedy this inconvenience, or attain any more perfect definition, which may point out that circumstance in the cause, which gives it a connexion with its effect. (76–7)

Both definitions are founded in experience, because they connect the idea to the impression that gives rise to it: the first implicitly, the second explicitly. They are, therefore, proper definitions, which, in their different ways, satisfy the requirements of Hume's version of the theory of ideas. Both are also imperfect, because they fail to identify the real power in the object that they aim to capture. Instead, they incorporate 'circumstances foreign to the cause' in order to capture the source of the idea: in the first case, the repeated instances of pairs of events; in the second, the transition of the mind when confronted by the object (the cause), once it has become accustomed to the further object (the effect) that has uniformly accompanied it in experience. The idea of necessary connection is meaningful, because it originates in an impression. This impression is a product of the customary principles of human nature when confronted by a world whose powers it cannot discern. The definition is thus a sceptic's definition, because it shows us to possess—and necessarily to possess—an idea that, although fundamental to our capacity to understand the world, does not reflect the nature of the world.[24] The definitions show, in short, not anything real about the world, but the central shortcoming of human nature, its inability to penetrate nature's secrets: 'No conclusions can be more agreeable to scepticism than such as make discoveries concerning the weakness and narrow limits of human reasoning and capacity.'[25]

There is one fly in the ointment. Hume adds, immediately after

[24] Flew observes that the definitions make no reference to necessary connection, but mistakenly thinks this a failure of nerve. It is, rather, the whole point. See *Hume's Philosophy of Belief*, 123 ff.; cf. Beauchamp and Rosenberg, *Hume and the Problem of Causation*, 11–12.

[25] Cf. Norman Kemp Smith: 'what [Hume] intends to assert is not that there is no such thing as necessity or agency outside the mind, but that the only *meaning* which we can attach to the terms "necessity", "efficacy", "agency", "power", "energy", is one which derives from what is no more than a feeling, i.e. from what is possible of existence only in some mind, and that we cannot therefore, by means of it, hope to have any kind of *understanding or comprehension* of what, through the processes of belief, we none the less come to locate in external happenings' (*The Philosophy of David Hume*, 397).

giving his definitions: 'We have no idea of this connexion, nor even any distinct notion what it is we desire to know, when we endeavour at a conception of it' (77). He here insists that the actual nature of the world, the nature of the real powers, is utterly beyond our reach: so much so that, in asking whether there are real causal powers in objects, we find ourselves caught on the eristic dilemma: how can we know how to search, when we do not know what it is for which we search? And, if we do not know for what we search, how can we know that *there is indeed something* for which to search? So does not Hume here rule out the sceptical realist interpretation? This is the conclusion drawn by Kenneth Winkler. He suggests that Hume's scepticism is to be understood as 'a *refusal to affirm* the existence of real powers'.[26] His ground is the one identified here. He observes: 'Hume needn't say that there is no such thing as objective connection; it is enough for him to say that we cannot *in any way* conceive of it, and that as a result we cannot believe in it.'[27] Hume does not, then, believe there to be real causal powers.

It will be useful to separate this objection into two parts. First of all, if what we have to go on in explaining Hume's views reduces to a catalogue of such comments, then Winkler is right. What we cannot conceive of we cannot conceive of, and there is an end to the matter. The burden of this study, however, is that we have a good deal more to go on, in the form of Hume's presentation of human nature as guided by custom and other associative processes, processes that are illuminated by reference to mechanical models of nature. Hume is, it has been argued, applying the results of the latest science to human nature. He thereby draws in a conception of the human mind as systematically cut off from nature's secrets, and so cut off precisely because its fundamental processes are themselves mechanical in kind. It is against this background, then, that we should interpret the remarks to which Winkler appeals, for it is equally clear that this whole picture cannot be justified by reference to any ideas we have of our own real nature. If Hume is engaged simply in a first-person phenomenological analysis, then there is no basis for affirming real powers. But this should not surprise, since it is also clear that, on this basis, thoroughgoing phenomenalism, and even solipsism, appear equally to be unavoidable.

If this is not Hume's project—if, instead, he is trying to marry a first-personal analysis of impressions with the best available third-

---

[26] Winkler, 'The New Hume', 567.   [27] Ibid. 576.

personal story about the nature of the world itself—trying to show that our first-personal experience conforms to a consistently applied third-personal mechanical conception of the world, then it will not surprise if his language runs up against the difficulties embedded in such an ambitious enterprise. In such circumstances, however, we already recognize that conceptual purity is not the solution when confronted by the difficulties of any such task. Thus we do not ridicule the physicists of a century ago for affirming what is inconceivable, the wave-particle duality of light; nor do we ridicule contemporary physicists who accept the Copenhagen interpretation of quantum mechanics, despite its affront to common sense. We instead accept that the world is, at the microlevel, a very strange place, and that such views, despite their obvious conceptual difficulties, are not *therefore* to be dismissed. An adequate account of the complexites of the world is no easy task, and we should not simply leap on infelicitous claims, and thereby reject investigative projects. My suggestion is that we should treat Hume's project in the same way.

This view needs a further support before it can be convincing: it needs to be established that Hume does go beyond the refusal to affirm or deny real powers, that he does in fact *accept* that there are real powers, despite the apparently inconsistent denial that we have any notion of such things. The fundamental question here, in the terminology of the *Treatise*, is whether belief in real powers is a *natural* belief. This is because Hume's mechanical theory, by separating perceptions from objects, confronts exactly the same problem with respect to the reality of the world itself, powers or no powers. He resolves that problem by affirming that, despite our lacking any idea of the world that causes our perceptions—we necessarily lack impressions of the causes of our impressions—still we cannot help but believe that there is a real world that is that cause: 'We may well ask, *What causes induce us to believe in the existence of body?* but 'tis in vain to ask, *Whether there be body or not?* That is a point, which we must take for granted in all our reasonings.'[28] The question is, is his account of causal powers to be assimilated to this conclusion?

The answer, I believe, is yes—and for a reason that has already been given. It has been argued above that Hume's account of the genesis of the idea of necessary connection is a *proof* from experience. Wherever our experience is uniform, there we come to expect things to go on in the same way, exceptionlessly; and this

<hr>

[28] *Treatise*, 187.

exception-denying expectation just *is* the belief that things are
necessarily thus and so. The belief in necessary connections is thus
unavoidable wherever experience is uniform, so we are therefore
beings who necessarily believe that regularities in experience are
the result of causal powers in the objects—no matter how much
analysis of perceptions fails to reveal such powers to us. Hume
believes in causal powers for the same reason that he believes
in the real world itself: it is a natural belief, a belief necessarily
generated in beings like us by the regularities of experience.
Experience *proves* the reality of causal powers to us, because those
regularities are, for us, 'arguments from experience as leave no
room for doubt or opposition'.[29] This is, then, the second part of
the reply to Winkler. Hume does not, because he cannot, refuse to
affirm the existence of real powers. He has no idea what real
powers in nature might be, but he believes they are there nonetheless. Belief is not voluntary: 'Nature is too strong for principle'
(160).

It is now possible to tie up some loose ends. Hume's gloss on his
first definition—'in other words *where, if the first object had not been,
the second never had existed*'—has caused puzzlement. In contrast
to the definition itself, it appears to specify only a necessary condition, and so seems not to mean the same thing at all. Obviously,
the 'second' object could occur for reasons quite independent of
the first, without the necessary regularities being in any way compromised. Thus bread always nourishes; and nourishment is therefore recognized as an effect caused by bread. But oranges and
apples also nourish, so nourishment is not dependent on eating
bread. Hume's gloss appears committed to denying this, and so
seems plainly false. One plausible solution is that Hume has in
mind that pair of objects that are the latest occurrence of a regular
pairing. This would fit his use in the first definition itself. So 'first

---

[29] Winkler claims that Hume does not accord causal belief the same degree of conviction
as belief in external bodies ('The New Hume', 561–6). This may be so, but is not a decisive
consideration. The central issue is not whether belief in causal powers cannot, in no matter
what circumstance, be shaken, but whether uniform experience by itself compels belief in
necessity. Hume allows that there can be 'proof against proof', in which case the weaker proof
gives way (114). This is a central step in the argument against belief in miracle reports. If it
is insisted that the weaker proof is thereby shown not to be a natural belief, the point can
be conceded without affecting the substance of the issue. The natural belief in the external
world is proven by the vivacity of present impression, and by the orderliness—the uniformity—of the succession of present impressions. Belief in causal powers has only the second
to underpin it, so we might expect that, in a contest between the two (should such a circumstance be possible), it would be belief in causal power that would give way before
the stronger proof of real things. But such a 'weakness' would in no way undermine, in
the normal case, the ability of the uniformity of experience to compel belief in causal powers.
Natural belief need not be restricted only to those beliefs that are inevitable *no matter
what*.

object' means that object we think of as the cause, and 'second object' the second of the pair, which we think of as the effect. His gloss then boils down to the observation that, if the cause does not exist, then neither will the effect, which is true.

Another possibility, not at bottom too dissimilar, offers a commonsensical resolution: that Hume is thinking of familiar discrete events, such as his occasional appeal to the billiard-ball example. I know that every time I hit the cue ball, it strikes the object ball and imparts motion to it. So when I now go to the table to hit the cue ball, the same effect will occur. If I do not hit the ball, nothing will happen—the balls will not move themselves. If the first does not occur, the second will not exist. Similarly, if I do not eat my usual meal—of bread, as it happens—nourishment will not follow. In both cases, what are being picked out are occurrences in the world, not customary transitions in the mind, so these are illustrations of the first definition, not of the second. On either of these interpretations, Hume's point is sound, and he is not guilty of denying the antecedent.

Another possibility is worth considering. If Hume is thinking of cases where the second object has been experienced only after experience of the first, then it would follow, on his own account, that, after a multitude of instances, we would believe that the second *could* occur only after the first. Constant conjunction would generate the belief that they are necessarily connected. The second without the first would be contrary to all experience, and in that sense would be judged impossible: experience would *prove* it impossible. So, whether the interpretation offered of Hume's gloss is correct or not, the gloss itself can be employed to show how it might be that the human mind is naturally prone to fallacious reasoning. The mind, confronted with unbroken regular pairings of objects, concludes not only that the first necessarily produces the second, but also that the first is necessary *for* the second—despite having no grounds for ruling out other roads by which the second could occur. In doing so it makes an inference that is not deductively valid. It would be a rich irony if Hume has himself been led into this error, at just the point when he is explaining the imperfections of our idea of necessary connection itself. But, as the preceding interpretations imply, this conclusion is itself not necessary.

To return to the central message of this section. Hume has previously argued that the human mind constructs, according to principles conformable to a mechanical conception of its fundamental workings, a picture of the world that goes beyond the

actual contents of the impressions given in immediate outer and
inner perception. In doing so it does not rely on any insight into
the nature of the world, nor on any process of the rational faculty,
the understanding. It relies on customary transitions. In this
section he argues that this applies even to our very idea of necessary connection, the cornerstone of the idea of cause and effect—
itself the basis of all our reasonings from experience, and, indeed,
of our reasonings *concerning* experience, that is, of its real causes.
We are creatures of habit, not insight, and are so even in the
forging of that idea designed to distinguish necessary connections
from merely habitual associations, the real from the imagined.
Since this idea is also fundamental to the search for a systematic
understanding of the real causes of things, its essential imperfection rules out entirely the dream of philosophical knowledge of
the world, or *scientia*. Custom thus hides from us, not merely the
extent of its influence on our practical behaviour, but also the
imperfections of the conceptual resources with which it has provided us, and on which we must rely—both in the common course
of life, and in our most grand intellectual ambitions.

Section VIII

Of Liberty and Necessity

In this section, Hume defends a compatibilist account of the relation between human freedom and necessary laws of human nature. The compatibilism itself is entirely unremarkable for a thinker influenced by the mechanist tradition—compatibilist interpretations of one form or another are offered by many mechanical philosophers, especially, of course, by materialists, such as Hobbes, or by those prepared to regard materialism as possible, such as Locke. It is unlikely, then, that Hume's readers would have found anything novel or startling in the broad commitments expressed here. It is reasonable to expect, then, that the point of the section lies in the details, rather than in the compatibilist conclusion itself. This hypothesis does bear fruit: approaching the section in such a spirit suggests Hume's main concerns to be the confirmation of his account of necessity by its ability to establish the compatibilist conclusion; to affirm and underline the compatibilist commitment to fitting human nature into a general account of physical nature; and to show both the advantages for moral philosophy and the problems for theology implicit in the compatibilist resolution. Hume's purposes, then, are metaphysical, moral, and religious: a consistent experimentalism will teach us our place in the world, affirm our status as responsible moral agents, and at the same time show the depth of the problem confronting any theodicy.

Part I

Hume begins, as he had done in the previous section, with a defence of the importance of conceptual clarification in moral and metaphysical matters. His promise is, however, a little startling: the difficult, if not intractable, problem of the apparent conflict between liberty and necessity will not only be resolved, but everyone, despite their differences, will be shown to be in agreement—

that is, 'according to any reasonable sense, which can be put on
these terms' (81). The 'reasonable sense' is, of course, Hume's own,
at least with respect to the meaning of 'necessity'. In contrast, his
account of the meaning of 'liberty' is standard fare for an early
modern compatibilist. So we should expect that the weight of
Hume's discussion will fall on spelling out the implications of the
idea of necessity as explained in the previous section. The expectation is not disappointed.

Everyone agrees, says Hume, that every natural effect is produced by a necessary force that brings about precisely the effect
we observe, a force that is 'precisely determined by the energy of
its cause' (82).[1] To understand what is contained in this belief, we
need to discover how the idea of necessity arises. As has been
argued above, it arises from the uniformity observed in natural
occurrences: similar objects occur in regular arrangements; and the
mind through habit infers connections between them. So, if it can
be shown that these two features are true of voluntary human
behaviour, then it will have been shown that necessity is implicitly recognized—that is, *proven* by experience—to govern human
voluntary actions. There can be, therefore, no genuine disagreement about liberty and necessity: 'If it appear . . . that all mankind
have ever allowed, without any doubt or hesitation, that these two
circumstances take place in the voluntary actions of men, and in
the operations of mind; it must follow, that all mankind have ever
agreed in the doctrine of necessity, and that they have hitherto
disputed, merely for not understanding each other' (83). Hume's
strategy, then, is to consider human affairs from the two standpoints provided by each of the definitions of the idea of necessity,
and to show they do apply to such affairs.

Hume begins by affirming that human affairs do exhibit regular
conjunctions of similar events. The affirmation reflects his well-
known view that human nature is uniform in its basic principles.
He holds that human beings, in all times and places, have been
actuated by the same fundamental motives, and that these motives
are uniform in their effects:

It is universally acknowledged that there is a great uniformity among the
actions of men, in all nations and ages, and that human nature remains still
the same, in its principles and operations. The same motives always produce
the same actions: The same events follow from the same causes. Ambition,
avarice, self-love, vanity, friendship, generosity, public spirit: these passions,

---

[1] Note that this is a principle of conservation characteristic of the mechanists, affirmed in
Rule I of Newton's Rules of Reasoning in Philosophy (*Principia*, 398). It is also given an important supporting role in Hume's argument in Section XI.

mixed in various degrees, and distributed through society, have been, from the beginning of the world, and still are, the source of all the actions and enterprises, which have ever been observed among mankind. (83)

Given the social scientific orthodoxies of our age, it is important to stress that Hume is not claiming that human beings in all times and places have been the same in every significant respect. He is certainly not claiming that they have always had the same beliefs, and have always acted in the same way. He is not, in short, denying the reality of cultural differences. The most casual acquaintance with his writings on law and culture reveals, on the contrary, an insistence on the necessity of cultural variations: the whole point of his argument in *An Enquiry concerning the Principles of Morals*, that justice is founded in utility, is that social rules and their attendant mores *rightly* vary from one culture to the next, according to their different circumstances.[2]

What Hume is denying is that differences between societies and psyches go all the way down. He is claiming that the *fundamental motives* of the human psyche have always been the same, and that historians (and, as we would now say, anthropologists) show this to be so. In all societies, people are motivated by the same bedrock concerns, such that the best way to understand some past or foreign people is to transfer *most* of what we have learnt about our own fundamental motivations, individual or social. Hume's point is, in other words, not a denial of obvious human differences, but a version of the principle of charity: we must presume, when confronted by other societies, that their behaviours and social practices *make sense*—that they accord with what are for us basic explanatory principles. This is why anthropological studies *illuminate* in a way that natural histories of other species do not: we learn to see how the world *looks* to the eyes of another human being, something we never learn from studies of the behaviour of other animals. (That is why, in contrast to the familiarity that is a consequence of studies of other humans, animal behaviour remains *fascinating*. Fascination depends on impenetrability.)[3]

Hume argues that we show our reliance on the supposition of regularity when we reject travellers' tales or histories that claim

---

[2] *An Enquiry concerning the Principles of Morals*, Sections III–IV, in *Enquiries*, 183–211. Note, in particular, Hume's summary remark that 'the laws have, or ought to have, a constant reference to the constitution of government, the manners, the climate, the religion, the commerce, the situation of each society' (196), and the approving reference to Montesquieu that immediately follows.

[3] How sharply the boundaries need to be drawn between ourselves and other species is a matter of contention. A case against a sharp boundary is Frans de Waal, *Chimpanzee Politics: Power and Sex amongst the Apes* (New York: Harper & Row, 1982).

radically different basic principles of action in different times or places: thus the supernatural courage attributed to Alexander the Great by Quintus Curtius[4] is as unbelievable as the supernatural power also attributed to him by that author. (That is, extraordinary mental capacities are no more believable than extraordinary physical powers.) Accounts that attribute to foreign men no tinge of familiar motives, whether vicious or virtuous, are for just that reason no more credible than stories full of centaurs and dragons.[5] Further, this reliance on regularity also explains the value of experience in everyday life. General observations derived from experience are our guide in judging the behaviour of others, so, were there no such uniformity in human actions, experience would have no value.[6] This is not to deny human diversity. Hume acknowledges diversity stemming from differences in character, belief, and situation. But these differences themselves reveal underlying general principles that explain the differences that arise. Thus differences in customs lead us to principles about the force of custom; differences in the behaviour of the sexes lead us to principles about sex-linked differences in behaviour and general character; changes in outlook at different stages of life lead us to principles about age-linked factors. Even the differences in character between individuals provide insight, because the regularity of each distinct character is the foundation of our knowledge of each of those individuals, and of the behaviour we can expect from them.

This is not the whole of the story, Hume adds, for there are irreducible irregularities in human behaviour. However, admitting this is no reason for abandoning what has been said above; rather, we can adopt towards those irregularities exactly the same attitude we have to irregularities in the natural world, and proportion our confidence in an expected outcome according to the probabilities founded in past experience. We should not take such irregularities in human nature to be evidence for any uncertainty in the hidden causal powers that operate on, or within, the human frame.

[4] Quintus Curtius [Quintus Curtius Rufus], *History of Alexander*, trans. J. C. Rolfe (Cambridge, Mass.: Harvard University Press, 1946).

[5] Hume thus puts himself at odds with romantic idealizations like the 'noble savage'. In fact, he shows rather little interest in the New Worlds of the Americas and the Pacific, and the lessons they might provide—his own examples of different cultures are mainly drawn from the ancient world. Diderot's interest in the newly encountered societies provides a useful contrast. See Denis Diderot, *Supplément au Voyage de Bougainville*, in *Political Writings*, ed. J. H. Mason and R. Wokler (Cambridge: Cambridge University Press, 1992).

[6] Where uniformity is less visible, the evident value of experience will also be undermined. Thus the rapid rates of technological and social change in modern societies diminish the value of accumulated experience. This is most plain across generations: high rates of change render the past unintelligible to the next generation.

Rather, we should follow the methods of the natural philosophers, who, when confronted by irregularities, resolve these into 'the secret operation of contrary causes' (87). The human body, like other material things, is governed by the regular operations of hidden powers, and physicians, like philosophers, rightly attribute irregularities to the great complexity of the human body:

They know that a human body is a mighty complicated machine: That many secret powers lurk in it, which are altogether beyond our comprehension: That to us it must often appear very uncertain in its operations: And that therefore the irregular events, which outwardly discover themselves, can be no proof that the laws of nature are not observed with the greatest regularity in its internal operations and government. (87)

The same line of reasoning applies also to voluntary human actions. Irregularities of behaviour can be resolved into the operations of special causes. Of course, *all* irregularities cannot be explained in this way, since one regular feature of human character is a certain degree of unpredictability or caprice. But this no more denies uniform underlying principles than the irregularities of the weather imply violation of natural laws. In both cases the limitation is our ignorance, not the absence of regular natural operations: 'The internal principles and motives may operate in a uniform manner, notwithstanding these seeming irregularities; in the same manner as the winds, rain, clouds, and other variations of the weather are supposed to be governed by steady principles; though not easily discoverable by human sagacity and enquiry' (88). From all this it can be concluded both that 'the conjunction between motives and voluntary actions is as regular and uniform as that between the cause and effect in any part of nature', and also that, notwithstanding assumptions to the contrary, this is not a subject of disputation: 'this regular conjunction has been universally acknowledged among mankind, and has never been the subject of dispute, either in philosophy or in common life' (88). What has not previously been recognized, of course, is that this regularity is the linchpin of the idea of necessity. Therefore the key to resolving the apparent conflict between liberty and necessity has always been ready to hand—proven by our practice— but not recognized as such.

Hume now turns to consider human affairs through the lens of the second definition of necessity, thereby to show that we do draw inferences from observed regularities in human actions. He begins by observing that, given the argument of the previous section, it is strictly speaking superfluous to provide further arguments for necessitation in human voluntary actions—but to do so is valuable, because it will 'throw the argument into a greater variety of lights' (88–9). The key insight here concerns the fact, and more particularly the presuppositions, of human interdependence. The social interdependence of human beings is so great that no act is entirely free from the influence of others. In fact, the greater the extent of their dealings with others, the more human beings rely on *expectations* concerning others' voluntary actions. These expectations are based on past experience in just the same way as are expectations about the behaviour of natural phenomena; and in the same way they imply belief in the regularity of human behaviour. Hume thus concludes that the problem is dissolved by his explanation of necessity: 'Have we not reason, therefore, to affirm that all mankind have always agreed in the doctrine of necessity according to the foregoing definition and explication of it?' (89). The resolution embraces the presuppositions of the intellectuals as fully as it does everyday life, for endeavours as different as history, politics, morals, and aesthetic criticism all depend on assumptions concerning regular patterns of behaviour: thus histories are rendered credible, legislation purposeful, and morals and criticism relevant and intelligible. In all such cases we rely on an '*inference* from motives to voluntary actions, from characters to conduct' (90).

To this point, Hume has been concerned to show that the same principles can be applied to voluntary human actions as to natural phenomena. He now presses the point with an important argument, directed against the possibility that the two necessities—physical and human—are similar but distinct: notions that are parallel, but different. Hume must deny this, if he is not to reclassify his definitions as merely partial. He argues that the two necessities are indeed the same, by showing that human and purely natural phenomena can be fitted indifferently into a *single* chain of causes: the two necessities can coexist not merely in parallel but in series. Thus he points out that causal chains composed entirely of physical elements do not differ in the necessity of their effects from those that incorporate judgements about human actions or characters:

A prisoner who has neither money nor interest, discovers the impossibility of his escape, as well when he considers the obstinacy of the gaoler, as the walls and bars with which he is surrounded; and, in all attempts for his freedom, chooses rather to work upon the stone and iron of the one, than upon the inflexible nature of the other . . . Here is a connected chain of natural causes and voluntary actions; but the mind feels no difference between them in passing from one link to another: Nor is less certain of the future event than if it were connected with the objects present to the memory or senses, by a train of causes, cemented together by what we are pleased to call a *physical* necessity. The same experienced union has the same effect on the mind, whether the united objects be motives, volitions, and actions; or figure and motion.   (90–1)[7]

Of course, we do not always place such whole-hearted confidence (or despair) in human constancy, but, Hume adds, this is also true of natural phenomena. I trust a friend to conform to my expectations as much as I expect my house not to fall on me, even though I may be mistaken on either or both counts. We can imagine all kinds of possibilities that might lead the friend to behave in strange or unexpected ways, but nature also is not immune to the extraordinary. And some of our judgements of human behaviour, just like many of our judgements about nature, do not allow of the least doubt: we 'know with certainty' that a man will not put his hand into a fire and leave it there until it is destroyed. This doubt is not weakened even when it is *only* human behaviours that are in view: 'A man who at noon leaves his purse full of gold on the pavement at Charing-Cross, may as well expect that it will fly away like a feather, as that he will find it untouched an hour after' (91). We can be confident that modern-day London would not disappoint him in this particular. Reasonings about human actions thus show the same range of probabilities displayed in our judgements of natural phenomena.

What explains the failure to recognize this conformity? Why has everyone agreed in practice, but not in theory? The short answer, of course, is that they have not held Hume's view of the foundations of judgements of necessity. He does offer a longer answer, in which the short answer plays a central role. He suggests that the problem arises because our mistaken belief that we can perceive the real powers binding material objects together in causal relationships generates a false contrast with our perceptions of the operations of our own will, because with respect to the latter we recognize that we do not perceive any necessary connections.[8] But once it is acknowledged that in neither case is the causal power directly perceived, it then becomes clear that there is no essential difference between the two cases. The trouble, he concludes, stems from the fact that enquiries into this question begin at the wrong

---

[7] Note here also the implicitly mechanical conception: physical qualities are comprehended under the heads of 'figure and motion'.

[8] Hume is here thinking of the common-sense view, which affirms necessity in nature but freedom in ourselves. Locke, it should be remembered, held precisely the opposite (*Essay*, II. xxi. 4–5).

end, with reflection on the powers of the soul. If the enquiry began at the other end, and examined what is known about material causes, the conclusion reached would not concern a gulf between free will and unfree nature, but would simply affirm the narrow extent of our knowledge of causes, volitional or material. We have no insight into such hidden causes, but we can discover that regularity underpins causal judgements, that the same regularity is discovered in the actions of the will as in material nature, and therefore that necessity reigns in both domains.

Hume now turns to consider the other side of his compatibilist coin, the nature of liberty. Liberty, he says, is not denied by the conclusion just reached, for, once it is properly understood, it will be clear that all disputes concerning the presumed conflict between liberty and necessity have been 'merely verbal': they have arisen because of inappropriate definitions of terms. This is Hume's 'reconciling project'. The argument depends simply on finding the right definition. He sets it out succinctly:

> what is meant by liberty, when applied to voluntary actions? We cannot surely mean that actions have so little connexions with motives, inclinations and circumstances, that one does not follow with a certain degree of uniformity from the other, and that one affords no inference by which we can conclude the existence of the other. For these are plain and acknowledged matters of fact. By liberty, then, we can only mean *a power of acting or not acting, according to the determinations of the will*; that is, if we choose to remain at rest, we may; if we choose to move, we also may. Now this hypothetical liberty is universally allowed to belong to every one who is not a prisoner and in chains. Here, then, is no subject of dispute. (95)

This 'reconciliation' will seem more a matter of arbitrary assertion unless it is recognized that here Hume is offering nothing new. The mechanical philosophers typically offered accounts of liberty of this kind, whether from within the experimental tradition (for example, Locke[9]) or from outside it (for example, Hobbes[10]). Hume's brevity would surprise no reader familiar with

---

[9] 'I think *the Question is not proper, whether the Will be free, but whether a Man be free*. Thus . . . so far as any one can, by the direction or choice of his Mind, preferring the existence of any Action, to the non-existence of that Action, and, *vice versâ*, make it to exist, or not exist, so far he is *free*. For if I can, by a thought, directing the Motion of my Finger, make it move, when it was at rest, or *vice versâ*, 'tis evident, that in respect of that, I am free . . . For such a preferring of Action to its absence, is the *willing* of it: and we can scarce tell how to imagine any *Being* freer, than to be able to do what he *wills*' (Locke, *Essay*, II. xxi. 21).

[10] 'LIBERTY, or FREEDOME, signifieth (properly) the absence of Opposition; (by Opposition, I mean externall Impediments of motion;) and may be applyed no lesse to Irrationall, and Inanimate creatures, than to Rationall . . . *A* FREE-MAN, *is he, that in those things, which by his strength and wit he is able to do, is not hindred to doe what he has a will to*. But when the words *Free*, and *Liberty*, are applyed to anything but *Bodies*, they are abused; for that which is not

this broad tradition; in fact, given the preceding hints, it is rea-sonable to suppose that the conclusion is just what the discerning reader would have expected.

Hume concludes that the account of liberty given here can be *proven*, by ruling out the available alternative. The argument is this: everything that exists has a cause, since what is uncaused exists merely by chance, and there are no chance events: 'chance . . . is a mere negative word, and means not any real power which has any-where a being in nature' (95). But, since all causes imply necessary connections, to define liberty in the alternative way, as what is not necessary, is to equate it with chance. The cost of this definition is thus very high, because, even if coherent, it amounts to denying that such liberty exists: 'liberty, when opposed to necessity, not to constraint, is the same thing with chance; which is universally allowed to have no existence' (96). Notice, first of all, that the argu-ment is astonishing indeed if Hume denies powers in nature; so it can be taken as strong, if indirect, evidence that he does not. Sec-ondly, the argument is indeed a *proof* in Hume's special sense of the term (56n.). To rule out the only available alternative by showing it to be universally rejected is to provide an argument that leaves 'no room for doubt or opposition'. To show what, on reflection, we find we do or must believe, given the cluster of convictions that we display—and cannot conceive abandoning—is not to demonstrate the truth of a principle, but to *prove* our commitments from our practice. Hume's general strategy, then, is wholly conformable to the probabilism of Academic scepticism—as set out in Section VI—and shows that scepticism to be capable of arriving at indubitable, if not infallible, conclusions.

Part II

To understand clearly the argument of Part II it is necessary to step back, and to consider the conclusion Hume has reached in Part I against a wider background of morals and theology. The moral issue is clear: if we are creatures governed by necessity, how is morality possible? Moral responsibility appears to depend on a strong version of free will, such that we are the *originators* of our actions—and not merely that we choose them, where choice is

subject to Motion, is not subject to Impediment . . . from the use of the word *Freewill*, no liberty can be inferred to the will, desire, or inclination, but the liberty of the man; which consisteth in this, that he finds no stop, in doing what he has the will, desire, or inclination to doe' (Hobbes, *Leviathan*, ch. XXI, 145–6).

itself under the regime of necessity. Hume directly attacks this viewpoint in the opening paragraphs of Part II. He also appears to be well aware of the main theological ramifications of his position, concerning the possibility of theodicy. However, his treatment of this latter issue is cautious and indirect. This makes the significance of his remarks easy to miss, so a brief sketch of the theological background, and of the implications of Hume's position, are appropriate.

In the Christian tradition, the tolerance of an omnipotent and morally perfect God for the observable evils in the world requires explanation. The first influential answer was that of Irenaeus (c.130–c.202), that present evil is to be explained and justified by future good, because the present evil is inseparable from the future good. This world is a 'vale of soul-making', and souls are made through the encounter with, and in the end overcoming of, evil. The solution offered thus has some affinities with the Stoic view that evils are, in a sense, only apparent, because reflection on the functioning of the entire system reveals its providential character, and thus justifies those evils that are part and parcel of a system with a beneficent purpose. The Irenaean theodicy is thus fully teleological. No less importantly, it implies that evil exists in the world because God wills it: God deliberately makes a world in which evil is an integral part.

The alternative, and ultimately more influential, account was that of Augustine. Augustine's theodicy places a strong doctrine of free will in the centre of the frame. Free will is the supremely valuable capacity, and genuinely free will must allow for the capacity to choose to do what is evil. On this account, then, evil is not a contributory element to an overall providential structure, but merely an inevitable feature of the best possible world: it plays no constructive role; it is simply an unavoidable consequence. The Augustinian theodicy is thus not wholly teleological. Although the creation is a providential order, the existence of evil is to be explained by direct reference not to this order, but to the unintended effects of its supremely valuable feature. For this feature, free will, although itself a deliberately bestowed divine benefit, has consequences that are quite distinct from the intentions of the divine creative act, because it is a power not constrained by any necessity; in particular, it is not constrained by divine power. The consequences of free human volitions, therefore, are not effects traceable back to an originating divine cause: free human actions are themselves genuine creations, and for this reason the evil they may cause are not to be attributed to the originating divine cause. On this account, God does not will evil.[11]

With this in mind, we can begin to see the theological stakes involved. Late medieval and reformed theologies of a strongly voluntarist cast abandoned theodicies of the Irenaean kind, thereby avoiding both divine responsibility for evil, and, with the rise of mechanist natural philosophies, teleology as well.[12] The compatibilist resolution of the nature of liberty, however, undercuts the distinctiveness of the Augustinian alternative, effectively transforming it into a particular version of the Irenaean theodicy. If free will is not a power that breaks human volitions out of the necessities of the natural order, then both the volitions and their consequences must be regarded as products of the divine will, and justification of the existence of evil must revert to teleology, by appealing directly to the overall beneficence of the providential order. So it seems that a credible theodicy must argue that experienced evils are to be justified by reference to an overarching providential order. If this cannot succeed, it must then be acknowledged that the evidence does not rule out the possibility that the creator is either not omnipotent, or not wholly good. With this in mind, it will become clear that there is a real sting in the tail of Hume's closing reflections on theodicy.

Hume begins by acknowledging that he is defending territory that many have thought fatal to morality and religion. His initial response is the rhetoric typical of the Enlightenment philosopher: that we should evaluate hypotheses according to their truth or falsity, and should not hide behind their real or supposed 'dangerous consequences to religion and morality'. It also, however, appears to be implicit acknowledgement that, in this case, there is substance to the charge, even though Hume seems to draw the sting by immediately insisting that the doctrines he has advanced of necessity and liberty 'are not only consistent with morality, but are absolutely essential to its support' (97). It is noticeable that here religion has quietly slipped from view, and, perhaps, not

---

[11] These different kinds of theodicy are discussed fully in J. Hick, *Evil and the God of Love* (London: Macmillan, 1966).

[12] Thus, for example, the philosophers associated with Gresham College in London (which later developed into the Royal Society) commonly adhered to theologies of a strongly voluntarist kind, and for that reason held reformed or puritan convictions. See C. Hill, *Intellectual Origins of the English Revolution* (Oxford: Clarendon Press, 1965), ch. 1. The connections between voluntarist theologies and the rise of the new science have attracted a vast literature. See e.g. R. Hooykas, *Religion and the Rise of Modern Science* (Edinburgh: Scottish Academic Press, 1984); A. Funkenstein, *Theology and the Scientific Imagination from the Middle Ages to the Seventeenth Century* (Princeton: Princeton University Press, 1986); Osler, *Divine Will and the Mechanical Philosophy*; and Menn, *Descartes and Augustine*.

accidentally. The positive implications of Hume's doctrines are almost—if not quite entirely—limited to morality, and he turns to spell out these advantages before returning to the religious question. Once again he structures his discussion by examining issues concerning necessity and liberty in turn.

Hume observes that necessity, on the account he has given of the term—'the constant conjunction of like objects, or in the inference of the understanding from one object to another'—has always been acknowledged to be a feature of human volitional activity: 'no one has ever pretended to deny that we can draw inferences concerning human actions, and that those inferences are founded on the experienced union of like actions, with like motives, inclinations, and circumstances' (97). It may be that this account of necessity, or even the sceptical interpretation of experience on which it rests, will be rejected; but, he says, to do so will not affect the point at issue, which is that the connections he refers to are universally recognized in moral judging, and of no consequence for 'the received orthodox system with regard to the will'. His point here seems to be merely that his account, like the 'received orthodox system', takes the will to be the cause of human actions. If his meaning is no more than this, it allows a straightforward reading of his further claim that religion also is (at this point at least) left untouched; for the wider ramifications of the sceptical solution must include acknowledging that the divine will is more thoroughly inscrutable than the theologians have supposed.[13] And, if this is the point, he can reasonably conclude: 'Nothing, therefore, can be more innocent . . . than this doctrine' (97).

Hume next applies the doctrine to three aspects of human moral practice. In the first place, we create laws in which rewards and punishments are built in, because we suppose that such rewards and punishments do exercise a reliable influence on human motivations, and therefore suppose that they cause human actions. Secondly, only if people are causes of their actions can they be answerable for them; and they can be answerable only if the cause itself can be understood to be some 'durable and constant' part of them. To deny necessity is to break any link between the behaviour and the person, and therefore to leave 'pure and untainted' even the person who commits 'the most horrid crime' (98). In contrast, by affirming the role of necessity, and therefore of stable principles of the individual character, in moral judgement, we are able

---

[13] The importance of this point for the interpretation of the argument from design will be brought out in Section XI.

to explain otherwise puzzling features of moral practice: the failure to blame what is brought about 'ignorantly and casually'; the lesser blame attached to hasty and unpremeditated behaviour; and the removal of blame following observably genuine repentance. Moral blame depends on proofs of 'criminal principles in the mind' (99); but there are no such proofs without supposing necessary connections between durable principles of character and the actions that attend them.

Hume now turns to consider the issues concerning liberty. They are quickly dispatched. The same arguments as those above will, he claims, show that liberty as here defined is a necessary condition for moral judgement. Thus, unless we suppose that people act on the basis of their choices, we make nonsense of our moral practices: we provide rewards and punishments on the assumption that they will underpin choices, rather than deny its exercise; we commend or blame only those actions that stem from choices, and not those that are the result of coercion; and the complexities of our judgements reflect the complex ways in which choices and constraints can be implicated in resultant behaviours. Actions are chosen in so far as they spring from our own 'internal character, passions, and affections', and only in so far as they spring from these causes, rather than from 'external violence', can they give rise to moral judgement. Morality depends, then, on necessity and liberty, and in precisely the senses Hume has defined them.

Hume now turns to consider questions of theodicy. He introduces a particular objection that might be brought against his account of necessity and liberty; and, by introducing the problem posed for theodicy in these terms, he veils the fact that theology does not fare so well at the hands of his 'reconciling project'. If the entire universe is governed by 'a continued chain of necessary causes, pre-ordained and pre-determined', then our volitions, like the rest of nature, have for their 'ultimate Author' the 'Creator of the world, who first bestowed motion on this immense machine, and placed all beings in that particular position, whence every subsequent event, by an inevitable necessity, must result' (99–100). And, since it cannot be said that God, unlike us, is ignorant or careless of the consequences of his actions, including their most remote consequences, it must follow that 'he foresaw, he ordained, he intended all those actions of men, which we so rashly pronounce criminal'. We are thus confronted with a dilemma: either the 'infinite perfection' of the creator means that such apparently criminal actions are not, in the end, to be judged criminal after all; or that 'the Deity, not man, is accountable for them'.[14] Hume sums up the situation in this way:

But as either of these positions is absurd and impious, it follows, that the doctrine from which they are deduced cannot possibly be true, as being liable to all the same objections. An absurd consequence, if necessary, proves the original doctrine to be absurd; in the same manner as criminal actions render criminal the original cause, if the connexion between them be necessary and inevitable.   (100)

Hume's point is not that both horns of the dilemma are equally absurd and impious: rather, the first is absurd, the second impious. The absurd consequence, that morality is undermined because the doctrine renders criminal actions non-criminal, can be regarded as a lapse into Pyrrhonism about moral judgement, and so avoidable by an Academic solution; the impious doctrine, that the creator's moral character may not differ from the perceived moral quality of the natural order, is not rejected, but left—for the time being at least—in sceptical darkness.

The absurd consequence, that our ordinary moral judgements are radically mistaken, has been held by various philosophers, all of whom held that 'to an enlarged view, which could comprehend the whole system of nature, every event became an object of joy and exultation', because every evil in the world is not eradicable without greater cost, but is instead 'an essential part of this benevolent system' (101). The *locus classicus* of this outlook is Stoicism. But it applies no less to Christian theologians of an Irenaean stamp; and, amongst the moderns, it clearly applies to Leibniz. Hume's sceptical solution is that nature is too strong for reason here as elsewhere, and thus, 'though this topic be specious and sublime, it was soon found in practice weak and ineffectual'.[15] Conclusions of this kind appeal to the academic in the ivory tower, but to those actually suffering serious pain it merely adds insult to injury. We do and must judge as our passions dictate; and our nature is such that we cannot shape our judgements according to such grand metaphysical designs. 'The affections take a narrower and more natural survey of their object; and by an economy, more suitable to the infirmity of human minds, regard alone the beings around us, and are actuated by such events as appear good or ill to the private system' (102).

The same reasoning applies also to moral ills. We are naturally

---

[14] Note that this objection is unintelligible unless it concerns the deity's causal powers; and that Hume's reply implicitly accepts it in these terms.
[15] Note again the use of 'specious' by Hume to mean attractive or plausible *simpliciter*.

disposed to approve or disapprove of particular characters or actions, and no disposition is more essential to our nature. We naturally approve of whatever tends to 'the peace and security of human society', and only with great difficulty can we subordinate our immediate judgements to 'remote and uncertain speculations'. Speculative philosophies can be no more successful in persuading us of the doubtfulness of our ordinary judgements of good and evil than in attempting to convince us that there is no difference between beauty and ugliness: 'Both these distinctions are founded in the natural sentiments of the human mind: And these senti-ments are not to be controuled or altered by any philosophical theory or speculation whatsoever' (103). Thus the 'absurd conse-quence', the denial of the veridicality of our normal moral judge-ments, is overcome. It is overcome not by refining our rational arguments, but by a sceptical solution that reminds us that the sentiments on which moral judgements depend are ultimately independent of the understanding, and thus reaffirms that human nature is too strong for reason.

The second horn of the dilemma is left unresolved. If human liberty is not a power that breaks the chain of necessity, but is merely the exercise of choice, then it is not clear how the creator, who is thus a 'mediate cause' of human action, including evil action, can avoid being stained by the same 'sin and moral turpi-tude' that attaches to human actions and characters. Hume reserves judgement; and, in doing so, acts wholly according to his sceptical insistence on the limits of human understanding. However, his proposal for modest philosophy can bring no comfort to the theist, amounting as it does to a recommendation to abandon all theological reflections:

These are mysteries, which mere natural and unassisted reason is very unfit to handle; and whatever system she embraces, she must find herself involved in inextricable difficulties, and even contradictions, at every step which she takes with regard to such subjects . . . Happy, if she be thence sensible of her temerity, when she pries into these sublime mysteries; and leaving a scene so full of obscurities and perpexities, return, with suitable modesty, to her true and proper province, the examination of common life; where she will find difficulties enough to employ her enquiries, without launching into so boundless an ocean of doubt, uncertainty, and contradiction! (103)

In the end, then, Hume denies that the key theological problem of theodicy is soluble. If we treat this conclusion at face value, as a general reflection on theology in the light of experimental prin-ciples, he might be thought merely to be reminding us of the necessity of keeping reason's wings clipped; that is, as the recommendation that we restrict reason to the narrow sphere of everyday life to which it is properly suited. As such, the passage would serve as a rebuke to the religious metaphysician, by insisting on the unfathomable depth of what lies beyond experience. There may be, however, more here than meets the eye. Placed in this particular context, Hume's remarks leave a specific and murky cloud hanging over Christian theology: the moral perfection of the first cause of the natural order can be called into question; and that question, it seems, cannot be removed. Here, then, we have Hume's first sally against the argument from design. This first, modestly sceptical, conclusion will later give rise to objections of a more specific and damaging nature.

Section IX

Of the Reason of Animals

This short section argues that animals as well as humans learn from experience by means of customary connections between causes and effects. The title is provocative, in that it implicitly denies that reason is the mark of the human. It is best regarded as debunking in intent, since the argument is to the effect that all learning from experience, whether by animals or humans, is founded not on reasoning, but on instinct; that is, animals learn from experience according to the same non-rational process by which human beings also learn. The section's modern career is characterized largely by neglect: its significance, and even the reason for its inclusion in the *Enquiry*, are rarely considered. This is, in part, because it advances views that have become congenial to the modern mind, and, in part, because Hume's observations, while they are intended to support his account of the principles underlying human functioning, do not add to that account. The section thus seems only to be filling in the details, not extending the fundamentals of his position.

To read the section thus is not to get it wrong, but it is to miss what matters. The sting in the tail—the rejection of human distinctiveness, and its wider implications and connections—would not have been lost on the eighteenth-century reader. There are several such implications worth drawing out. In the first place, to emphasize similarities between human and animal mental capacities is to signal affinities with the sceptical tradition. The rejection of any sharp divide between animal and human natures is a distinguishing feature of the sceptical tradition. Thus Sextus, in discussing the First Mode employed by Pyrrhonists as an aid to suspension of judgement, adds, 'for good measure', a comparison of 'the so-called irrational animals with humans in respect of appearances'. The 'appearances' in question are not merely perceptions, but the apparent (manifest) qualities of animals with respect to reasoning, and even moral virtue. The relevant point here is the former, an animal's reasoning powers, and on this head

Sextus observes that a dog 'does choose what is appropriate and avoid what is harmful to himself: he pursues food and retreats from a raised whip'. Moreover, 'he has an expertise which provides what is appropriate to him: hunting'.[1]

The *value* of the division between human and animal rational powers was also a target for some sceptics. Thus Cicero's spokesman for Academic scepticism in *De Natura Deorum*, Gaius Cotta, argues that reason is more commonly put into the service of evil than of good, and is therefore to be judged a burden rather than a benefit to the human race. Further, because this burden has been imposed by the immortal gods, Cotta concludes that it shows the gods to *lack* concern for human welfare.[2] Both these themes— the similarities between human and animal capacity, and the dubious value of rationality—are then taken up by Montaigne in his discussion of the extent of human powers in 'An Apology for Raymond Sebond'.[3]

Of course, Montaigne's brand of Pyrrhonism is intended to shore up faith, not to destroy it, so, unlike Cicero's Cotta, he does not conclude that the doubtful value of reason suggests that human beings are unloved by God. Nevertheless, the connections here are significant. The sceptical arguments against the sharp separation of animals and humans on the basis of rationality—whether by arguing that animals are rational too, or that reason is a much overrated possession—implicitly deny either the fact, or the significance, of the Aristotelian definition of the human being as the rational animal. The sceptical tradition thus typically denies the distinctively religious doctrines built on that definition: most importantly, the Christian doctrine of Man as *Imago Dei*, especially in Catholic orthodoxy.[4] The sceptical stance on the comparative insignificance of human reason, then, is no mere epistemological subtlety, but an implicit rejection of much in the way of orthodox religious opinions.[5] Hume, for his part, does not, in this section,

---

[1] Sextus Empiricus, *Outlines of Scepticism*, I, 62–6.
[2] Cicero, *De Natura Deorum*, III. xxvii, in *De Natura Deorum and Academica*, 353–5.
[3] Montaigne, 'An Apology for Raymond Sebond', in *The Complete Essays*, ed. Screech, 505–42.
[4] The qualification is necessary because orthodox (Thomist) Catholicism has been the more inclined to spell out the meaning of that doctrine in terms of rational capacities. In contrast, the more emphatically Augustinian views that have been a subcurrent in Catholicism (surfacing, not least, amongst the Cartesians), and, more generally, the nominalist and voluntarist tradition stemming from Ockham that came to dominate the Protestant world, focus more on the human capacity for free will as the 'divine spark' in human nature. Edward Craig fails to notice this alternative tradition in his discussion of the early modern fate of the 'Image of God' doctrine in *The Mind of God and the Works of Man*, ch. 1.
[5] It need hardly be added that it is also a simultaneous rejection of both Aristotelian and Cartesian conceptions of human nature, as we should expect of a sceptical attack on dogmatism in general (as discussed in chs. 2 and 3 above).

argue directly for both theses, since he does not address Cotta's argument that reason is overvalued. It is worth noting, however, that he *does* share the conception of reason that leads Cotta to his conclusion: that reason is an instrument that serves desires—and that therefore is valuable in so far as it serves worthy desires.[6] There is thus no bar to his offering an argument of the same kind, even though here he chooses not to do so.

Hume begins by observing that conclusions concerning factual matters depend on analogical arguments: where causes are similar, we expect similar effects; and the greater the similarity, the better the analogy, and the more confidence we can place in the conclusion drawn. However, even where the analogy is not perfect, reasoning of this kind still has weight: thus anatomical discoveries can be extended from one species to all animals, as, for example, in the case of the circulation of the blood. The appeal here is to the second of Newton's Rules of Reasoning in Philosophy: 'to the same natural effects we must, as far as possible, assign the same causes', a principle illustrated by, among other things, 'respiration in a man and in a beast'.[7] Hume's use of this principle is considerably more ambitious than anything Newton would have imagined possible—or, for that matter, desirable. This is because Hume does not merely mean to apply it to cases of human and animal bodily function—as with Newton's respiration example—but to cases of comparative mental function as well. He is explicit about this, holding that analogical reasoning of this kind can be employed in his own enquiry into human mental functioning:

These analogical observations may be carried farther, even to this science, of which we are now treating; and any theory, by which we explain the operations of the understanding, or the origin and connexion of the passions in man, will acquire additional authority, if we find, that the same theory is requisite to explain the same phenomena in all other animals. We shall make trial of this, with regard to the hypothesis, by which we have, in the foregoing discourse, endeavoured to account for all experimental reasonings; and it

---

[6] The *locus classicus* is *Treatise* Book II Section III, 'Of the influencing motives of the will', and is encapsulated in the famous remark: 'Reason is, and ought only to be the slave of the passions, and can never pretend to any other office than to serve and obey them' (*Treatise*, 415). The same basic position also underpins Hume's insistence, in both the *Treatise* (Book III) and *Enquiry concerning the Principles of Morals* (Appendix I), on the foundational role of sentiment in morals. The famous *is-ought* paragraph in the *Treatise* (469–70) also reflects this position. (I have discussed these connections in my *Natural Law and the Theory of Property: Grotius to Hume* (Oxford: Clarendon Press, 1991), 280–3.) The instrumental conception of reason is both well fitted to, and even exhibited in, the sceptical understanding of human powers. Hume acknowledges the fact by making the subordination of reason to feeling a central element of sceptical philosophy in 'The Sceptic' (*Essays*, 159–80).

[7] Newton, *Principia*, 398.

is hoped, that this new point of view will serve to confirm all our former observations. (104–5)

In this passage the experimental method of reasoning is explicitly invoked ('we shall make trial of this') in order to resolve a 'moral subject' of no small importance: the distinctiveness—or not—of human beings with respect to the rest of the animal kingdom.

In fact, at this point it is possible to step back from the specific example and identify the general threat implicit in Hume's philosophical strategy—the introduction of experimental reasoning into moral subjects—to important established beliefs. The experimental method is appropriate where essences are not revealed, where rational intuition of natures is impossible, and so where analogies drawn between like objects is useful and necessary. The rationale for experimental natural philosophy is that this is the case with physical bodies. To extend this approach to the mind, then, is to hold the same to be true of the mind—or, at the very least, for the same to be true of it in the relevant respects. Hume accepts that this is so—that the essence of the mind, and its powers, are unknown to us[8]—and follows Locke in thinking of inner reflection as 'internal Sense',[9] as comparable in some way to ordinary sense perception. The analogy is revealing, because it suggests that the applicability of the experimental method to minds reflects analogies between mental and physical operations. This need not imply materialism, because a sufficient explanation is that such analogies exist where the mind is *passive*, where mental phenomena are the result of bodily processes that are simply *received* by the mind—as, for example, in sense perception itself. But to treat reasoning after the same fashion is implicitly to extend this model to realms of mental life that had long been thought to be wholly distinct from animal natures. In the hands of the Cartesians, it is even classed as a power wholly foreign to matter and its processes. The introduction of experimental method to moral subjects, then, treats mental functioning as importantly analogous to bodily functioning; and, by discerning similarities between animals and humans in this respect, likewise treats animal and human natures as analogous. Several significant boundaries are thus threatened by the adoption of experimental method in the moral domain: the boundary between the human and the animal, and between the mental and the physical. It is no accident, then, that this section of the *Enquiry* implies that human beings are (as we would put it) part of nature; Hume's experi-

---

[8] *Treatise*, xvii; cf. also ch. 3 above.   [9] Locke, *Essay*, II. i. 4.

mental method is itself built on the supposition that this is a plausible outlook.[10]

The argument itself is brief and familiar in its outlines. Hume observes, first, that animals learn from experience, and do so by 'inferring' that the same effects will follow from the same causes. In this way they become acquainted with the 'obvious properties' of objects, and so come in time to 'treasure up a knowledge of the nature of fire, water, earth, stones, heights, depths, &c., and of the effects which result from their observation' (105). The effects of this learning are clearly visible in the 'cunning and sagacity' that older animals display, and that are entirely the fruit of experience. He adds, in similar vein to Sextus, that such learning is even more clearly revealed in the effects of training on dogs and other domestic animals—from their fear of punishment when threatened, to their response to being called by their name. These responses are due entirely to experience; and in each case the animal judges of facts that lie beyond immediate sense perception, and does so by means of the analogies drawn from similarities in past experience.

Secondly, he argues that such learning from experience is not founded on 'any process of argument or reasoning'. No animal reasons to the effect that 'like events must follow like objects, and that the course of nature will always be regular in its operations'. This is certain, because, if there *are* arguments to this effect, they lie beyond the capacities of all brutes, since 'it may well employ the utmost care and attention of a philosophic genius to discover and observe them'. Animals, then, are not guided by reasoning in arriving at these conclusions. Nor, as argued in previous sections, are human beings—whether child or adult, intellectually simple-minded or sophisticated. Even philosophers themselves, 'in all the active parts of life, are, in the main, the same with the vulgar, and are governed by the same maxims' (106). So these conclusions— since they *are* reached by animals, children, and adults, irrespective of intellectual sophistication—must depend on some natural principle that is more reliable and accessible than the uncertain processes of reasoning. Hume concludes that, even if it were not

[10] Notice that the argument of Section VIII Part I also situates human beings firmly within the natural (physical) world, treating voluntary and physical components of causal chains indifferently. Of course, the argument there is how we *do* treat human volitions, not what they are in themselves; but the moral can readily be drawn that, in doing so, we reveal more than we realize—that, despite our metaphysical or religious commitments, we discover that we do in fact think of ourselves as part of the wider natural order. As Hume observes in another context: 'A concession thus extorted, in opposition to systems, has more authority than if it had been made in prosecution of them' (*An Enquiry concerning the Principles of Morals*, in *Enquiries*, 195).

certain in humans, it seems scarcely questionable in the case of animals; but since it *has* been established in the case of humans, the rules of analogy already referred to should persuade us that it must apply to all creatures—animal and human—without exception. Animals 'infer' effects from causes, and thus form new factual beliefs, entirely through customary or habitual connections. In both higher and lower classes of 'sensitive beings'—humans and animals—this process is the same.[11]

The final paragraph spells out a moral that is, by now, familiar: the similarities between humans and animals exist because, at bottom, the processes that underpin human practice are non-rational, and are so because they are ultimately grounded in mechanical operations. Thus Hume argues that we recognize that many aspects of animal behaviour are not due to experience, but 'derive from the original hand of nature'. These behaviours we call *instincts*, and we are inclined to find them both remarkable and inexplicable. However, our sense of wonder at such animal capacities will perhaps be reduced when we realize that the ability to learn from experience, which we share with (higher) animals, and which is absolutely crucial to our practical existence, is itself a kind of instinctive ability. It is thus best understood as a set of mechanical operations, which work in ways we do not comprehend:

the experimental reasoning itself, which we possess in common with beasts, and on which the whole conduct of life depends, is nothing but a species of *instinct or mechanical power*, that acts in us unknown to ourselves; and in its chief operations, is not directed by any such relations or comparisons of ideas, as are the proper objects of our intellectual faculties. Though the instinct be different, yet still it is an instinct, which teaches a man to avoid the fire; as much as that, which teaches a bird, with such exactness, the art of incubation, and the whole economy and order of its nursery. (108; emphasis added)

The capacity of human beings to conduct their lives in the light of experience does not distinguish them from the animal kingdom, since animals function in the same way. In neither case is such learning grounded on processes of reasoning; it is instead

---

[11] In the second (1750) edition, Hume added a long footnote to show how, on his account, the great differences in reasoning capacity between humans and animals, and between different human beings, are to be explained. The details of this account need not concern us. The point of the explanations offered is mainly to show that an appeal to custom is not an appeal to a principle that is only able to operate uniformly across all cases: rather, custom produces different effects when it operates on different raw materials. It is also interesting to note that Locke, in the *Essay*, discusses the differences in capacity between humans, and between animals and humans, in a passage that stresses both the importance of analogy, and also the difficulties of discerning the boundary between the rational and the irrational (Locke, *Essay*, IV. xvi. 12).

founded on the non-rational process of customary connection. The similarity, and the non-rational foundation, are both explained by the same supposition: human beings, like animals, are, not only in their physical being, but also in (at least) all those mental processes on which the formation of factual beliefs and the conduct of life depends, best understood to operate according to mechanical principles. Human beings are not semi-divine beings set apart from the natural world, but are, at least in very large part,[12] part of that world—a world of mechanical processes.

[12] The qualification is necessary because Hume recognizes, in the passage just quoted, that 'the comparisons of ideas' that are 'the proper objects of our intellectual faculties' cannot, by the preceding arguments, be incorporated within a single—mechanical—domain. Hume does not go so far as to deny dualism; rather, by arguing that much of what had been taken to be distinctively rational human capacities is explicable in terms of mechanical processes, he indicates the *possibility* of an entirely material, mechanical universe.

Section X

Of Miracles

This famous section has suffered from its own success. In the first place, it has been so frequently anthologized in collections of readings in the philosophy of religion that it is most frequently read out of context. Restoring it to its place within Hume's wider argument aids in understanding the argument itself, and in assessing both its value and its contribution to the overall argument of the *Enquiry*. Secondly, its success means that it is now far more widely read than other critical discussions of miracles from the same period, so its distinguishing features are easily missed: not least, some limitations of the argument that were noted by contemporary critics. One limitation stems from the kind of argument Hume employs. Another reflects the fact that the argument of the section presupposes principles expounded in preceding sections of the *Enquiry*. It will be shown that both these features limit the independent significance of the argument: it is not the case, nor does Hume intend, that his critique of miracles can stand alone as a source of religious, or even of Christian, unbelief.

The first task, then, is to place this section in context. There are two aspects that need to be considered, one forward looking, and one backward looking. The forward-looking aspect is that, although the question of the defensibility of religious belief is directly addressed for the first time in this section, religious issues are also pursued in the succeeding section, 'Of a particular Providence and of a future State'. So we will get a better sense of Hume's overall aims by considering how the two sections together contribute to an assessment of religious belief. This is readily settled. Section XI is framed by a discussion of the political implications of philosophical enquiry, but the body of the discussion concerns the religious conclusions that can be extracted from the argument from design. Since, after Newton, the argument from design enjoyed the pre-eminent position among the purely rational arguments for religious belief, it is reasonable to conclude that Section XI is meant to be an assessment not merely of the design argument *per se*, but of the case for natural religion in general.[1] Miracles, in contrast, belong to revealed religion. In fact—as will become clear—from Hume's point of view miracles constitute the foundation of revealed religion. Section X can therefore be regarded as Hume's assessment of the case for revealed religion. Further, since each section treats its subject matter as if self-contained, it seems that Hume's purpose is to determine, first, what religious beliefs can be established purely through revelation, and, secondly, what beliefs can be established purely through reason. That is, his ambition appears to be to determine whether revelation and reason function as *independent* foundations for religious belief. If the answer is that *neither* source can alone provide a justification for a system of religious beliefs, then neither will it be clear how some combination of the two can overcome the difficulty.[2] I suggest that this is Hume's strategy in Sections X and XI; and therefore that the two sections *together* constitute his critique of religion.

This hypothesis resolves an otherwise puzzling feature of the miracles section: when it is compared to views that it might be thought to be arguing against, it is very obviously inadequate, because it appears to argue against a position that sophisticated religious thinkers—conventional or otherwise—did not hold. Thus Hobbes, for example, argues that the role of miracles is to identify prophets. Clearly, such a claim presupposes independently established religious views, since belief in the existence of prophets themselves needs first to be grounded. Further, Hobbes also argues that miracles alone are not sufficient to establish a possible prophet's *bone fides*: it is also necessary that the prophet's message be theologically orthodox.[3] So, for Hobbes, the significance of miracles is to be judged from *within* a religious point of view; miracles are not independent grounds for religious beliefs.

Of course, Hobbes's contemporary reputation as an atheist, or as, at best, dangerously heterodox, means that his position cannot be the most compelling example. Although that reputation may

[1] 'We know [God] only by his most wise and excellent contrivances of things, and final causes' (Newton, *Principia*, 546 (General Scholium)). Cf. Locke's *Essay*, which provides a negative illustration. Largely composed before the *Principia* appeared, the *Essay* frequently alludes to the religious significance of natural order, but his central argument for God's existence is the argument from a first cause (*Essay*, IV. x).
[2] That is, it would not be clear to Hume's readers how to overcome the difficulty. My concern is with Hume's strategy, not to rule out a priori those arguments that seek an inductive basis for religious belief by assessing the totality of the evidence derivable from the various, individually inadequate, arguments. See e.g. R. Swinburne, *The Existence of God* (Oxford: Clarendon Press, 1979), and J. Houston, *Reported Miracles: A Critique of Hume* (Cambridge: Cambridge University Press, 1994).
[3] Hobbes, *Leviathan*, ch. XXXII, 257–8; see also ch. XXXVII, 300–6.

be undeserved,[4] it is true that his opinions are too unconventional to establish any general point. However, the same cannot be said against Locke: although his views were undoubtedly less conventional than he was prepared to admit, he was nevertheless a sincere Christian, and, importantly, recognized as such. So it is significant to note that he, too, denies that miracles can stand alone as a basis for religious belief. This is evident from an observation in the *Essay*—an observation that Hume is unlikely to have missed, since it is set within a discussion of the ordinary sources of belief. Locke says:

Though the common Experience, and the ordinary Course of Things have justly a mighty Influence on the Minds of Men, to make them give or refuse Credit to any thing proposed to their Belief; yet there is one Case, wherein the strangeness of the Fact lessens not the Assent to a fair Testimony given of it. For where such supernatural Events are suitable to ends aim'd at by him, who has the Power to change the course of Nature, there, under such Circumstances, they may be the fitter to procure Belief, by how much more they are beyond, or contrary to ordinary Observation. This is the proper Case of *Miracles*, which well attested, do not only find Credit themselves; but give it also to other Truths, which need such Confirmation.[5]

This passage, with its recognition of the conflict between the miraculous and the ordinary course of events, which is then resolved in favour of the miraculous, gives a precise statement of the view Hume has in his sights. It is all the more striking, then, that the argument of Section X does not fully address the position being put, since Locke clearly supposes (and as his explicit discussion of the grounds for belief in God illustrates) that belief in God—a God with 'the Power to change the course of Nature'—is established on other, rational, grounds.[6] This view has significant implications for determining the extent and nature of the reliance we can place on the observed regularities in experience: for, if experience habituates us to expect regularities to be maintained, but at the same time provides the grounds for rational conviction that our experience of order reflects the activity of a designer

[4] The view that Hobbes was an atheist has recently been argued by E. Curley, ' "I Durst Not Write So Boldly", or, How to Read Hobbes's *Theological–Political Treatise*', in D. Bostrenghi (ed.), *Hobbes e Spinoza* (Naples: Bibliopolis, 1992). For the case for regarding Hobbes as an unconventional, but nevertheless orthodox (in the sense of adhering to the creeds of the first four church councils), Calvinist Christian, see A. P. Martinich, *The Two Gods of* Leviathan (Cambridge: Cambridge University Press, 1992). Martinich replies directly to Curley in his Appendix A (339–53). A further exchange is Curley, 'Calvin and Hobbes, or, Hobbes as an Orthodox Christian', Martinich, 'On the Proper Interpretation of Hobbes's Philosophy', and Curley, 'Reply to Professor Martinich', in *Journal of the History of Philosophy*, 34 (1996), 257–71, 273–83, and 285–7.
[5] Locke, *Essay*, IV. xvi. 13.   [6] Ibid. IV. x.

capable of modifying that order in instances where it suits his purposes, then the assurance we can maintain in our mental habits is substantially undercut. 'Of Miracles', taken alone, ignores this complication, and for this reason the argument against miracles seems to make an easy target for critics of a Lockean stamp.

The opportunity was not missed. In 1751, three years after the publication of the *Enquiry*, Thomas Rutherforth responded to Hume's argument along precisely these lines:

A firm and unalterable experience of the common course of nature is indeed a direct proof, that no event, which is inconsistent with the usual train of causes and effects, can be brought about by any of the ordinary powers of nature, which are the objects of experience. But we have already shewn ... that the same experience is no proof at all, against the likelihood or possibility of bringing about such an event by a power, which is superior to the common course of nature, a power which we can demonstrate to exist, and which is consequently the object of our knowledge.[7]

Hume's argument thus failed to impress at least one notable churchman, and so failed because the argument simply did not address an established English view—a view of which he cannot be imagined to have been unaware. Moreover, the view was established not merely because it was defended by Locke, for Locke's argument is itself an updated version of an argument stemming from Aquinas.[8] So, if Hume has somehow not noticed, or not recognized the significance of, this objection, then he has quite failed to address a central Christian view—an oversight that would be nothing less than astonishing.

The problem is resolved, and Hume's general strategy explained, however, if we suppose that 'Of Miracles' is not intended to stand alone as a critique of religious belief; that his strategy is, first, to argue that miracles do not provide an independent foundation for religious belief, and *then* to argue that the best-supported rational foundation also fails—leaving it to the reader to draw the obvious conclusion. Whether or not Hume's argument is judged to be ultimately successful, this two-pronged strategy seems to be the minimum that charity requires, since only such a strategy is *adequate* to the task of addressing the Christian view, as exemplified in Aquinas and Locke. It seems necessary to conclude, then, that 'Of Miracles' is not intended to stand alone as a critique of religion, nor even of the possible grounds for belief in miracles

---

[7] Thomas Rutherforth, *The Credibility of Miracles Defended against the Author of* Philosophical Essays (Cambridge: J. Bentham Printer to the University, 1751), 13.

[8] For a discussion of Aquinas's view—and of the use later made of it by William Paley in his *Evidences of Christianity* (1794)—see Penelhum, *David Hume*, 174–5.

themselves. This is important for more than historical reasons, since it is still the case that a common objection to Hume's argument is precisely to the effect that he ignores background knowledge gained through rational means.[9] The conclusion must be that Hume's critique of religion in the *Enquiry* has two parts, and they are interdependent parts of a whole.[10]

The second, backward-looking, contextual aspect concerns the extent to which Hume relies, in this section, on arguments and conclusions reached in preceding sections. In fact, throughout this section Hume relies on the sceptical interpretation of experience characteristic of the experimental philosophers, and the solution he provides is again a 'sceptical solution'. That is, the argument proceeds on the assumption that experience does not deliver knowledge of the essences or natures of things, or, therefore, of their causal powers.[11] The solution is sceptical because it does not depend in any way on rational insight into how the world really is, but appeals to the standard of proper functioning—and therefore of, among other things, credibility—for instinctive, mechanical beings like us. That standard is of course probability. Probability is the inertial transference to present and future experience of past regularities, and thus the natural (inductive and fallible) standard by which human beings do and must measure all that they encounter. Probabilities are human norms: they are the degrees of conviction that determine the credibility of any and all empirical claims. It is against these fallible but unavoidable degrees of conviction that putative miracles must be tested.[12] The argu-

[9] See e.g. Houston, *Reported Miracles*, ch. 10.

[10] It is well known that Hume removed a version of the miracles argument from the *Treatise* before publishing it. Does this mean that the two-pronged strategy I have suggested was only belatedly recognized by Hume, when writing the *Enquiry*? Not necessarily. M. A. Stewart has suggested, with respect to an early manuscript fragment on evil, that it originally formed part of a section on natural religion intended for the *Treatise*. See 'An Early Fragment on Evil', in M. A. Stewart and J. P. Wright (ed.), *Hume and Hume's Connexions* (Edinburgh: Edinburgh University Press, 1994), 164.

[11] This explains his otherwise very unsatisfactory handling of Archbishop Tillotson's argument (to which we will return below).

[12] Cf. Christine Korsgaard's observation that, for Hume, reflection on our capacities and mode of functioning 'shows that *human nature* ... is intrinsically normative, in a negative [sense] ... there is *no intelligible challenge* that can be made to its claims' (Korsgaard, *The Sources of Normativity*, 66). This is in the right spirit, but Hume's account has a more positive air, as Kant noticed: 'in a being that has a reason and a will, if the proper end of nature were its *preservation*, its *welfare*, in a word its *happiness*, then nature would have hit upon a very bad arrangement in selecting the reason of the creature to carry out this purpose. For all the actions that the creature has to perform for this purpose, and the whole rule of its conduct, would be marked out for it far more accurately by instinct ... and if reason should have been given, over and above, to this favored creature, it must have served it only to contemplate the fortunate constitution of its nature, to admire this, to delight in it, and to be grateful for it to the beneficent cause ...' (Immanuel Kant, *Groundwork of the Metaphysics of Morals*, trans. and ed. M. Gregor (Cambridge: Cambridge University Press, 1997), iv. 395). This passage appears to be a gloss on Hume's remarks at the end of Section V Part II (*Enquiries*, 54–5).

ment of this section is a sceptical solution to the problem of miracle claims. For this reason it is an explicit application of principles of probability.

Two consequences flow from recognizing this feature of the argument. In the first place, Hume explicitly identifies the argument of Part I as a 'full *proof*' against miracles, in the experiential (and thus quasi-probabilistic) sense of 'proof' explained in Section VI. Proofs are 'arguments from experience as leave no room for doubt or opposition' (56 n.). They are distinct from probable arguments only in the conviction they establish; both are arguments from experience—differing only in degree—and so both are sharply opposed to demonstrative arguments that concern only relations of ideas, not matters of fact. Proof is, in Hume's hands, a concept specifically adapted to scepticism, especially its Academic variety. It is an appeal to experience, which, like all such appeals, is fallible; but, by concealing its fallibility in the undisturbed conviction it (typically) produces, it is inherently deceitful. (Custom conceals from us our dependence on its effects.) Nevertheless, the whole-hearted confidence we place in what experience proves is not misplaced: we *properly* place our confidence therein. The Academic affirms that we must live by fallible appearances, and that we live rightly by living according to those appearances that are, in Sextus' words, 'plausible and scrutinized and undistractable'.[13] Proofs are precisely those appearances that are plausible and scrutinized and undistractable. They are, for us, compelling standards; but they do not disclose the nature of reality.

The moral is that the reader who comes to this section without a clear understanding of the nature or point of Hume's distinctions between proof, probability, and demonstration is all too likely to misunderstand both the argument and its presuppositions. Admittedly, Hume does attempt to ease the problem by restating, in the opening paragraphs, what a proof is. However, he distinguishes it there from probability only; he does not similarly insist on the contrast with demonstrations. So the temptation to read the argument as an attempted demonstration—and therefore as concluding that miraculous events are logical impossibilities—remains strong. This is a temptation into which even prominent interpreters have fallen, as will be shown below. No argument will be properly understood if the central terms are not explained, or the reasons for their deployment not recognized. So separating the

[13] Sextus Empiricus, *Outlines of Scepticism*, I. 229.

argument of this section from the context necessary for a proper understanding, in the manner of the anthologists, is an invitation to confusion.

In fact, Hume himself worried about how readily intelligible the original version of the argument would be when set outside its context. He makes this clear in the famous letter to his older cousin, Henry Home, Lord Kames, where he comments that (in removing the original miracles section from the final version of the *Treatise*) he is engaged in 'castrating' his work, 'that is, cutting off its noble Parts'. In a preceding paragraph in the same letter, he says he is sending Kames 'some Reasonings concerning Miracles' that he 'once thought of publishing with the rest, but . . . [is] afraid will give too much Offence even as the World is dispos'd at present'. He then adds: 'There is Something in the turn of Thought and a good deal in the Turn of Expression, which will not perhaps appear so proper for want of knowing the Context.'[14] Hume's introductory paragraphs to the *Enquiry* version of the argument are certainly intended to overcome the problem; but they are not wholly successful in doing so.

The second consequence worth noting is that, because the argument is an application of principles of probability, it can be seen as a species of a genus; and to recognize this is to illuminate many of its distinctive features.[15] Probability theory itself was a success story: it advanced in leaps and bounds in the 1650s, after the pioneering efforts of Pascal and others (and thus after the writing of *Leviathan*). It was quickly recognized that questions of the credibility of testimony, and therefore also of miracles, fell within the purview of probability, so the newly sophisticated theory was set to work on these issues, and its implications frequently discussed.[16] The terms of the discussion were set by Arnauld and Nicole in their

[14] David Hume to Henry Home, 2 Dec. 1737, in *New Letters of David Hume*, ed. R. Klibansky and E. Mossner (Oxford: Clarendon Press, 1954), 3; see also *Letters*, ed. Greig, i. 24–5.

[15] For the following comments on the importance of setting the section within the context of antecedent probability arguments, I am indebted to two very valuable recent studies: D. Wootton, 'Hume's "Of Miracles": Probability and Irreligion', in Stewart (ed.), *Studies in the Philosophy of the Scottish Enlightenment*, 191–229; and M. A. Stewart, 'Hume's Historical View of Miracles', in Stewart and Wright (eds.), *Hume and Hume's Connexions*, 171–200. Wootton emphasizes the importance of French sources on Hume's argument: Arnauld and Nicole, and also libertine *samizdat* literature. Stewart, in contrast, sees Hume as essentially engaged in rewriting Locke. The two positions are not wholly opposed—Locke was, in all likelihood, himself influenced at this point by Arnauld and Nicole—but the emphases are quite different. Stewart's position is close to the view to be put here—and, indeed, anticipates and complements some aspects of the argument.

[16] For an accessible account of the development of probability theory from Pascal to Hume, see I. Hacking, *The Emergence of Probability* (Cambridge: Cambridge University Press, 1975). For an account of the state of probability theory in Hume's day, and of its application to practical and moral matters, see L. Daston, *Classical Probability in the Enlightenment* (Princeton: Princeton University Press, 1988).

widely read textbook, *Logic or the Art of Thinking* (1662),[17] and the influence of this work is visible in Locke's handling of the issues in the latter parts of the *Essay*.[18]

Hume's argument reflects some of the more widely established aspects of contemporary probability arguments, and this fact helps to explain what otherwise might seem a surprising feature. This feature has been observed above, in the case of Hobbes. It is that the discussion of miracles in theological debate was very commonly subordinated to, or treated alongside, the question of prophecy—but Hume mentions prophecy only when summing up his argument. This surprising fact is, however, explained when the argument is recognized as an exercise in the theory of probability. The new probability theory's approach to miracles tended to relegate questions of prophecy to the margins, because it undercut any significant distinction between miracles and prophecies. It did so because of its particular slant on what it is about a miracle that is miraculous: because miracles are rare, and therefore, in terms of ordinary experience, improbable, they can be defined precisely in terms of their improbability. Miracles are improbable; and, indeed, are to be distinguished from mere marvels in terms of their (much) greater *degree* of improbability. Once this interpretation of what it is for something to be a miracle is in place, then, considered in terms of their improbability, marvels and prophecies—in the sense of foretelling the future—are much of a piece. So, from this perspective, a discussion of miracles could include, in its purview, both marvellous events and the foretelling of the future.

This is precisely how Hume sees things, as he shows when summing up his argument against miracle reports:

What we have said of miracles may be applied, without any variation, to prophecies; and indeed, all prophecies are real miracles, and as such only, can be admitted as proofs of any revelation. If it did not exceed the capacity of human nature to foretell events, it would be absurd to employ any prophecy as an argument for a divine mission or authority from heaven. (130–1)

The qualification here, that 'as such only, can be admitted as proofs of any revelation', needs to be noted, since the term 'prophecy' was applied not only to foretelling, but also to religious teaching. The latter, however, has no authority unless supported in other ways; and these other ways must be by the tests of either natural or revealed religion. So, as Hobbes had insisted, conformity with theological orthodoxy must be the test for the authority of

[17] Arnauld and Nicole, *Logic or the Art of Thinking*, 260–75.
[18] Locke, *Essay*, IV. xv, and following chapters.

religious teachings, at least where such orthodoxy stems from accepted conclusions of rational theology. In contrast, the credibility of prophecy in the sense of foretelling the future is tested by the same principles that test reports of other purported revelations. So prophecy, as a distinct subject of intellectual enquiry, is dissolved into other branches of natural or revealed theology. Prophecy is a distinct question for Hobbes, but not for Hume, since the former, unlike the latter, wrote before the significant developments in, and applications of, probability theory in the latter half of the seventeenth century.

Two further features of Hume's account reflect the influence of probability theory. In the first place, 'Of Miracles' is divided into two parts, a division that, to some degree at least, reflects the established division of probability arguments into 'internal' and 'external' evidences. The division is drawn in *Logic or the Art of Thinking*, where it is explained as follows:

In order to decide the truth about an event and to determine whether or not to believe in it, we must not consider it nakedly and in itself, as we would a proposition of geometry. But we must pay attention to all the accompanying circumstances, internal as well as external. I call those circumstances internal which belong to the fact itself, and those external that concern the persons whose testimony leads us to believe in it.[19]

Locke makes a similar distinction. In the *Essay*'s chapter on probability, he distinguishes two 'grounds' of probability in the following terms: '*First*, The conformity of any thing with our own Knowledge, Observation, and Experience. *Secondly*, The Testimony of others, vouching their Observation and Experience.'[20] He then proceeds to contrast the knowledge gained by first-hand experience with the degrees of probability we attach to others' testimony, according to its degree of conformity with our own.[21] Hume's discussion reflects this established division, although he modifies it for his own purposes. Part I examines the 'internal' credibility of the miracle report, and then weighs it against the strongest possible 'external' evidence, where the credibility of the testimony is beyond doubting.[22] Part II then examines the quality of the *actual* testimony (external evidence) available for miraculous events, especially for miracles capable of founding a religion.

---

[19] Arnauld and Nicole, *Logic or the Art of Thinking*, 264.   [20] Locke, *Essay*, IV. xv. 4.

[21] Cf. Stewart, 'Hume's Historical View of Miracles', for a close comparison of the similarities and differences between the distinctions as drawn in Locke's *Essay* and Arnauld and Nicole's *Logic*; and for Hume's closer connections to Locke (177–83).

[22] Hume describes his conclusion at the end of Part I as a 'direct and full *proof* . . . against the existence of any miracle' that stems 'from the nature of the fact' (*Enquiries*, 115).

Locke's handling of the issues also reveals the complex pattern of influences at work in the young tradition of applying probability theory to testimony. He observes, in a spirit now identified with Hume, that where there is no conformity between the fact itself and the testimony—where, as he puts it, 'Experience has been always quite contrary'—there 'the most untainted Credit of a Witness will scarce be able to find belief'. He then illustrates the point with the story of the Dutch ambassador who failed to convince the King of Siam that water froze in cold climates, and could then easily bear the weight of a man—and even 'an Elephant, were he there'.[23] This is intriguing, in that the same basic story turns up in the second (1750) edition of the *Enquiry*, except for the fact that the King of Siam has become an Indian prince, and the Dutch ambassador is nowhere to be seen. The surprise is eased when it is recognized that the tale had become something of a standard example, having appeared in a number of eighteenth-century discussions of miracles. Despite the divergence from Locke's version, however, there is some evidence that Hume has Locke in mind, in part because he offers a refinement of Locke's terminology.[24] He points out that, since the events observable in cold climates were quite outside the experience of the tropical personage, they were not, in fact, contrary to it: 'Though they were not contrary to his experience, they were not conformable to it' (114).[25]

The second further influence of probability on the argument concerns Hume's definition—or definitions—of 'miracle'. At first, he defines a miracle as 'a violation of the laws of nature' (114). Since he immediately adds that laws of nature are 'established' by 'a firm and unalterable experience', it is plain that miracles violate laws in the sense that they are sharply at odds with the normal course of nature. That is, they are defined in terms of their

[23] Locke, *Essay*, IV. xv. 5.

[24] David Wootton discusses the light these other accounts throw on Hume's sources. He suggests that the absence of this example from the first edition, despite its widespread discussion in England, bespeaks a French background to Hume's argument. This is not impossible, but the *Enquiry* arrives a full ten years after Hume's French sojourn to write the *Treatise*, and in all other sections the *Enquiry* versions have been thoroughly rewritten. So the suggestion is not irresistible. (See Wootton, 'Hume's "of Miracles"', 193 ff.) Stewart plausibly suggests that 'Hume may have conflated it in his memory with another Locke anecdote, about the "*Indian* Philosopher" who wondered what the world stood on (*Essay*, II. xiii. 19; xxiii. 2): both anecdotes involve elephants' (Stewart, 'Hume's Historical View of Miracles', 200 n. 48).

[25] Of course, the proper application of such a distinction is considerably more difficult than its mere recognition, and Hume concedes as much: the Indian prince, he claims, 'reasoned justly' (113), even though he was in fact mistaken. The Indian prince therefore *justly believed* that the testimony was contrary to his experience, even though, *in fact*, it was simply not conformable to it. He thus correctly applied a fallible standard, and thereby fell into error.

improbability. But Hume offers more than one definition, and to some this has seemed like carelessness. This is not the case. When he does amend the definition—'A miracle', he says, 'may be accurately defined, *a transgression of a law of nature by a particular volition of the Deity, or by the interposition of some invisible agent*' (115 n.)—the clue to this shift is, once again, the lens of probability through which the topic is being viewed. Hume amends the definition as he goes along to reflect the fact that the miracle reports that matter are those that can serve as the foundation for a religion, and such miracles—those that must be attributable to nothing less than the interposition of a deity—are those events that must be *maximally* improbable. There can be no other ways of explaining them—no 'analogies' drawn from nature—if they are to be interpreted as acts of a divine hand. In the end, only unique exceptions to 'firm and unalterable experience' will satisfy this requirement, so in this way Hume is led to the view that religion-grounding miracles must be unique.[26]

Hume amends his definition as he goes along because the argument begins with lesser improbabilities before moving on to an examination of greater improbabilities. This is why Hume opens his argument by initially considering 'the extraordinary and marvellous' (113)—those events that are dramatically different, but not so rare as to beggar belief—before moving on to consider the 'really miraculous' (114). And it is why, in the latter parts of Part II, he allows a distinction between the report of a miraculous occurrence that may be judged possible in principle, and the report of any miracle 'so as to be the foundation of a system of religion', which may not (127). Hume concludes thus, in part, because of 'external' evidences—that is, because such claims have so often been fabricated, so often promoted by playing on religious hopes and fears. But the conclusion owes no less to the fact that miracle reports capable of serving as the basis for such claims must resist even analogies with natural processes. He illustrates the point by comparing one miraculous event—eight days of darkness in midwinter—that is explicable as an extreme instance of the 'decay, corruption, and dissolution of nature' characteristic of midwinter, with another miraculous event—a resurrection after a month—that defies any such explanation (127–8). Hume's shifts in defini-

---

[26] Of course, if the grounds for regarding an event as having a divine cause can be established independently of degree of improbability, uniqueness will not be the marker of the religiously significant miracle. Cf. S. Clarke, 'When to Believe in Miracles', and 'Hume's Definition of Miracles Revised', *American Philosophical Quarterly*, 34 (1997), 95–102, and 36 (1999), 49–57.

tion of the miraculous are, then, evidence not of carelessness, but of a steady tightening of the screws.

The influence of probability theory provides an independent indication that Hume's critique of miracles is part of the *Enquiry*'s larger critique of religion arising from his interpretation of the implications of experimental philosophy. The larger critique itself is not exhaustive—it does not attack all possible foundations for religious belief—but the targets are carefully chosen for maximum effect. Hume uses his experimental principles to attack the independent evidential basis of revealed religion, and then turns to a critique of the main plank of natural religion. His aim is not to establish atheism, since no sceptic could intend any dogmatic settlement—even a negatively dogmatic settlement—of such an ultimate question.[27] Instead, he aims to show that the moderately sceptical interpretation of experience he has argued to be required by experimental philosophy—that experience cannot deliver to us knowledge of natures or causal powers—further implies that neither revealed nor natural theology can deliver the goods they promise: a significant body of religious doctrine. Hume the Academic sceptic argues, first, that the probabilities on which we do and must rely in judging our experience *prove* that miracle reports, because incredible to a properly functioning human mind, cannot be independent foundations for a revealed religion. The same sceptical interpretation of experience also implies that considerations of order or design deliver only forms of natural theism that are too uncertain, and too meagre in content, to be a basis for any system of religious doctrine. With this framework in place, it is now possible to turn to the arguments of 'Of Miracles'.

Part I

Hume begins by introducing a former Archbishop of Canterbury's argument against the Catholic doctrine of the 'real presence', or transubstantiation. Tillotson's argument is, he says, 'as concise, and elegant, and strong as any argument can possibly be supposed against a doctrine, so little worthy of a serious refutation' (109). The air of Protestant anti-Catholicism is unmistakable: Hume presents himself, in these opening remarks, as a good British Protestant joining in the favourite national pastime of attacking Catholic 'superstition'. Of course, the disguise is thin, but it is never entirely

---

[27] The sceptic and the atheist are distinguished as two different kinds of critic of religion at the beginning of Section XII (*Enquiries*, 149).

discarded—to the plain annoyance of some critics.[28] Recognizing this feature is important, however, because an attack on superstitious belief in miracles was itself an established avenue of Protestant critique of Catholicism. For the Catholic, unlike the Protestant, holds that miracles are an ongoing presence in mundane events—sanctification, for example, depends, in part, on the performance of miracles—rather than decisive divine acts that belong to the biblical period, especially to the life and mission of Jesus. For this reason, the Catholic can be thought to be more inclined to see the divine hand at work in occurrences that the Protestant—at least, the Protestant not infected by 'enthusiasm'— will view as natural, if unusual.[29] In this respect the Protestant self-image was of being more congenial to careful, experimental investigation of strange reports, and less inclined to precipitate declarations of divine intervention. A critique of miracle reports thus has itself a Protestant air, and to begin by invoking a former Archbishop underlines the fact, and encourages the attendant expectations.

The first task, before turning to Tillotson's 'concise, and elegant' argument, is to explain the unworthy doctrine that is its target. The doctrine of the real presence is the claim that, in the sacrament of the Eucharist, the bread and wine genuinely become the body and blood of Christ. They do so in a special sense, reliant on scholastic concepts and distinctions: the respective substances or essences of the bread and wine are changed, but not their 'accidents', their merely sensible properties. So, although there is no change to the appearance of either the bread or the wine, the underlying substances, in which the accidents 'inhere', do change. The bread and wine are really transformed into the body and blood of Christ. So, in the Eucharist, Christ is made a *real presence*.

Hume sets out Tillotson's critique (from the *Discourse upon Transubstantiation* (1684)) as follows: the authority of Scripture and Church tradition depends on the eye-witness accounts of the apostles to the miracles of Christ, 'by which he proved his divine mission'. That is, it depends entirely on the evidence of the senses. However—as Locke had affirmed[30]—the evidential value of reported experiences must diminish when they pass along a chain

---

[28] Thus, for example, A. A. Sykes, a rationalist Protestant apologist, distancing himself from Hume's opinions, complained of the Christian guise that: 'Such a mask, such a Disguise is so very thin, that every one may see the Features of the Man through the Veil he has put on' (quoted by Wootton, 'Hume's "of Miracles"', 221).

[29] Hume considers the two kinds of defective religiosity in 'Of Superstition and Enthusiasm', in *Essays*, 73–9.

[30] Locke, *Essay*, IV. xvi. 10, 11.

of testimony, so our evidence for the truth of Christianity is less than the evidence for the truth of our senses. Further, since a weaker evidence can never destroy a stronger, any Christian doctrines that conflict with the evidence of our senses must be rejected. The doctrine of the real presence *does* contradict sense; therefore it must be rejected. The argument, Hume concludes, is 'decisive' (110).

In fact, the argument so obviously fails to address the Catholic doctrine that one is at first tempted to think that neither Tillotson nor Hume knew it at all. The doctrine of transubstantiation does not at all contradict what is ordinarily meant by sense perception—what we see, smell, taste, and so on—since it accepts that the sensible qualities, the 'accidents', are not changed. In fact, it *affirms* that participants in the mass see, smell, and taste bread and wine, and nothing else. The point had been emphasized by Arnauld and Nicole in *Logic or the Art of Thinking*, written twenty years before Tillotson's work.[31] How then can the doctrine be thought to contradict sense? Antony Flew's judgement of the issue seems irresistible: 'It is astonishing that Tillotson, only seven years before his elevation to the See of Canterbury, should have put forward this argument. It suggests that he failed to appreciate what the nub of the peculiarly Roman Catholic doctrine of transubstantiation really is.'[32] Flew's later judgement on the matter shows his view to be unchanged: Hume begins, he says, with 'a mischievous reference to an intellectual indiscretion of the Latitudinarian theologian and [then] future Archbishop Tillotson'.[33]

However, there is a way to avoid concluding that Tillotson and Hume were ignorant or silly. The very fact that Tillotson's argument is itself an application of principles of probability to testimony suggests sophistication rather than ignorant prejudice, as indeed does its application to the question of transubstantiation. The doctrine had been a delicate issue for the Cartesians, since the Sorbonne and the Vatican both suspected that Descartes's radical new theory of substances was not compatible with theological orthodoxy on this point—one reason why Descartes's works were

[31] 'In the Eucharist the senses clearly show us roundness and whiteness, but they do not inform us whether it is the substance of bread that causes our eyes to perceive roundness and whiteness in it. Thus faith is not at all contrary to the evidence of the senses . . .' Arnauld and Nicole, (*Logic or the Art of Thinking*, 262). (This work was first published in 1662, and went through five editions by 1683.)

[32] Flew, *Hume's Philosophy of Belief*, 172. Flew quotes from the second Canon of the Council of Trent to illustrate that it is substance, but not appearance, that is said to change. Note therefore how ill this particular miracle claim fits the category of miracle *report*, i.e. of a marvellous occurrence observably at odds with the ordinary course of nature.

[33] A. Flew, *David Hume: Philosopher of Moral Science* (Oxford: Basil Blackwell, 1996), 80.

put on the Index shortly after his death. Even sympathizers saw the difficulty: Arnauld raises the question in the Fourth Set of Objections to the *Meditations*, to which Descartes offers a careful reply;[34] and, as noted above, Arnauld and Nicole address the question in *Logic or the Art of Thinking*.[35]

These considerations encourage the thought that Tillotson knew what he was doing; that the apparent ignorance is really evidence of a deliberately provocative stance. If we suppose him to have been as well informed on the experimental philosophy of the Royal Society, then we can explain his argument by supposing that he accepted the conclusions of Robert Boyle, the leading experimentalist, that the essences of the Aristotelians were not discovered by sense perception, and that a philosophy based on sound principles of sense could find no place for such notions. If we do suppose this, then his argument hangs together: for, on this view, what is received by the mind in perception are sensible qualities only—no forms or essences of substances are communicated to the mind through sense perception—and so sensory experiences have to be considered at face value. Thus the way is cleared to assess Church traditions against our own sense experience; that is, against our own experience of sensible qualities. Interpreted thus, it is indeed plausible to conclude that transubstantiation 'contradicts sense', and should therefore be rejected.[36]

If this interpretation seems plausible, then it must be admitted that most of the real work in the argument happens off the page. However, even if this were thought to be a problem for Tillotson (or at least for this interpretation of him), it is not a problem with respect to Hume. For 'Of Miracles' is Section X of an extended argument to precisely the conclusion that sense does not and cannot deliver knowledge of the essences of substances. So, even if Tillotson is not to be taken in this way, Hume's use of him certainly can. It makes perfect sense for Hume to argue that, given his own preceding arguments concerning the limitations of knowledge deriving from sense perception, Tillotson's argument is indeed decisive. Hume's use of Tillotson thus presupposes the sceptical interpretation of experience he has already expounded (and as

---

[34] *The Philosophical Writings of Descartes*, ii. 152–3, 172 ff.

[35] Arnauld and Nicole, *Logic or the Art of Thinking*, 2, 36, 71–2, 112–13.

[36] This enables thinking of Tillotson's argument as embodying a hermeneutic principle for interpreting scripture and tradition. Understood thus, it looks like a direct response to the concerns of Arnauld and Nicole. For, in their discussions of transubstantiation, they are much exercised by the question: what is the *this* of which Christ speaks in the Last Supper, when he says, bread in hand, 'This is my body which is broken for you'? Tillotson's argument implies that such questions have to be answered in ways that do not conflict with our experience of sensible qualities.

such provides a specific illustration of the dangers of extracting this section from its original setting).

One other feature of Hume's handling of Tillotson's argument deserves noting. Immediately after setting out the conclusion, he inserts a qualification: scripture and tradition have less weight than sense, but only 'when they are considered merely as external evidences, and are not brought home to everyone's breast, by the immediate operation of the Holy Spirit' (109). Modern readers tend not to take this remark at face value. Neither did a conspicuous number of his contemporaries, who regarded it as a mere smoke-screen. This is, I believe, correct (and will attempt to show why below). For present purposes, what is noteworthy about the remark is its 'fideistic' character: it suggests that there is a way of knowing which is the special deliverance of faith, even to the point of being contrary to reason. As such, it prefigures the famous concluding remark to Part II, that Christian faith is itself a miracle, being contrary to sound principles of experiential evidence (131).

Hume now turns to the serious business of his main argument, which, 'if just, will, with the wise and learned, be an everlasting check to all kinds of superstitious delusion, and consequently, will be useful as long as the world endures. For so long, I presume, will the accounts of miracles and prodigies be found in all history, sacred and profane' (110). The argument will always be useful because, not only will there always be such stories, there will also always be found superstitious minds to embrace them.

He begins with some reminders about the reliance to be placed on past experience: while our only guide in factual reasoning, experience is not infallible, since, as we know, it sometimes leads us into error. However, we have some prior idea of the likelihood of error, since experience also teaches us of the degree of uncertainty of particular events. 'A wise man, therefore, proportions his belief to the evidence': where past experience has been entirely consistent, he regards this experience as *proof* that future experience will be the same; where it has been variable, he concludes what the future will *probably* be like, judging the probability entirely on the ratios of past events. So probability—in the sense of a degree of assent that falls short of assurance[37]—presupposes variability in past experience, and the degree of probability reflects the actual experienced variability.

These principles, says Hume, can be applied to testimony, including first-hand eye-witness reports. Our confidence in such

[37] And so to be contrasted to both proof and demonstration. See also Locke, *Essay*, IV. xvi. 6.

reports is itself founded entirely in experience. This means that a given testimony itself constitutes a proof or a probability, according to its degree of fit with past experience: 'according as the conjunction of any kind of report and any kind of object has been found to be constant or variable' (112). Judging the credibility of testimony, then, requires proportioning it to the degree of confidence that can be placed in the evidence. The credibility of the testimony can be weakened by either internal or external circumstances. The former occurs where reports conflict with the degree of uniformity of our own experience. The latter occurs where the quality of the testimony itself can be called into question: for example, where witnesses disagree, where they are few or of doubtful character, where they stand to gain from their story, or where their manner gives cause for doubt: 'when they deliver their testimony with hesitation, or, on the contrary, with too violent asseverations' (113).[38]

If we restrict ourselves, for the time being, to internal circumstances, and test reports against our past experience, it is clear that testimony concerning any event that 'partakes of the extraordinary and the marvellous' must, for that very reason, be of less evidential value. That is, the evidential value of testimony decreases in direct proportion to the unusualness of the reported fact, because the unusualness of a fact is a measure of its lack of conformity with past experience. In such cases, a contest of credibilities is set up: 'when the fact attested is such a one as has seldom fallen under our observation, here is a contest of two opposite experiences; of which the one destroys the other, as far as its force goes, and the superior can only operate on the mind by the force, which remains' (113). The uniformity of our experience is always the test: and so the very same experience that establishes the *general* credibility of eye-witness reports simultaneously undermines the credibility of those *particular* reports that are not conformable to it.[39] In fact, incredible reports can and should be

---

[38] Cf. Locke's list of factors that affect the quality of testimony (*Essay*, IV. xvi. 9).

[39] This is certainly a crucial move in the argument. In Hume's view, the Indian prince 'reasoned justly' when denying the reality of ice—even though he was wrong in fact—because he rejected what was not *conformable* to his experience. He was wrong in fact because, given his inexperience of cold climates, the freezing of water was not *contrary* to his experience. However, the very fact that this is a genuine distinction means that it should be drawn where appropriate. The cautious reasoner, who wishes to be guided by what experience *does* teach, and not merely by what it *seems* to teach to the careless observer, will therefore want to *test* anomalous reports precisely in order to determine whether experience has been violated, or merely enriched. In other words, at this point alternative explanatory hypotheses need to be considered. This is just the point stressed by C. S. Peirce in his response to Hume's argument. See his 'The Laws of Nature and Hume's Argument against Miracles', in C. S. Peirce, *Selected Writings (Values in a Universe of Chance)*, ed. P. P. Wiener (New York: Dover, 1966), 289–321, esp. 308 ff. Further, Peirce's inductive strategy, which seeks to find the best explanation of

rejected even when they are affirmed by sources who would, in normal circumstances, be beyond reproach.

This brings us to the nub of Hume's argument: its application not merely to the marvellous, but to the truly miraculous. The most incredible of all reports, he insists, are those that are completely at odds with past experience, and they may remain incredible even when the testimony in their favour cannot be faulted. This is because in such a case we have 'proof against proof'—that is, a direct contest between an otherwise unbelievable report and an irreproachable source. In such a case 'the strongest must prevail, but still with a diminution of its force, in proportion to that of its antagonist' (114). Hume now proceeds to argue that the miracle report cannot be the strongest, that it cannot override the evidence of past experience.

The first, and most important, step to this conclusion concerns the degree of improbability that necessarily attaches to miracles. This is because they are, by definition, violations of the laws of nature: that is, putative exceptions to principles of experience that *cannot* be doubted, because they are backed by the highest degree of uniformity of experience. In Hume's words:

A miracle is a violation of the laws of nature; and as a firm and unalterable experience has established these laws, the proof against a miracle, from the very nature of the fact, is as entire as any argument from experience can possibly be imagined . . . There must . . . be a uniform experience against every miraculous event, otherwise the event would not merit that appellation. And as a uniform experience amounts to a proof, there is here a direct and full *proof*, from the nature of the fact, against the existence of any miracle; nor can such a proof be destroyed, or the miracle rendered credible, but by an opposite proof, which is superior.   (114–15)

In short, miracle reports, in order to be believed, must overcome the strongest possible evidence against them, because what constitutes a report as miraculous is its opposition to a law of nature; and the uniformity of experience that establishes laws of nature *as* laws is such that they cannot be doubted. So miracle reports can be believed only where the evidence for them is wholly beyond reproach, in fact as perfect as any testimony could be, in order to constitute a proof superior to the proof that, in the nature of the fact, attaches to the laws of nature. Hume gives the clear impression that such a degree of confidence in a testimony cannot be

what cannot be determined with certainty, is readily conformable to the spirit of Academic scepticism—more so, it might seem, than is Hume's approach. But Hume has more to say about 'analogies'—and therefore, in modern terms, best explanations—in Part II.

achieved; that the strongest case that could be hoped for would be
'a mutual destruction of arguments' (116), in which, presumably,
belief is disabled on both fronts. Nevertheless, he does not argue
at this stage that all miracle reports are unbelievable—only that it
is highly uncertain that, even with the best possible testimonial
evidence, such reports could outweigh common experience.[40] It is
left to Part II to argue that the best possible evidence has never
been provided for any reported miracle, and that the shortcomings of evidence are all the more pronounced in the case of religious miracle claims.

(Hume acknowledges, in a footnote, that it is not always possible to tell whether common experience has been violated. Sometimes events may be genuinely miraculous, even if undetected,
such as the 'raising of a feather, when the wind wants ever so little
of a force requisite for that purpose'. The doctrine of the real presence is, of course, a miracle claim of this kind. However, miracles
that can serve to *establish* a religion are, in the nature of the case,
readily detectable, and the key question there becomes whether
the marvellous events might not be genuinely miraculous, because
(for example) just a remarkable coincidence. This question itself
would have to be settled by probabilities. If, for example, a man
speaks out against a storm and the storm then abates, has he stilled
the waves by his voice? If coincidence can be ruled out—for
example, by an improbable number of other remarkable events
connected up to that man—then the event is truly at odds with
laws of nature, because human voices do not normally have that
effect. This occurrence then qualifies as a divinely caused act,
because it fits the 'accurate definition' of a miracle as '*a transgression of the law of nature by a particular volition of the Deity, or by the
interposition of some invisible agent*' (115 n.). Hume does not spell
things out fully here, but he does make it clear at the end of Part
II that the evidence for believing an event contrary to the law of
nature to be due to the action of an invisible agent is simply the
unqualified opposition between the event and the ordinary course
of things. Remarkable events that resist even analogies with
natural processes are those that are properly attributable to invisible agents, and it is the credibility of reports of these sorts of
events that is at issue in this section.)

It is important to recognize what Hume is and is not arguing

---

[40] Cf. Hume's comment, in a letter to Hugh Blair: 'The proof against a miracle, as it is
founded on invariable experience, is of that *species* or *kind* of proof, which is full and certain
when taken alone, because it implies no doubt, as is the case with all probabilities; but there
are degrees of this species, and when a weaker proof is opposed to a stronger, it is overcome'
(*Letters*, ed. Greig, i. 350).

here, not least because a plausible but mistaken interpretation is not without notable adherents. He is *not* arguing that, because a law of nature has been established by 'a firm and unalterable experience', any exceptional event is not an exception to a law because laws are, by definition, exceptionless—the exception showing that the putative law is, in fact, no law at all. This interpretation has tempted many. David Fate Norton's account is a notable recent example:

the very perfection of the proof that a miracle has occurred implies that what has occurred is not in fact a miracle. A miracle is a violation of the laws of nature; a law of nature is established by a firm and unalterable experience. The champion of miracles is arguing, however, that this experience is not firm and unalterable; at least one exception is, he claims, known. From this exception it follows, Hume reminds us, that there is no violation of a law of nature because there is no law of nature, and hence, there is no miracle.[41]

This is not Hume's argument; in fact, it *cannot* be. The argument described is a form of demonstration, seeking to rule out miracles on the basis of relations of ideas: a miracle is defined as a violation of a law of nature; but a law of nature is defined as exceptionless, inviolable; therefore the 'miracle' shows the putative law not to be a law after all; therefore no law has been violated; therefore no miracle has occurred. The argument depends wholly on the meaning of the terms—on the relations of ideas. It is a demonstrative argument a priori, not an argument from experience. It is therefore not a proof in Hume's sense—and therefore not his argument.[42] The point can be clarified by remembering that, for Hume, laws of nature are the most general of those beliefs about the natural world that are 'established'—that is, *proven*—by experience; that what is proven is, *for us*, certain, even though not infallibly the case; and Hume's argument is to show that miracle reports are *disproven* by the fact that they violate the principles of experience, and are thus incredible to a properly functioning mind.[43]

Antony Flew also argues that the logical impossibility

[41] Norton, *David Hume*, 299.

[42] That interpretations of this kind must be mistaken is supported, from a different direction, by Antony Flew. As he rightly observes, although Hume does talk of the 'impossibility' of miracles, 'he is still careful never to say or to imply, either that the events described are inconceivable, or that the notion of a miracle is self-contradictory' (Flew, *Hume's Philosophy of Belief*, 186).

[43] In this context, note how Hume opposes testimony to miracles—sometimes even supported by a 'cloud of witnesses'—by employing terminology that *appears* question-begging because of implicit appeal to proper functioning: Cardinal de Retz rejected the testimonies because 'he . . . concluded, *like a just reasoner*, that such an evidence carried falsehood upon the very face of it'; '*the wise* lend a very academic faith to every report which . . .'; and 'the absolute impossibility or miraculous nature of the events' is decisive 'in the eyes of *all reasonable people*' (*Enquiries*, 124–5; emphases added).

interpretation is mistaken. He argues that Hume means, not that miracles are logically impossible, but that they are *physically* impossible: 'And the criterion of physical as opposed to logical impossibility simply is logical incompatibility with a law of nature, in the broadest sense.'[44] This is, rightly, to construe the argument as concerning matters of fact: laws of nature describe how the world works, and so what physically can occur; miracle claims violate these standards; thus miracles are impossible, and miracle claims are false. This is much closer to Hume's meaning, but it nevertheless goes astray, and again because the notion of proof, and above all its sceptical (or fallibilist) character, is not adequately appreciated. The central point is that even though—in fact, *because*—laws of nature are proven by experience, they do not, for Hume, tell us how the world *is*—but only how we must believe it to be. They are, indeed, our best explanations of how things are, but still they are *our* best explanations: and so vulnerable to all the errors and inductive frailties characteristic of the natural, mechanical beings that a sound experimental philosophy judges us to be.[45] So, although we will certainly *believe* that reports of miracles are reports of physical impossibilities, the impossibility is, in the final analysis, psychological rather than physical. That is, miracle reports are *incredible* to a mind that judges according to the principles of experience—that is, to a properly functioning, if fallible, mind. Thus Hume is not, as Flew elsewhere claims, guilty of 'lapsing from his own high corrigibilist principles . . . [and] taking it for granted that everything which an eighteenth-century man of sense believed to be impossible must in truth actually be impossible'.[46] Rather, what Hume accepts is that an eighteenth-century man of sense must *judge* miracle reports to be reports of impossibilities, and that in so judging he is 'a just reasoner', because he judges by the best available, and therefore by authoritative, standards—even though he may fall into error by so doing.[47]

Hume's argument is more subtle, and more informed by his Academic scepticism, than has commonly been realized. His argument is not a conceptual argument to the effect that miracles are logically impossible, nor a dogmatic argument to the effect that they

[44] Flew, *Hume's Philosophy of Belief*, 187.

[45] The difference between Hume and Newton can be brought out here. Both agree that laws of nature are summaries of (accurate measurement of) experience, and so are not unchangeable in principle. However, for Hume, the laws are *for us* unchangeable— necessary—because a firm experience has habituated us to expect the world to go in the same way. Newton has no such account of the (subjective) necessity of laws. See *Opticks*, Query 31, 400–1.

[46] Flew, *David Hume*, 84.

[47] This is why Hume commends the Indian prince (*Enquiries*, 113–14).

are physically impossible.[48] He is, rather, applying his experimental principles to show (in Part I) that, even where the supporting testimony is irreproachable, miracle reports are very unlikely to be credible; and (in Part II) that, given the special problems created by religious interests, irreproachable testimony is not to be found, so miracle reports sufficient to found a religion are *not* credible. Hume insists, over and over again, that what he is offering is a 'direct and full *proof*' against miracles. There is no trace of any purely conceptual argument, nor of what can or cannot exist, in his concluding summation. The fundamental question is, rather, what can 'command my belief or opinion':

> When anyone tells me, that he saw a dead man restored to life, I immediately consider with myself, whether it be more probable, that this person should either deceive or be deceived, or that the fact, which he relates, should really have happened. I weigh the one miracle against the other; and according to the superiority, which I discover, I pronounce my decision, and always reject the greater miracle. If the falsehood of his testimony would be more miraculous, than the event which he relates; then, and not till then, can he pretend to command my belief or opinion. (116)

Miracles are weighed, and the superiority judged, according to the evidence of experience; that is, according to the processes by which different 'views or glimpses' imprint ideas more or less strongly on the imagination, thereby rendering them, *for us*, proofs or probabilities (57). This is an account not of what is or is not possible—logically or physically—but of the proper functioning of mechanisms of belief formation in an instinctive being.

Part II

The argument to this point is not intended to be conclusive. Hume has allowed that testimony for a miracle may be irreproachable, but that such a circumstance is not sufficient to establish belief in the miracle, because of the complete confidence we place in the law of nature that the purported miracle violates. We find ourselves caught between two competing claims, and belief can attach only to the stronger claim. Since the confidence placed in a law of

[48] David Wootton concurs, although his choice of terms is not entirely happy. He says: 'Laws of nature are proofs against miracles, not because they show them to be impossible ... but because they show such events to be in the highest degree improbable.' His discussion suggests that by this comment he means that the key issue is probability with respect to belief—that is, credibility (Wootton, 'Hume's "of Miracles"', 204–5). Stewart does not directly address the issue, but his account is congenial to the interpretation offered here ('Hume's Historical View of Miracles', 185 ff.).

nature is as strong as any belief can be, it seems impossible that the miracle report could triumph. Hume does not press the point, however: he allows it to be *possible* that, where the testimony is irreproachable, the miracle report *could* triumph. The argument of Part II is that the condition is excessively charitable. Testimony in support of a miracle is, in fact and in the nature of the case, never irreproachable: there never has been, nor could be, any testimony sufficient to outweigh belief in the relevant law of nature. All miracle reports are therefore incredible.

Hume offers four main reasons for this conclusion. The first of these is the orthodox concern of probability theory: the quantity and quality of the witnesses. The very orthodoxy of the issue makes it a little surprising that Hume's treatment is so brief. It can only be presumed that he thought his conclusions obvious— perhaps even uncontroversially so—and therefore ill-deserving of any extended discussion. His claim is simply historical: there is not to be found, in history, any miracle attested by a sufficient number of witnesses who were sufficiently sensible and well educated to rule out any suspicion that they might have been deluded; of such good character as to rule out the possibility of deceit; of sufficient reputation to protect, so that they would have had much standing to lose if discovered to be wrong; and where the facts reported occurred in public circumstances and in an important centre of human affairs, where sensible and educated critics would quickly detect any falsehoods. These conditions, concludes Hume, are never met, but all 'are requisite to give us a full assurance in the testimony of men' (117).

The second flaw in testimonies concerning miracles, Hume argues, is a flaw in human nature itself, which undermines the confidence we might otherwise have in testimonies concerning remarkable events of all kinds. This flaw is a tendency to abandon our normal principles of experience, just when they are most needed. In common life, we draw conclusions on the basis of analogies, and place greatest confidence in the most usual or most regular occurrences. When we proceed in this way, we reject the extraordinary. However, the human mind sometimes works in a quite contrary way, and, by taking pleasure in what is most surprising, tends towards belief in the strange precisely because of its strangeness. This is the *love of wonder*, a tendency quite at odds with the principles of ordinary experience. It is, says Hume, visible in the reception of extraordinary travellers' tales; but, when combined with 'the spirit of religion', all good sense is abandoned. This is because the religious believer is especially prone to a range of failings: to the illusions engendered by 'enthusiasm'—that is, emotionally intense religious experience that clouds judgement at the same time as it augments self-confidence;[49] to a neglect of truthfulness for the sake of the great ends of religion; to an excessive vanity prompted by the importance of the cause and of his place in it; and (like everyone else) to self-interest. To compound these problems, he also has an audience that is ignorant, and that is prone to sacrifice its judgement in the face of perceived ultimate mysteries, or due to the effects of excessive passion. The evidence of all this is plain in history: forged miracles, priests leading a gullible populace by inflaming their passions, and so on. The love of wonder, combined with the peculiar temptations and opportunities provided by religious beliefs, conspire to unhinge human judgement when confronting precisely those topics that seem to exhibit the greatness of human nature—its concern for the 'ultimate questions'. Hume's point here can thus be understood as an application of his more general view, that human beings are not fallen semi-divinities but instinctive creatures who function properly when dealing with the ordinary concerns of daily life. When confronted by extreme cases, however, their principles of judgement, not being fitted to these circumstances, send them seriously awry: sober and sound judgement vanishes, and gives way to the violent and disabling effects of disordered passions.

Hume's third argument against the quality of testimony for miracles develops a point he has mentioned in the course of his first objection: that testimony to miracles emanates from remote, uneducated parts of the world. He claims that it counts strongly against miracle stories that they occur mainly among 'ignorant and barbarous nations', or, where adopted by civilized nations, are so because inherited from 'ignorant and barbarous ancestors'. Thus the histories of modern nations begin with remote times when miracles were thick on the ground, but as we approach 'enlightened ages' they 'grow thinner every page' (119). This fact alone, he concludes, is enough to show that these founding marvels are nothing mysterious, but just one more evidence of the human love of wonder and marvels, which, although it can be kept in check in enlightened times, can never be entirely eliminated. In fact, in ignorant times—where critical examination is uncommon—they flourish in fertile soil, so much so that over time they shoot up

[49] Cf. Hume's treatment of this psychological type, and its religious manifestations, in 'Of Superstition and Enthusiasm' (in *Essays*, 73–9).

'into prodigies almost equal to those which they relate'. That is, belief in them can be regarded to be almost as remarkable—almost as miraculous—as the original miracle story itself.[50]

These three objections are similar in spirit. All breathe the air of Enlightenment certitudes, as evidenced by the regular contrast of civilized to barbarian, educated to ignorant. Up to a point, the objections are sound: miracle stories are more common in stories of remote origins; they are strikingly less common (but not absent) in the literature produced in ancient Athens and Rome in their heydays, where hard-headed attitudes born of exposure to a wide variety of societies and their practices are visibly present. They provide a sharp contrast with the vivid examples of peasant superstitions in all ages. Nevertheless, the contrasts are overplayed. They may tell us as much about the complacent self-understanding of the eighteenth-century *philosophe* as they do about the 'barbarous' times or societies themselves. The origins of Christianity itself fit poorly with these claims: although Augustine and other defenders of Christianity had drawn attention to Christianity's origins amongst uneducated fishermen, in order to emphasize its remarkable success in the ancient world,[51] it seems not to have been the case that Christianity developed as a religion of the social margins. Its principal propagator, Paul of Tarsus, was an educated Roman citizen; the Christian communities he established in Rome and the Greek cities seem to have included many aristocratic or genteel women and their households; and, in time, it developed into something of a middle-class affair before Constantine transformed it into the state religion in the fourth century.[52] Despite an abundance of fishermen, then, early Christianity seems to have been less of a 'barbarous' affair than has commonly been imagined. The objection can perhaps be reconstructed in more modest fashion, for many of the miracle stories connected to the life of Jesus occur in the countryside, and for that reason

---

[50] This objection anticipates Hume's concluding remark to this section that, for the believer, faith is itself 'a continued miracle in his own person' (*Enquiries*, 131).

[51] Augustine, *The City of God against the Pagans*, ed. R. W. Dyson (Cambridge: Cambridge University Press, 1998), 1113 (XXII. v).

[52] See e.g. P. Brown, *Authority and the Sacred* (Cambridge: Cambridge University Press, 1995). The point here applies equally against Nietzsche's critique of Christianity as the religion of slave morality, of *ressentiment*. Unfortunately, despite the mountains of Nietzsche literature, this question seems rarely to be seriously addressed. An exception is F. A. Lea, *The Tragic Philosopher: Friedrich Nietzsche* (London: Methuen, 1957). (It is also worth considering, in opposition to Nietzsche, whether Christianity's rejection of warrior ideals, and emphasis on pacific virtues, itself reflects the values of the urban middle class, for whom the 'modern' life of the Greek city required the abandoning of the rustic ideals of the Heroic Age. Much the same point can be made concerning Plato's subordination of Homeric *thumos* to the rule of reason. Niezsche's opposition to both thus appears not to be heroic resistance to slavishness, etc., but nostalgic anti-modernity.)

could be said to precede the religion's transmission to the educated world. However, even here there are problems, because the argument relies on an image of Jesus as a simple carpenter, brought up in an environment of almost Homeric simplicity. Since Nazareth was situated quite close to the Roman towns of Capernaum and Caesarea Philippi, however, this image may itself owe more to folklore than fact.[53]

A second problem with Hume's argument to this point concerns the 'love of wonder'. There is no doubt that love of wonder is a readily observable human trait, but this fact alone does not justify Hume's argument. This is because it is not so readily observable that the love of wonder results in *belief*; nor, given Hume's own principles, is it clear how it can do so. What is the present impression that transforms a merely hypothetical state of affairs into something actively believed, a stable and vivid idea? Further, it seems less than fair dealing on Hume's part to introduce this human trait at this point of the argument, having ignored it in the positive account of belief in Section V. What he has to say here may well be right, but questions remain about how well it fits with his principles, and whether the attempt to make it fit would, by complicating the psychological story about human functioning, do collateral damage to the argument of this and other sections.

It is also worth asking just how Hume's audience would have reacted to these arguments. There is little doubt but that the reaction would have been largely hostile; but not necessarily wholly so. It has already been noted that the educated, largely Protestant, readership would have had some reasons for sympathy with these objections: both Catholic 'superstition', and non-conforming, quasi-anarchistic Protestant 'enthusiasm', with all their attendant political consequences (from the Revolt of 1745 back to the Civil War), could be considered examples of religious pathology, generated by the sorts of vices Hume lists here. A moderate Protestant, educated, like Hume, in Cicero and other ancient authors, and with the requisite distaste for the excesses of Catholics and enthusiasts, would have shared at least some of Hume's Enlightenment attitudes. It cannot be presumed, in other words, that the audience

---

[53] The Gospels report Jesus popping into these towns on a regular basis. He also drops in on the busy Mediterranean ports of Tyre and Sidon. These were all, in varying degrees, cosmopolitan towns of the Empire. Jerusalem must also be regarded in the same light, since it was the centre of Roman administration as well as of Jewish religious culture. Moreover, the fact of Jerusalem's religious function cannot count against it without begging the question at issue: Hume's claim is that religious origins are in 'barbarous' environments, not that religious culture *is* barbarism. The same point applies to Jerusalem's Jewishness.

would have found all the arguments objectionable; even if they would have lamented the author's failure to make the necessary distinctions between barbarians, on the one hand, and divinely appointed apostles—even if fishermen—on the other.

Hume's fourth objection is different from the first three. At first sight, it seems not to be another argument against the quality of testimony, but a further case of 'proof against proof'. The conclusion is that testimony offered in support of miracles is self-destroying, because, given the diversity of miracle reports offered in support of different religions, any testimony in support of a particular miracle is opposed by an 'infinite' number of contrary testimonies. This gives us the clue as to why Hume treats it as a problem of the reliability of testimony. Testimony is undermined if different witnesses disagree, and the different miracle stories of different religions are treated by Hume as competing reports. His argument begins with the claim that, 'in matters of religion, whatever is different is contrary' (121). A given miracle, he claims, is supposed to establish the truth of some particular religious doctrine or system, but it cannot do this unless it simultaneously overthrows every other religious system, and, in so doing, also overthrows the miracles on which those other systems were founded. So all the miracles of different religions are to be regarded as competing claims, and, considered as such, they are mutually destructive.

Hume seems to be assuming that all religions are built on miracles. This is dubitable, but need not detain us: in so far as religions are built on miracles, the argument will be relevant. The nature of the argument itself is revealed by the analogy with which Hume concludes the objection:

This argument may appear over subtle and refined; but is not in reality different from the reasoning of a judge, who supposes, that the credit of two witnesses, maintaining a crime against any one, is destroyed by the testimony of two others, who affirm him to have been two hundred leagues distant, at the same instant when the crime is said to have been committed. (122)

Hume's meaning is that different miracle reports are contrary because they require a wonder-working divinity to be at different places at the same time, performing different actions to establish contrary creeds. Making this explicit shows that this argument against the credibility of miracle testimonies is more precisely focused. This is because, although the first three objections can be understood to be directed against miracles in the sense of overwhelmingly improbable events, this fourth objection is directed against the specifically religious, 'accurate' definition of a miracle as *'a transgression of a law of nature by a particular volition of the Deity'* (115n.). This is worth noting, because the argument is plainly inadequate as an objection to unlikely events themselves. If every religion has its collection of miracle stories, then it remains possible to conclude that the number of marvels is greater than imagined, and that confidence in natural regularity, expressed in belief in the necessity of the laws of nature, is overplayed; that the natural world is less uniform than often supposed, and that the laws of nature hold only in general and for the most part.

This possibility may appear to undermine Hume's case, for it would weaken his prior arguments against testimony to allow that marvels might be more common than even any one religion supposes. The evidence for the operations of the 'love of wonder' itself would then be undermined, for, if marvellous events are more common, then there is less reason to suppose that reports of them are to be explained away, by invoking a distinct form of human weakness or gullibility. Further, by undermining the claimed uniformity of ordinary experience, it would also undermine the plausibility of any critique based on applying principles of probability, since, without uniformity, no probability argument could attain the force of a proof. However, Hume would have little cause for embarrassment because there is another more general respect in which the multiplication of marvels is 'contrary' to religious miracles: if marvellous events are more common, then there would appear to be *no* events that were so contrary to ordinary experience—so thoroughly at odds with all natural analogies—that they would demand a religious interpretation. A multiplicity of marvels is not evidence of a busy, caring deity. It is, rather, evidence of variable natural processes: of chance. A multiplicity of marvels undermines Hume's specific argument only as it undermines the general case for miracle itself.

This completes the empirical case Hume brings against miracle reports in Part II, so we can step back and ask why these objections have been introduced. They are not, as may be supposed, simply a list of Hume's additional objections to miracles and the religious mentality. They are that, but they also serve an important purpose. The argument of Part I has been that, according to the principles of probability grounded in experience, miracle reports are not credible. That is, a properly functioning human mind *simply will not believe* reports of miracles. But it is plain that very large numbers of people *do* believe such reports, and, most importantly, ground their religious beliefs thereon. So Hume needs to provide evidence that these beliefs are indeed due to malfunctioning of some kind or other. The psychological and sociological theses advanced here are designed to serve this end. His argument is, at bottom, that the hopes and fears on which religion is built cause us to mishandle the evidence pertinent to the 'religious hypothesis'. Most notably, the 'love of wonder' is a principle of the human frame at odds with the durable principles of interpretation on which we rely in judging experience, and as such one further evidence of the frailties of the natural processes that underpin human mental functioning.

The remainder of the section consists of illustration, clarification, and an important qualification. The role of these remarks will be better appreciated if the contrast between proper and improper functioning is kept in mind. To begin with the illustrations. They are three historical examples to show that, even where testimony is as good as one could hope for, still we see that, as long as we are not blinded by our own religious attachments, or by the special temptations religion brings in its train—as long, in short, as we function properly, according to the canons of ordinary experience—we do accept the principle he has laid down, and reject the extraordinary reports as unbelievable. Thus Cardinal de Retz, for example, in rejecting a miracle report as unbelievable despite the evidence offered for it, 'concluded, like a just reasoner, that such an evidence carried falsehood upon the very face of it, and that a miracle, supported by any human testimony, was more properly a subject of derision than of argument' (124).[54]

In fact, Hume argues, belief in miracles reflects an error concerning the value of testimony. Because human testimony sometimes has 'the utmost force and authority' (125), it is tempting, but mistaken, to conclude that it always has the same level of authority.[55] In particular, it is wise to test very carefully every report that is in the interests of the reporter: and nothing is more flattering to a person than to be cast in the role of an ambassador from heaven. Not only does this seduction lead the reporter astray, but 'the gazing populace', with their love of wonder, 'receive greed-

---

[54] Hume is effectively offering a challenge: if, like the Cardinal, we do not accept that a leg will grow back 'by the rubbing of holy oil upon the stump' (123), no matter what the 'cloud of witnesses' (125), we show by our response that experience has *proved* to us the impossibility of the event; that is, that it is impossible for us to believe it.

[55] The discriminatory attitude to testimony recommended here shows clearly that Hume does not suppose that testimony is intrinsically unreliable. His point is that we should test it against our other information—including, of course, other testimony—and judge all in the light of the principles founded in experience. Thus Hume's view is not the 'epistemological individualism' that simply denies testimony the status of first-hand experience. Cf. Coady, *Testimony*.

ily, without examination, whatever sooths superstition' (126). These two factors help to explain why miracle stories flourish for a time before fading into oblivion: their popularity is never due simply to the quality of evidence for them, and therefore fluctuates according to the impact of the other factors. Moreover, to illustrate the difficulty of proper testing, it is only necessary to recall just how difficult it is to establish what actually happened in the past or in some remote place—even for a court of law set up for precisely that purpose. With new religions, he adds, the problems are very pronounced, since they are usually ignored by the educated until they have established a secure grip on the minds of the masses. So, by the time an independent assessment of the religions' miraculous credentials becomes socially important, it is almost impossible to establish their falsehood—and far too late to have any effect on mass belief.[56]

Hume now offers a summary conclusion before introducing his important qualification. The conclusion is that there are so many shortcomings in the testimonies provided for miracles that they are not credible to a 'just reasoner', a person whose natural judgements have not been contaminated by religious hopes and fears. In Hume's terminology, actual miracle reports do not amount to a probable argument, let alone a proof. And, of course, even if they did amount to a proof, they would be opposed by another proof, of the most powerful kind possible: the contrary evidence of common experience. Since experience is the source of the authority of testimony, and also the basis for the laws of nature, when they come into conflict we have no option but to weigh them against each other, and accept the weightier. The miraculous reports of all popular religions fail this test: 'therefore we may establish it as a maxim, that no human testimony can have such force as to prove a miracle, and make it a just foundation for any such system of religion' (127).

It is at this point that the qualification is introduced. The conclusion concerns miracles that are capable of founding a religion, and, although Hume does not give a general specification of such miracles, it is clear that they are characterized by their maximal improbability. He illustrates the difference between these and other miracles by contrasting two different cases. It is, he says, allowable that there could be proof, by testimony, of miracles in the broader sense of violations of the laws of nature, 'though, perhaps, it will be impossible to find any such in all the records of

---

[56] Again, Hume's Enlightenment conviction that religions arise through ignorance and fear—as argued at length in *The Natural History of Religion*—lies in the background here.

history'. If, for example, there were well-attested reports of eight days of darkness from 1 January 1600—that is, in the middle of the northern winter—this would have to be accepted, and the task for the scientists would be to discover the causes of such a remarkable occurrence. This is because such a testimony is less at odds with the course of nature than may at first appear, since 'the decay, corruption, and dissolution of nature, is an event rendered probable by so many analogies, that any phenomenon, which seems to have a tendency towards that catastrophe, comes within the reach of human testimony, if that testimony be very extensive and uniform' (128). Some miracles, that is, although strictly violations of natural laws, nevertheless are not *entirely* disanalogous to natural processes or tendencies, and so may be credible, provided the supporting testimony is of sufficient quality.

The case is different with religion-grounding miracles, simply because such miracles owe their significance precisely to the absence of any such analogies. This means that the contest between the miracle report and the laws of nature must be direct and unqualified; a situation where the careful reasoner will inevitably judge the balance of proof to lie with the law of nature. Thus, if the historians of England agreed that Queen Elizabeth died on 1 January 1600, but reappeared after a month and governed for a further three years, we should not believe it. It is simply more probable that, although it *seemed* that she had died, in fact she had not. And even if the evidence for a genuine death was strong, it would still be more likely that someone has tried to dupe us than that the laws of nature were so dramatically violated. This probability *rises* if the miracle were supposed to establish a new religion, because the long history of the exploitation of human religious hopes by the unscrupulous or foolish is sufficient to cause suspicion that we are being conned. We must, Hume concludes, remember the basic principle: that it is far more likely that the testimony is false, than that the laws of nature have been violated.

These remarks go some way towards meeting an important criticism of Hume's handling of extraordinary reports, brought by C. S. Peirce. Peirce describes Hume's method as one of 'balancing likelihoods', and contrasts it with a more fruitful alternative, the employment of abductive reasoning (argument to the best explanation) to generate alternative hypotheses capable of further comparison and testing.[57] Although he may not have thought Hume's version of the method of 'balancing likelihoods' as disreputable as

[57] Peirce, 'The Laws of Nature and Hume's Argument against Miracles', in Peirce, *Selected Writings*, 289–321.

other versions of the same basic method, he does make it very clear, in another place, that this method is an obstacle to fruitful enquiry, principally because of its obduracy in the face of contrary evidence. He thus condemns this method as a prejudice of the eighteenth century. It is evidenced in

the refusal of Laplace and Biot in the closing years of the previous century to accept the evidence that stones fall from heaven (evidence proving that they do so daily), simply because their prepossessions were the other way. One of the geologist brothers De Luc declared that he would not believe such a thing though he saw it with his own eyes; and a scientifically given English ecclesiastic who happened to be sojourning in Siena when a shower of aerolites were dashed in broad daylight into an open square of that town, wrote home that having seen the stones he had found the testimony of eye-witnesses so unimpeachable and so trustworthy—that he accepted the fact, you will say? by no means—that he knew not what to think! Such was the *bon sens* that guided the eighteenth century—a pretty phrase for ineradicable prejudice.[58]

Whatever the prejudices of Hume the man, his argument does not commit him to this kind of rigidity. If the miracle does not pander to the human foibles that promote and are promoted by religion, the question is whether there are sufficiently strong analogies between the miraculous event and the observable course of nature. In this case it is clear that there are, since experimental practice (Galileo's telescopic viewings of the planets) and mechanical philosophy (the heavens, like the earth, judged to be composed of material objects in motion) both affirm that there are lumps of rock moving through the heavens, and so capable of crashing into the earth's atmosphere and penetrating to the earth's surface. Hume may or may not have handled such a case in this way: but it is clear that he could have done so.[59]

Hume winds up the section with some famous remarks about faith. He argues that the preceding discussion shows it to be a mistake for the Christian to seek to defend Christianity by means of reason: 'our most holy religion is founded on *Faith*, not on reason; and it is a sure method of exposing it to put it to such a trial as it is, by no means, fitted to endure' (130). He supports the claim by examining the Pentateuch (that is, the traditionally described Books of Moses, the first five books of the Old Testament). If considered 'not as the word or testimony of God himself,

---

[58] Peirce, 'The Century's Great Men in Science', in ibid. 268–9.

[59] The same can be said of Richard Whately's critique of Hume in his *Historic Doubts Relative to Napoleon Buonaparte* (1819), in which he argues that Hume's principles would commit him to denying that Napoleon ever existed. Whately misses the importance of these qualifications about analogies. His argument is briefly discussed by Coady in *Testimony*, 187.

but as the production of a mere human writer or historian' (130),
it must fare very poorly when measured against the principles he
has provided. The extraordinary events recorded there—the original perfections of Eden, the Fall, the immense lifespans enjoyed
in that time, the Deluge, the selection of the Jews as the Chosen
People ('and that people the countrymen of the author'), of their
deliverance by Exodus to the Promised Land—all these are reports
both at odds with our ordinary experience, and also dubitable
by reference to the effects of the love of wonder, self-interest,
etc. They therefore must fail when judged by sound standards of
probability:

I desire any one to lay his hand upon his heart, and after a serious consideration declare, whether he thinks that the falsehood of such a book, supported
by such a testimony, would be more extraordinary and miraculous than all
the miracles it relates; which is, however, necessary to make it be received,
according to the measures of probability above established.   (130)

The conclusion must be that faith is itself miraculous, since it
can only be maintained by suspending judgement of probabilities:

upon the whole, we may conclude, that the *Christian Religion* not only was
at first attended with miracles, but even at this day cannot be believed by any
reasonable person without one. Mere reason is insufficient to convince us of
its veracity: And whoever is moved by *Faith* to assent to it, is conscious of a
continued miracle in his own person, which subverts all the principles of his
understanding, and gives him a determination to believe what is most contrary to custom and experience.   (131)

The strong fideism of this passage has usually been read as
heavily ironical. I think the judgement is correct: that the 'continued miracle' refers to a *malfunction* in the human organism, not
to evidence of a supernatural mystery. However, this cannot be too
quickly concluded, for things are not quite as simple as may
appear.

It cannot, in the first place, simply be *assumed* to be ironical,
because it is a view with a significant pedigree. The argument goes
back at least to Augustine, and had also been deployed by Aquinas
and Dante, amongst others. Augustine had argued that the rise of
belief in the resurrection of 'the earthly body of Christ' was as
remarkable as the original event, not least because it was publi-
cized by the uneducated:

we shall find, if we consider it, that the manner in which the world came to
believe is itself even more incredible [than the resurrection]. A few fishermen,
uneducated in the liberal arts, completely uninstructed in the doctrines of

their opponents, with no knowledge of grammar, not armed with dialectic, not adorned with rhetoric: these were the men whom Christ sent out with the nets of faith into the sea of this world. And in this way He caught all those fish of every kind, including—more wonderful still, because more rare— even some of the philosophers themselves . . . Here, then, we have three incredible things; yet they have all come to pass. It is incredible that Christ rose in the flesh and with His flesh ascended into heaven. It is incredible that the world believed so incredible a thing. And it is incredible that a few obscure men, of no standing and no education, should have been able so effectively to persuade the whole world, including the learned.[60]

In addition, sceptical defences of Christian fideism had been provided by Michel de Montaigne and Pierre Bayle, and their views had helped make fideism and scepticism seem like natural bedfellows.[61] There is, then, some reason for taking these remarks as evidence of a genuine fideism.

Some reason, but not enough. This can be seen by considering, first, an apparently toothless qualification. Hume says that his argument applies only to biblical writings considered as human writings, rather than as 'the word or testimony of God himself'. The fideistic reader would concur with Hume here, and would indeed end up marvelling that faith is so miraculous when judged by reason's standards. The reader of a more 'experimental' cast of mind, however, would conclude that it is the word or testimony of men that underpins belief in the Bible as the word or testimony of God—as Hume himself accepts when discussing Tillotson's argument (109). So the distinction is, in the end, without a difference, and the principles of probability are not, after all, legitimately suspended in this case. From the experimental point of view, then, the fideist's conclusion is untenable; Hume's experimentalism thus rules out fideism, and reveals his conclusion to be indeed ironic.

In another respect, however, fideism seems to be just the sort of

[60] Augustine, *The City of God*, 1113–14 (XXII. v). Cf. Dante: ' "If the world turned to Christ without the help / of miracles," I said, "then that would be / a miracle far greater than them all . . ." ' (Dante Alighieri, *The Divine Comedy*, iii. *Paradise*, trans. M. Musa (Harmondsworth: Penguin Books, 1986), XXIV. 106–8). Stewart points out that the argument had been popular in the seventeenth century, having been put by Hugo Grotius (*De Veritate Religionis Christianæ*, 1627), Edward Stillingfleet (*Origines Sacræ*, 1662), and Ralph Cudworth (*The True Intellectual System of the Universe*, 1678). See Stewart, 'Hume's Historical View of Miracles', 176, 197 n. 21.

[61] Montaigne's conclusion to 'An Apology for Raymond Sebond' illustrates the connection between fideism and scepticism: both depend on limiting human rational powers. He concludes, against Seneca, that it is impossible for a man to 'mount above himself or above humanity: for he can see only with his own eyes, grip only with his own grasp. He will rise if God proffers him—extraordinarily—His hand; he will rise by abandoning and disavowing his own means, letting himself be raised and pulled up by purely heavenly ones. It is for our Christian faith . . . to aspire to that holy and miraculous metamorphosis' (*The Complete Essays*, ed. Screech, 683).

position a sceptic should hold, for, as Hume has insisted, nothing is more congenial to scepticism than conclusions that show the narrow range and limited powers of reason and the understanding. Fideism holds just this—Montaigne and Bayle are not *accidentally* fideist—so is not fideism precisely the kind of view a sceptic should embrace? To some degree this point must be conceded: by denying knowledge and living according to appearances, even plausible and scrutinized and undistractable appearances, the sceptic affirms the necessity of trusting processes that remain unfathomable. The sceptic must recognize, to some degree; 'the whimsical condition of mankind': we 'must act and reason and believe', even though unable to explain and justify doing so (160). Nevertheless, there are two objections that can be made to allowing a fideistic interpretation of Hume's concluding remark.

First, the fideism appealed to in this passage is very strong. It does not merely restrict reason to its proper province, but seeks to *override* a conclusion of reason. To appeal to faith *against* an argument opposing the legitimacy of a certain practice or belief is very different from an appeal to faith justified by reason's alleged impotence in the face of religious questions. Fideism of this kind is dogmatic anti-rationalism: it denies reason's sway not by showing its limits, but by *asserting* such limits. It is to propose faith as an alternative foundation for knowledge—faith has its reasons, of which reason knows nothing—but to do so when the question of just what reason knows remains the very point at issue. For the fideist to hold, in such circumstances, that the deliverances of faith are secure—and are secured by the ways of knowing peculiar to faith, which reason cannot penetrate—is simply to dogmatize. Fideism of this kind thus embodies an attitude to what can be known quite at odds with the enquiring outlook of the moderate sceptic, and clearly shows itself to be anti-rational dogmatism—irrationalism—not scepticism.

The second objection is related. The kind of reason rejected in Hume's 'fideistic' conclusion is not the metaphysical reasoning based on alleged insight into natures and essences that is the stock in trade of the philosophical dogmatist, and the basis for natural theology. To oppose faith to reason in this sense is not obviously mistaken, since it amounts to denying that religious belief stands or falls according to the validity of the various a priori arguments for God's existence. In this sense, to oppose faith to reason is, at least in part, to claim a place for revelation. But the reason that is (apparently) rejected in Hume's conclusion is precisely that type of reasoning that his sceptical enquiries have sought to establish—the probabilistic principles of experimental reasoning—and by which any putative revelation is properly to be judged. So to oppose faith to reason in this manner is not to make space for revelation, but to deny all standards by which evidence is to be judged—and therefore to leave us at the mercy of any unscrupulous self-styled messiah into whose orbit we should have the misfortune to fall. It is not plausible to think that Hume does not see this, and so it must be concluded that the 'fideistic' conclusion is indeed ironic.

Support for this conclusion can also be reached by another route. Locke argues in the *Essay* that faith, which he describes as assent to revelation,[62] is separate from reason, even above reason—but not contrary to it. He argues, in 'balance of probabilities' fashion, that an 'evident *Revelation*' overrides probability, but not because faith overrides reason. Rather, 'clear' revelation is stronger than reason in those and only those cases where reason delivers only probabilities. His point is that, where revelation is clearly established, it overrides the merely probable. Nevertheless, it remains for reason to determine whether revelation has occurred: 'whether it be a divine Revelation, or no, *Reason* must judge; which can never permit the mind to reject a greater Evidence to embrace what is less evident'.[63]

Hume's argument is that, not only can it be argued, as does Locke, that a priori reason rules out alleged revelations that are absurdities, logical contradictions; it is also true that *experimental* reason rules out all miracle reports, by showing that the miracle report is always the 'less evident'. So his argument clearly aims to show that experimental reason denies that there is any space for faith—assent to revelation—at all; and to appeal to the mysteries of faith at this point is not, therefore, to retreat to higher ground, but to fail to be rational. This does not, perhaps, rule out the possibility of a sceptical solution, by means of a 'religious instinct'—but this seems unlikely to have been Hume's point. The instincts he proposes in advancing his theory of human nature are precisely the problem for religion, not its solution. Moreover, this is ground a Christian cannot occupy, since it allows in every religion and superstition discovered in human history. It is most probable, then, that Hume would endorse Locke's conclusion that the opposition of faith to reason is not to be tolerated:

---

[62] Locke, *Essay*, IV. xvi. 14.
[63] Ibid. IV. xviii. 9, 10. Cf. the similar position of Arnauld and Nicole, *Logic or the Art of Thinking*, 260 ff.

to this crying up of *Faith*, in opposition to *Reason*, we may, I think, in good measure, ascribe those Absurdities, that fill almost all the Religions which possess and divide Mankind. For Men having been principled with an Opinion, that they must not consult *Reason* in the Things of Religion, however apparently contradictory to common Sense, and the very Principles of all their Knowledge, have let loose their Fancies, and natural Superstition; and have been, by them, led into so strange Opinions, and extravagant Practices in Religion, that a considerate Man cannot but stand amazed at their Follies, and judge them so far from being acceptable to the great and wīse GOD, that he cannot avoid thinking them ridiculous, and offensive to a sober, good Man. So that, in effect Religion which should most distinguish us from Beasts, and ought most peculiarly to elevate us, as rational Creatures, above Brutes, is that wherein Men often appear most irrational, and more senseless than Beasts themselves. *Credo, quia impossibile est: I believe, because it is impossible*, might, in a good Man, pass for a Sally of Zeal; but would prove a very ill Rule for Men to chuse their Opinions, or Religion by.[64]

It seems not unlikely that many of Hume's readers would have remembered this passage, as they read his apparently fideistic closing sentences. If so—despite the mitigations possible by considering cases like those of Montaigne and Bayle—they would have felt considerable unease and distrust, and would rightly have felt so. The conclusion must be that Hume would have agreed with Locke's judgement that to adhere to a faith not tempered by rational judgement of what is, and what is not, divine revelation, is to 'expose our selves to all the Extravagancy of Enthusiasm'.[65] Hume's 'fideistic' conclusion is, then, an ironical allusion to the errors of the religious 'enthusiasts'. The miracle of faith is the marvellous (astonishing and improbable) fact of human epistemic malfunctioning in the face of ultimate questions: religious hopes and fears unhinge the principles of experience by which human beings are normally, and properly, guided.

---

[64] Locke, *Essay*, IV. xviii. 11. (The *credo* Locke quotes here—a more extreme version of the Augustinian type of argument—is from Tertullian.)
[65] Ibid. IV. xvi. 14.

Section XI

Of a particular Providence and of a future State

The explicit subject of this section is the prospect of those special future rewards and punishments—beyond the ordinary rewards and punishments to be expected in the common course of life—that are the stuff of religious systems. That is, it is concerned with the grounds for believing in *particular*, as distinct from *general*, Providence. The latter lies open to view: it is the implications, for human beings, of the general economy of the created order—the fortunes and misfortunes that arise predictably from the normal course of human affairs in the world. The former, in contrast, concerns the special stuff of religious hopes and fears, especially of Christian hopes and fears: of divine judgement, of the reward of the virtuous and punishment of the wicked, of heaven and hell.[1]

The concerns of the section are, however, rather broader than this may suggest. Although the obvious target is Christian theology, the larger aim is to assess the significance of the argument for a divine creator from the evidence of design in the world. Since, as noted in the previous section, this argument was commonly understood to be the most powerful of the purely rational arguments for theism, the section can be seen to be an assessment of the prospects for natural theology. Further, the religious question is framed within a discussion of intellectual freedom: can the granting of intellectual liberty to the philosopher endanger the state, and thereby justify restriction of intellectual enquiry for

---

[1] The distinction between general Providence and particular Providence, and of their sources in God's general will and particular will, respectively, had been pressed hard by Malebranche, who had argued that, not only were there general laws governing nature, but also general laws of divine grace. See Nicolas Malebranche, *Treatise of Nature and Grace*, trans. with an introduction and notes by P. Riley (Oxford: Clarendon Press, 1992). Riley points out, in his very enlightening Introduction, that, for Malebranche, belief that one was the beneficiary of miracles, and therefore of particular Providence, was to be suffering from acute egomania (19). This is, in essence, Hume's critique of 'enthusiasm' in 'Of Superstition and Enthusiasm' (in *Essays*, 73–9), and may have been its source.

the sake of political security? Hume's answer—that it cannot, because philosophers are quiet souls, and the masses do not understand them—can, to a degree, be understood as a response to Bayle's suggestion that a society of atheists is possible. Hume's position is that *philosophical* agnostics or atheists are no threat to public order, because the irreligious conclusion depends on taking the world as it is, and as such *leaves* everything as it is. For the unphilosophical, in contrast, the conclusion shakes their view of the world—not least their view of the foundations of legitimate social order—and so makes them more prone to abandon restraints on their passions, and more inclined to 'the infringement of the laws of society' (147). Hume would thus sympathize with that famous Enlightenment willingness to doubt the existence of God—as long as it was not in front of the servants. More charitably expressed, his position is that a society of atheists is indeed possible; but the peaceful transition from a religious to an atheistical society may not be so.

Of course, to claim that this is Hume's position requires a degree of interpretative licence, since the section is in dialogue form, and the main arguments are presented not by the person of the author, but by a friend—and, for that matter, by a friend who speaks for Epicurus rather than for himself. The arguments are therefore framed several times over, and this could be taken to present insuperable interpretative difficulties. However, a closer look eases this worry, since there is little evidence that the role of the framing is to obscure Hume's own views. It is true that some of the devices employed—the framing of the religious questions in a moral and political context, and the transference of the discussion to the ancient world—may help to distance the discussion from contemporary concerns.[2] Nevertheless, the initially plausible assumption that the dialogue form is an attempt by the author to detach himself from the views expressed cannot be sustained. For a start, it is (partially) undercut in the text itself: the person of the author remarks at an important stage of the discussion that his friend has adopted the debating trick of couching the argument in terms of his (the author's) own doctrines: 'you insinuate yourself into my favour by embracing those principles, to which, you know, I have always expressed a particular attachment' (142). So, although the text later makes clear that the friend's conclusions are not the author's considered views, there is no strenuous attempt to distance the friend's outlook from that of the author. Further, the most damaging remark against the argument from design is

---

[2] The point is made by Penelhum, *David Hume*, 178.

made not by the friend, but by the author. This is the observation at the end of the section, that, as previously argued, causes and effects are identified only by multiple instances, whereas the argument from design attempts to argue from a single instance to a presumed causal connection. The conclusion is not spelt out, but the point is clear: the argument from design appears to depend on an unjustifiable assumption for its very formulation, and to trade on (merely) presumed analogies for its execution. Thus one contemporary critic, with (it seems) this observation in mind, remarked that 'some of the worst parts of this essay are directly proposed in his own person'.[3] It seems unlikely, then, that Hume's aim in employing the dialogue form was to put up a smokescreen, since it is quite unlikely that he would have done such a bad job of it.[4]

In fact, an acquaintance with the conventions governing the philosophical dialogue of the period reinforces the point. The dialogue form had been revived, most notably, by Shaftesbury: he had lamented its decline since the Ancients, and attributed the fact to the closeting of philosophy in the Schools. Moderns who wished to emulate the Ancients—particularly those who sought an engaged philosophy for social improvement and enlightenment—were those most concerned to master the dialogue form and its conventions. Hume certainly belongs in this camp.[5] So it is no surprise to discover that, in the *Dialogues concerning Natural Religion*, he closely adheres to the principal conventions of the period governing the construction of philosophical dialogue.[6] For present purposes, the most important of those conventions is that the

---

[3] John Leland, *A View of the Principal Deistical Writers of the Last and Present Century* (London: B. Dod, 1755), ii. 27.

[4] This is not to say that considerations of prudence played no role at all: for, although it would not have fooled the intelligentsia, it does seem sufficiently indirect and subtle to be safe from the eyes or ears of the servants. As noted above, to be guilty of irreligion is one thing; but to be brazenly guilty of irreligion, and therefore to endanger public order, is quite another. Even so, it is unconvincing to hold, as does Wootton, that Hume resorts to dialogue form 'to avoid having to take full responsibility for irreligious arguments' ('Hume's "Of Miracles"', 191–2). It is more plausible to conclude that Hume manipulates the dialogic conventions of the period in order the better to *expose* his position: they provide him with a means of distinguishing his view from the Epicurean—a view with which it could easily be confused.

[5] See his remarks about the disastrous consequences of philosophy's setting itself apart in the Schools: 'The Separation of the Learned from the conversible World seem to have been the great Defect of the last Age, and must have had a very bad Influence both on Books and Company ... Learning has been as great a Loser by being shut up in Colleges and Cells, and secluded from the World and good Company ... Even Philosophy went to Wrack by this moaping recluse Method of Study, and became as chimerical in her Conclusions as she was unintelligible in her Stile and Manner of Delivery ... 'Tis with great Pleasure I observe, That Men of Letters, in this Age, have lost, in a great Measure, that Shyness and Bashfulness of Temper, which kept them at a Distance from Mankind ...' ('Of Essay Writing', in *Essays*, 534–5).

[6] See M. Malherbe, 'Hume and the Art of Dialogue', in Stewart and Wright (eds.), *Hume and Hume's Connexions*, 201–23.

dialogue must be 'authorless': 'it is of the very essence of *l'art classique* that there cannot be in the text any manifest mark of the author himself. The dialogue develops by its own formal necessity.'[7] Plainly, this convention is violated in this section. One possible explanation is that it is a very clumsy attempt at the genre. It is more convincing, however, to conclude that Hume here deliberately manipulates the established convention in order to serve his own ends: first, to enable the successful insertion of a dialogue within a larger work, without destroying continuity; and, secondly, to allow the full exposition of a view not his own, but with which he is—and, as he acknowledges, must be— sympathetic. Hume flouts the convention the better to serve his own purposes.[8]

There is a further reason for the use of the dialogue form at this point. The dialogue is the ideal form for exposition of contrary, or at least diverse, views, on topics that admit of no certain answer. In this respect, dialogue is the literary form, *par excellence*, of sceptical thought. Plato chose the dialogue to present the enquiries of Socrates, and the common interpretation of Socrates as a sceptic led to the Academy's identification with a variety of scepticism. This connection between dialogue and scepticism was subsequently strengthened through the works of Cicero, who advocated the Academic philosophy, and argued that the undogmatic exposition that dialogue allowed was especially suitable for enquiries into the most difficult of all subjects, the nature of the gods: 'This is a topic on which it seems proper to summon all the world to sit in judgement and pronounce which of these doctrines is the true one. If it turn out that all the schools agree, or if any one philosopher be found who has discovered the truth, then but not before I will convict the Academy of captiousness.'[9] This concern for an overtly undogmatic method when dealing with ultimate questions is the best explanation for Hume's use of the dialogue form in this section. In fact, it seems likely that Cicero's dialogue on the gods

---

[7] Ibid. 207. In the *Dialogues concerning Natural Religion*, this is achieved by giving the role of narrator to Pamphilus, a student of Cleanthes. Cf. C. Battersby, 'The *Dialogues* as Original Imitation: Cicero and the Nature of Hume's Skepticism', in Norton et al. (eds.), *McGill Hume Studies*, 240–1.

[8] Hume offers a faithfully Shaftesburian account of the canons of the dialogic form in the letter from Pamphilus to Hermippus that introduces the *Dialogues concerning Natural Religion*. In fact, he specifically remarks on the undesirability of conveying 'the image of *pedagogue* and *pupil*' (*Dialogues and Natural History of Religion*, ed. J. C. A. Gaskin (Oxford: Oxford University Press, 1993), 29). As Battersby notes ('The *Dialogues*', 243–5), this is *not* entirely avoided there! The *Enquiry* section is free of this problem, however, because, although the Epicurean employs the author's arguments, there is no sense of a deferential relationship.

[9] Cicero, *De Natura Deorum*, I. vi, in *De Natura Deorum* and *Academica*, 17. See also Battersby, 'The *Dialogues*', 247.

provided the basic problematic of Hume's discussion here, since *De Natura Deorum* addresses both what can be known of the gods, and also the consequences for social order.[10] Cicero observes that some believe that 'the disappearance of piety towards the gods will entail the disappearance of loyalty and social union among men as well, and of justice itself, the queen of all the virtues'.[11]

Bringing the Ciceronian connection to the fore is helpful in another way as well: it reminds us to take seriously the fact that the friend speaks as an Epicurean. In the first place, the Epicureans were not primarily concerned to argue that the gods did not exist, but that they were remote, and largely indifferent to human affairs. This serves as a reminder that the argument of the Epicurean friend is directed not against the existence of a deity (this is allowed to be a possibility), but against religion: that is, against any attempt to draw further conclusions concerning the nature of such a being, and concerning implications for human life. Secondly, Hume has already signalled his commitment to sceptical principles, and so the alert reader is in a position to interpret the remarks made by the person of the author in the dialogue, since they can be expected to embody the response of the Academic (in Cicero's dialogue, Gaius Cotta) to Epicurean doctrines. Viewed in this light, the relationship between the author and the Epicurean friend becomes clearer. The Epicurean presents a plausible argument against religion, but does so dogmatically.[12] The person of the author replies to 'his harangue' (142) by acknowledging its resemblances to his own principles, but challenging its conclusions. The Epicurean responds with another speech, providing a plausible reply, but is then met with some further problems, the last of which challenges a central premiss of the design argument itself.

From this perspective, then, the dialogue form indicates less of an attempt to cover over Hume's real opinions than a way of addressing a difficult subject. It allows the presentation of a plausible argument, Epicurean in spirit, and then the sceptical

[10] Another influence also needs to be acknowledged: M. A. Stewart has claimed that Pierre Bayle's presentation of a debate, before the Athenian public, between Stratonicians and Stoics 'was clearly Hume's model for *Enquiry* XI'. See Stewart, 'An Early Fragment on Evil', 169 n.

[11] Cicero, *De Natura Deorum*, I. ii, in *De Natura Deorum and Academica*, 7.

[12] Thus Hume observes, in a letter to Gilbert Elliot, that 'a profest Atheist, & . . . an Epicurean . . . is little or nothing different' (*Letters*, ed. Greig, i. 155; repr. in *Dialogues and Natural History of Religion*, ed. Gaskin, 26). Gaskin provides a helpful gloss on this passage: 'for the Epicureans, the gods are a refined part of the natural universe, not its external cause or its creators. They exist in self-sufficient blessedness, inactive and unrelated to man and the processes of the world. See Lucretius, *The Nature of the Universe*, iii. 18–24. Thus Hume concludes that the Epicureans might just as well say that there are no gods: at least the gods *matter* no more for the Epicurean than for the atheist' (199).

identification of some dubitable assumptions. This way of looking
at the matter has been overlooked because of an impression of
authorial insincerity. The impression arises because the sceptical
probing does not weaken the anti-religious tendency of the Epicurean argument: the author's first objection seems fairly comfortably overcome, and the last objection, by picking out a
presupposition of the argument from design, strengthens the case
against religion even though it chips away at the Epicurean
argument itself. This does show that Hume's sympathies are with
the *tendency* of the argument, if not with its precise conclusion.
The good Academic holds back from dogmatic certainties on such
difficult questions, and remains sensitive to the limited confidence
we can place in argumentative strategies like analogy when
addressing questions that push beyond the limits of experience.

Scepticism is not, however, the timid refusal to draw conclusions
from plausible premisses; it is the willingness to challenge the
presuppositions of arguments themselves. Thus we should not be
surprised when the author, after objecting to the Epicurean's conclusions, challenges the assumptions about causation on which
the design argument depends. He has not (or has not *simply*) been
softening up the reader in order to slip in a knockout blow at
the end; he has been playing the part of the good Academic
throughout. The Epicurean asserts that the gods are entirely
remote from human affairs, and that all the hopes of religion are
misplaced. The sceptic, in reply, denies knowledge of such ultimate
mysteries, and reaffirms the limitations from which reasoning
from experience cannot escape. He further observes that, given its
premisses, the Epicurean argument mounts a plausible critique of
the case for natural religion, sufficient to shift the burden of proof
onto the defenders of the religious hypothesis. The conclusion of
the section, implied rather than stated explicitly, is that the argument from design does not succeed in providing a foundation for
any contentful natural religion. Since this is the most persuasive
of the arguments of natural theology, natural theology itself must
therefore be presumed to fail. Reason cannot, that is, provide convincing grounds for belief in a God 'who has the Power to change
the course of Nature'.[13] The argument of this section thus removes
the foundation on which objections to the miracles argument
characteristically rest, and thereby completes Hume's critique of
religion. With Hume's strategy now clarified, we can turn to consider the specific arguments, and their meaning.

[13] Locke, *Essay*, IV. xvi. 13.

The section opens with an exchange about the fortunes and misfortunes of philosophy. The author remarks that philosophy was fortunate to be born in the tolerant society of ancient Greece, since philosophy is a tender plant that depends on an agreeable climate. Even today, he adds, robust modern philosophy has trouble coping with her persecutors. The Epicurean friend's reply is a surprise: the bigotry that confronts philosophy is actually its own product. It is the 'speculative dogmas of religion' that are 'the present occasions of such furious dispute', and they could not have existed in 'the early ages of the world' (133). Before philosophers started speculating on the nature of things, religious views were little more than collections of traditional tales. It was, he says, the creation of *philosophical religion*, through the alliance of philosophy with superstition, that produced modern religious dogmatists and bigots.[14]

Our author responds: does this mean that philosophy alone is never a threat to society? This is at odds with the view, brought against Epicurus, that, by denying 'providence and a future state', he undercut 'the ties of morality' and threatened 'the peace of civil society' (133–4). The Epicurean friend replies that trouble is never caused by philosophy ('calm reason') alone, that passion and prejudice have always played a role. To show the truth of this claim, he proposes to make a speech on behalf of Epicurus that would satisfy the philosophically inclined audience of ancient Athens: it 'will fill all the urn with white beans, and leave not a black one to gratify the malice of my adversaries' (134).[15] The offer is immediately accepted, and the friend now speaks as Epicurus, arguing against, not the existence of divine beings, but the possibility of drawing distinctively religious conclusions from the main argument proposed in support of divine existence: the argument from design.

The Epicurean's argument is as follows. Speculative questions about the origin and government of the universe do not, he observes, affect the public interest, in that they do not undermine the peace of society or the security of government. For this reason, the philosophers should be left in peace 'to examine, at leisure, the question the most sublime, but at the same time, the most speculative of all philosophy' (135). This truth has been obscured by the religious philosophers, who, by seeking to go

---

[14] Hume's conception of Christianity as a philosophical religion is filled out in 'Of Parties in General', in *Essays*, 62–3. Cf. the discussion above, in Ch. 2.

[15] 'In Athens beans were used in ballotting: white ones for election or agreement, black for rejection or opposition' (P. H. Nidditch's editorial note, *Enquiries*, 371).

beyond religious traditions and to establish religion on principles of pure reason, have achieved the opposite of their aim: instead of easing doubts, they have stimulated them. Their method is this: they observe the order of the universe, and then ask whether it could be produced by collisions of atoms, or otherwise by chance. They, and their followers, conclude that the observed order of nature reveals such evidence of intelligence or design that it would be reckless to conclude that it could have arisen by chance or any undirected material processes. This is an argument from an effect to its cause: the observed order implies the work of an intelligent cause, a designer. Since this is the main argument for the existence of a designer, it follows that, if the argument fails, then there remains no sound reason for believing the conclusion. In addition, it needs to be noted that, if the argument is to work, it cannot build more into the conclusion than is contained in the premises: it cannot attribute more to the cause (the designer) than is implied by the effect (the observed order of nature). The consequences deserve noting.

When we reason from an effect to its cause, continues the Epicurean, the cause we identify must be *sufficient* to produce the effect. However, since our evidence for the cause is no more than that effect, we cannot ascribe to the cause any further properties than are *necessary* to produce the effect: 'we must proportion the one to the other' (136). So, by such an argument, we cannot discover any further facts about the cause, nor infer other effects it might have. Any further claims, then, must be reached by means other than this argument. This applies equally to all kinds of causes, whether material processes, or the activites of an intelligent being. So, if the existence or order of the universe is attributed to the gods, then we can and must attribute to them the same degree of power, intelligence, and benevolence that we discern in the world itself: 'The supposition of farther attributes is mere hypothesis' (137). In like manner, neither can we, on the basis of the observed order, suppose there to be other, more perfect worlds elsewhere in space or time. To do so is to suppose what is *entirely imaginary* (137): a product of the faculty of imagination, not of reason. Nevertheless, the limitation is frequently violated. It is one thing for 'priests and poets' to speak of past ideal states, 'a golden or silver age' of perfect harmony or happiness. But when the same is done by philosophers, who claim to base their views on reason rather than authority, the claims must be examined. If they ground these claims purely on reason, by arguing from effects to causes, the claims must fail. Such an argument cannot produce such additional knowledge, and so they must be dressing up what reason delivers with additional products supplied by their imagination.[16] Arguing from the world we know, to the nature of the gods, cannot produce reasons for believing in any world other than the one we already know.

So, concludes the Epicurean, since we have to recognize the real imperfections of the world, it is a fruitless exercise to seek to save the honour of the gods, by making them more perfect than the world we know. Arguments that do attempt to rescue the divine nature from the evidence of imperfection that surrounds us—such as the Platonic view that the imperfections of the world are due to the inherent imperfections of matter, or the Malebranchian claim that the deity cannot but act according to general laws— these arguments must presuppose precisely what they seek to justify. If we make the necessary assumptions, then these arguments do offer coherent explanations of the imperfections of the world. But why make the assumptions? Why seek to explain the course of nature by means of hypotheses that may be entirely false, and for which we have no evidence? The religious hypothesis, then, is only one possible explanation for the world we encounter, and it cannot authorize any additional conclusions. While it is true that in such difficult subjects no theory can be scorned, nevertheless no argument can be allowed to overstep its proper bounds. In this case, the bounds are clear: no argument from effect to cause can give reason for believing that there is a being more perfect than the imperfect world with which we are familiar.

This completes the main thrust of the Epicurean argument. The Epicurean friend now proceeds to points of detail, political and theological. The political point is that, because this argument depends on taking the world as it is, it therefore also leaves the world just as it is. In no way, says the Epicurean, does it deny, or disturb, what can be discovered to be true by any observer: that the virtuous life is the path to peace of mind, that friendship is the greatest pleasure, and moderation the way to lasting tranquillity. These facts are plain, whether they stem from intelligent design or not. However, if one were to argue that there is some *particular* providence—for example, that the good are rewarded, and the bad punished, beyond the general, or natural, rewards and punishments already described—this would be to commit precisely the error in question. Such arguments 'have aided the ascent of reason by the wings of the imagination' (138). Of course, it *may*

---

[16] Notice here that the imagination is identified as a source of errors, as argued above (Section III).

be true that the divinity has a whole array of features of which we are ignorant: but to assert it is to rely on 'mere *possibility* and hypothesis' (141). The Epicurean concludes that the great standard of practical life is the experienced train of events. To argue from this experience to the existence of 'a particular intelligent cause' responsible for the order of the universe, while not necessarily mistaken, is nevertheless to 'embrace a principle, which is both uncertain and useless':

It is uncertain; because the subject lies entirely beyond the reach of human experience. It is useless; because our knowledge of this cause being derived entirely from the course of nature, we can never, according to the rules of just reasoning, return back from the cause with any new inference, or making additions to the common and experienced course of nature, establish any new principles of conduct and behaviour.   (142)

The argument for an intelligent cause of the world leaves everything as it is; its denial must therefore do the same. The 'religious hypothesis' cannot change this without abandoning reason for flights of imagination. In like manner, a rational rejection of religious systems can constitute no threat to public order or social unity. So philosophy—even an anti-religious philosophy like Epicureanism—is no threat to the state. The conclusion of the Epicurean argument is, then, that philosophers should be left in peace, to pursue their enquiries wherever they lead them.

The most striking feature of the Epicurean argument, at least for present purposes, is its invocation of recognizably experimental principles. This is to be seen in its Newtonian echoes, and in its heavy reliance on a central Newtonian principle. First, the echo: Hume has the Epicurean refer to any conclusion that goes beyond the data provided by experience as 'hypothesis'. Thus he says that 'the supposition of farther attributes is mere hypothesis' (137), and refers to the most significant of such suppositions as 'the religious hypothesis' (139). The Newtonian echo here is unmistakable, for Newton's famous rejection of 'hypotheses' in the General Scholium is precisely a rejection of conclusions that go beyond the phenomena: 'I frame no hypotheses; for whatever is not deduced from the phenomena is to be called an hypothesis; and hypotheses, whether metaphysical or physical, whether of occult qualities or mechanical, have no place in experimental philosophy.'[17] Religion is a hypothesis, in this sense of the term, because it does not rest content with the possibility of an intelligent designer, in so far as that is established by the observable order of the world, but

---

[17] Newton, *Principia*, 547.

imagines further attributes of such a being, and infers from these attributes many conclusions for which there is no evidence at all. Religion, in other words, is not the coin of the cautious and accurate experimental philosopher.

Secondly, the argument relies directly on a central Newtonian principle. He sets out the first of the 'Rules of Reasoning in Philosophy' as follows:

We are to admit no more causes of natural things than such as are both true and sufficient to explain their appearances.

To this purpose the philosophers say that Nature does nothing in vain, and more is in vain when less will serve; for Nature is pleased with simplicity, and affects not the pomp of superfluous causes.[18]

The identification of religion as a 'hypothesis' is a particular case of the rule presented here, since in this case the hypothesis is a 'superfluous' cause. However, it is not only in this way that the Newtonian rule is behind the Epicurean argument. A careful inspection of the argument shows it to be nothing other than a direct application of the rule. The argument insists that reason can invest no more power in the cause than is required for the effect; and this is also the point of the frequent appeals to *proportionality*, as is made explicit in the initial presentation of the argument: 'When we infer any particular cause from an effect, we must proportion the one to the other, and can never be allowed to ascribe to the cause any qualities, but what are exactly sufficient to produce the effect' (136).

The example Hume chooses to illustrate the point—two weights in a scale balance—underscores the background influence of physical science. This principle is clearly Newton's first rule, and Hume makes it plain that the argument is just the application of the rule to divine actions. The point should be visible from the summary of the argument already given, but selective quotation renders it almost irresistible:

The same rule holds, whether the cause assigned be brute unconscious matter, or a rational intelligent being . . . The cause must be proportional to the effect; and if we exactly and precisely proportion it, we shall never find in it any qualities, that point farther, or afford an inference concerning any other design or performance . . . Allowing, therefore, the gods to be the authors of the existence or order of the universe; it follows, that they possess that precise degree of power, intelligence, and benevolence, which appears in their workmanship . . . The supposition of farther attributes is mere hypothesis. (136–7)

---

[18] Ibid. 398.

The mark of the 'just reasoner' (139) is 'sound philosophy' (146), and the first rule of sound philosophy, as practised by the 'wise man' (110), is to proportion belief to evidence—in this case, to proportion believed causes to experienced effects. The Epicurean argument is thus a clear application of the experimental method of reasoning to divine existence and human destiny. It is to turn Newton against himself: if we know God 'only by his most wise and excellent contrivances of things, and final causes', and if 'to discourse of whom from the appearances of things, does certainly belong to Natural Philosophy',[19] then the verdict of an accurate experimental philosophy is that, beyond reflection on the general economy of nature, there is nothing at all to say.

The distinctiveness of Hume's Newtonian-inspired Epicurean argument can be brought out by comparing it with the related arguments of Descartes and Locke. In the Third Meditation, in a passage already referred to in Part One above, Descartes prepares the ground for his cosmological proof of divine existence with the remark that

it is manifest by the natural light that there must be at least as much <reality> in the efficient and total cause as in the effect of that cause. For where, I ask, could the effect get its reality from, if not from the cause? And how could the cause give it to the effect unless it possessed it? It follows from this both that something cannot arise from nothing, and also that what is more perfect—that is, contains in itself more reality—cannot arise from what is less perfect.[20]

In this passage, and throughout the exposition of the cosmological argument itself, Descartes stipulates that the reality of the cause cannot be less than that of the effect. Whether this is a way of speaking licensed by the mechanical philosophy has already been questioned. At this point, what is noteworthy is that he does not limit our knowledge of the cause to what is revealed by the effect. Rather, the effect indicates a *minimum* to which the cause must measure up, and may well exceed. The whole point of the argument is precisely to arrive at knowledge of the cause that is *not* contained in the effect: the existence (the 'formal reality') of God. The moral is summed up in a version of the Epicurean maxim, *ex nihilo nihil fit* (nothing comes from nothing).[21]

---

[19] Newton, *Principia*, 546.   [20] Descartes, *Philosophical Writings*, ii. 28.
[21] Cf. Lucretius' employment of the principle to *avoid* appeals to divine causes: 'Our starting-point shall be this principle: / *Nothing at all is ever born from nothing / by the gods' will*. Ah, but men's minds are frightened / Because they see, on earth and in the heaven, / Many events whose causes are to them / Impossible to fix; so, they suppose, / The gods' will is the reason. As for us, / Once we have seen that *Nothing comes from nothing*, / We shall perceive with greater clarity / What we are looking for, whence each thing comes, / How things are caused, and no "gods' will" about it' (Lucretius, *The Way Things Are* [*De Rerum*

Locke employs a similar argument, although in his case all talk of degrees of reality has been purged. Instead, he argues that the cause must possess the *properties* exhibited by the effect. His reliance on the Epicurean maxim is very marked. The argument runs as follows: nothing comes from nothing ('Nonentity cannot produce any real Being'); there is, and has always been, something; therefore there is a cause of something that is itself something, and that has always been. And, since the powers of the effects must be owing to their cause, the first cause is the most powerful of all beings. Finally, since human beings possess the powers of perception and knowledge, they must have received these from the first cause, and so there must exist a perceiving and knowing being who has existed for all eternity. He thus concludes that, 'from the Consideration of our selves, and what we infallibly find in our own Constitutions, our Reason leads us to the knowledge of this certain and evident Truth, that *there is an eternal, most powerful, and most knowing Being*'.[22]

So, like Descartes, Locke employs this form of reasoning to argue what must be necessary to produce certain effects, but without *limiting* it to powers sufficient for the purpose. Neither does he address the question that for Hume is of most significance, that of the moral qualities discoverable in a creator of the order we experience: he considers only power and intelligence. Without Hume's strict proportionality requirement, he does not perceive the problem lurking in the question of a creator's moral qualities. Hume certainly does: he is concerned to identify 'that precise degree of power, intelligence, and benevolence' necessary and sufficient for a world with the properties of our own. So, in presenting the Epicurean argument, Hume does not reject the connection between properties in the cause and in the effect on which Descartes and Locke had relied.[23] Instead, he applies to it the proportionality test derived from Newton's first rule, and, by explicitly including moral qualities in his purview, turns the argument against its religious employment. He thus arrives at a conclusion congenial both to scepticism and to liberty of thought and discussion.[24]

Natura], trans. R. Humphries (Bloomington, Ind.: Indiana University Press, 1968), 24 (I. 150 ff.)). Hume's rejection of the maxim (164) is therefore all the more striking—but not problematic. He is there, as he is in this section, rejecting the dogmatism of the Epicureans, even though he is not without sympathy for many of their principles.

[22] Locke, *Essay*, IV. x. 6.

[23] When, in his own person, he makes his final response to the argument, this connection is called into question; as indeed it must be, given his insistence that 'every effect is a distinct event from its cause' (30).

[24] This is not the place to pursue the details of Hume's politics, but it is worth noting that these comments in favour of liberty are by no means a rarity in his writings, and offer support to thinking of him as a cautious liberal, rather than a conservative. J. C. Laursen (*The Politics of Skepticism in the Ancients, Montaigne, Hume, and Kant* (Leiden: E. J. Brill, 1992))

The remainder of the section addresses some possible weaknesses of the argument. The author responds, in the first place, by raising an objection that seems easily met. As mentioned above, this helps to give the impression that Hume is not being sincere, but it is more instructive to think that Hume's aim here is to raise, and meet, a set of objections that would naturally occur to his readers, and to save the more damaging objections to the author's second response. The first objection raises the possibility that experience, rather than supporting the Epicurean conclusion, will support a stronger conclusion:

If you saw, for instance, a half-finished building, surrounded with heaps of brick and stone and mortar, and all the instruments of masonry; could you not *infer* from the effect, that it was a work of design and contrivance? . . . Consider the world and the present life only as an imperfect building, from which you can infer a superior intelligence; and arguing from that superior intelligence, which can leave nothing imperfect; why may you not infer a more finished scheme or plan, which will receive its completion in some distant point of space or time?   (143)

The Epicurean's response is that arguments of this kind depend on unrecognized analogies between human beings and the deity. When we encounter some object that is recognizably a human product, we are able to call on the *other sources* of our knowledge of human beings, and thereby make plausible inferences about the proper interpretation of the object—including, it should be noted, the purposes both of the object and of its maker.[25] In the case of the deity, however, there are no alternative sources of knowledge, only the singular entity of the world itself, considered as the effect of some cause. Analogies on which to build up interpretations of the purpose of this entity, and of the aims, and character, of the maker, are therefore not available, and the objection fails.

illustrates the durable connections between liberalism and the sceptical tradition. This connection is still visible in Mill, but it is his emphasis on 'negative liberty' that has in recent times been taken as the hallmark of the liberal: the primary influence in this direction is of course Isaiah Berlin's 'Two Concepts of Liberty' (*Four Essays on Liberty* (Oxford: Oxford University Press, 1969), 118–72). Berlin's essay, perhaps because of its covert preoccupation with the totalitarianisms of the mid-twentieth century, finds no place for scepticism in liberalism's sources. It is therefore forced to extract the essence of liberalism from a concept of liberty denied by some of liberalism's founding fathers (e.g. Locke and Kant) and held by some of its opponents (e.g. Hobbes). An adequate account of the rise of liberalism must include reference to the contribution of sceptical philosophies, Hume's included.

[25] Hume does not develop this point, concentrating instead on (what he judges) the illegitimate anthropomorphism of such arguments. The mechanical conception of the world does allow a further challenge: the world, thus interpreted, has no intrinsic purposes, no natural *telos*; it is simply discrete events causing others, *ad infinitum*. Outcomes are predictable—if not with certainty—but such evidence of orderliness is not to be confused with intrinsic purposes. Rather, purposes arise through human beings, who then illegitimately read their own concern for purposes back into the merely mechanical world.

This reply will not work if design is considered only one among several possible rational arguments for a divine existence, and so comprises indirect evidence that Hume thought no serious alternative argument was available.[26] It also will not work if the world does furnish us with analogies after all. This objection is raised by Joseph Priestley, in his *Letters to a Philosophical Unbeliever*. Priestley objects that to conclude that there is an intelligent designer is by that fact to show the deity not to be unique, but 'to be placed in the general *class of intelligent and designing agents*'; therefore, to appeal to analogies with the other intelligent and designing agents of whom we have experience—ourselves—is not misplaced. Perhaps; but he then cruels his pitch by adding that the deity is 'infinitely superior to all others of that kind'.[27] If so, Hume could rejoin, that being is also infinitely disanalogous to that class of beings after all. Priestley also argues that we do not know merely *one* effect of divine action, but many, and 'we see that all of them advance to some state of perfection'.[28] But the many creatures with which we are acquainted come into being, as far as we can see, by natural causes—so there is no need in such cases to appeal to a hidden cause. It is the order of the whole that seems to stand in need of explanation, and this is indeed one unique thing. The moral or teleological aspect of the argument fares no better: creatures do grow towards actualizing their potential, and in this sense 'advance to some state of perfection'; but they do not always achieve it, and, more tellingly, even when they do they soon come to death and decay.

The Epicurean argument thus survives these assaults. It fares less well against the second round of objections the author brings against it. The political objection shows how Hume's principles lead him into the 'not in front of the servants' view. It runs as follows: while it may be true that religion can exercise no *proper* influence on political behaviour, nevertheless it does have such an influence. The masses believe that the deity does reward virtue and

---

[26] One notable absentee is the ontological argument, revived by Descartes. It is plausible to suppose that Hume shared Locke's judgement of its significance. Locke had expressed doubts about placing too heavy a reliance on it: '*How far the* Idea *of a most perfect Being,* which a Man may frame in his Mind, does, or does not prove the *Existence of a* GOD, I will not here examine . . . But yet, I think, this I may say, that it is an ill way of establishing this Truth, and silencing Atheists, to lay the whole stress of so important a Point, as this, upon that sole Foundation' (*Essay*, IV. x. 7). His reasons are partly because of reservations about the effectiveness of the argument, but also partly because he considers the arguments from the order of the world to be compelling. The ontological argument is thus both dubitable and unnecessary.

[27] Joseph Priestley, *Letters to a Philosophical Unbeliever* (2nd edn., 1787; New York: Garland Publishing, 1974), Part I, Letter X, 155.

[28] Ibid.

punish vice, and they moderate their own behaviour accordingly. To deny these views, then, will be to undermine a principal restraint on their conduct, with damaging effects: 'those, who attempt to disabuse them of such prejudices, may, for aught I know, be good reasoners, but I cannot allow them to be good citizens and politicians; since they free men from one restraint upon their passions, and make the infringement of the laws of society, in one respect, more easy and secure' (147).

Nevertheless, the author does not judge this to be grounds for restricting philosophers' freedom of enquiry. 'There is', he observes, 'no enthusiasm among philosophers', and their views 'are not very alluring to the people'. For this reason they cause no harm—but restricting them may do so, since to limit such liberties of thought may in the end encourage politicians to impose further restrictions on liberty that are resented by 'the generality of mankind', and thereby to create the very disorder they sought to avoid.

Unfortunately, this attractive conclusion has one striking flaw. Hume has stressed in a number of places that 'religion . . . is nothing but a species of philosophy' (146), so it is not the case that philosophies cannot be enthusiastic. Clearly, some are; but it is still possible for Hume to argue that, although religion is a species of philosophy, the religious philosopher is not an enthusiast, and the religious enthusiast is not a philosopher. This is a credible conclusion—but it is of doubtful practical help in this situation. This is because a religious philosopher can have enthusiastic followers, and there may be no way of controlling the political excesses of the followers without controlling the philosopher; moreover, the attempt to control the philosopher could then bring out the least desired result, by inflaming the followers' enthusiasm to dangerous levels. It seems difficult to deny that the issue of liberty of thought and enquiry is more problematic than Hume allows.[29]

The final objection cuts the deepest, both philosophically and religiously. It builds on Hume's account of our knowledge of causes, and is introduced in these terms:

I much doubt whether it be possible for a cause to be known only by its effect (as you have all along supposed) or to be of so singular and particular a nature

[29] It is also difficult to harmonize Hume's claim that religion is 'a species of philosophy' with some of his other remarks. For example, he sometimes speaks of philosophy as if the same as the conclusions of an enlightened scepticism: 'superstition is a considerable ingredient in almost all religions, even the most fanatical; there being nothing but philosophy able entirely to conquer these unaccountable terrors' ('Of Superstition and Enthusiasm', in *Essays*, 75).

as to have no parallel and no similarity with any other cause or object, that has ever fallen under our observation. It is only when two *species* of objects are found to be constantly conjoined, that we can infer the one from the other; and were an effect presented, which was entirely singular, and could not be comprehended under any known *species*, I do not see, that we could form any conjecture or inference at all concerning its cause. (148)

The point here depends on the argument of Section IV that knowledge of causes and effects is entirely due to experience, and so cannot be inferred from any single case. This is true whether the event under consideration is a cause or an effect, so the earlier account of the distinctness of causes is applicable to the present case:

every effect is a distinct event from its cause. It could not, therefore, be discovered in the cause, and the first invention or conception of it, *a priori*, must be entirely arbitrary. And even after it is suggested, the conjunction of it with the cause must appear equally arbitrary; since there are always many other effects, which, to reason, must seem fully as consistent and natural. In vain, therefore, should we pretend to determine any single event, or infer any cause or effect, without the assistance of observation and experience. (30)

The world is not some effect that we have experienced to follow after some preceding event, nor do we have any experience of any other worlds, or of their relations to their causes. Since on Hume's account it is not possible to inspect an object's perceptible properties to arrive at conclusions about its causes or effects, neither then is it possible to inspect the world to discover features in it that reveal the cause from which it sprang.

Indeed, we cannot, by scrutinizing the world, come to see that it is an *effect* at all. The conception of the world as an effect—essential to the argument from design—does not arise from experience and observation. So the argument from design, which appears to be an a posteriori argument from the observed order of nature, is in fact an a priori argument: it presupposes that the world is the effect of some cause, and therefore that the observed orderliness of the world is the effect of some intelligent cause. The special affection of the Newtonians for the argument from design is therefore misplaced: experimental philosophy, properly understood, grants it no special status. It is no less 'hypothetical' than any other metaphysical argument for divine existence, and, like those other arguments, depends on an exalted sense of reason's powers that an accurate experimental philosophy denies. None of this means, of course, that the world is *not* the effect of some cause, even of some intelligent cause. So the conclusion of the argument cannot be shown to be false. For the sceptic, however, this is not a disagreeable state of affairs: scepticism is not negative dogmatism, nor therefore is religious scepticism atheism. The point is, if the sceptical interpretation of experience is correct, then the negative dogmatism of the Epicurean argument can be resisted; but this is no comfort to the religionist, since the very same sceptical interpretation shows the argument from design itself to be dependent on a religious 'hypothesis'. The author does not press the point: it is left to the reader 'to pursue the consequences of this principle' (148).

The section concludes by affirming that, since it is the religionist who appeals to the argument from design, the Epicurean's objections to the conclusions commonly drawn from that argument do indeed 'merit our attention'. This may seem evasive on Hume's part, but it is, in fact, sound argumentative strategy. The Epicurean argument does not rely on the details of his account of the sceptical implications of mechanism, but only on the application of Newton's first rule of reasoning. And, since it was precisely the Newtonians who championed the argument from design, the Epicurean argument is designed to cut where the defences are thin, and where it will most hurt. The dialogue form, then, far from being a way of obscuring Hume's real position, frees him to press hard an argument that is denied him by his own principles. If this seems deceitful, it should not: it is merely the practice of internal critique. And internal critique, because it invokes no dogma, is a method very congenial to scepticism.

Hume's arguments in Sections X and XI thus comprise a unity. Section X argues that miracle reports sufficient to found a religion are, taken on their own merits, incredible to any properly functioning mind. Section XI then removes the sole ground for thinking that miraculous events might nevertheless occur: the belief that natural reason can independently establish that there is a God 'who has the Power to change the course of Nature'.[30] If this account is sound, the question arises: Why is it so rarely recognized? Why, in particular, is 'Of Miracles' so often taken to be a free-standing critique of religion? The answer must explain the relative neglect of Section XI itself. One factor is simply the dialogue form itself: it is difficult for the casual modern reader to take dialogue seriously as a philosophical form, and the background influence of the common view of Hume's intellectual biography—

[30] Locke, *Essay*, IV. xvi. 13.

that is, of the 'merely literary' tendencies of the mature Hume—no doubt reinforces the difficulty.

The substantial reason, however, is the shift in the intellectual landscape concerning religious topics since the eighteenth century. Natural theology no longer commands the respect it previously enjoyed. In the eighteenth century, this respect was considerable. Newton had affirmed in the General Scholium, as noted above, that we know God 'only by his most wise and excellent contrivances of things, and final causes', and that 'to discourse of [him] from the appearances of things, does certainly belong to Natural Philosophy'[31]—and his followers certainly took him at his word. The natural philosophers turned themselves to the task of showing the harmony of the new science with Christian belief. The institution of the Boyle Lectures in England—of which Samuel Clarke's *A Discourse concerning the Being and Attributes of God* (1704)[32] is the best known—is testimony to the fact. In fact, so great was the prestige of natural theology, that, in the more extreme versions fostered by the new science, it even provided religious grounds for *resisting* belief in miracles. The instructive example here is Malebranche. So great was his emphasis on the unvarying will of the omnipotent and omniscient creator—that is, on the divine *general will* that underpinned *general* Providence in the form of the invariant laws of nature themselves—that his theology had great difficulty in finding a place for law-violating miracles (*particular* Providence) at all. By ultimately resolving this tension in favour of the miraculous, Malebranche remained within the Christian framework; but, in making the tension so explicit, he helped lay the foundations for the rise of French Deism.[33]

For our purposes, the important point is that the religious interpretation of the new natural philosophy generated a tension *within* the religious outlook itself. This tension, between the general orderliness of design and the particularity of miracles, therefore provided *religious* grounds for doubts about miracles. Of course, these doubts, if uncontained, would lead to Deism. But, since the stress on general orderliness derived from the perspective of the new science, no believer sympathetic to that science could be entirely untouched by the sense of tension. It is

---

[31] Newton, *Principia*, 546.

[32] See Samuel Clarke, *A Demonstration of the Being and Attributes of God and Other Writings*, ed. E. Vailati (Cambridge: Cambridge University Press, 1998).

[33] Malebranche, *Treatise of Nature and Grace*; and Patrick Riley's Introduction in particular. See also Riley, *The General Will before Rousseau* (Princeton: Princeton University Press, 1986), for the remarkable adventures of the idea of the general will from Malebranche to Rousseau.

therefore reasonable to suppose that criticisms of miracles emanating from self-styled supporters of the new scientific outlook could expect a more tolerant reception than the modern reader might suppose. Hume himself provides some evidence that this was indeed the case. He remarks, in his letter to Kames where he speaks of 'castrating' the *Treatise* by removing the miracles section, that publication is not wise, 'even as the World is dispos'd at present'.[34] The (Christian) world was, it seems, disposed towards tolerance of criticisms of special revelation—a fact, if true, explicable by the contemporary high standing of natural theology.[35]

Natural theology's subsequent decline can be attributed, in part, to the very success of Hume's critique in this section and, of course, in the *Dialogues concerning Natural Religion*. The principal factor, however, is undoubtedly the apparently irresistible rise of evolutionary theory, especially in its dominant form, Darwinian natural selection. It is this that has relegated natural theology to the margins of modern intellectual life, because, according to natural selection, the order we see in nature is not design—not even *evidence* of design—but the random, blind, adaptations of organisms—or of their genes—to environmental pressures. Further, it commonly *denies* the perfect orderliness of the world: that orderliness—including biological adaptation—is at best only a rough and ready affair.[36] The consequence of the triumph of this view is that natural theology is now almost entirely absent from public culture, so much so that it is a matter of surprise and curiosity to the public when an intellectual who takes it seriously—and for serious reasons—is discovered.[37] In fact, such are the hard times on which it has fallen that critiques of Darwinism seem often to be resisted precisely because they are thought to be back-door attempts to reintroduce natural theology, and *therefore* not credible. The reasoning is, of course, circular; but the relevant point here is simply just how profound has been natural theology's fall from grace. The consequence of the fall is that religious critics and apologists alike are now inclined to see the test of religious belief

[34] *Letters*, ed. Greig, i. 24–5.
[35] Cf. David Wootton's contrary view that such remarks show Hume to be tapping into a groundswell of clandestine religious unbelief ('Hume's "Of Miracles"'). I have discussed the issues more fully in 'Marvels, Miracles, and Mundane Order: Hume's Critique of Religion in *An Enquiry concerning Understanding*', *Australasian Journal of Philosophy*, 79 (2001).
[36] See e.g. R. Dawkins, *The Blind Watchmaker* (New York: Norton, 1986), for an emphasis on the imperfections of the evolutionists' world. Adaptationism has been attacked by Stephen Jay Gould and Richard Lewontin in a number of works: for a summary, see K. Sterelny and P. E. Griffiths, *Sex and Death: An Introduction to Philosophy of Biology* (Chicago: University of Chicago Press, 1999), 224 ff.
[37] These are mostly to be found amongst the physicists. See e.g. P. Davies, *God and the New Physics* (Harmondsworth: Penguin Books, 1990), esp. ch. 12.

to lie wholly in claims of special revelation, and to assume, where no evidence persuades them to the contrary, 'twas ever thus. Herein, I suggest, lies the origin of the powerful tendency to read 'Of Miracles' as a self-contained critique of religious belief, of Christianity in particular; and to read 'Of a particular Providence and of a future State' hardly at all. Hume's very different intellectual environment is not always forgotten, but its implications for the reading of his critique of religion in the *Enquiry* are all too frequently overlooked.

Section XII

Of the academical or sceptical Philosophy

The interconnected essays that make up this work have displayed a clear tendency: sceptical doubts have been raised, and sceptical solutions proposed. This is true not only of the two sections that explicitly bear this tag, but also of those succeeding sections that appeal to custom, probability, and proof as the foundation of judgement. Free will, in the sense of some contracausal power possessed only by human beings and other higher creatures, has been denied, and human freedom has been relocated within the natural order. Human rationality itself has been humbled, as the ancient sceptics and Montaigne had humbled it, by being treated as, in large part, a quality possessed also by animals. Finally, religion, the defining mark of the human soul, has been attacked: first, by undermining the evidential basis for miracles, and then by denying that religious explanations are a justified response to the observed orderliness of the natural world. True, these anti-religious conclusions are not to be confused with atheism; and the attack on religion is itself mitigated by several fideistic avowals. Even if credibility were to be granted to these avowals, however, this would do nothing to dilute the sceptical air of the work, since such fideism was precisely the retreat of the Christian sceptic, as exemplified in Bayle and Montaigne. *An Enquiry concerning Human Understanding* is openly and avowedly a work of philosophical scepticism.

The question that needs to be addressed, then, is whether scepticism can be a credible philosophy. The problem is that those sceptics who have sought to resist all beliefs—to accept 'no opinion or principle concerning any subject, either of action or speculation' (149)—have succeeded only in making themselves ridiculous. Is this an inevitable consequence of the attempt to live the sceptical life? Is scepticism a wholly negative doctrine that leaves nothing standing, not even itself? And that the sceptical principles outlined in this work must therefore be wholly rejected, even if they cannot be refuted? The task of this final section is to show that these common responses, although not without their point, do not apply to the view outlined and defended in this work: that there is, indeed, a credible scepticism; and that it has a sharp cutting edge.[1]

Part I

Hume begins by observing a peculiar difficulty that the sceptic shares with that other enemy of religion, the atheist. Both inspire the ire of the religious philosophers, even though their genuine existence is doubted by those philosophers themselves. This strange situation comes about in the following way. The religious philosophers divide their time between proving the existence of God—thus routing the atheists—while simultaneously pondering whether anyone could be so irrational as to be genuinely atheistic. In similar fashion, even though no one has ever met someone so absurd as to have 'no opinion or principle concerning any subject, either of action or speculation', the figure of the sceptic still manages to provoke 'the indignation of all divines and graver philosophers' (149). The former issue is not relevant here, but what of the latter? Is the sceptic an absurd figure? What exactly is scepticism? And how far can sceptical doubt be pushed without collapsing under the weight of its own questions?

Hume suggests that the first thing to do is to notice that there are two kinds of scepticism. The first of these is *'antecedent* to all study and philosophy'. This is the method of doubt proposed by Descartes as a way of avoiding error. It stipulates that, before attempting scientific enquiries, we doubt everything, even our sensory and intellectual powers themselves, if they cannot assure us of their veracity. This method overcomes doubt and uncertainty by accepting only those beliefs that can be deduced from an indubitable starting point. The fundamental flaw in this enterprise, says Hume, is that there is no such starting point; and, even if there were, it would be impossible to get beyond it without calling on the very capacities that have been rejected. The Cartesian doubt, then, if it were possible, would be 'entirely incurable': 'no reasoning could ever bring us to a state of assurance and conviction on any subject' (150).

---

[1] Thus understood, this section is not simply a substitute for *Treatise* Book I Part IV; so Flew's complaint that it is 'entirely inadequate'—because it omits discussion of the causes that induce us to believe in the existence of body, and of personal identity—is not to the point. See Flew, *Hume's Philosophy of Belief*, 243.

This brisk dismissal of the Cartesian strategy reveals rather more about Hume's perception of Descartes's method than of its actual weaknesses. The objection is certainly not without force, but it does seem to imply that it is the *cogito* on which Descartes builds his edifice. This is not so. The *cogito* arrests the doubt, but it is only a stage on the way to establishing the solid foundation on which Descartes will build: the existence of God. The foundation of Descartes's metaphysics is the conclusion that the perfections of the divine nature guarantee that God is no deceiver, and therefore that my essence, and therefore also my basic capacities, are not fundamentally flawed. God's existence guarantees that my own essence is not inherently deceptive, and that my faculties are therefore capable, when correctly employed, of attaining to genuine knowledge of the world: of the essence and existence of the kinds of things there are, and the relations between them: of *scientia*.

Of course, this is not to say that Descartes's strategy works. In reaching his conclusion, he must appeal to a *criterion* that can assure him that his idea of God is itself truthful; and clarity and distinctness, the criterion on which he relies, is not beyond doubt. In fact, since he himself can affirm it wholeheartedly only *after* establishing God's existence, it seems that, as Arnauld objected, he is here forced to argue in a circle.[2] Nor does the *cogito* establish as much as Descartes supposes, since he accepts, without examination, that the fact of thinking from which it begins includes the knowledge that there is an *I* that *has* these thoughts, which is thus distinct from, and prior to, them: the essence of which they are accidents. These are certainly flaws in the Cartesian strategy, but drawing them out nevertheless suffices to show that Hume's attack on Descartes at this point is too swift to be compelling.[3] Hume does, however, concede that this form of scepticism has its use, and just the use that Descartes had proposed: to free enquiry from preconceptions. If kept within sensible limits, this form of scepti-

---

[2] Antoine Arnauld, Fourth Set of Objections, in Descartes, *Philosophical Writings*, ii. 150.
[3] Taken most charitably, his remarks could be thought to be affirming that the 'Cartesian circle' is indeed viciously circular; but it does seem that his objection is the simpler one, that once one has arrived at the *cogito* there is nowhere else to go. Of course, if the circle is inescapable, then the *cogito* indeed leads nowhere: so he might be right, even though his objection is itself too elliptical. Of course, Hume's own account of impressions and ideas, and their association, and of belief in terms of steadiness of the relevant perception (Sections II, III, V), implicitly denies that there is any criterion of truth given in experience. Thus Descartes's strategy in the *Meditations*—of scrutinizing ideas for marks of their truth—is ruled out from the start. In the *Treatise*, Hume addresses both of these issues explicitly: the sceptical solution of the problem of the criterion in terms of experience and habit (265); and the absence of any directly experienced *I* in the famous chapter on personal identity (251–63), and in the confession of failure to explain the source of the idea in the Appendix (633–6).

cism frees us from prejudices we may have unwittingly imbibed.[4]
It also teaches us the importance of a systematic and critical
method. Beginning from self-evident principles, proceeding cautiously, and testing each conclusion as it is obtained—although
progress by these means is slow, it is the only path to solid and
stable conclusions. 'Antecedent' scepticism, then, as long as it is
kept within the bounds of moderation, is an important servant of
philosophical science.

The second kind of scepticism is '*consequent* to science and
enquiry'. This form is close to Hume's experimental heart, and so
he devotes to it a more thorough, and more careful, examination.
This form of scepticism arises when the attempt to understand the
world by investigating its features undermines itself, by undermining the very certitudes from which enquiry began, and on
which it depends. It arises

when men are supposed to have discovered, either the absolute fallaciousness
of their mental faculties, or their unfitness to reach any fixed determination
in all those curious subjects of speculation, about which they are commonly
employed. Even our senses are brought into dispute, by a certain species of
philosophers; and the maxims of common life are subjected to the same
doubt as the most profound principles or conclusions of metaphysics and
theology. (150)

Scepticism of this kind, because it may call into question the
most basic of our convictions, may seem fantastic. However,
because it is not simply spun out of the head of some metaphysical crank in his closet, but grounded in empirical research,
it cannot be simply ignored or lightly dismissed. These are views
that require careful assessment; so to this assessment Hume now
turns.

He begins by sweeping aside one type of sceptical argument: that
which attempts to undermine faith in our faculties by showing
their limitations or imperfections. Thus, for example, sensory illusions, such as 'the crooked appearance of an oar in water', or 'the
double images which arise from the pressing one eye' cannot legitimately destroy all confidence in the senses; what they show is
that the senses have their limitations, and stand in need of cor-
rection by reason and experience:

These sceptical topics . . . are only sufficient to prove, that the senses alone
are not implicitly to be depended on; but that we must correct their evidence

---

[4] For this reason, Descartes was hailed by the eighteenth-century *philosophes* as a hero of
Enlightenment. See Voltaire, *Letters on England*, 68–72; d'Alembert, *Preliminary Discourse*,
77–80; and Schouls, *Descartes and the Enlightenment*.

by reason, and by considerations, derived from the nature of the medium, the distance of the object, and the disposition of the organ, in order to render them, within their sphere, the proper *criteria* of truth and falsehood. (151)

In this passage, we see Hume distancing himself from one kind of argument commonly employed by the ancient sceptics.[5] For example, the Ten Modes of Aenesidemus, which are discussed at some length by Sextus Empiricus, include precisely such variabilities in the deliverances of the senses.[6] Hume's concluding remark that, 'within their sphere', the senses can provide '*criteria* of truth and falsehood' thus signals a divergence from a characteristic argument of the ancient sceptics. The question is, how significant is this divergence? It is, I suggest, less than it seems.

The ancient sceptics denied that the senses could provide a criterion of truth, because the senses revealed only the appearance of a thing. Since appearances are conditioned by the varieties of sense organs themselves, and as such vary according to extrinsic factors, they do not reveal truths about things. As such, appearances are obstacles to truth, and so there can be no criterion of truth appropriate to the senses. Truth concerns the nature of a thing—its essence—and the criterion of truth is the standard by which the essence is discovered. The sceptics and their opponents did not differ on this point; only on whether there was such a criterion, and therefore such truth. Hume's retreat on this point is a limited concession to the Lockean argument that the senses can be classed as delivering knowledge within their (admittedly narrow) proper sphere: particular matters of fact. Locke argues that 'sensitive knowledge of particular existence' is properly regarded as a species of knowledge because it cannot effectively be doubted; and, he adds, Descartes's reflections about dreaming only succeed in underlining the fact. Nevertheless, because it gives the lowest degree of certainty of the various species of knowledge, it must be ranked beneath the other species, intuition and demonstration.[7]

Hume does not go so far: he agrees that the existence of things present to the senses cannot be doubted, but does not conclude therefrom that such existence is thereby *known*.[8] However, *some-*

---

[5] His objection is precisely that brought by the anti-sceptical Hobbes, in his impatient response to Descartes in the Third Objections. See Descartes, *Philosophical Writings*, ii. 121.

[6] Sextus Empiricus, *Outlines of Scepticism*, I. 35–163.　　[7] Locke, *Essay*, IV. ii. 14.

[8] The indubitability of present perceptions is implicit in Hume's account of belief in Section V. It is made explicit in the famous remark in the *Treatise* that ''tis in vain to ask, *Whether there be body or not?* That is a point, which we must take for granted in all our reasonings' (187). That is, we cannot successfully doubt the existence of the objects that appear to the senses—whatever the relation of the perceptions to their causes. Hume thus allows—as Locke does not—the possibility of an ineliminable tension between the natural beliefs about the objects and the best answer reason can give about the existence and nature of such objects.

thing is certainly discovered in such cases: that there is a perception with particular qualities; qualities that are settled, and that
can be the subject of orderly discourse and classification. In other
words, it is possible to establish accurate standards concerning the
ideas themselves, and therefore concerning experience: fruitful
empirical enquiry, with its own standards for assessing empirical
claims, is a genuine possibility, despite our propensities to error.[9]
Hume does not devote much space to this point in the *Enquiry*—
his main preoccupations are elsewhere—but he does affirm it in
the closing paragraphs of the work. At this stage of the argument,
he is signalling his acceptance of an outlook more qualified than
that of the Ten Modes—that is, of an outlook that does not reduce
all perceptions to mere equality. He is thus also signalling that the
sceptical arguments on which he will place weight will not simply
be recycled versions of the ancient sceptical arguments: 'There are
other more profound arguments against the senses, which admit
not of so easy a solution.' Indeed; and they derive precisely from
where, for the uninitiated, they would be least expected—from the
modern philosophy, the great triumph of the age.

The 'more profound' argument against the senses is a model of
sceptical argumentation. This is because it develops by drawing out
tensions between our instinctive commitments and our best interpretations of the world, and producing that 'amazement and irresolution and confusion, which is the result of scepticism' (155
n.). The instinctive commitment is our common-sense belief in the
reality of the various properties of objects as revealed by our senses.
The opposed view stems directly from the new philosophy's apparent implications for perception: the theory of ideas. The distinctive feature of this theory, as pressed by Locke in the *Essay*, is that
perceptions are distinct from the real objects that cause them—
that the contents of consciousness are ideas *rather than* real objects.
As explained above (in Chapter 3), this seems an irresistible conclusion from the mechanical principles embraced by the new

---

[9] Hume thus endorses the phenomenological strand in his predecessors. Descartes had
emphasized that the intellect, in so far as it restricts itself to ideas themselves—that is, as
long as judging of the reality of causes is avoided—cannot err (Fourth Meditation, in *Philosophical Writings*, ii. 39). Similarly, Locke and Berkeley both accepted that perceptions in
themselves are not deceptive, but only the judgements or inferences we draw from them—
and that we will avoid error by coming to a more accurate understanding of what it is the
senses reveal. Cf. Locke, *Essay*, IV. xiv. 3–4. See also Berkeley's Third Dialogue, where Philonous observes, concerning a man's mistaken judgement a half-submerged oar is crooked: 'He
is not mistaken with regard to the ideas he actually perceives; but in the inferences he makes
from his present perceptions. Thus in the case of the oar, what he immediately perceives by
sight is certainly crooked; and so far he is in the right. But if he thence conclude, that upon
taking the oar out of the water he shall perceive the same crookedness; or that it would affect
his touch, as crooked things are wont to do: in that he is mistaken' (George Berkeley, *Three
Dialogues between Hylas and Philonous*, ed. J. Dancy (Oxford: Oxford University Press, 1998),
121).

philosophy, because these principles deny the formal identity between real object and perception guaranteed by the Aristotelian account. Instead, the new philosophy must regard the mind's perception of the object as an *effect* brought about by the (efficient) cause, the real object itself. And, as Hume does not tire of telling us, an effect and its cause are distinct existences. So common-sense beliefs about objects, and the best available account of our perceptual processes, commit us to incompatible conclusions. Hume then argues that the attempt to resolve the sceptical 'amazement and irresolution and confusion' caused by this opposition only succeeds in getting us deeper into the mire. The sceptic must therefore win the day.

Hume develops the argument as follows. It seems clear, he begins, that men have an instinctive reliance on their senses, and so always suppose that there is an external world that exists independently of their perceptions. Animals show the same tendency: their confidence in the independent reality of the world is implied in all their thoughts and actions. It also seems clear that, when men follow this instinctive belief, they always suppose that their perceptions are the very same things as the objects. They do not consider that their perceptions are merely representations of the objects; they always suppose that the white and hard table that they perceive just *is* the real table, 'uniform and entire'. But this universal opinion is swept away by the slightest acquaintance with natural philosophy (that is, with the new science and its mechanical principles), which holds that what is present to the mind is not the object itself but an image or perception, and that the senses are merely inlets to the mind, and do not put us in immediate contact with the objects. An illustration will help: our perception of a table becomes smaller as we move away from it, but the table itself does not become smaller, so we can conclude that our perception is an *image* of the table, not the real table itself. Our perceptions are merely *representations* of objects, and these representations vary in ways that the objects do not.

This may seem a very weak argument to a philosopher steeped in modern debates on perception. After all, it simply ignores the possibility that what we see is indeed the real object, and that when we move away from it it does not *become* smaller, but only *looks* smaller. To respond in this way is, however, to fail to recognize the argument's target, the Aristotelian and Scholastic account of perception. For Hume, to distinguish, as does this objection, between how the thing *is*, and how it *looks*, is to concede all that he needs: for it concedes that what is before our eyes is an appearance, not the being of the thing. The argument is simply that the being of the thing does not change; the perception does; therefore the perception is not of the being of the thing. The argument here is directed against the chief alternative to the mechanical account of perception, for which perceptions are appearances—that is, phenomena distinct from the objects that are their cause. It is, that is, directed against the Aristotelian conception of perception as the communication of the form of the object, such that the perception and the object are formally identical; the perception is of the very being of the thing. Hume seeks simply to deny this identity, to establish that the perception and the real thing are not (formally) identical, and so to establish the superiority of the mechanical account of perception.[10]

It is because he is here following orthodoxies about the new natural philosophy that Hume is able simply to announce that his conclusions are irresistible: they are 'the obvious dictates of reason'. They show that, to this extent, reason compels us to give up our instinctive picture of the world, and to adopt a new interpretation of sense experience: we are 'necessitated by reasoning to contradict or depart from the primary instincts of nature, and to embrace a new system with regard to the evidence of our senses' (152). But, once we do so, a new problem arises: we find that our defences against the sceptic have been weakened. Previously it was possible to oppose the arguments of the sceptics by appealing to the irresistibility of our instinctual judgements; but now instinctual authority has been deposed. The new interpretation must therefore be defended by reason alone. In Hume's view, however, this cannot be done.

His argument runs as follows. How can it be *proved*—how can experience establish beyond doubt—that the mind's perceptions are caused by external objects that resemble them, even though entirely distinct from them? That they could not be produced either by the mind itself, or by some other spirit, or by 'some other cause still more unknown to us'? After all, we already accept, in the cases of dreams and of delirium, that some perceptions arise independently of an external object. The problem is compounded by the fact that we have no way of explaining how body can influence mind in the first place, since (according to the established theories) body and mind are supposed to be completely different substances, even to have quite 'contrary' essences. So how can it

---

[10] For a similar argument against Scholastic substantial forms as incapable of coping with the variability of the natural world, see Locke's discussion of changelings and monsters (*Essay*, IV. iv. 13–16).

be determined whether the mind's perceptions are produced by objects that *resemble* the perceptions? Only experience can do the job—but it is clear that, in this case, experience is impotent. This is because the mind, being acquainted only with perceptions, cannot have experience of how its perceptions are connected to the objects that are their presumed causes. So no reasoning from experience can establish that there are such causes. Nor, he adds, can the problem be resolved by appealing to the veracity of the Deity: 'If his veracity were at all concerned in this matter, our senses would be entirely infallible; because it is not possible that he can ever deceive.'[11] Further, if the reality of the external world is called into question, the principal argument for the existence of the Deity is simultaneously undercut. It makes no sense to argue for a Deity on the basis of the natural order, if we cannot establish that that order does really exist.

Hume thus concludes that, on the question of the reality of the external world, the philosophical sceptics must triumph. We find that if, on the one hand, we follow our natural instincts, we are led to the conclusion that the mind's perception just *is* the physical object. If, on the other hand, we adopt the more rational principle, taught by natural philosophy, that our perceptions are merely representations of external objects, then we abandon our natural sentiments—but without finding an alternative foundation, since we cannot find any sound argument from experience to *prove* that our perceptions are connected with independently existing objects. The reality of the external world remains subject to reasonable doubt.

The difficulty is compounded by considering a further question, 'derived from the most profound philosophy'. The profound philosophy in question is Bishop Berkeley's: Hume spells out Berkeley's central arguments against Locke's attempt, by means of the distinction between primary and secondary qualities, to build a bridge from perceptions to the real objects. It is agreed, he says, that

[11] Again Hume shows himself to be no careful reader of Descartes. Descartes's argument is that simple perceptual errors (like illusions) are not incompatible with God's veracity, because the proper limits of the senses have to be established before confidence is to be reposed in them. That is, our senses do not come with a maker's instruction sheet, telling us to treat their information as infallible guides to the natures of objects. Their role in conveying information needs to be understood; and, once this role is properly understood (as spelt out in Descartes's mechanical principles), it can be concluded that, in their own way, the senses *are* infallible: we feel a pain in the leg whenever the relevant nerve is stimulated in the relevant way, whether or not we still have the leg to which that nerve is normally attached. So, as long as we understand that our sensations tell us that certain nerves are being stimulated, we can place our faith in them. We go astray by falsely concluding that our sense organs are more than mechanical devices, and that the information they provide can stand independently of reason or judgement. So Descartes's response to the problem of illusion for divine veracity is strikingly similar to Hume's own solution to the problem of illusion in general, as described above.

the 'sensible qualities' of objects, such as their hardness or colour, are merely *secondary*, in that they do not exist in the objects themselves, but are perceptions of the mind that do not represent real features of objects.[12] However, if this is accepted for secondary qualities, it must also be true of primary qualities, such as extension and solidity.[13] For example, the idea of extension derives entirely from sense perception; and 'if all the qualities, perceived by the senses, be in the mind, not in the object, the same conclusion must reach the idea of extension',[14] because it is 'wholly dependent on the sensible ideas or the ideas of secondary qualities'.[15] The only way to avoid this conclusion is to argue that ideas of primary qualities arise by *abstraction*. However, it is quite impossible to form such abstract

[12] In putting the argument in this way, Hume thus also accepts, without complaint, that Berkeley's characterization of Locke's distinction is just. In this he is mistaken, since Locke's distinction turns on the claim that *ideas of* secondary qualities, in contrast to ideas of primary qualities, do not resemble the qualities in the objects by which they are caused. But secondary qualities, no less than primary qualities, reside in the objects themselves; while ideas of both belong in the mind. This should be plain enough from the terminology: ideas are mental entities, whereas qualities, whether secondary or primary, are modifications of substances (they 'inhere in' substances, in Aristotelian terminology), and thus reside in the real objects themselves. (See Locke, *Essay*, II. viii).

[13] Locke differs from Descartes on the essential properties of material substance, arguing that 'solidity' (or 'impenetrability'—not to be confused with hardness or with being in a solid state) is no less essential a part of matter than extension, and that matter can not therefore be defined, as Descartes had claimed, as *res extensa* (see Locke, *Essay*, II. iv). So this reference is incidental evidence that it is not merely Berkeley's arguments, but also their specific target—Locke's version of mechanical philosophy—that Hume has in mind here.

[14] This remark also exhibits the tendency to elide the distinction between ideas (in the mind) and qualities (in the object). Berkeley—and, following him, Hume—would have made life considerably less frustrating for their readers if they had instead argued that the distinction between 'idea' and 'quality' itself presupposes precisely the realism being called into question, and had offered a revamped terminology to avoid the almost-inevitable pitfalls.

[15] Here we see Hume—as his stance on the fundamental role of the imagination requires—following Berkeley's 'imagist' conflation of conceptions and perceptions. The idea of extension is wholly dependent on the ideas of secondary qualities if that idea is an image not merely in the sense of representing a quality of an object, but also in the sense of being *pictured* by the imagination. It is indeed impossible to picture an extended figure in one's mind without investing it with further qualities—particularly colour—in order to distinguish it from the field within which it is perceived. This view is made more explicit in the argument against abstraction that follows. It needs to be emphasized that the failure sharply to distinguish conception from perception is not necessarily a lapse by these philosophers. Early modern experimental philosophy was not an exercise in conceptual clarification. So for Hume at least the task is to work out the methods of functioning possible for a radically stripped-down model of the mind. His project is the attempt to show the extent and implications of mechanical processes in the mind: *copying* through *impressing* is one aspect of that model (associating is the other)—and it is an aspect that implies that conceptions and perceptions will not be sharply distinct. The conflation of the two, in other words, is not a confusion, but a theory-driven conclusion: the mind is under the empire of the imagination, that is, under the power of *images*; so conception is properly to be seen in imagist terms. This connection may have led philosophy down some blind alleys, but the experimentalist response to Descartes will not be understood if the enhanced role of the imagination—of bodily processes on mental functioning—is treated, as it has often been, as mere conceptual muddle. (Can this defence be extended to include Berkeley? Only with difficulty, since he takes over experimental doctrines without taking over the programme, and so can be assessed wholly on the phenomenology. This leaves him with little room to respond to Descartes's observations concerning the relative reach of the imagination and of the intellect. See, for example, the remarks on understanding versus imagining a chiliagon in the Sixth Meditation (*Philosophical Writings*, ii. 50–1).)

ideas: 'An extension, that is neither tangible nor visible, cannot possibly be conceived: and a tangible or visible extension, which is neither hard nor soft, black nor white, is equally beyond the reach of human conception' (154–5). In the same way, it is impossible to think of a triangle *in general*—we have to think of a *particular* triangle, complete with all its particular properties, 'primary' or 'secondary'. The doctrine of abstraction must be abandoned, and the distinction between primary and secondary qualities must therefore suffer the same fate.[16]

In this passage, Hume displays a durable attachment to a number of Berkeley's central arguments. His purposes, however, are quite at odds with Berkeley's own. He notes that Berkeley claimed 'to have composed his book against the sceptics as well as against the atheists and free-thinkers',[17] but adds that, whatever Berkeley's intentions, the force of his arguments is sceptical after all, because '*they admit of no answer and produce no conviction*', instead causing only 'that momentary amazement and irresolution and confusion, which is the result of scepticism' (155 n.). For Hume, it is precisely this sceptical tendency that is important here. His purpose in this section has been to make a case for taking scepticism seriously, mainly by showing that the best interpretation of the new experimental philosophy separates our perceptions from the real world, which, we presume, causes them; even to the extent of leaving us with no way of determining whether or not there is a connection at all. The quasi-Berkeleian argument strengthens this case. It argues that, even if it is conceded that there is an independently existing world that lies behind our perceptions, the properties that we attribute to that world are best understood as belonging not to that world at all, but merely to our perceptions: the world may exist independently, but the 'worldliness' of the world is in the mind. The real existence of an independent world, conceded on these terms, is thus too shadowy to be worth defending: 'Bereave matter of all its intelligible qualities, both primary and secondary, you in a manner annihilate it, and leave only a certain unknown, inexplicable *something*, as the cause of our perceptions; a notion so imperfect, that no sceptic will think it worth while to contend against it' (155). So, far from being an absurd

---

[16] For Berkeley's attack on Lockean abstraction, see *Principles*, ed. Dancy, Introduction, §§6–25; for the attack on the distinction between primary and secondary qualities, see *Principles*, Part I, §§9–15. For discussion, see Dancy's 'Editor's Introduction' to each of the *Principles* and *Three Dialogues*; Berkeley, *Philosophical Works, Including the Works on Vision*, ed. M. R. Ayers (London: Dent, 1975), Introduction; Dancy, *Berkeley: An Introduction* (Oxford: Blackwell, 1987); K. Winkler, *Berkeley: An Interpretation* (Oxford: Clarendon Press, 1989); D. Berman, *George Berkeley: Idealism and the Man* (Oxford: Clarendon Press, 1994).

[17] Cf. Ch. 3 above.

figure, the sceptic is able to mount powerful arguments from experience; arguments that rely, not on the traditional appeals to
sensory illusions, but on persuasive arguments based on insights
drawn from the new physical science.

How persuasive are they? One objection can be brought. The
quasi-Berkeleian argument builds on the insight, derived from
mechanical philosophy, that ideas are distinct from real objects,
and drives home the conclusion that the 'reality' we invest in the
objects—their properties—actually belongs to the ideas. In this
way the realist starting points of the enquiry are undermined.
However, the very fact that the starting points are realist should
now give us pause: if those starting assumptions are denied, can
the distinction between ideas and objects be maintained? Does not
that distinction depend on realist assumptions? After all, the view
that perception is a mechanical process implies that such processes
really occur. It also requires that they really are mechanical. So,
giving an account of these processes requires regarding the world
as more than an 'unknown, inexplicable *something*': it requires, it
seems, that the world must be regarded as possessing at least the
primary qualities. This does not mean, of course, that there is a
world that *does* possess these properties; only that the mechanical
philosophy is committed to such a world. For this reason, though,
to argue from insights drawn from the mechanical philosophy
to conclusions that deny such a world is more to embarrass mechanical philosophy—to reveal its unexpected flaws—than to
make a strong case for the shadowiness of the independent world.
The argument shows that something has to give; but what, and
why, is not thereby settled.

Of course, this conclusion may satisfy the sceptic, who need
only undermine the confident claims of dogmatic philosophy,
without seeking to establish an alternative case. There is some evidence that this is in fact Hume's aim. The quasi-Berkeleian argument is, as pointed out above, a gloss on the earlier argument that,
once the 'more rational opinion' of the new science is adopted, it
is no longer possible to *prove* that perceptions are connected to
independently existing objects. So what is denied is proof—argument from experience that leaves no room for doubt or uncertainty—that perceptions are connected to real objects, and the
quasi-Berkeleian argument is introduced to show that conceding
the connection is not enough to allay sceptical worries. And, even
if the connection between perceptions and objects were somehow
proven, there would still remain the further task of proving that
the connection is one of resemblance.

Considered in this way, Hume's argument does not depend on committing himself to the conclusions of the sceptical arguments, the quasi-Berkeleian argument included. It is enough for the arguments to serve as a challenge to the dogmatist: if the arguments cannot be met, then the sceptic must win the day, by showing that the best available interpretation of the world is flawed. It is only necessary, then, for the sceptical philosopher to treat these arguments as plausible, as in play until a successful rejoinder can be made. This is, I think, Hume's attitude to them. They clearly engage his sympathies, but he does not attempt to establish them beyond doubt. Nor do his purposes require that he do so. The aim of Part I is merely to set out the sceptic's case against experience. Parts II and III will consider, first, the case against reason, and then defend the mitigated scepticism that avoids the excesses of Pyrrhonism. The sceptical case against reason will turn out to be weaker than that against the senses, but this neither shows the former to be misguided nor the latter to be invulnerable. Fortunately, the precise status of the two critiques need not be settled definitively. What does need stressing, though, is that the sceptical arguments of this first part are components of a larger whole, and are properly to be interpreted in the light of that larger argument.

Part II

The task of this part is to examine the sceptical objections to reason. Hume remarks that 'It may seem a very extravagant attempt of the sceptics to destroy *reason* by argument and ratiocination; yet is this the grand scope of all their enquiries and disputes' (155). The enterprise does have a paradoxical air, when described thus—but there are other ways of conceiving of this task that dissolve the paradox. The sceptical enterprise can be understood as a rational critique of Reason—of the apotheosis of rationality—rather than of reasoning itself; that is, as an examination of the extent of human rational powers. The results of this enquiry can then be employed to test claims made on behalf of reason. Most importantly, it opens up the possibility of a critique of the grand theories built, explicitly or implicitly, on strong assumptions about reason's powers: speculative theology and metaphysics. This is Hume's aim.

The sceptical critique of reason can be applied both to abstract reason, and also to reasoning concerning matters of fact. Hume's discussion of the first can be treated fairly briefly, not least because he rehearses arguments about infinities and the paradoxes thus generated that had been thoroughly canvassed by his predecessors.[18] The chief objections against abstract reasonings, he observes, arise from contradictions and absurdities in theories concerning space and time. For example, nothing is more contrary to common sense than the doctrine of the infinite divisibility of extension, and its consequences. That there is a real quantity that is infinitely less than a given quantity, and that contains within it quantities that are infinitely less than itself, and so on: such claims, says Hume, are no less shocking to common sense than those 'priestly *dogmas*, invented on purpose to tame and subdue the rebellious reason of mankind'. In this case, however, the scandal is all the greater because 'these seemingly absurd opinions are supported by a chain of reasoning, the clearest and most natural' (156). Examples of similarly incredible but irresistible deductions can be given on other topics concerning space and time, such as the infinitely small angle of contact of a tangent to a circle, and the infinitely smaller angles of contact of tangents to other curves. The clear arguments seem to demand assent, but the conclusions are so bizarre that assent is scarcely possible.

The situation seems even worse if we turn to doctrines about time. For example, the idea that there is 'an infinite number of real parts of time, passing in succession, and exhausted one after another' (157)[19] seems so absurd that it seems necessary first to have been corrupted (rather than improved) by philosophy in order to take it seriously. So, Hume concludes, absurdities like these must push us towards scepticism. However, even in such a scepticism, reason cannot rest content, because it is incomprehensible to us that such clear ideas and deductions can contain contradictions. Thus scepticism about these paradoxes is *itself* subject to sceptical doubts: 'nothing can be more sceptical, or more full of doubt and hesitation, than this scepticism itself, which arises from some of the paradoxical conclusions of geometry or the science of quantity' (158).

The sceptical critique having left geometry and mathematics in disarray, Hume now turns to reasoning concerning factual (or 'moral') matters. He divides these into two kinds, the popular and

---

[18] See e.g. Descartes, *Principles*, I. 26–7, in *Philosophical Writings*, i. 201–2; Arnauld and Nicole, *Logic or the Art of Thinking*, 230–2; Locke, *Essay*, II. xvii; and Berkeley, *Principles*, Part I, §§128–32.

[19] Hume probably has in mind Augustine's discussion of time and its paradoxes. See Augustine, *Confessions*, trans. with an introduction and notes by H. Chadwick (Oxford: Oxford University Press, 1992), Book XI (221 ff).

the philosophical. The division corresponds to the division, in Part I, between the 'trite' and the 'profound' objections to sensory evidence (151); that is, between the traditional objections deriving from ancient scepticism, and the more sophisticated objections generated by an accurate understanding of the modern philosophy.

The *popular* objections to factual reasoning are the following: the natural weakness of human understanding; the contradictory views held in different times and places; the variations in judgements that reflect health, age, and so on; and the internal contradictions in the set of any given person's views. The dependence of this short list on traditional sceptical arguments can be drawn out by comparing it with Sextus' account of Aenesidemus' Ten Modes. The First Mode illustrates the weakness of human understanding by showing its resemblances to animal understanding; the Second Mode illustrates the contradictory views held by different groups of human beings by reference to the irreconcilable claims of the various Dogmatic schools; and the Fourth Mode illustrates the variations in judgements that are due to 'circumstances'—that is, extrinsic factors such as health, age, wakefulness, drunkenness, and so on.[20] With this in mind, Hume's comment that these are weak objections shows him, once again, to be signalling to the reader that the best case for scepticism does not derive from the arguments familiar from the ancient sceptics.

The actual objection he brings, however, *seems* simply to be the tried-and-true complaint that scepticism must be rejected because the sceptic cannot live his scepticism.[21] In fact, there is more to Hume's objection than this alone, but it is worth noting at this point that the objection is prone to misunderstanding by the modern reader, who will object that what is true is not therefore livable. This can be conceded, provided we stick with equally modern notions of truth. But this point itself gives the clue: for the ancient philosopher, truth concerns reality, and therefore also the proper way to conduct oneself in the world.[22] A philosophy was not, in the ancient world, merely a set of factually accurate statements, but a way of life. So if the ancient sceptic was unable

[20] Sextus Empiricus, *Outlines of Scepticism*, I. 62–78, 85–90, 100–14. (The Third Mode concerns variations in the senses, and so belongs to the objections to sensory evidence canvassed in Part I.)

[21] The issue (with reference to Hume and the Pyrrhonians) is spelt out in these terms by M. Burnyeat, 'Can the Sceptic Live his Scepticism?', in M. Schofield, M. Burnyeat, and J. Barnes (eds.), *Doubt and Dogmatism: Studies in Hellenistic Epistemology* (Oxford: Clarendon Press, 1980), 20–53.

[22] The transformation of the idea of truth in the history of western philosophy is spelt out in considerable detail in R. Campbell, *Truth and Historicity* (Oxford: Clarendon Press, 1992).

to live his scepticism, this amounted to the failure of scepticism *as philosophy*. What of Hume's own concern for this question? First, it should be noted that the demise of this outlook is more recent than the demise of the ancient notion of truth. It held sway in the modern world too, until philosophy 'professionalized'. And, secondly, since, as has been argued above, Hume's aim in the *Enquiry* is to outline a 'philosophy of life' for modern times, it is entirely appropriate for him to assess the sceptical way of life in terms of its livability.

The argument itself is as follows. He points out that reasonings about fact and existence are necessary for everyday life to continue at all: so it would be rash to conclude, on the basis of specific short-comings in those reasonings, that we should abandon them altogether. The great failing of *'Pyrrhonism* or the excessive prin-ciples of scepticism' is its inability to translate into everyday life. In debate it is hard, if not impossible, to defeat the Pyrrhonian outlook; but in the employments of daily life it is just over-whelmed by our natural responses to the world we encounter and with which we interact. Thus the sceptic ends up engaging with the world not according to the principles of sceptical philosophy, but in the same way as everyone else: 'the most determined sceptic' is left 'in the same condition as other mortals' (158–9).

It was mentioned above that Hume's point is not simply that excessive scepticism fails because it cannot be lived. The further aspect of the objection is implicit in the very argument of the *Enquiry* itself. The foregoing sections of the work have argued not only that human reason is weak, and less influential in human life than commonly imagined, but also that the non-rational founda-tion of habit is *itself* a foundation for a form of reasoning—prob-able reasoning—the proper employment of which is a reliable, if not infallible, guide in shaping our beliefs and practices. So not only must excessive scepticism be judged to fail the test of practi-cal life; it must also be severely embarrassed by the ability of a moderate scepticism to build a thoroughly practical outlook on the basis of sceptical principles. For the moment, though, this point is deferred. Hume proceeds instead to spell out the *philosophical* objections brought by the sceptic against factual reasoning, and these turn out to be the destructive arguments of the first half of the *Enquiry*: that is, the arguments, deriving from the insights of experimental philosophy, against the dogmatists' conception of human rational powers. (The positive argument, including par-ticularly the role of proof and probability, Hume delays until Part III.)

The *philosophical* objections brought by the sceptic are as follows: that all our evidence for factual beliefs that are not part of present experience depend on causal reasoning; that the evidence for causal connections is entirely a matter of regular conjunctions in experience; that we have no argument to show that what has been regularly conjoined in experience will continue to be so; that here we rely entirely on habit or natural instinct; and that, although this instinct is very hard to resist, it may lead us into error.[23] On these topics, Hume concludes, the sceptic's case is strong: the arguments 'arise from more profound researches' than the popular objections, because they depend on working out the consequences of the experimental method of reasoning when applied to moral subjects, and they seem 'to have ample matter of triumph' because they are carefully drawn conclusions from the central—sceptical—message of experimental philosophy.[24]

Having limited his exposition to the negative phase of the *Enquiry*'s scepticism, it is no surprise that Hume should observe at this point that the sceptic's victory seems to be merely Pyrrhic. It shows only 'his own and our weakness; and *seems, for the time at least*, to destroy all assurance and conviction' (159; emphasis added). The qualification is important, for this appearance will be shown to be overcome by the mitigated scepticism spelt out in Part III. Hume's aim, at this point, is to hammer home the objection that, by threatening 'assurance and conviction', unqualified scepticism is useless, and therefore to be rejected:

For here is the chief and most confounding objection to *excessive* scepticism, that no durable good can ever result from it; while it remains in its full force and vigour. We need only ask such a sceptic, *What his meaning is? And what he proposes by all these curious researches?* He is immediately at a loss, and knows not what to answer. A Copernican or Ptolemaic, who supports each his different system of astronomy, may hope to produce a conviction, which will remain constant and durable, with his audience. A Stoic or Epicurean displays principles, which may not only be durable, but which have an effect on conduct and behaviour. But a Pyrrhonian cannot expect, that his philosophy will have any constant influence on the mind: or if it had, that its influence

[23] This instinct may be, he says, 'fallacious and deceitful' (159): the choice of terms itself suggesting a further attempt to rebuke Descartes for his appeal to a non-deceiving God (cf. 153).
[24] The arguments thus correspond, in the sphere of fact and experience, to the sceptical arguments deriving from the theory of ideas, the perceptual theory implied by mechanical philosophy. In this respect, these arguments provide a clear picture of Hume's primary project.

would be beneficial to society. On the contrary, he must acknowledge, if he will acknowledge anything, that all human life must perish, were his principles universally and steadily to prevail.   (159–60)[25]

So, because useless, unqualified scepticism fails as a philosophy of life, and therefore as philosophy. A related, but weaker (more internal) objection, in the idiom of the late twentieth century, would be to describe scepticism as *unmotivated*. The objection is weaker and more internal than Hume's because it is usually applied to arguments or standpoints that serve no broader theoretical purpose, no 'programme'. Hume's point is stronger not only because it reflects the general requirement that philosophy has a practical existential point, but also because of the special emphasis placed on this feature by the philosophers of the Enlightenment. For the secularizing French *philosophe* in particular, social usefulness replaced salvation as the central concern for a human life, and the *philosophe* himself, as the high priest of the dawning new age, took a particular pride in discovering and advancing useful truths and useful arts. Hume's emphasis on the uselessness of unqualified scepticism shows him to share this Enlightenment outlook: such scepticism is to be rejected because it is useless; the peculiar glory of philosophy is that it teaches us useful truths, or useful principles, for the better conduct of life.[26]

With this in mind, we can conclude with a small but useful point, concerning the memorable passage with which Hume closes Part II:

[25] It seems likely that, in this passage, Hume has in the back of his mind the example of Pyrrho himself, who, according to Diogenes Laertius, 'led a life consistent with his doctrine, going out of his way for nothing, taking no precaution, but facing all risks as they came, whether carts, precipices, dogs or what not, and, generally, leaving nothing to the arbitrament of the senses; but he was kept out of harm's way by his friends who, as Antigonus of Carystus tells us, used to follow close after him'. Diogenes also mentions the alternative account of Pyrrho's life offered by Aenesidemus, which is worth noting at this point because it suggests that even Pyrrho learnt the value of a *mitigated* scepticism: 'Aenesidemus says that it was only his philosophy that was based upon suspension of judgment, and that he did not lack foresight in his everyday acts' (Diogenes Laertius, *Lives of Eminent Philosophers*, trans. Hicks, ii. 475).

[26] This outlook seems to have been particularly pronounced in the attitude to history. Thus the philosophers insisted that history should be written by them—otherwise it could be nothing but a catalogue of dull facts. Voltaire illustrates the attitude well: 'You prefer that philosophers should write ancient history because you wish to read it as a philosopher. You seek only useful truths, and have found, as you say, scarcely anything but useless errors.' Diderot's commendation of Voltaire as a historian is in the same vein: 'Other historians relate facts to inform us of facts. You relate them to excite in our hearts an intense hatred of lying, ignorance, hypocrisy, superstition, tyranny; and this anger remains even after the memory of the facts has disappeared' (quoted in Becker, *The Heavenly City of the Eighteenth-Century Philosophers*, 91–2). Hume's subsequent career as a historian—and the explicit moral tendency of his historical labours—becomes, in this light, a natural development. The Enlightenment philosophers' desire to teach useful truths rendered the writing of histories an almost inevitable ambition.

Nature is always too strong for principle. And though a Pyrrhonian may throw himself or others into a momentary amazement and confusion by his profound reasonings; the first and most trivial event in life will put to flight all his doubts and scruples, and leave him the same, in every point of action and speculation, with the philosophers of every other sect, or with those who never concerned themselves in any philosophical researches. When he awakes from his dream, he will be the first to join in the laugh against himself, and to confess, that all his objections are mere amusement, and can have no other tendency than to show the whimsical condition of mankind, who must act and reason and believe; though they are not able, by their most diligent enquiry, to satisfy themselves concerning the foundation of these operations, or to remove the objections, which may be raised against them. (160)

The sheer charm of this passage makes it all the easier to iden-tify the view expressed as Hume's own view—but it is not. The passage is wholly concerned with the response of the excessive sceptic, when brought back to good sense by the intercourse of common life; and the joke he shares is with the common people themselves, who are inclined to accept that theirs is indeed a whimsical condition. ('It's a rum old world.') It cannot, however, be identified as Hume's own view—unless, of course, by 'founda-tion' he means the *ultimate* foundations that would be provided by rational insight into natures or essences—since the very purpose of the *Enquiry* is precisely to show that there is a (mani-fest) foundation of our beliefs, and reasonings from experience, in the habitual tendencies of the human mind, and to show how probable judgements based thereon can even amount to full proofs. The human condition is whimsical if the Pyrrhonian's inability to live his scepticism is the last word. But it is not. From the ashes of unbounded scepticism a new philosophy can arise, a philosophy that is able to draw constructive conclusions—espe-cially about the limits of our rational powers—from the failings of dogmatic and Pyrrhonian philosophy alike; and, by a careful application of the principles of experimental philosophy and its mechanical picture of the world, forge principles of probable judgement on which we can confidently rely in the conduct of life. Expounding this new and constructive version of *Academic* scepticism is the task of the final part of Hume's work.

Part III

Hume opens this final part by affirming that there is a mitigated or Academic scepticism that avoids the central failing of Pyrrhonism: Academic philosophy is 'durable and useful'. It achieves this usefulness not because it rejects Pyrrhonian arguments outright, but because it learns from their failings. Academic scepticism corrects the 'undistinguished doubts' of Pyrrhonism through 'common sense and reflection'. According to Hume, it does this in two main ways.

First, it corrects the tendency to dogmatism in human judgements. 'The greater part of mankind', says Hume, 'are naturally apt to be affirmative and dogmatical in their opinions.' This is because they tend to see only their own point of view, and so are unable to engage sympathetically with the views of others. They are thus ill-equipped to weigh one view against another, and rapidly become uncomfortable and impatient with complications that interfere with their plans and actions, resorting to ever more dogmatic stances in an effort to distance themselves from the pangs of uncertainty. If they could become aware of the weaknesses of human intellectual capacities, even when applied most carefully, they would come to acknowledge these limits in their own thinking, and adopt a more moderate approach both to their own views, and to those of others. A 'small tincture of Pyrrhonism' is thus able to correct the disposition of the enquirer, by keeping in view 'the universal perplexity and confusion, which is inherent in human nature' (161). The first lesson that mitigated scepticism learns from Pyrrhonism, concludes Hume, is that 'there is a degree of doubt, and caution, and modesty, which, in all kinds of scrutiny and decision, ought for ever to accompany a just reasoner' (162).

This conclusion can be misconstrued. Hume clearly does not mean that firmly held conclusions on any topic are impossible. This would be to make nonsense both of the arguments of the *Enquiry* as a whole, and especially of the implications of the second lesson that mitigated scepticism learns from Pyrrhonian doubts. This second lesson concerns the limitations of human intellectual capacities, which, once settled, can then be used as a critical— indeed, sharply critical—tool against various kinds of putative knowledge. The famous denunciation of certain pretended sciences in the closing paragraph of the *Enquiry* shows this lesson of scepticism to allow very firm judgements indeed. How is the sharply critical edge of mitigated scepticism to be squared with the first conclusion that 'a degree of doubt, and caution, and modesty . . . ought for ever to accompany a just reasoner'? Some reconciling comments are in order.

It is probable that at this point Hume would benefit from the vocabulary of the modern scientist, or (what comes to much the

same thing) of modern inductive logic. The scientist who insists
that scientific conclusions are held tentatively does not mean to
imply that confidence should not be placed in, say, Darwinian
explanations; and in particular does not mean to imply that such
explanations are on a level with 'creation science'. Rather, the
scientist accepts that Darwinian explanations are to be held with
confidence, and are to be preferred to the proposals of 'creation
science'. Nevertheless, they are held tentatively, in the sense that
they are based on specific evidence, and so are revisable to the
extent that further evidence, or persuasive reinterpretations of the
meaning of that evidence, become available.[27] Of course, it is not
true that individual scientists always manage to behave in this way.
The point is that physical science, and other practices that seek to
determine the best explanation in the light of the best understanding of the evidence, *properly* function in this way. They
develop standards for assessing alternative explanations, and arrive
at judgements concerning the relative value of these alternatives.
The explanation established as the best *is* the best explanation,
and as such ought to be accepted. However, the grounds of this
explanation are not set in concrete, and the 'just reasoner' recognizes the fact. So, in holding that the best explanation is indeed
the best, the 'just reasoner' recognizes both that this explanation
ought to be accepted, and also that it is fallible—subject to revision or replacement.

To apply this to Hume's own case. Since the standards for determining the best interpretation of an author's remarks include
coherence with his other views—especially, of course, other views
that are *immediately* expressed—and since Hume turns to the
second lesson discoverable through sceptical doubt immediately
following his comments about the intellectual modesty, and so on,
of the 'just reasoner', the best explanation is that the two lessons
are not incompatible, and that the preferred interpretation is precisely that which allows a harmonized account. (True, he does say
that the second lesson of sceptical doubt gives rise to *another*
species of mitigated scepticism, but the point still holds, since
coherence requires that, even if there are two species, they are not
to be supposed incompatible.) The account of the 'tentative' character of the theories advanced by the scientist (the experimental

[27] 'Creation science' itself is, of course, an attempt to provide such a reinterpretation, and
so cannot be ruled out *a priori*. To recognize this does not, however, mean that all interpretations are to be treated as equal, that, for example, every different view has a right to equal
time in the curriculum. To think so is to sound the death knell of education entirely, since
it requires admitting every imaginable hypothesis—from astrology to voodoo—into the curriculum on equal terms.

natural philosopher) offered above does allow both an insistence on intellectual caution together with a critical edge, and so is the best interpretation of Hume's meaning. The 'degree of doubt, and caution, and modesty' of the 'just reasoner' is not, therefore, an unwillingness to reach conclusions or assess the relative merits of alternative views, but the recognition that all views, including one's own, must always be subject to the authority of the evidence, and that the evidence is itself subject to change.

With this problem settled, it is now possible to address Hume's remarks on the second lesson of sceptical doubt. There is, he says, a second useful form of mitigated scepticism that insists that our enquiries be restricted to 'such subjects as are best adapted to the narrow capacity of human understanding'. The need for this insistence arises because the human imagination is naturally inclined to roam in regions beyond the familiar world of the everyday, whereas sound judgement works in precisely the opposite direction, confining itself to 'such subjects as fall under daily practice and experience'. Coming to see the force of the Pyrrhonian doubt—even to the extent of recognizing that it is defeated not by reason but by natural instinct—is the best way of ensuring that judgement will rule over flighty imagination.[28] This insight will still allow the philosophically minded appropriate avenues of enquiry. They will realize that 'philosophical decisions are nothing but the reflections of common life, methodized and corrected', and so will remember to keep their enquiries within their proper bounds: those set by 'common life'. Such philosophers, aware of their ignorance of why the familiar everyday world functions as it does, will not be tempted to advance extravagant theories concerning 'the origin of worlds, and the situation of nature, from, and to eternity' (162).

The value of restricting intellectual endeavours in this way, Hume adds, is made plain by spelling out the kinds of capacities possessed by the human mind, and then matching these powers

[28] This is, admittedly, an unexpected conclusion for a philosopher so keen to emphasize 'the empire of the imagination' (*Treatise*, 662). However, it is no part of Hume's philosophy that this empire's dominion is absolute, nor that it should be. How is its influence to be contained? If this seems a hard question to answer, it is only because of a tendency to think of the mind's faculties as discrete entities with their own powers—as Hume's own talk of 'empire' itself invites. As Locke emphasized, however, 'faculty' means only a power or ability, not something that possesses that ability. The mind has faculties, and therefore has abilities; faculties themselves do not. (See Locke, *Essay*, II. xxi. 17–20.) We know, from experience, that we can act on the basis of our judgement—that judgement can come to exercise control over imagination's flights of fancy—and that we function more successfully when this is so. Pyrrhonian doubt thus has a therapeutic function, not unlike another famous therapy: where imagination was, there judgement will be. Or, more accurately if less catchily: where the flights of imagination were, there stable if not infallible judgements will be.

to the corresponding branches of human knowledge. This process will enable us to distinguish the proper subjects of human enquiry from the improper, or bogus: it will establish criteria for distinguishing science from pseudo-science. So the *Enquiry* concludes with a taxonomy of legitimate forms of research, and the identification of some conspicuous pretenders.

First, the human mind has the capacity to construct pure or abstract sciences through its power of rational demonstration. Hume claims, however, that the only objects capable of treatment by this means are 'quantity and number'; and that any attempt to apply this method in other fields produces 'mere sophistry and illusion'. The method can be applied to these subjects because 'the component parts of quantity and number are entirely similar'—that is, they are purely quantities or purely numbers. Thus complex relations can be deduced between these components. Where objects differ in more complex ways—along many dimensions—such computations are no longer possible, and we can do no better than observe the fact of their difference. The realm of application of the 'geometrical method', then, does not extend to the complex objects of the natural world, still less to the world of human affairs. The theorems of geometry are genuine insights arrived at by deductive reasoning. In contrast, Locke's suggestion that there can be a demonstrative science of morals, and that the proposition '*that where there is no property, there can be no injustice*' is part of such a science, is mistaken. The proposition is indeed true, but because it is an (imperfect) definition, not because it is part of a demonstrative system, a science. That this is so becomes clear when we recognize that injustice is accurately defined as violation of property.[29] What presents itself as an important moral insight gained by rational deduction turns out, on closer inspection, to be merely a veiled definition of the terms. The same is true, Hume concludes, of 'all those pretended syllogistical reasonings, which may be found in every other branch of learning' (163).[30]

---

[29] The point here depends on the (natural law) view that property is what lawfully, and thus justly, belongs to someone, and that injustice is taking what justly belongs to another. Locke accepts this view, and so is well aware that the truth of the proposition is guaranteed by the meaning of the terms (see *Essay*, IV. iii. 18). Hume's point might be put by saying that, because a true proposition is produced by an inference from an accurate definition, it does not follow that the two propositions are part of a deductive *system*. Applying *modus tollens* to a true proposition does generate a true conclusion, but it does not thereby generate the constituents of a new science.

[30] Hume does not spell out all the casualties of this argument, but it clearly applies to all *a priori* metaphysics—for example, Spinoza's (aspects of which come in for some rough treatment in the *Treatise*, 240 ff.)—and also to the seventeenth century's dalliances with geometrical social science, such as Samuel Pufendorf's *Elementa Jurisprudentiae Universalis* (1660).

Hume now turns to address factual enquiries, and argues that in this sphere demonstration can have no place. This is because the existence or non-existence of any thing (and the occurrence or non-occurrence of any event) cannot be determined by purely logical considerations. This applies, he says, to any being whatsoever: 'Whatever *is* may *not be*. No negation of a fact can involve a contradiction. The non-existence of any being, without exception, is as clear and distinct an idea as its existence. The proposition, which affirms it not to be, however false, is no less conceivable and intelligible, than that which affirms it to be' (164).[31]

The immediate target here is plain enough: Descartes's revival of the ontological argument. That argument holds that the idea of God is itself sufficient to establish God's existence, and thus implies that the idea of a non-existing God is contradictory, and as such not a clear and distinct idea at all. In this passage, Hume rejects this view outright. God's existence, whether true or not, is no more necessary than the existence of 'Caesar, or the angel Gabriel'. Questions concerning what exists, not excluding immortal or divine beings, can be settled only by arguments from cause or effect, and these depend entirely on experience, not on any a priori reasonings.[32]

The method of reasoning appropriate to all empirical enquiries is therefore probable reasonings from cause and effect. Hume provides a brief classification of these enquiries, according to whether they are concerned with general or particular facts. The natural sciences, medicine, and 'politics' are all concerned with relations between *kinds* of thing, and thus with general facts.[33] History, geography, and astronomy, in contrast, deal only in particular facts, whether Caesar's conquest of Gaul or the motions of Jupiter's moons. This is interesting up to a point; but, given Hume's characteristic preoccupations, we should expect a brief foray into

[31] Hume contrasts this state of affairs with that in 'the sciences, properly so called', meaning geometry and mathematics. That is, the sciences 'properly so called' are bodies of deductive knowledge—*scientiae*—not empirical enquiries.

[32] In a footnote, Hume observes that the 'impious maxim of the ancient philosophy, *Ex nihilo, nihil fit*, by which the creation of matter was excluded, ceases to be a maxim, according to this philosophy.' True; but his own conclusion—'Not only the will of the supreme Being may create matter; but, for aught we know *a priori*, the will of any other being might create it, or any other cause, that the most whimsical imagination can assign'—although it is not a *maxim*, seems equally deserving of the epithet 'impious'. The suspicion that this footnote is ironical is confirmed when it is remembered that this allegedly impious maxim is the foundation on which both Descartes and Locke had built their arguments for God's existence: see the Third Meditation, where it is invoked implicitly (*Philosophical Writings*, ii. 28), and Locke's explicit appeal to it in his primary argument (*Essay*, IV. x. 3).

[33] 'Politics' here is not politics in the modern sense. It does include political theory, but more particularly refers to jurisprudence and public administration (cf. 'police', which was also used to cover these topics).

taxonomizing the sciences to have a further purpose. The expectation is not disappointed.

Theology is less easily classified from this standpoint, since it 'is composed partly of reasonings concerning particular, partly concerning general facts'. Hume's explicit point here is that the question of the existence of God concerns a particularity, whereas the question of the immortality of souls is a general question about the existence of a kind of thing. This appears to be no idle observation. Hume's point appears to be that, when classified according to the objects of study—a form of classification usual for the sciences— theology is discovered to be something of a dog's breakfast. It seems, therefore, not to be a distinctive discipline of enquiry at all. Worse is to come. Hume remarks: 'It has a foundation in *reason*, so far as it is supported by experience. But its best and most solid foundation is *faith* and divine revelation.' There is a real sting in this tail. The task Hume is engaged in is to classify kinds of enquiry based in experience. To hold that theology is such an enquiry *so far as* it is supported by experience, but that its main supports lie elsewhere, is to imply that it does not unequivocally belong in this list of (as we would say) the sciences. Hume has already emphasized, in his discussion of design, the very uncertain conclusions that experience can deliver on these sublime topics, so theology can hope only to be a limited enquiry without solid conclusions. The appeal to faith and divine revelation at this point merely rubs salt into the wound, since the discussion of miracle reports, despite its corresponding fideistic endnote, has denied the existence of any credible body of experiential data from which conclusions can be drawn. Theology, in other words, has no credible claim to inclusion amongst the parts of experimental philosophy. It is just another species of dogmatic metaphysics.

What then of morality? Does not the experimental philosophy, by undermining the scientific pretensions of theology, thereby undermine 'the true ground of Morality; which can only be the Will and Law of a God, who sees Men in the dark, has in his Hand Rewards and Punishments, and Power enough to call to account the Proudest Offender'?[34] No it does not. Morality is not an externally imposed law on self-seeking behaviour, as supposed by Hobbes and Locke, and other advocates of 'the selfish system of morals'.[35] It is, rather, a natural disposition of the human mind, which, like aesthetic judgement, belongs more properly to 'taste and sentiment' than to the understanding—and as such requires

[34] Locke, *Essay*, I. iii. 6.
[35] Hume, *An Enquiry concerning the Principles of Morals*, Appendix II, in *Enquiries*, 296.

no divine policeman for its exercise.[36] There is room for reasoned enquiries concerning morality, but these must begin, like all empirical endeavours, from the experiential data; in this case, 'the general taste of mankind, or some such fact, which may be the object of reasoning and enquiry' (165). Moral philosophy, that is to say, must begin from facts of psychology, sociology, anthropology, and the like; and, by subjecting these facts to scrutiny and decision—by methodizing and correcting common life—it will arrive at standards for the proper conduct of life. This is an experimental procedure that is entirely independent of theology or any other metaphysical principles.

The conclusion must be that theology and dogmatic metaphysics are pseudo-sciences. Both make claims about the kinds of thing that exist, but in neither case can the claims be made good. What exists can be known only through reasoning from experience, not from abstract demonstrations. The abstract deductions to conclusions concerning real existence, the hallmark of the dogmatic metaphysicians, are entirely bogus. Theology, as long as it reasons from experience, survives this criticism; but as long as it reasons *accurately* from experience it will arrive at no conclusions. Theology is empty; dogmatic metaphysics is the blindness of delusion. For this reason, the philosopher who has properly absorbed the lessons of experience discovers, among other things, the principles of quality control in libraries. But just in case the point has been missed, the future librarian closes with his own advice to the profession.[37]

A properly mitigated scepticism, then, far from being useless or ridiculous, develops principles of probable reasoning that, by distinguishing the credible from the fantastic, provide the only reliable guide for the conduct of life. The Academic sceptic is protected 'either from the fruitless efforts of human vanity, which would penetrate into subjects utterly inaccessible to the human understanding, or from the craft of popular superstitions, which ... break in upon every unguarded avenue of the mind, and overwhelm it with religious fears and prejudices' (11). Mitigated

---

[36] The 'general providence' of common life provides a degree of independent motivation, as Hume observes in Section XI (140), and also at the end of *An Enquiry concerning the Principles of Morals* (*Enquiries*, 283–4). And *particular* supports are provided by a wise legislator, who builds additional incentives to virtue into the institutions of the well-contrived republic.

[37] Hume's incendiarism at this point seems more extreme than it is. The modern reader's delicacy about such practices is a response to the history of twentieth-century totalitarianism. Hume's point is a simple turning of the tables against those who destroyed books on the basis of their false opinions. What the principles of experience teach us, he concludes, is that it is the books by which such destruction was sanctioned that are those actually deserving of destruction.

scepticism is a 'durable and useful' philosophy that has learnt, and so can teach, the lessons of experience. It thus returns us to the practices of common life, and safeguards us from the delusions of dogmatic metaphysics, and of its 'delirious and dismal' offspring.[38]

---

[38] That is, if we count its human, as well as its institutional, offspring: 'A gloomy, hair-brained enthusiast, after his death, may have a place in the calendar; but will scarcely ever be admitted, when alive, into intimacy and society, except by those who are as delirious and dismal as themselves' (*Enquiries*, 270).

PART THREE

Conclusion

Hume's Enlightenment Tract

The best explanations of the physical world are provided by experimental philosophy. This philosophy denies knowledge to make room for enquiry. That is, it rejects the extravagant claims made on behalf of human reason by the dogmatic philosophers, and therefore also of the knowledge of the essences of objects derived from rational insight into their natures, or delivered a priori by alleged innate principles in the mind. Without such knowledge, we must make do with experience and what can be gleaned from it. We must, that is, make do with what is adequate for practice, but which leaves us without wisdom.[1] We must examine carefully the evidence of experience, and build up from this examination an account of the observed regularities of the natural world, the laws of nature. The explanations that best fit the experimental evidence are that the world works according to mechanical principles: most simply, that change occurs because objects in motion collide with other objects, and impart motion to them; that the distinctive patterns of behaviour of complex objects are to be explained by the structure and relation of their simplest parts (their mechanism), where these simplest parts are probably microscopic but indivisible *atoms* or *corpuscles*; and that events are explicable in terms of wholly distinct efficient causes and their effects, not final causes.

Although the nature of the mind is not revealed by this philosophy, it is not the case that mechanical explanations cannot illuminate mental capacities and processes.[2] By eschewing innate knowledge, experimental philosophy must found all thought and belief ultimately on sense perception, interpreted as a mechanical process: ideas arise in the mind because the external world impinges on the sense organs, *impressing* on them the perceptions that the mind then copies or combines. This process implies that the objects that cause ideas are entirely distinct from them, and,

---

[1] See Aristotle, *Metaphysics*, I. i, in *A New Aristotle Reader*, ed. Ackrill, 255–7.
[2] *Treatise*, p. xvii; *Enquiries*, 13–15, 64–9. See Locke, *Essay*, II. i. 4; IV. iii. 27, 29.

in particular, that the essences of objects are not transmitted to the mind.[3] Perceptions are mere appearances.[4] There is no knowledge of substances or real essences.[5] Further, the imaginative powers of the mind are stimulated by the relations between different ideas, connecting together ideas that are similar, or contiguous in space or time, or causally connected. This is a mechanical process, called the *association of ideas*. These two features—the distinct existence of ideas and objects, and the generation of new ideas by association—mean that the mind confronts systematic obstacles in its attempts to comprehend the world. These obstacles are formidable, because they leave the mind with no *criterion* by which to judge of reality. Mechanism plus association thus seems to require the revival of something like Cicero's moderate scepticism: 'Our position is not that we hold that nothing is true, but that we assert that all true sensations are associated with false ones so closely resembling them that they contain no infallible mark to guide our judgement and assent.'[6]

An examination of experiential beliefs confirms this general picture. All our evidence for factual beliefs that go beyond present experience depend on causal reasoning. The evidence for causal connections, however, is entirely reducible to regular conjunctions in experience, and it is impossible to establish that what has been regularly conjoined in experience will continue to be so. We rely instead on habit or natural instinct; and, although this instinct is very difficult to resist, it may lead us into error. In fact, our vulnerability in this respect is redoubled by the instinctive character of our processes of belief formation themselves. In so far as we aim at certainty—at philosophical knowledge of underlying causes—we are doomed to failure; human life must proceed without certain foundations.

This may seem a counsel of despair, but there is a way ahead. The habitual reliance on past regularities allows a standard that is as nuanced as the regularities themselves. We judge of the probabilities of events according to the relative frequencies of the relevant conjunctions. These probabilities are, of course, rigidly inductive, and so not infallible. Nevertheless they are our only possible standard; and, because they are grounded firmly in experience, and because there is no credible alternative to their claims, they are therefore our *rightful* standard. The idea of causation itself

---

[3] Cf. Aristotle, *On the Soul*, II. xii, in *A New Aristotle Reader*, ed. Ackrill, 186.
[4] See also Bayle, 'Pyrrho', in *Historical and Critical Dictionary*, 197.
[5] See also Locke, *Essay*, II. xxiii. 1; II. vi. 3–18. See further Ayers, 'The Foundations of Knowledge and the Logic of Substance', 62–5; and Buckle, 'British Sceptical Realism'.
[6] Cicero, *De Natura Deorum*, I. v, in *De Natura Deorum* and *Academica*, 15.

arises by probabilistic means: where conjunctions have been entirely regular, we come, by habit of mind, to feel their necessity, and from this internal impression arrive at the idea of cause and effect. Once we recognize this relation, we can dissolve the apparent conflict between liberty and necessity. This implicitly builds a bridge between animal and human natures, and the gap can be bridged explicitly by showing that animals draw conclusions from experience in the same way as do human beings. Principles of probability applied to human testimony also show the impossibility of believing miraculous reports sufficient to serve as a foundation of religion, even if (as is almost never the case) the testimony is of the highest order. Thus revealed religion is shown to be incapable of establishing its credentials. Natural religion also feels the weight of these principles: the argument from design must presuppose that the world can be regarded as the effect of some cause, whereas the above principles deny that any unique entity or occurrence can be so regarded. Even if this point is not pressed, the argument has a further weakness, since, in arguing from the perceived world to a perfect designer, it contravenes Newton's First Rule of Reasoning in Philosophy, which stipulates that we must invest no more reality in any cause than is sufficient to bring about the effect. Nevertheless, social order is not—or is not *properly*—threatened by these conclusions, for, as long as we are guided by the principles of experience, the rejection of the religious hypothesis leaves the world as it is, including the moral principles on which everyday life is built.

These are all sceptical arguments: they build, on the non-rational foundation of instinct, principles of practice and judgement that are probable rather than certain. There is thus a form of scepticism that, despite the (rationally irrefutable) excesses of the Pyrrhonians, can lay claim to being a philosophy that is 'durable and useful'. The mitigated or Academic sceptic can overcome the dangerous and self-destructive pretensions of reason to construct a philosophy that is cautious and modest, but that also possesses a sharp critical edge: by carefully examining the powers of the human mind, it is able to separate the credible forms of enquiry from the bogus, and thereby promises to free human life from the burdens of metaphysical fantasy and superstition.

This is the argument of the first *Enquiry*. It is not simply a rewriting of some unrelated topics from (primarily) Book I of the *Treatise*, but a carefully constructed work designed to reach an important and useful conclusion. It is both better written, and considerably better focused, than the earlier work, with which it is so frequently and unfavourably compared. Admittedly, the critical purpose of *Treatise* Book I was partly obscured by Hume's late decision to castrate the work, by 'cutting off its noble Parts',[7] including the original version of the miracles argument, and (perhaps) a lost section on natural religion.[8] If those sections had not been removed, the role of *Treatise* Book I (and, in particular, of Part III, 'Of knowledge and probability') to clear away impediments to a non-metaphysical philosophy—a constructive defence of the reasonings of common life—would have stood out more clearly. The *Enquiry*, in contrast, makes these connections visible—even if Hume's polemical purpose means that the constructive aspects are not emphasized—and in this sense must be judged a better guide to the point and purpose of Hume's philosophy.

Ironically, the under-appreciation of the *Enquiry* may partly be due to Hume's own efforts to remedy the defects of the earlier work. The *Treatise* is a long and complicated work, in which it is sometimes difficult to see the forest for the trees. No casual reader has any trouble seeing why it failed to take the reading public by storm. Hume attempted to overcome the problems of length and complexity by reducing the treatment of the issues to sometimes very short sections that were, in their first manifestation, presented as a series of linked but apparently independent essays: the *Philosophical Essays concerning Human Understanding*. In rewriting the work this way he may have adapted the subject matter to the attention span of the reading public, but he recreated the problem of unity in a different form. The further attempt to overcome the perception of disunity, by renaming the work *An Enquiry concerning Human Understanding*, divided into 'sections' rather than 'essays', did ease the problem; but it did not overcome it.

Nevertheless, the *Enquiry* is, indeed, a unified whole; and, once that whole is discerned, the character of the work, as a tract for the times, becomes very clear. The foundations on which the work is built are wholly sceptical, but the structures thus supported are typical Enlightenment doctrines: the new philosophy of nature has swept away the old view of the world; properly understood, the new philosophy also shows that religion and the systems of morals built thereon are inextricably wedded to the old philosophy, and must share the same fate. Superstition and vain speculation must give way to experimental enquiries that alone can promise 'durable and useful' results. This is not a dream of Utopia, but a practical programme for genuine progress in human affairs. Philosophy must rise to this challenge by extricating itself from

---

[7] *New Letters*, ed. Klibansky and Mossner, 3; *Letters*, ed. Greig, i. 25.
[8] See Stewart, 'An Early Fragment on Evil', 160–70.

the closets of the Schools, in which its very language was rendered barbarous and unintelligible, and must speak to the people in the 'easy' terms of everyday life, so that true philosophy and its fruit, civilized social order, can flourish.[9]

Thus, in its own suitably modest way, the *Enquiry* heralds a new order based, first of all, on publicly accessible principles, and, secondly, on (what we would call) scientific principles. In its confidence in the new science, its confidence in the fallible but durable mechanisms of human nature and the standards of judgement proper to it, its hostility to religion, and, not least, its sense of a break with the medieval past, it breathes the air of Enlightenment. When read sympathetically—that is, in its own right—the work reveals a unified argument with a polemical purpose: it moves from the implications of the new natural philosophy for perception, and for the doxastic processes of human nature, to the criticism of religion and the practical principles built thereon. Along the way, it affirms the possibility of social improvement through experimental enquiry, and affirms human standards as the only rightful standards. This is the outlook of the Enlightenment: *An Enquiry concerning Human Understanding* is Hume's Enlightenment tract.

The conclusion may seem to have been reached altogether suddenly. But this is not so. Hume has presented us with a work that follows the contours described, and that ends, as it begins, with the call to purge society of the dismal fruits of discredited philosophy. If the larger picture escapes us, despite this plain and repeated message, two causes—not unconnected—recommend themselves. The first is that Hume's avowal of scepticism has been so thoroughly misunderstood that it has barred thinking of him as possessing constructive purposes, still less as a (cautious) fellow-traveller with contemporary, philosophically dogmatic, reformers. The second is that the fault lies in us, in our standard approach to the philosophical works of the past, and that such misunderstandings arise not by chance but by necessity. The problem, in brief, is that we have read too selectively, and with our eyes too close to the page; as a result, we have failed to address the fundamental interpretative question, concerning the coherence of our author's mind.[10] It is with an eye to the influence of factors such as these that this study is best ended, not with further arguments

---

[9] See also Livingston's emphasis on these connections in *Philosophical Melancholy and Delirium*.

[10] And have even invented distinctions to bar the way. Bernard Williams's distinction between 'history of philosophy' and 'history of ideas'—a distinction loved too much by too many—is one instructive example. See Williams, *Descartes: The Project of Pure Enquiry* (Harmondsworth: Penguin Books, 1978), 9–10.

for the conclusion reached, but by appealing to an apposite remark of Hume's own:

I know not whether the reader will readily apprehend this reasoning. I am afraid that, should I multiply words about it, or throw it into a greater variety of lights, it would only become more obscure and intricate. In all abstract reasonings there is one point of view which, if we can happily hit, we shall go farther towards illustrating the subject than by all the eloquence and copious expression in the world. This point of view we should endeavour to reach, and reserve the flowers of rhetoric for subjects which are more adapted to them. (79)

BIBLIOGRAPHY

ADORNO, T., and HORKHEIMER, M., *Dialectic of Enlightenment*, trans. J. Cumming (New York: Herder & Herder, 1972).

ANNAS, J., and BARNES, J., *The Modes of Scepticism* (Cambridge: Cambridge University Press, 1985).

ARIEW, R., and GRENE, M. (eds.), *Descartes and his Contemporaries* (Chicago: University of Chicago Press, 1995).

ARISTOTLE, *A New Aristotle Reader*, ed. J. L. Ackrill (Oxford: Clarendon Press, 1987).

ARNAULD, ANTOINE, and NICOLE, PIERRE, *Logic or the Art of Thinking*, ed. J. V. Buroker (Cambridge: Cambridge University Press, 1996).

ATKINSON, R. F., 'Hume on Mathematics', *Philosophical Quarterly*, 10 (1960), 127–37.

AUGUSTINE, *Confessions*, translated with an introduction and notes by H. Chadwick (Oxford: Oxford University Press, 1992).

——*The City of God against the Pagans*, ed. R. W. Dyson (Cambridge: Cambridge University Press, 1998).

AYERS, M. R., 'Substance, Reality, and the Great, Dead Philosophers', *American Philosophical Quarterly*, 7 (1970), 38–49.

——*Locke*, 2 vols. (London: Routledge, 1991).

——'The Foundations of Knowledge and the Logic of Substance: The Structure of Locke's General Philosophy', in G. A. J. Rogers (ed.), *Locke's Philosophy: Content and Context* (Oxford: Clarendon Press, 1994), 49–73. Reprinted in V. C. Chappell (ed.), *Locke* (Oxford: Oxford University Press, 1998), 24–47.

——*Locke: Ideas and Things* (London: Phoenix, 1997).

BACON, FRANCIS, *The Essays*, ed. J. Pitcher (Harmondsworth: Penguin Books, 1985).

BAIER, A., *A Progress of Sentiments: Reflections on Hume's* Treatise (Cambridge, Mass.: Harvard University Press, 1991).

BARFOOT, M., 'Hume and the Culture of Science', in M. A. Stewart (ed.), *Studies in the Philosophy of the Scottish Enlightenment* (Oxford: Clarendon Press, 1990), 151–90.

BATTERSBY, C., 'The *Dialogues* as Original Imitation: Cicero and the Nature of Hume's Skepticism', in D. F. Norton *et al.* (eds.), *McGill Hume Studies* (San Diego: Austin Hill Press, 1979), 253–78.

BAYLE, PIERRE, *Historical and Critical Dictionary: Selections*, trans. R. H. Popkin and C. Brush (Indianapolis: Hackett, 1991).

BEAUCHAMP, T., and ROSENBERG, A., *Hume and the Problem of Causation* (New York: Oxford University Press, 1981).

BECK, L. W., *Essays on Kant and Hume* (New Haven: Yale University Press, 1978).

BECKER, C. L., *The Heavenly City of the Eighteenth-Century Philosophers* (New Haven: Yale University Press, 1932).

BEISER, F. C., *The Fate of Reason* (Cambridge, Mass.: Harvard University Press, 1987).

BERKELEY, GEORGE, *Philosophical Works, Including the Works on Vision*, ed. M. R. Ayers (London: Dent, 1975).

——*A Treatise Concerning the Principles of Human Knowledge*, ed. J. Dancy (Oxford: Oxford University Press, 1998).

——*Three Dialogues between Hylas and Philonous*, ed. J. Dancy (Oxford: Oxford University Press, 1998).

BERLIN, I., *Four Essays on Liberty* (Oxford: Oxford University Press, 1969).

BERMAN, D., *George Berkeley: Idealism and the Man* (Oxford: Clarendon Press, 1994).

BIRO, J., 'Hume's New Science of the Mind', in D. F. Norton (ed.), *The Cambridge Companion to Hume* (Cambridge: Cambridge University Press, 1993), 33–63.

BLACKBURN, S., 'Hume and Thick Connexions', *Philosophy and Phenomenological Research*, 50 (supp.) (1990), 237–50; reprinted in Blackburn, *Essays in Quasi-Realism* (New York: Oxford University Press, 1993), 94–107.

BOX, M. A., *The Suasive Art of David Hume* (Princeton: Princeton University Press, 1990).

BOYLE, SIR ROBERT, *The Sceptical Chymist* (London: Everyman, 1964).

BROAD, C. D., 'Hume's Theory of the Credibility of Miracles', *Proceedings of the Aristotelian Society*, NS 17 (1916–17), 77–94.

BROUGHTON, J., 'Hume's Ideas about Necessary Connexion', *Hume Studies*, 13 (1987), 217–44.

BROWN, P., *Authority and the Sacred* (Cambridge: Cambridge University Press, 1995).

BROWN, S., *Leibniz* (Brighton: Harvester Press, 1984).

BUCKLE, S., *Natural Law and the Theory of Property: Grotius to Hume* (Oxford: Clarendon Press, 1991).

——'Hume's Biography and Hume's Philosophy: "My Own Life" and *An Enquiry concerning Human Understanding*', *Australasian Journal of Philosophy*, 77 (1999), 1–25.

——'British Sceptical Realism: A Fresh Look at the British Tradition', *European Journal of Philosophy*, 7 (1999), 1–29.

——'Marvels, Miracles, and Mundane Order: Hume's Critique of Religion in *An Enquiry concerning Human Understanding*', *Australasian Journal of Philosophy*, 79 (2001).

BURKE, EDMUND, *A Philosophical Enquiry into the Origin of our Ideas of the Sublime and Beautiful* (1757), ed. J. T. Boulton (Notre Dame, Ind.: University of Notre Dame Press, 1958).

BURNYEAT, M., 'Can the Sceptic Live his Scepticism?', in M. Schofield *et al.* (eds.), *Doubt and Dogmatism: Studies in Hellenistic Epistemology* (Oxford: Clarendon Press, 1980), 20–53.

——(ed.), *The Skeptical Tradition* (Berkeley and Los Angeles: University of California Press, 1983).

BURTT, E. A., *The Metaphysical Foundations of Modern Physical Science* (Atlantic Highlands, NJ: Humanities Press, 1952).

CAMPBELL, R., *Truth and Historicity* (Oxford: Clarendon Press, 1992).

CAPALDI, N., and LIVINGSTON, D. W. (eds.), *Liberty in Hume's History of England* (Dordrecht: Kluwer, 1990).

CASSIRER, E., *The Philosophy of the Enlightenment*, trans. F. C. A. Koelln and J. P. Pettegrove (Princeton: Princeton University Press, 1979).

CHAMBERS, EPHRAIM, *Cyclopaedia: or, an Universal Dictionary of Arts and Sciences* (London: 1728).

CHAPPELL, V. C. (ed.), *Hume: A Collection of Critical Essays* (London: Macmillan, 1966).

——*Locke* (Oxford: Oxford University Press, 1998).

CHRISTENSEN, J., *Practicing Enlightenment: Hume and the Formation of a Literary Career* (Madison: University of Wisconsin Press, 1987).

CICERO, MARCUS TULLIUS, *De Natura Deorum* and *Academica*, trans. H. Rackham (Cambridge, Mass.: Harvard University Press, 1951).

CLARK, W., GOLINSKI, J., and SCHAFFER, S. (eds.), *The Sciences in Enlightened Europe* (Chicago: University of Chicago Press, 1999).

CLARKE, D., *Descartes' Philosophy of Science* (Manchester: Manchester University Press, 1982).

——*Occult Powers and Hypotheses: Cartesian Natural Philosophy under Louis XIV* (Oxford: Clarendon Press, 1989).

CLARKE, SAMUEL, *A Demonstration of the Being and Attributes of God and Other Writings*, ed. E. Vailati (Cambridge: Cambridge University Press, 1998).

CLARKE, S., 'When to Believe in Miracles', *American Philosophical Quarterly*, 34 (1997), 95–102.

——'Hume's Definition of Miracles Revised', *American Philosophical Quarterly*, 36 (1999), 49–57.

CLATTERBAUGH, K., *The Causation Debate in Modern Philosophy 1637–1739* (London: Routledge, 1999).

COADY, C. A. J., *Testimony* (Oxford: Clarendon Press, 1992).

COLERIDGE, SAMUEL TAYLOR, *Biographia Literaria; or, Biographical Sketches of my Literary Life and Opinions* (1817) (Menston, UK: Scolar Press, 1971).

COSTA, M. J., 'Hume and Causal Realism', *Australasian Journal of Philosophy*, 67 (1989), 172–90.

COTTINGHAM, J., *The Rationalists* (Oxford: Oxford University Press, 1988).

CRAIG, E., *The Mind of God and the Works of Man* (Oxford: Clarendon Press, 1987).

CUNNINGHAM, A. R., 'Getting the Game Right: Some Plain Words on the Identity and Invention of Science', *Studies in History and Philosophy of Science*, 10 (1988), 365–89.

CURLEY, E., '"I Durst Not Write So Boldly", or, How to Read Hobbes's *Theological–Political Treatise*', in D. Bostrenghi (ed.), *Hobbes e Spinoza* (Naples: Bibliopolis, 1992).

——'Calvin and Hobbes, or, Hobbes as an Orthodox Christian', *Journal of the History of Philosophy*, 34 (1996), 257–71.

CURLEY, E., 'Reply to Professor Martinich', *Journal of the History of Philosophy*, 34 (1996), 285–7.

CURTIUS, QUINTUS [QUINTUS CURTIUS RUFUS], *History of Alexander*, trans. J. C. Rolfe (Cambridge, Mass.: Harvard University Press, 1946).

D'ALEMBERT, JEAN LE ROND, *Preliminary Discourse to the Encyclopedia of Diderot* (1751), trans. R. N. Schwab (Chicago: University of Chicago Press, 1995).

DANCY, J., *Berkeley: An Introduction* (Oxford: Blackwell, 1987).

DANTE ALIGHIERI, *The Divine Comedy*, 3 vols., ed. M. Musa (Harmondsworth: Penguin Books, 1986).

DASTON, L., *Classical Probability in the Enlightenment* (Princeton: Princeton University Press, 1988).

DAVIE, G., 'Edmund Husserl and "the as yet, in its most important respect, unrecognised greatness of Hume"', in G. P. Morice (ed.), *David Hume: Bicentenary Papers* (Edinburgh: Edinburgh University Press, 1977), 69–76.

DAVIES, P., *God and the New Physics* (Harmondsworth: Penguin Books, 1990).

DAWKINS, R., *The Blind Watchmaker* (New York: Norton, 1986).

DEAR, P. (ed.), *The Scientific Enterprise in Early Modern Europe: Readings from* Isis (Chicago and London: University of Chicago Press, 1997).

DESCARTES, RENÉ, *Descartes: Philosophical Writings*, trans. E. Anscombe and P. T. Geach (London: Thomas Nelson, 1954).

—— *The Philosophical Writings of Descartes*, trans. J. Cottingham, R. Stoothoff, and D. Murdoch, 2 vols. (Cambridge: Cambridge University Press, 1985).

DE WAAL, F., *Chimpanzee Politics: Power and Sex amongst the Apes* (New York: Harper & Row, 1982).

DICKER, G., *Hume's Epistemology and Metaphysics* (London and New York: Routledge, 1998).

DIDEROT, DENIS, *Political Writings*, ed. J. H. Mason and R. Wokler (Cambridge: Cambridge University Press, 1992).

DIOGENES LAERTIUS, *Lives of Eminent Philosophers*, trans. R. D. Hicks (2 vols.; Cambridge, Mass.: Harvard University Press, 1925).

DOUGLAS, M., *Purity and Danger* (London: Routledge, 1991).

EDELMAN, G., *Bright Air, Brilliant Fire: On the Matter of the Mind* (New York: Basic Books, 1992).

EWIN, R. E., *The Moral Philosophy of Thomas Hobbes* (Boulder, Colo.: Westview Press, 1991).

FAUVEL, J., FLOOD, R., SHORTLAND, M., and WILSON, R. (eds.), *Let Newton Be!* (Oxford: Oxford University Press, 1988).

FLEW, A., *Hume's Philosophy of Belief* (London: Routledge & Kegan Paul, 1961; repr. Bristol: Thoemmes Press, 1997).

—— *David Hume: Philosopher of Moral Science* (Oxford: Basil Blackwell, 1986).

FOGELIN, R., 'Hume's Scepticism', in D. F. Norton (ed.), *The Cambridge Companion to Hume* (Cambridge: Cambridge University Press, 1993), 90–116.

FORBES, D., *Hume's Philosophical Politics* (Cambridge: Cambridge University Press, 1975).

FORCE, J. E., 'Hume's Interest in Newton and Science', *Hume Studies*, 13 (1987), 166–216.

FOSL, P. S., 'The Bibliographic Bases of Hume's Understanding of Sextus Empiricus and Pyrrhonism', *Journal of the History of Philosophy*, 36 (1998), 261–78.

FRASCA-SPADA, M., *Space and the Self in Hume's* Treatise (Cambridge: Cambridge University Press, 1998).

FUNKENSTEIN, A., *Theology and the Scientific Imagination from the Middle Ages to the Seventeenth Century* (Princeton: Princeton University Press, 1986).

GARBER, D., *Descartes' Metaphysical Physics* (Chicago: University of Chicago Press, 1992).

GARRETT, D., *Cognition and Commitment in Hume's Philosophy* (New York: Oxford University Press, 1997).

GAUKROGER, S., *Descartes: An Intellectual Biography* (Oxford: Clarendon Press, 1995).

——(ed.), *The Uses of Antiquity* (Dordrecht: Kluwer, 1992).

GROTIUS, HUGO, *De Jure Belli ac Pacis Libri Tres* (1625), trans. F. W. Kelsey (New York: Oceana Publications, 1964).

HABERMAS, J., *The Philosophical Discourse of Modernity*, trans. F. G. Lawrence (Cambridge, Mass.: MIT Press, 1987).

HACKING, I., *The Emergence of Probability* (Cambridge: Cambridge University Press, 1975).

HATFIELD, G., 'Metaphysics and the New Science', in D. C. Lindberg and R. S. Westman (eds.), *Reappraisals of the Scientific Revolution* (Cambridge: Cambridge University Press, 1990), 93–166.

HICK, J., *Evil and the God of Love* (London: Macmillan, 1966).

HILL, C., *Intellectual Origins of the English Revolution* (Oxford: Clarendon Press, 1965).

HOBBES, THOMAS, *Metaphysical Writings*, ed. M. W. Calkins (La Salle, Ill.: Open Court, 1989).

——*Leviathan*, ed. R. Tuck (Cambridge: Cambridge University Press, 1991).

HOOYKAS, R., *Religion and the Rise of Modern Science* (Edinburgh: Scottish Academic Press, 1984).

HOUSTON, J., *Reported Miracles: A Critique of Hume* (Cambridge: Cambridge University Press, 1994).

HUME, DAVID, *The Philosophical Works of David Hume*, ed. T. H. Green and T. H. Grose, 4 vols. (London: Longmans, Green, 1889).

——*The Letters of David Hume*, ed. J. Y. T. Greig, 2 vols. (Oxford: Clarendon Press, 1932).

——*New Letters of David Hume*, ed. R. Klibansky and E. Mossner (Oxford: Clarendon Press, 1954).

——*A Letter from a Gentleman to his Friend in Edinburgh*, ed. E. C. Mossner and J. V. Price (Edinburgh: Edinburgh University Press, 1967).

——*Enquiries concerning Human Understanding and concerning the Principles of Morals*, 3rd edn., ed. L. A. Selby-Bigge, rev. P. H. Nidditch (Oxford: Clarendon Press, 1975).

——*A Treatise of Human Nature*, 2nd edn., ed. L. A. Selby-Bigge, rev. P. H. Nidditch (Oxford: Clarendon Press, 1978).

——*The History of England*, 6 vols. (Indianapolis: Liberty Fund, 1983).

HUME, DAVID, *Essays, Moral, Political, and Literary*, rev. edn., ed. E. F. Miller (Indianapolis: Liberty Fund, 1987).

——*Dialogues and Natural History of Religion*, ed. J. C. A. Gaskin (Oxford: Oxford University Press, 1993).

——*Four Dissertations* (1757) (Bristol: Thoemmes Press, 1995).

——*An Enquiry concerning Human Understanding*, ed. T. L. Beauchamp (Oxford: Oxford University Press, 1999).

HUTCHESON, FRANCIS, *An Essay on the Nature and Conduct of the Passions and Affections. With Illustrations on the Moral Sense* (1728) (Hildesheim: Georg Olms, 1969).

JOHNSON, O. A., *The Mind of David Hume: A Companion to Book I of A Treatise of Human Nature* (Urbana, Ill.: University of Illinois Press, 1995).

JONES, P., *Hume's Sentiments: Their Ciceronian and French Context* (Edinburgh: Edinburgh University Press, 1982).

——(ed.), *Philosophy and Science in the Scottish Enlightenment* (Edinburgh: John Donald Publishers, 1988).

——(ed.), *The 'Science of Man' in the Scottish Enlightenment* (Edinburgh: Edinburgh University Press, 1989).

KANT, IMMANUEL, *Critique of Pure Reason*, trans. N. Kemp Smith (London: Macmillan, 1933).

——*Groundwork of the Metaphysics of Morals*, trans. and ed. M. Gregor (Cambridge: Cambridge University Press, 1997).

KEMP SMITH, N., *The Philosophy of David Hume* (London: Macmillan, 1941).

KORSGAARD, C. M., *The Sources of Normativity* (Cambridge: Cambridge University Press, 1996).

KUYPERS, M. S., *Studies in the Eighteenth Century Background of Hume's Empiricism* (New York: Russell & Russell, 1966).

LAPLACE, PIERRE SIMON, MARQUIS DE, *A Philosophical Essay on Probabilities*, ed. E. T. Bell (New York: Dover, 1951).

LAURSEN, J. C., *The Politics of Skepticism in the Ancients, Montaigne, Hume, and Kant* (Leiden: E. J. Brill, 1992).

LEA, F. A., *The Tragic Philosopher: Friedrich Nietzsche* (London: Methuen, 1957).

LEAR, J., *Aristotle: The Desire to Understand* (Cambridge: Cambridge University Press, 1988).

LEIBNIZ, G. W., *Discourse on Metaphysics and Related Writings*, ed. R. N. D. Martin and S. Brown (Manchester: Manchester University Press, 1988).

——*New Essays on Human Understanding*, ed. P. Remnant and J. Bennett (Cambridge: Cambridge University Press, 1996).

——*Philosophical Texts*, ed. R. S. Woolhouse and R. Francks (Oxford: Oxford University Press, 1998).

LELAND, JOHN, *A View of the Principal Deistical Writers of the Last and Present Century*, 2 vols. (London: B. Dod, 1755).

LENMAN, B., *The Jacobite Cause* (Glasgow: Richard Drew Publishing, 1986).

LENNON, T. M., *The Battle of the Gods and Giants: The Legacies of Descartes and Gassendi, 1655–1715* (Princeton: Princeton University Press, 1993).

LEVINE, J. M., *The Battle of the Books: History and Literature in the Augustan Age* (Ithaca, NY: Cornell University Press, 1991).

LINDBERG, D. C., and WESTMAN, R. S., (eds.), *Reappraisals of the Scientific Revolution* (Cambridge: Cambridge University Press, 1990).

LIVINGSTON, D. W., *Hume's Philosophy of Common Life* (Chicago: University of Chicago Press, 1984).

——'Hume on the Natural History of Philosophical Consciousness', in P. Jones (ed.), *The 'Science of Man' in the Scottish Enlightenment* (Edinburgh: Edinburgh University Press, 1989), 68–84.

——*Philosophical Melancholy and Delirium: Hume's Pathology of Philosophy* (Chicago: University of Chicago Press, 1998).

LOCKE, JOHN, *An Essay concerning Human Understanding*, ed. P. H. Nidditch (Oxford: Clarendon Press, 1975).

LONG, A. A., *Hellenistic Philosophy: Stoics, Epicureans, Sceptics*, 2nd edn. (London: Duckworth, 1986).

——and SEDLEY, D. N. (eds.), *The Hellenistic Philosophers*, i (Cambridge: Cambridge University Press, 1987).

LUCRETIUS [TITUS LUCRETIUS CARUS], *The Way Things Are* [*De Rerum Natura*], trans. R. Humphries (Bloomington, Ind.: Indiana University Press, 1968).

——*On the Nature of the Universe*, trans. R. E. Latham, rev. J. Godwin (Harmondsworth: Penguin Books, 1994).

MCCRACKEN, C. J., *Malebranche and British Philosophy* (Oxford: Clarendon Press, 1983).

MACINTYRE, A., *Against the Self-Images of the Age* (London: Duckworth, 1971).

——*After Virtue*, 2nd edn. (London: Duckworth, 1984).

——*Whose Justice? Which Rationality?* (London: Duckworth, 1988).

MALEBRANCHE, NICOLAS, *The Search after Truth* and *Elucidations of the Search after Truth*, trans. T. M. Lennon and P. J. Olscamp, with Philosophical Commentary by T. M. Lennon (Columbus, Oh.: Ohio State University Press, 1980).

——*Treatise on Nature and Grace*, trans. with an introduction and notes by P. Riley (Oxford: Clarendon Press, 1992).

MALHERBE, M., 'Hume and the Art of Dialogue', in M. A. Stewart and J. P. Wright (eds.), *Hume and Hume's Connexions* (Edinburgh: Edinburgh University Press, 1994), 201–23.

MARTINICH, A. P., *The Two Gods of Leviathan* (Cambridge: Cambridge University Press, 1992).

——'On the Proper Interpretation of Hobbes's Philosophy', *Journal of the History of Philosophy*, 34 (1996), 273–83.

MATES, B., 'The Skeptic Way', Introduction to B. Mates (trans.), *The Skeptic Way: Sextus Empiricus's Outlines of Pyrrhonism* (New York: Oxford University Press, 1996).

MENN, S., 'Descartes, Augustine, and the Status of Faith', in M. A. Stewart (ed.), *Studies in Seventeenth-Century European Philosophy* (Oxford Studies in the History of Philosophy, 2; Oxford: Clarendon Press, 1997), 1–31.

——*Descartes and Augustine* (Cambridge: Cambridge University Press, 1998).

MERCER, C., 'The Vitality and Importance of Early Modern Aristotelianism', in T. Sorell (ed.), *The Rise of Modern Philosophy* (Oxford: Clarendon Press, 1993), 33–67.

MILLER, D., *Philosophy and Ideology in Hume's Political Thought* (Oxford: Clarendon Press, 1981).

MILLICAN, P. J. R., 'Hume's Argument Concerning Induction: Structure and Interpretation', in S. Tweyman (ed.), *David Hume: Critical Assessments*, 4 vols. (London: 1995), ii. 91–144.

——(ed.), *Reading Hume on Human Understanding: Essays on the First* Enquiry (Oxford: Oxford University Press, 2000).

MONTAIGNE, MICHEL EYQUEM, SEIGNEUR DE, *The Complete Essays*, trans. M. A. Screech (Harmondsworth: Penguin Books, 1991).

MOORE, G. E., *Philosophical Papers* (London: Allen & Unwin, 1959).

MOSSNER, E. C., *The Life of David Hume*, 2nd edn. (Oxford: Clarendon Press, 1980).

MOUNCE, H. O., *Hume's Naturalism* (London: Routledge, 1999).

MULLER, J. Z., *Adam Smith in his Time and Ours: Designing the Decent Society* (New York: Free Press, 1993).

NADLER, S. (ed.), *Causation in Early Modern Philosophy: Cartesianism, Occasionalism, and Preestablished Harmony.* (University Park, Pa.: Pennsylvania State University Press, 1993).

NEWTON, SIR ISAAC, *Sir Isaac Newton's Mathematical Principles of Natural Philosophy and his System of the World*, trans. A. Motte, rev. F. Cajori (Berkeley and Los Angeles: University of California Press, 1934).

——*Opticks, or A Treatise of the Reflections, Refractions, Inflections, & Colours of Light*, 4th edn. (1730) (New York: Dover, 1979).

——*Newton's Philosophy of Nature: Selections from his Writings*, ed. H. S. Thayer (New York: Hafner, 1974).

NOONAN, H. W., *Hume on Knowledge* (London: Routledge, 1999).

NORTON, D. F., *David Hume: Common-Sense Moralist, Sceptical Metaphysician* (Princeton: Princeton University Press, 1982).

——(ed.), *The Cambridge Companion to Hume* (Cambridge: Cambridge University Press, 1993).

——and POPKIN, R. H. (eds.), *David Hume: Philosophical Historian* (Indianapolis: Bobbs-Merrill, 1965).

——CAPALDI, N., and ROBISON, W. L. (eds.), *McGill Hume Studies* (San Diego: Austin Hill Press, 1979).

NOXON, J., *Hume's Philosophical Development* (Oxford: Clarendon Press, 1973).

OSLER, M. J., 'John Locke and the Changing Ideal of Scientific Knowledge', *Journal of the History of Ideas*, 31 (1970), 3–16.

——'Galileo, Motion, and Essences', *Isis*, 64 (1973), 504–9.

——*Divine Will and the Mechanical Philosophy: Gassendi and Descartes on Contingency and Necessity in the Created World* (Cambridge: Cambridge University Press, 1994).

OUTRAM, D., *The Enlightenment* (Cambridge: Cambridge University Press, 1995).

PANNENBERG, W., *Basic Questions in Theology*, 2 vols. (London: SCM Press, 1971).

PASSMORE, J., *Hume's Intentions*, 3rd edn. (London: Duckworth, 1980).

PEARS, D., *Hume's System: An Examination of the First Book of his* Treatise (Oxford: Oxford University Press, 1990).

PEIRCE, C. S., *Selected Writings (Values in a Universe of Chance)*, ed. P. P. Wiener (New York: Dover, 1958).

PENELHUM, T., 'Hume's Skepticism and the *Dialogues*', in D. F. Norton *et al.* (eds.), *McGill Hume Studies* (San Diego: Austin Hill Press, 1979), 253–78.

——*David Hume: An Introduction to his Philosophical System* (West Lafayette, Ind.: Purdue University Press, 1992).

PHEMISTER, P., 'Locke, Sergeant, and Scientific Method', in T. Sorell (ed.), *The Rise of Modern Philosophy*, (Oxford: Clarendon Press, 1993), 231–49.

PHILLIPSON, N., *Hume* (London: Weidenfeld & Nicolson, 1989).

PLATO, *Plato's Phaedo*, ed. R. S. Bluck (London: Routledge & Kegan Paul, 1955).

POMPA, L., *Human Nature and Historical Knowledge: Hume, Hegel and Vico* (Cambridge: Cambridge University Press, 1990).

POPE, ALEXANDER, *Alexander Pope*, ed. P. Rogers (Oxford Authors; Oxford: Oxford University Press, 1993).

POPKIN, R. H., 'The Philosophy of Bishop Stillingfleet', *Journal of the History of Philosophy*, 9 (1971), 303–19.

——*The History of Scepticism from Erasmus to Spinoza* (Berkeley and Los Angeles: University of California Press, 1979).

——*The High Road to Pyrrhonism*, ed. R. A. Watson and J. E. Force (Indianapolis: Hackett, 1993).

POPPER, K. R., *The Logic of Scientific Discovery* (London: Hutchinson, 1959).

——*Objective Knowledge: An Evolutionary Approach* (Oxford: Clarendon Press, 1972).

PRIESTLEY, JOSEPH, *Letters to a Philosophical Unbeliever* (2nd edn., 1787; New York: Garland Publishing, 1974).

RAND, B. (ed.), *The Life, Unpublished Letters, and Philosophical Regimen of Anthony Ashley Cooper, Earl of Shaftesbury* (London and New York: Sonnenshein, 1900).

RANDALL, J. H., 'David Hume: Radical Empiricist and Pragmatist', in S. Hook and M. R. Konvitz (eds.), *Freedom and Experience* (Ithaca, NY: Cornell University Press, 1947).

RAPHAEL, D. D. (ed.), *British Moralists 1650–1800*, 2 vols. (Oxford: Oxford University Press, 1969).

RÉE, J., *Descartes* (London: Allen Lane, 1974).

——AYERS, M., and WESTOBY, A., *Philosophy and its Past* (Hassocks, Sussex: Harvester Press, 1978).

RICHETTI, J. J., *Philosophical Writing: Locke, Berkeley, Hume* (Cambridge, Mass.: Harvard University Press, 1983).

RILEY, P., *The General Will before Rousseau* (Princeton: Princeton University Press, 1986).

ROGERS, G. A. J. (ed.), *Locke's Philosophy: Content and Context* (Oxford: Clarendon Press, 1994).

RUSSELL, B., *History of Western Philosophy*, 2nd edn. (London: George Allen & Unwin, 1961).

RUSSELL, P., 'Hume's *Treatise* and Hobbes's *The Elements of Law*', *Journal of the History of Ideas*, 46 (1985), 51–64.

RUTHERFORTH, THOMAS, *The Credibility of Miracles Defended against the Author of* Philosophical Essays (Cambridge: J. Bentham Printer to the University, 1751).

SACRED CONGREGATION FOR THE DOCTRINE OF THE FAITH, *Instruction on Respect for Human Life in its Origin and on the Dignity of Procreation: Replies to Certain Questions of the Day* (Homebush, NSW: St Paul Publications, 1987).

SANCHES, F., *That Nothing Is Known*, ed. E. Limbrick and D. F. S. Thomson (Cambridge: Cambridge University Press, 1988).

SCHMITT, C., 'Towards a Reassessment of Renaissance Aristotelianism', *History of Science*, 2 (1973), 159–93.

SCHOFIELD, M., BURNYEAT, M., and BARNES, J., *Doubt and Dogmatism: Studies in Hellenistic Epistemology* (Oxford: Clarendon Press, 1980).

SCHOULS, P. A., *Descartes and the Enlightenment* (Edinburgh: Edinburgh University Press, 1989).

——*Reasoned Freedom: John Locke and Enlightenment* (Ithaca, NY: Cornell University Press, 1992).

SEXTUS EMPIRICUS, *Outlines of Scepticism*, trans. J. Annas and J. Barnes (Cambridge: Cambridge University Press, 1994).

SHER, R. B., *Church and University in the Scottish Enlightenment: The Moderate Literati of Edinburgh* (Edinburgh: Edinburgh University Press, 1985).

——'Professors of Virtue: The Social History of the Edinburgh Moral Philosophy Chair in the Eighteenth Century', in M. A. Stewart (ed.), *Studies in the Philosophy of the Scottish Enlightenment* (Oxford Studies in the History of Philosophy, 1; Oxford: Clarendon Press, 1990), 87–126.

SORELL, T., 'Hobbes without Doubt', *History of Philosophy Quarterly*, 10 (1993), 121–35.

——'Hobbes's Objections and Hobbes's System', in R. Ariew and M. Grene (eds.), *Descartes and his Contemporaries* (Chicago: University of Chicago Press, 1995), 83–96.

——(ed.), *The Rise of Modern Philosophy: The Tension between the New and Traditional Philosophies from Machiavelli to Leibniz* (Oxford: Clarendon Press, 1993).

STERELNY, K., and GRIFFITHS, P. E., *Sex and Death: An Introduction to Philosophy of Biology* (Chicago: University of Chicago Press, 1999).

STERN, G., *A Faculty Theory of Knowledge: The Aim and Scope of Hume's First Enquiry* (Lewisburg, Pa.: Bucknell University Press, 1971).

STEWART, J. B., *Opinion and Reform in Hume's Political Philosophy* (Princeton: Princeton University Press, 1992).

STEWART, M. A., 'An Early Fragment on Evil', in M. A. Stewart and J. P. Wright (eds.), *Hume and Hume's Connexions* (Edinburgh: Edinburgh University Press, 1994), 160–70.

——'Hume's Historical View of Miracles', in M. A. Stewart and J. P. Wright (eds.), *Hume and Hume's Connexions* (Edinburgh: Edinburgh University Press, 1994), 171–200.

——'Two Species of Philosophy: The Historical Significance of the First *Enquiry'*, in P. J. R. Millican (ed.), *Reading Hume on Human Understanding: Essays on the First* Enquiry (Oxford: Oxford University Press, 2001).

——(ed.), *Studies in the Philosophy of the Scottish Enlightenment* (Oxford Studies in the History of Philosophy, 1; Oxford: Clarendon Press, 1990).

——(ed.), *Studies in Seventeenth-Century European Philosophy* (Oxford Studies in the History of Philosophy, 2; Oxford: Clarendon Press, 1997).

——and WRIGHT, J. P. (eds.), *Hume and Hume's Connexions* (Edinburgh: Edinburgh University Press, 1994).

STRAWSON, G., *The Secret Connexion: Causation, Realism, and David Hume* (Oxford: Clarendon Press, 1989).

STROUD, B., *Hume* (London: Routledge, 1977).

SUCHTING, W. A., 'Hume and Necessary Truth', *Dialogue*, 5 (1966–7), 47–60.

SWIFT, JONATHAN, *A Tale of a Tub. Written for the Universal Improvement of Mankind. To which is added, An Account of a Battel between the Antient and Modern Books in* St James's *Library* (1704) (New York: Garland, 1972).

SWINBURNE, R., *The Existence of God* (Oxford: Clarendon Press, 1979).

TOOLEY, M., *Abortion and Infanticide* (Oxford: Clarendon Press, 1983).

TUCK, R., 'Hobbes and Descartes', in G. A. J. Rogers and A. Ryan (eds.), *Perspectives on Thomas Hobbes* (Oxford: Clarendon Press, 1988), 11–41.

——*Hobbes* (Oxford: Oxford University Press, 1989).

VOLTAIRE, FRANÇOIS-MARIE AROUET, *Letters on England*, trans. L. Tancock (Harmondsworth: Penguin Books, 1980).

WAXMAN, W., *Hume's Theory of Consciousness* (Cambridge: Cambridge University Press, 1994).

WESTFALL, R. S., *The Construction of Modern Science: Mechanisms and Mechanics* (Cambridge: Cambridge University Press, 1977).

WHATELY, R., *Historic Doubts Relative to Napoleon Buonaparte*, 9th edn. (London: John Parker, 1849).

WHELAN, F. G., *Order and Artifice in Hume's Political Philosophy* (Princeton: Princeton University Press, 1985).

WILLIAMS, B., *Descartes: The Project of Pure Enquiry* (Harmondsworth: Penguin Books, 1978).

WINKLER, K. P., *Berkeley: An Interpretation* (Oxford: Clarendon Press, 1989).

——'The New Hume', *Philosophical Review*, 100 (1991), 541–79.

WOJCIK, J. W., *Robert Boyle and the Limits of Reason* (Cambridge: Cambridge University Press, 1997).

WOKLER, R., 'Apes and Races in the Scottish Enlightenment: Monboddo and Kames on the Nature of Man', in P. Jones (ed.), *Philosophy and Science in the Scottish Enlightenment* (Edinburgh: John Donald Publishers, 1988), 145–68.

——'Enlightenment, Continental', in E. Craig (ed.), *The Routledge Encyclopedia of Philosophy* (10 vols.; London: Routledge, 1998), iii. 315–20.

WOOD, P. B., 'Science and the Aberdeen Enlightenment', in P. Jones (ed.), *Philosophy and Science in the Scottish Enlightenment* (Edinburgh: John Donald Publishers, 1988), 39–66.

WOOD, P. B., 'The Natural History of Man in the Scottish Enlightenment', *History of Science*, 27 (1989), 89–123.

——'Science and the Pursuit of Virtue in the Aberdeen Enlightenment', in M. A. Stewart (ed.), *Studies in the Philosophy of the Scottish Enlightenment* (Oxford: Clarendon Press, 1990), 127–49.

WOOLHOUSE, R. S., *Locke* (Brighton: Harvester Press, 1983).

——*The Empiricists* (Oxford: Oxford University Press, 1988).

WOOTTON, D., 'Hume's "Of Miracles": Probability and Irreligion', in M. A. Stewart (ed.), *Studies in the Philosophy of the Scottish Enlightenment*, (Oxford: Clarendon Press, 1990), 191–229.

WRIGHT, J. P., *The Sceptical Realism of David Hume* (Manchester: Manchester University Press, 1983).

——'Hume's Academic Scepticism: A Reappraisal of his Philosophy of Human Understanding', *Canadian Journal of Philosophy*, 16 (1986), 407–35.

——'Hume's Rejection of the Theory of Ideas', *History of Philosophy Quarterly*, 8 (1991), 149–62.

YOLTON, J. W., *John Locke and the Way of Ideas* (Oxford: Clarendon Press, 1956).

——*Thinking Matter: Materialism in Eighteenth-Century Britain* (Oxford: Basil Blackwell, 1983).

——*Perceptual Acquaintance: From Descartes to Reid* (Oxford: Basil Blackwell, 1984).

——(ed.), *Philosophy, Religion and Science in the Seventeenth and Eighteenth Centuries* (Rochester, NY: University of Rochester Press, 1990).

INDEX